When should I travel to get the best airfare?
Where do I go for answers to my travel questions?
What's the best and easiest way to pl━━ ━━━ ━━━k my trip?

frommer━━━━━━━━━━━━ m

Frommer's, the travel guide l━━━━━━━━━━━━━━━━━━━**city.com**,
the leader in online travel, to b━━━━━━━━━━━━ ━y-to-use resource
designed to help you plan and ━━━━━━ ━p online.

At **frommers.travelocity.com**, you'll find free online updates about
your destination from the experts at Frommer's plus the outstanding travel
planning and purchasing features of Travelocity.com. Travelocity.com
provides reservations capabilities for 95 percent of all airline seats sold,
more than 47,000 hotels, and over 50 car rental companies. In addition,
Travelocity.com offers more than 2,000 exciting vacation and cruise
packages. Travelocity.com puts you in complete control of your travel
planning with these and other great features:

> **Expert travel guidance from Frommer's** - over 150 writers
> reporting from around the world!

> **Best Fare Finder** - an interactive calendar tells you when to
> travel to get the best airfare

> **Fare Watcher** - we'll track airfare changes to your favorite
> destinations

> **Dream Maps** - a mapping feature that suggests travel
> opportunities based on your budget

> **Shop Safe Guarantee** - 24 hours a day / 7 days a week live
> customer service, and more!

Whether traveling on a tight budget, looking for a quick weekend getaway,
or planning the trip of a lifetime, Frommer's guides and Travelocity.com
will make your travel dreams a reality. You've bought the book, now book
the trip!

Alaska Cruises
& Ports of Call

2002

by Fran Wenograd Golden
& Jerry Brown

Hungry Minds™

Best-Selling Books • Digital Downloads • e-Books • Answer Networks
e-Newsletters • Branded Web Sites • e-Learning
New York, NY • Cleveland, OH • Indianapolis, IN

Published by:

Hungry Minds, Inc.
909 Third Ave.
New York, NY 10022

ISBN 0-7645-6557-5
ISSN 1520-5525

Editor: Amy Lyons
Production Editor: Suzanna R. Thompson
Photo Editor: Richard Fox
Cartographers: Elizabeth Puhl and John Decamillis
Production by Hungry Minds Indianapolis Production Services

Front cover photo: The *Yorktown Clipper* at Misty Fjords National Monument, Rudyerd Bay.
Back cover photo: Brown bear catching salmon.

Special Sales

For general information on Hungry Minds' products and services, please contact our Customer Care department; within the U.S. at 800-762-2974, outside the U.S. at 317-572-3993, or fax 317-572-4002. For sales inquiries and reseller information, including discounts, bulk sales, customized editions, and premium sales, please contact our Customer Care department at 800-434-3422.

Manufactured in the United States of America

5 4 3 2

Contents

Appendix: Alaska in Depth   200

Index   216

List of Maps

An Invitation to the Reader

In researching this book, we discovered many wonderful places — hotels, restaurants, shops, and more. We're sure you'll find others. Please tell us about them so that we can share the information with your fellow travelers in upcoming editions. If you were disappointed with a recommendation, we'd love to know that, too. Please write to:

Frommer's Alaska Cruises & Ports of Call 2002
Hungry Minds, Inc. • 909 Third Avenue • New York, NY 10022

An Additional Note

Please be advised that travel information is subject to change at any time — and this is especially true of prices. We therefore suggest that you write or call ahead for confirmation when making your travel plans. The authors, editors, and publisher cannot be held responsible for the experiences of readers while traveling. Your safety is important to us, however, so we encourage you to stay alert and be aware of your surroundings. Keep a close eye on cameras, purses, and wallets, all favorite targets of thieves and pickpockets.

The following abbreviations are used for credit cards:

AE	American Express	DISC Discover	V Visa
DC	Diners Club	MC MasterCard	

FROMMERS.COM

Now that you have the guidebook to a great trip, visit our website at **www.frommers.com** for travel information on nearly 2,000 destinations. With features updated regularly, we give you instant access to the most current trip-planning information available. At Frommers.com, you'll also find the best prices on airfares, accommodations, and car rentals — and you can even book travel online through our travel booking partners. At Frommers.com, you'll also find the following:

- Daily Newsletter highlighting the best travel deals
- Hot Spot of the Month/Vacation Sweepstakes & Travel Photo Contest
- More than 200 Travel Message Boards
- Outspoken Newsletters and Feature Articles on travel bargains, vacation ideas, tips & resources, and more!

About the Authors

Fran Wenograd Golden is the author of *Cruise Vacations For Dummies, Frommer's European Cruises & Ports of Call,* and *TVacations: A Fun Guide to the Sites, the Stars and the Inside Stories Behind Your Favorite TV Shows.* She's also a contributor to concierge.com and the *Boston Herald,* as well as to *Frommer's Greece, Frommer's Greek Islands,* and *Honeymoon Vacations For Dummies.* Fran lives north of Boston with her husband, Ed, and their two teenagers.

Scottish-born **Jerry Brown** was a news reporter for London's *Daily Mail,* and, later, West Coast bureau chief of a U.S. travel trade publication, a position he held for more than 30 years. He is now happily retired. An avid Alaskaphile, Brown is married and has two grown sons, two daughters-in-law, and a granddaughter. His family shares his fascination with the 49th state.

Contributors

Jan Halliday wrote the essay on Alaska's Native peoples in chapter 2. A journalist for 25 years and a former editor of *Alaska Airlines Magazine,* Jan is the author of *Native Peoples of the Northwest* (Sasquatch Books, 2nd edition, 2000) and *Native People of Alaska: A Traveler's Guide to Land, Art, and Culture* (Sasquatch Books, 1998).

Text on whales and land mammals excerpted from *Frommer's Alaska 2002* by **Charles Wohlforth.**

Illustrations of whales, mountain goat, sea otter, sea lion, caribou, and Dall sheep by **Giselle Simons.** All other wildlife illustrations by **Jasper Burns.**

Acknowledgments

Thanks also to small-ship-cruising fans **Matt Hannafin, Ben Wenograd,** and **Shannon Wegele,** and all the cruise-line public relations departments.

What's New in Alaska Cruising

Just like the glaciers, the world of Alaska travel is always changing. New ships come, and others go. Hotels open, and others change hands. Cruise lines add new shore excursions and land packages and enhance their onboard offerings. And in our travels, we discover new places of interest. In writing this book we've tried to keep track of the latest and greatest.

The following are some of the highlights.

SHIPS In late 2001, P&O Princess Cruises and Royal Caribbean announced plans for a monumental merger that would create the world's largest cruise vacation company, with 41 ships and more on the way. The deal was to close in the second quarter of 2002. Officials said they would continue to operate the Princess and Royal Caribbean brands as separate entities. It was unclear at the time of publication what the combined company would do in terms of its other brands, which include Celebrity Cruises, P&O Cruises, and Swan Hellenic.

Other big news is the introduction of the biggest ship ever to cruise Alaska waters, the 109,000-ton, 2,600-passenger *Star Princess*. She will join an already big fleet that was expanded still further in the wake of the September 11, 2001, terrorist attacks when several lines, based on a belief that passengers may prefer to stay closer to home, moved ships that had been scheduled to cruise in Europe to Alaska instead. **Holland America** and **Princess** both added a ship, bringing their number of vessels in the Alaska market to six each. (Holland America added its flagship *Amsterdam* on weeklong itineraries from Seattle, and Princess is bringing back the *Regal Princess* on 10-night cruises from San Francisco.) **Celebrity,** which had planned to deploy the *Mercury* in Europe, returned the ship, instead, to Alaska, where it had been for several years previously.

Luxury line **Seabourn** also said it would return to Alaska following a five-year absence, diverting its *Seabourn Spirit* from previously planned Mediterranean cruises. In the luxury end, this means passengers will have more options than ever before, with Seabourn offering a formal cruising experience on a small ship, **Crystal** doing the same on a bigger ship, and **Radisson** offering a more casual brand of luxury.

Four extra ships may not seem like a lot, but think of it in these terms: It's 6,058 berths that nobody expected to be available. This means more competition in the market, which promises (a) to make life difficult for cruise-line marketers and (b) to produce what may be some incredible bargains for consumers as the cruise lines do battle along price lines.

Cruise lines also moved ships around a tad. **Radisson Seven Seas,** for instance, is bringing back to the market the all-suite *Seven Seas Navigator,* which replaces the bigger all-suite, all-balcony cabin *Seven Seas Mariner,* the line's ship in the Alaska market in 2001. (The *Mariner* is scheduled to cruise Europe in 2002.) Royal Caribbean is bringing its beautiful new *Radiance of the Seas* back to

Alaska for a second year, where it will be joined by the older megaship *Legend of the Seas.* (Interestingly, both the *Radiance,* introduced in 2001, and *Legend,* introduced in 1995, were the first in their respective classes.)

In small ship news, **American Safari Cruises** adds a 12-passenger yacht, expanding its fleet to three vessels. In 2001, Cruise West retired the *Spirit of Glacier Bay.* And Alaska's Glacier Bay Tours & Cruises officially changed its name to **Glacier Bay Cruiseline.**

ONBOARD CHANGES Cruise lines, of course, did all sorts of tweaking of their onboard products. Among the more noteworthy changes, Carnival introduced on its *Carnival Spirit* a new tipping policy in which passengers are automatically charged $9.75 per day.

Educationally-oriented World Explorer introduced an enhanced education program on its *Universe Explorer* that offers a series of classes for up to 40 participants and field trips personally guided by experts. (The fee for the program is $180–$240 per person.)

With the *Star Princess,* Princess introduces to its Alaska fleet reservations-only alternative dining, with the ship boasting both upscale Italian and Mexican venues. (A fee is charged at both.)

A new casual dining option, in the form of an open-air grill, was introduced on the *Crystal Harmony.* And Glacier Bay's *Wilderness Discoverer* now boasts four recently added suites (the first such accommodations in that line's fleet).

CRUISETOURS The big news for Alaska cruisetours in 2002 is Princess' addition of optional add-on land tours to Wrangell–St. Elias National Park, previously a rather inaccessible area, where Princess is building a new hotel (see below).

You'll see us talking more about Royal Caribbean/Celebrity's new land programs introduced in 2001. Jerry tried them, twice taking the company's new domed railcar between Anchorage and Fairbanks, by way of Denali Park, and was very impressed.

And World Explorer introduced a new **Canadian Rockies rail-tour program,** from Calgary to Vancouver, available as a pre- or post-cruise option.

HOTELS Princess plans to open in the spring, just in time for the 2002 season, its new 85-room **Copper River Princess Wilderness Lodge.** The property is in Wrangell–St. Elias National Park, where Princess will also offer a new series of land tours (see above).

And note these hotel name updates: The Regal Alaskan in Anchorage is now the Millennium Alaskan; Hotel Vancouver and the Waterfront Hotel in Vancouver are now The Fairmont Hotel Vancouver and The Fairmont Waterfront Hotel; the Baranof Hotel in Juneau is now the Westmark Baranof Hotel; and the Empress Hotel in Victoria (B.C.), one of the Pacific Northwest's (if not the world's) greatest addresses, is now The Fairmont Empress Hotel.

We've also added the Seward Windsong Lodge in Seward because the property offers incredible views as the only lodge in Kenai Fjords National Park.

ATTRACTIONS Not a new attraction, but new in our book, for those who want to venture out of Vancouver is the touristy but fun **Capilano Suspension Bridge** (a narrow, high-up crossing of the Capilano River in North Vancouver). We've also added as organized tour options in Vancouver: **Vancouver Stanley Park Horse-Drawn Tours,** a firm that, as the name implies, offers horse-drawn tours of gorgeous Stanley Park; and **Vancouver Trolley Company,** which offers city tours using an old-fashioned street trolley.

In Victoria, we tried and liked a tour in a classic convertible on a beautiful sunny day, and that's why we've added the new tour option of **Classic Car Tours.** And because Fran's brother and sister-in-law particularly enjoyed it, we've added in Victoria the **Miniature World** attraction, located in back of The Fairmont Empress Hotel.

In Sitka, there's the additional organized tour option of a cultural tour by Native American–run **Tribal Tours.** In Skagway, we describe the new home and collection of the **Skagway Museum & Archives.** And in Valdez, we've added the Valdez Museum Annex, which is slightly off the beaten path—if you can be off the beaten path in such a small town. (It's 4 blocks from the main Valdez Museum.)

SHORE EXCURSIONS We're pretty excited about some of the new shore excursion options in Alaska, although we haven't gotten to try them all yet. These including a snorkeling adventure in Ketchikan ($79, including the use of an insulating wet suit), a rain-forest walk in Juneau ($60–$64), horseback riding outside of Skagway ($120–$139), a bike excursion in Haines ($42), and sport fishing in Valdez ($129), which, despite its fame as an oil-spill capital, offers some excellent fishing opportunities.

GLACIER BAY There was great debate at press time over how many ships should be allowed to visit Glacier Bay, based on concerns over the environmental impact. We detail the latest as we know it. The issue, of course, is the effect of ship traffic on the wildlife of the bay. And the question is how many permits the National Park Service will be allowed to issue. A federal court ruled last summer that access should be reduced by about 30, which caused a late season diversion of a few ships to Icy Straits, Hubbard Glacier, and other alternative spots. The lines hope that Congress will reverse the court's decision in time to allow them to operate a full schedule of Glacier Bay visits this year. But that's by no means certain. Whether the ship you're on will get to travel there remains to be seen (no matter what it says in the brochure). But don't worry, there are plenty of other fabulous glaciers to see. (You won't miss much if you skip Glacier Bay.)

READER'S SUGGESTION We do listen, and one reader pointed out that small ships have tipping guidelines that can be different from those of big ships. So to help avoid any confusion, we've included a guideline on how to tip on a small ship. See chapter 6.

1

Cruising the Great Land:
An Introduction

Alaska is one of the top cruise destinations in the world, and when you're sailing through the calm waters of the Inside Passage or across the Gulf, it's easy to see why. The scenery, in what is one of the nation's few remaining frontiers, is simply breathtaking.

Much of the coastline is wilderness, with snowcapped mountain peaks, immense glaciers that create thunderous noise as they calve into the sea, emerald rain forests, fjords, icebergs, soaring eagles, lumbering bears, and majestic whales all easily viewed from the comfort of your ship.

Visit the towns, and you'll find people who retain the spirit of frontier independence that brought them here in the first place. Add Alaska's colorful history and heritage, with its European influences, its gold-rush spirit of discovery, and its rich Native culture, and you have a destination that is utterly and endlessly fascinating.

The fact that approximately 750,000 cruise passengers arrive annually in this last great frontier has had its impact, of course, turning some towns in summer into tourist malls populated by seasonal vendors and imported souvenirs. However, the port towns you'll visit—from Juneau, the most remote state capital in the country, to Sitka, with its proud reminders of Native and Russian culture—retain much of their rustic charm and historical allure. Sure, you may have to jostle for a seat in Juneau's popular Red Dog Saloon (a must-do beer stop) or ask other visitors to step out of the way as you try to snap a picture of Skagway's historic gold-rush buildings, but these are minor hassles for cruise-ship passengers.

There may be even bigger crowds in Alaska in 2002. Following the September 11 terrorist attacks, and based on changes in travel patterns and the premise that travelers would probably want to stick closer to home, several lines announced plans to move ships that were to cruise in the Mediterranean and other parts of Europe to the Alaska market. Celebrity Cruises, for instance, is repositioning its *Mercury* to Alaska and will now have three ships in the market in 2002. Holland America and Princess are each adding a ship: HAL repositioning its flagship *Amsterdam* to Seattle for weeklong Alaska itineraries, and Princess repositioning *Regal Princess* to San Francisco, from where it will offer 10-night Alaska sailings. The moves bring the total number of ships both HAL and Princess will have in Alaska for the summer of 2002 to six. But the biggest news is the return of Seabourn Cruise Line to the Alaska market. The ultra-luxury, small-ship line will offer 10- and 11-night cruises on its *Seabourn Spirit*, which had earlier been scheduled to spend the summer in the Mediterranean.

All this adds a considerable number of berths to the Alaska market, but how these cruises will sell and what they will do to the actual number of travelers in Alaska remains to be seen.

Unfortunately, the hordes of visitors and the environmental impact of so many cruise ships are beginning to take their toll on the psyches of some Alaska residents. Haines, for instance, has put a limit on the amount of cruisetour traffic it will tolerate, and Juneau, the state's beautiful capital, imposed a $5-per-passenger head tax in 2000, ostensibly to pay for the essential services (police, sewage, roadways, and so on) used by the estimated 630,000 cruisers who visit there annually.

The vexing question of cruise-ship taxation in Alaska—at both local and state levels—is one that is not likely to go away in a hurry. In 2000, one energetic state legislator went so far as to introduce a bill that would have imposed a $50-per-person head tax on all cruise passengers. Half of the money collected was to have been given to the first five ports on any itinerary, at the rate of $5 per passenger; the remaining $25 was to have gone into the general exchequer. That tax would have superseded all local cruise passenger fees, of course. The bill never got out of committee and, so, never came to a vote of the legislature, and although it wasn't reintroduced in the 2001 session of the legislature, the cruise industry fears that it, or something like it, is liable to pop up again sometime in the future. In fact, a group of citizens in Anchorage is trying to get signatures on a petition that would allow a proposal to be put to the voters next year to levy a $75 head tax on cruise passengers! That would no doubt seriously impact pricing. Although the lines can absorb a few bucks here and there, there's no way they can underwrite a $75 tax without passing it on to customers.

Nor is taxation the only challenge. At the same time as all this taxing is going on, the state legislature has enacted a series of pollution-mitigating restrictions on cruise lines, increasing environmental reporting requirements, for example, and restricting the number and size of the areas in which they may legally discard treated waste. Most of these laws were little more than guidelines, policed by the cruise operators themselves. So determined was Governor Tony Knowles to give the state real power to deal with polluters that, in 2001, he called the legislature back into session after its summer recess began, to thrash out a new set of laws giving the job of enforcement to the state itself, not the lines. To some extent, the cruise lines have themselves to blame. Some of them have been a little less than diligent in their pollution abatement efforts.

The fact that Alaska faces a deficit caused by volatility in the price of North Slope oil has something to do with the rush to tax. Some cruise executives believe environmental concerns, serious though they are, are being overplayed by way of creating an "excuse" to make cruise lines and their passengers pay to reduce the budget shortfall. Be that as it may, Alaska's (and Alaskans') perception of cruising and efforts to make cruise passengers pay more are matters that concern ship operators greatly. It all adds up to an uneasy situation, which both Alaska and the cruise lines are eager to resolve. To this end, Princess began in September 2000 to shut down its ships' engines while at dock in Juneau, drawing electrical power instead from the city grid and thus reducing the pollution coming from its ships' smokestacks. This is a new practice in cruising and signifies a willingness in the industry to help preserve its most valuable asset: the pristine destinations that people are coming to see.

Word to the wise: Don't let all this legislative wrangling frighten you off. On the whole, you'll find the residents of Alaska remain warm to visitors, whether they come from cruise ships or travel independently.

A variety of ships exists in the Alaska market. On the small ones, you can get closer to the natural sights and wildlife, visit out-of-the-way ports, and really get to know your fellow passengers. On the big ships, you can enjoy all the

Alaska

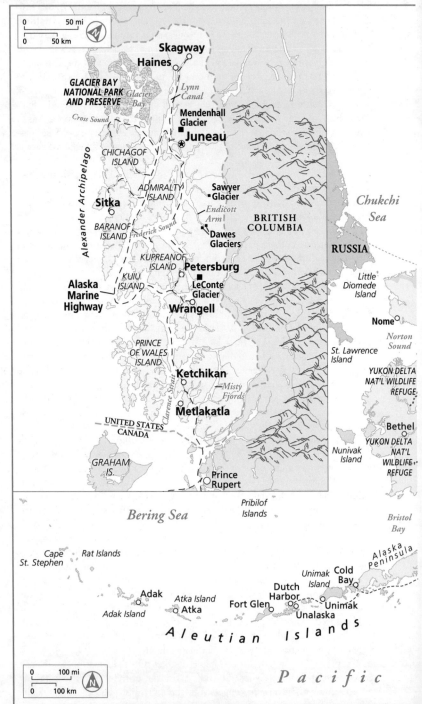

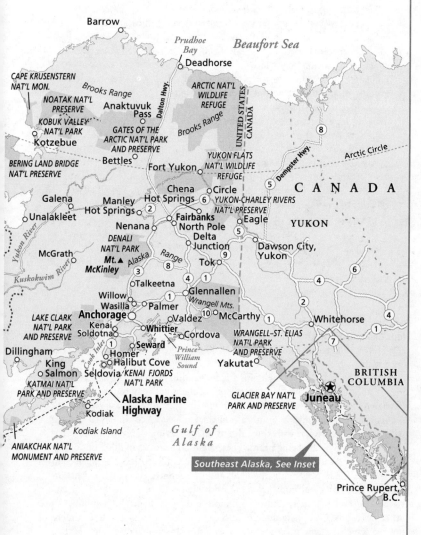

Paved Road
State or Provincial Route
Dirt Road

Arctic Ocean

Barrow

Prudhoe Bay

Beaufort Sea

Deadhorse

CAPE KRUSENSTERN NAT'L MON.

Brooks Range

ARCTIC NAT'L WILDLIFE REFUGE

NOATAK NAT'L PRESERVE

Anaktuvuk Pass

Brooks Range

KOBUK VALLEY NAT'L PARK

Kotzebue

GATES OF THE ARCTIC NAT'L PARK AND PRESERVE

Bettles

YUKON FLATS NAT'L WILDLIFE REFUGE

Fort Yukon

UNITED STATES / CANADA

Dempster Hwy.

Arctic Circle

BERING LAND BRIDGE NAT'L PRESERVE

8

Circle

Chena Hot Springs

6

YUKON-CHARLEY RIVERS NAT'L PRESERVE

5

C A N A D A

Galena

Manley Hot Springs

2

Fairbanks

Eagle

YUKON

Unalakleet

Nenana

North Pole

5

Yukon River

DENALI NAT'L PARK

Delta Junction

Dawson City, Yukon

McGrath

Mt. ▲ McKinley

Alaska Range

3

8

9

Tok

6

Kuskokwim River

4

1

4

Talkeetna

Glennallen

Willow

1

Wrangell Mts.

2

Wasilla   Palmer

Whitehorse

Anchorage

Valdez

10

McCarthy

1

4

LAKE CLARK NAT'L PARK AND PRESERVE

Kenai

Soldotna

Whittier

Cordova

WRANGELL-ST. ELIAS NAT'L PARK AND PRESERVE

7

1

Dillingham

Cook Inlet

Homer

Seward

Prince William Sound

Yakutat

BRITISH COLUMBIA

King Salmon

Halibut Cove

Seldovia

KENAI FJORDS NAT'L PARK

KATMAI NAT'L PARK AND PRESERVE

Alaska Marine Highway

Kodiak

GLACIER BAY NAT'L PARK AND PRESERVE

★ Juneau

Kodiak Island

Gulf of Alaska

ANIAKCHAK NAT'L MONUMENT AND PRESERVE

Southeast Alaska, See Inset

Ocean

To Vancouver & Seattle ↘

Prince Rupert, B.C.

Considering the Environment

Environmental issues involving passenger ship entry into Glacier Bay continue to pit conservationists against the cruise lines, most recently with the courts and Congress putting in their two cents worth, as well. The subject of how many ships can safely enter the vast wilderness area without upsetting the whales and other forms of aquatic life that inhabit it in the summer has been hotly debated—and disputed— for at least a decade and, at this writing, has reached a new fever pitch.

The latest round of controversy began way back in 1997 when the National Park Service upped the number of cruise ships authorized to enter the bay from 107 to 139. The increase was challenged in federal court by a group known as the National Parks Conservation Association, which argued that any Glacier Bay entry increase should have been preceded by an environmental impact study. The court rejected the argument, and the environmentalists appealed.

Last February—almost 4 years after the NPS decision—a three-member federal appeals court found in favor of the National Parks Conservation Association and ordered that the number of Glacier Bay tickets issued each year be trimmed back to 107, pending the outcome of a study of the cruise industry on the life of the bay. It left it to the lower court to decide when the cuts should be made. It was not until July that a judge, responding to the appeals court ruling, told the NPS to prorate the remainder of the 2001 season and reduce access in the last few weeks of August by a total of nine ships.

(For the purposes of Glacier Bay permitting, the season lasts 92 days— June, July, and Aug. May and Sept entries do not require permits nor, at any time, do small boats, such as those operated by Cruise West, Glacier Bay Cruiseline, and the like.)

amenities of a resort—spas, gyms, casinos, show lounges, swimming pools—and tour the state at the same time. And the big ships in Alaska are getting even bigger: New in the market in 2002 is the 2,600-passenger *Star Princess,* one of the biggest ships in the world.

Back in the early 1970s, there was a mere handful of ships, the largest carrying only about 600 passengers, virtually all of them in 7-day round-trip Inside Passage rotation out of Vancouver. The route along the Inside Passage (through the part of Alaska known as Southeast, or the Panhandle) continues to be a big seller. But this summer, with three dozen vessels serving the state, more variations on the theme are being heard. There are Alaska cruises in 2002 out of San Francisco and Seattle; one-way cruises across the Gulf of Alaska between Vancouver and Anchorage (with disembarkation in Seward, the port for Anchorage); and all-Alaska cruises beginning and ending in places such as Juneau, Ketchikan, and Whittier; cruises to remote Indian villages; and a number of other variations. And by signing up for the cruise lines' pre- or post-cruise land-tour packages (known as "cruisetours"), you can also visit such inland destinations as Denali National Park, Fairbanks, the Yukon Territory, or the Canadian Rockies.

Thus, some cruise passengers last year found that their itineraries were rejiggered at short notice in order to steer their ships away from the popular Glacier Bay. Holland America Line was the hardest hit, losing five entry authorizations; Princess gave up two; and Norwegian Cruise and World Explorer Cruises one apiece. The lines rerouted these ships to other scenic glacier wilderness areas, most particularly Disenchantment Bay, where sits Hubbard Glacier.

What comes next? What happens this year? No environmental impact study could possibly be completed in time for the coming season. If it were, the courts would need months to consider it, and the environmentalists would certainly challenge it again because, they would say, it was done in haste. The cruise lines printed their 2002 brochures on the basis of their share of the 139 Glacier Bay entries they expected to receive. Now they may receive fewer than they expected and be forced to explain to prospective cruisers that they're not going to Glacier Bay after all, but to Hubbard Glacier or Icy Bay or Misty Fjords or Tracy Arm instead.

That, the lines do *not* want to have to do.

Congress may prove to be their savior. At press time, the U.S. Senate had before it a bill, authored by Alaska Senator Ted Stevens, that would mandate a return to the original, higher level of Glacier Bay entry authorizations, regardless of what the courts say. Until that bill is discussed on Capitol Hill, we don't know for sure what we're dealing with in Glacier Bay cruising this year.

A word about Glacier Bay, though. Don't be put off if the cruise you choose is rerouted away from the park. There are many other totally satisfying, visually delightful wilderness areas that can substitute Glacier Bay, including, but not restricted to, those mentioned above. Whisper it: We would rather visit Hubbard Glacier any day!

Even before you cruise, we predict you'll want to visit again. Jerry first visited almost 30 years ago and claims he's never been the same—the place put such a spell on him that he's gone back every year since, sometimes two or three times. Fran's first visit to the state wasn't quite that long ago, but she also noticed her view of the world was forever changed, and she quickly put the state at the top of her list of cruise destinations. Alaska is like that. It grabs you by the scruff of the neck and won't let you go.

The Best of Cruising Alaska

Whether you're looking for pampering and resort amenities or a you-and-the-sea adventure experience, you'll find it offered by cruise ships in Alaska. Here are some of our favorites, along with our picks of the best ports, shore excursions, and sights.

- **The Best Ships for Luxury:** Crystal Cruises' 940-passenger *Crystal Harmony* is the big luxury ship in the Alaska market. We're talking superb cuisine, elegant service, lovely surroundings, great cabins, and sparkling entertainment. The 204-passenger *Seabourn Spirit* offers competition—but on a smaller scale. Guests onboard the sleek, modern vessel can expect

Personal Reminiscence

One of the great delights of Alaska is that you're never quite certain what to expect. Just when you think you've seen it all—there's more! Never was that point more vividly illustrated than on my visit late last summer. Both during the cruise portion, on Celebrity's magnificent *Infinity,* and on land, during a Denali Park rail ride on Celebrity's new domed cars, one wonder followed another.

You should know that I have cruised in Alaskan waters at least once a year since the early 1970s and have done the Denali trip umpteen times—often by rail, sometimes by coach. Yet last year, I saw things I had never seen before.

I was with a small group of people, some of whom were visiting Alaska for the first time. My wife, Margaret, was with me, and although she's not new to Alaska cruising, she had somehow missed out on Denali all these years. A few in the group regretted that *Infinity*'s itinerary did not include Glacier Bay but featured, instead, Hubbard Glacier. I offered the opinion that I'd rather visit Hubbard any day. I'm not sure many of them believed me, but it's true. The approaches to the mouth of Yaku-tat Bay and Hubbard, I told them, are scenically spectacular, with the St. Elias Mountain Range stretching as far as the eye can see. And I added that, in my experience, Hubbard was more active in calving than other glaciers I had seen.

"Be on deck early and don't forget your cameras," was my sage advice.

Fortune smiled on us on the day of our visit. The air was chilly, but the sun was bright, and the peaks—Mt. Vancouver, Mt. Logan, Mt. Hub-bard, Mt. St. Elias, and the other snow-capped sentinels by the bay—stood out in sharp relief against a clear blue sky. When we got into Enchantment Bay, at the top of Yakutat, in which Hubbard is located, the glacier was every bit as active as I had predicted. In fact, even I had to admit that its calving—both in the size of the falls and the accompa-nying thunderous sounds—was more impressive than I had seen in the past.

At dinner that night, my advice to the group was validated by their reaction to what they had seen. There was so much activity on the ice wall, complained one man, that he wore himself out running from one side of the deck to the other trying to capture that perfect picture.

His wife, a sun lover, admitted that she didn't expect to stay on deck long once she realized how cold it was. "But I didn't dare leave," she said. "There was so much going on." Hubbard Glacier had been, in every respect, a success.

And then came the whales!

In my 3 decades of savoring Alaska, I had seen whales—hundreds of them. But until last year, I had never seen one breaching. (That's what it's called when these creatures hurl themselves out of the water and drop in again on their backs with a mighty splash. Scientists aren't sure exactly why they do it. According to various theories, the whales may be communicating, playing, or warning off enemies. It's also believed that they may be trying to dislodge barnacles and parasites clinging to their bellies.) I had seen the pictures of the activity but never experienced it firsthand. Until last fall!

On a wildlife cruise (a shore excursion) out of Juneau, we watched two whales breach in rapid succession. Each must have been 6 feet clear of the water. It seemed almost orchestrated—like something from a Samuel Goldwyn extravaganza. I sort of expected Esther Williams to put in an appearance. It was an awesome sight, made all the more awesome by the fact that it was my first experience of the phenomenon.

But it was left to Denali Park to put on the biggest show of all. I eyed that segment of the cruisetour with some trepidation. Margaret had never been there before and was so excited at the prospect that I worried she would be disappointed. I cautioned her and the others that I had been in that area for days on end on previous trips without so much as a glimpse of Mt. McKinley. Its 20,320-foot summit—and for that matter, its entire bulk—is often shrouded in clouds and impossible to see. For Margaret's sake, and for the sake of the others, I didn't want that to happen on this occasion.

I needn't have worried. The photogenic mountain was as clear as a bell the whole time. And the best was yet to come.

In the past, I've taken wildlife tours of the park—and seen precious little wildlife! If you see Mt. McKinley, a moose, a caribou, a Dall sheep, and a grizzly bear on the same day, you are said to have seen "The Grand Slam." I had seen four of the five and three of the five and, on a really bad day, just two of the five. But this time—bingo!

Not only did we see all components of The Grand Slam, but we also saw them at close range. A mother grizzly and her cub foraged, unconcerned, along the side of the road as our bus stopped not 10 feet from them, with passengers' cameras clicking and whirring. The caribou and moose were just 40 or 50 yards from us, and Dall sheep were everywhere. As a bonus, we also had a very clear sighting of a red fox and numerous brushes with the state bird, the willow ptarmigan.

So there we were, one old Alaska/Denali hand and a number of neophytes. And the neophytes had seen on their first cruisetour what it took me 30 years to see!

Alas, the joy of discovery we had felt during our trip was quickly forgotten. We were scheduled to fly home from Fairbanks in the early morning of September 11. We got the news of the World Trade Center atrocity as we were handing our baggage over to the airline clerk. A supervisor whispered the news to her that all flights to and in the U.S. were scrubbed indefinitely, and the clerk returned our bags. We went back to our hotel to await the lifting of the ban; our check-in did not come until 6 days later. During our enforced stopover, we toured Fairbanks as best we could—with heavy hearts and little enthusiasm.

Margaret and I will always vividly remember that vacation. Unfortunately, for all of Alaska's splendor and visual excitement, we will remember it mostly for tragic reasons.

doting service, suite accommodations, free booze, and the finest cuisine at sea. If you want a more casual kind of luxury (a really nice ship with a no-tie-required policy), Radisson Seven Seas Cruises' **Seven Seas Navigator** offers just that, including plush all-suite cabins (most with private balconies) and excellent cuisine. (Plus, you get complimentary wine with dinner.)

- **The Best of the Mainstream Ships:** Everyone's most recent ships are beautiful, but Celebrity's new **Infinity** is a stunner, as will be, no doubt, its brand-new sister ship, **Summit** (due at press time). These modern vessels, with their extensive art collections, cushy public rooms, and expanded spa areas will give Celebrity a formidable presence in Alaska in 2002.

- **The Best of the Small Ships:** Clipper Cruise Line's newest vessel, the **Clipper Odyssey,** is a really stunning little ship, offering a higher level of comfort than most of the other small ships in this category. The most adventurous small-ship itineraries in Alaska are offered by Glacier Bay Cruiseline, whose **Wilderness Adventurer** and **Wilderness Explorer** both concentrate on kayaking, hiking, and wildlife, hardly visiting any ports at all over the course of their itineraries.

- **The Best Ships for Families:** All the major lines have well-established kids' programs. Holland America and Norwegian Cruise Line win points in Alaska for their special shore excursions for kids and teens, and Carnival offers special shore excursions for teens.

- **The Best Ships for Pampering:** It's a toss-up: Celebrity's **Infinity** and **Summit** offer wonderful AquaSpas complete with thalassotherapy pools and a wealth of soothing and beautifying treatments, while **Crystal Harmony** pampers all around, and the solariums on Royal Caribbean's **Vision of the Seas, Legend of the Seas,** and new **Radiance of the Seas** offer relaxing indoor pool retreats.

- **The Best Shipboard Cuisine:** Seabourn, Radisson, and Crystal (in that order) are tops. Of the mainstream lines, Celebrity is the best, with its cuisine overseen by renowned French chef Michel Roux. And there are signs of a new and rather surprising challenger for the cuisine award: Carnival. Although the line had not hitherto been especially noted for its food, it has upgraded both its main dining room and buffet offerings. And the line's new **Carnival Spirit,** which debuted in Alaska last year, has raised the company's standards considerably.

- **The Best Ships for Onboard Activities:** The ships operated by Carnival and Royal Caribbean offer a very full roster of onboard activities, that range from the sublime (lectures) to the ridiculous (contests designed to get passengers to do crazy things).

- **The Best Ships for Entertainment:** Look to the big ships here. Carnival and Royal Caribbean are tops when it comes to an overall package of show productions, nightclub acts, lounge performances, and audience-participation entertainment. And Princess offers particularly well-done stage shows.

- **The Best Ships for Whale-Watching:** If they come close enough, you can see whales from all the ships in Alaska. Smaller ships, though—such as those operated by Glacier Bay Cruiseline—and Cruise West may actually change course to follow a whale. Get your cameras ready!

- **The Best Ship for a Great Itinerary:** World Explorer Cruises'

Universe Explorer is unmatched in this area with its 14-day, round-trip itineraries from Vancouver that include all the major ports of call and a few others, too. Included is an extended port call at Metlakatla, a Tsimshian Indian village on Annette Island, just south of Ketchikan, and a visit to Kodiak Island, famous for its bear population. (No other cruise ships visit there regularly.)

- **The Best Ships for Cruisetours:** Princess and Holland America are the entrenched market leaders in getting you into the Interior either before or after your cruise. They own their own hotels, deluxe motor coaches, and railcars, and after many years in the business, they both really know what they're doing. Some of the other lines actually buy their cruisetour products from them. Holland America's cruisetours strength is its 3- and 4-night cruises combined with an Alaska/Yukon land package, while Princess is arguably stronger in 7-day Gulf of Alaska cruises in conjunction with Denali/Fairbanks or Kenai Peninsula land arrangements. Royal Caribbean also last year introduced its own land-tour operation (complete with hugely impressive, custom-built, double-decker railcars) to go with cruises on its Royal Caribbean and Celebrity brands.

- **The Best Ports: Juneau** and **Skagway** are our favorites, but we also really like Haines. Juneau is one of the most visually pleasing small cities anywhere and certainly the prettiest capital city in the United States. It's fronted by the Gastineau Channel and backed by Mount Juneau and Mount Roberts, offers the very accessible Mendenhall Glacier, and is otherwise surrounded by wilderness— and it's a really fun city to visit,

too. As for Skagway, no town in Alaska is more historically significant, and the old buildings are so perfect, you might think you stepped into a Disney version of what a gold-rush town should look like. If, that is, you can get over the decidedly turn-of-the-millennium Starbucks coffee vendor in the Mercantile Center and all the upscale jewelry shops that have followed cruise passengers from the Caribbean. For a more low-key Alaska experience, take the ferry from Skagway to Haines, a great place to spot eagles and other wildlife. (Some ships also stop at Haines as a port of call.)

- **The Best Shore Excursions:** Flightseeing and helicopter trips in Alaska are really unforgettable ways to check out the scenery if you can afford them. A helicopter trip to a dogsled camp at the top of a glacier (usually the priciest of the offerings) affords both incredibly pretty views and a chance to try your hand at the truly Alaskan sport of dogsledding. For a less extravagant excursion, nothing beats a ride on a clear day on the aforementioned White Pass and Yukon Route railway out of Skagway. And we also like to get active with kayak and mountain-biking excursions offered by most lines at most ports; in addition to affording a chance to work off those shipboard calories, these excursions typically provide optimum opportunities for spotting eagles, bears, seals, and other wildlife.

- **The Best Natural Sights Seen from Onboard:** There are so many in Alaska, it's hard to choose, but Glacier Bay, Hubbard Glacier, College Fjord, and Misty Fjords National Monument (into which big ships can only get a short distance) would have to appear on anyone's top-10 list.

2

Alaska 101:
A Cruise-Goer's Companion

Alaska has a story to tell. Ten thousand years of Native culture. Magnificent glaciers and wildlife. Colorful gold-rush history. The list goes on.

So you'll know what to expect when you arrive (and so you can drop a few well-informed words on your fellow cruise passengers your first day out), we've put together a short primer on the major Alaskan subjects you're likely to be curious about during your cruise. (For further information, see the appendix.)

1 An Introduction to Southeast Alaska's Native Culture

This essay was written for us by Jan Halliday, a former editor of *Alaska Airlines Magazine* and author of *Native Peoples of the Northwest* (Sasquatch Books, 2nd edition, 2000) and *Native People of Alaska: A Traveler's Guide to Land, Art, and Culture* (Sasquatch Books, 1998), both of which describe Native tours, interpretive centers, museums, art galleries, artists' studios, lodges, B&Bs, and restaurants in their area of coverage, and provide detailed contact information.

Welcome to the islands of the Inside Passage, the traditional and contemporary home of the **Tlingit** (pronounced *klink*-get) Indians. Although the Tlingit's language is related to the Athabascan of interior Alaska and Canada and to the Navaho of the American Southwest, no one knows for sure when they settled this strip of Alaska coastline and islands. The Tlingit may be descendants of the first wave of ice-age travelers who crossed the Bering Sea from Asia into North America, or they may descend from a later wave of immigrants who returned to this fish-rich area from the interior of the North American continent more than 10,000 years ago, after ice-age glaciers retreated.

No matter how they came here, until this century Tlingits used these inland channels between islands and river passageways through the barrier mountains as their highways. In the 1700s, Tlingit paddlers, steering huge cargo canoes carved from cedar logs, were sighted as far south as the Channel Islands off the coast of Los Angeles, reportedly to take slaves. In the 18th and 19th centuries, before epidemics decimated their communities, the Tlingit people were trade partners with the Russians, British, Americans, and interior tribes of Canada, controlling the waterways of Southeast Alaska and demanding tolls for their use. For example, in the 1800s, the Tlingits allowed gold miners to travel over the rugged **Chilkoot Pass** between Skagway and the Klondike goldfields, but only after they paid a substantial fee.

Newcomers to Southeast Alaska include the **Haida** and **Tsimshian** Indians, who came into Tlingit territory from British Columbia in the last 2 centuries. The Haida, from the Queen Charlotte Islands, settled on Prince of Wales Island in the late 1700s; Tsimshian Indians, from the Prince Rupert area, settled Annette Island as a utopian Christian community in the late 1800s.

Today, many Natives live in small villages on remote islands (such as **Angoon** on Admiralty Island, **Hoonah** on Chichagof Island, and **Kake** on Kupreanof Island) and in centers of commerce such as Juneau, Ketchikan, and Sitka. In smaller villages, away from the bustle of larger towns, you may see Natives drying seaweed in front of their houses on a sheet of plywood or filleting and drying salmon, both traditional foods. But visitors should not expect people, villages, or towns to look as they did when photographers froze their images in the last century, any more than you'd expect to see people in Oregon dressed in pioneer garb, making soap over a wood fire. Many do live traditional subsistence-level lifestyles, gathering and preserving fish and shellfish, beach greens, and berries, as well as ordering bulk groceries from Costco in Juneau. The primary source of income for villagers is logging and commercial fishing. All small communities use fuel-burning generators for electrical power and also have well-stocked stores, with larger items arriving by barge and cargo jet and fresh goods arriving daily by smaller planes.

It's important for visitors to remember that Native history and culture are entwined with the cultural and economic impact of the Russian, British, and American traders of the early 1800s, the gold miners of the late 1800s, and the timber, fishing, canning, and mining industries of the 20th century. Southeast Alaska clans led (and won) in the fight for civil rights years before Martin Luther King, Jr., led the civil rights movement for blacks in the 1960s. Many clan members have served in the U.S. military, many own businesses, and several are Alaska state legislators.

In 1971, Natives gained economic clout when the **Alaska Native Claims Settlement Act** settled the 100-year-old question of aboriginal land rights. Under dispute were 375 million acres of land in Alaska. Under provisions of the act, Congress deeded title to 44 million acres, spread throughout the state, to Alaska Natives, and a payment of close to $1 billion was made to compensate the loss of the remaining 331 million acres. The act created 13 regional corporations and more than 230 village corporations to receive federal money and manage land on behalf of Native shareholders. In Southeast Alaska, Native corporations such as Goldbelt, Cape Fox, and Huna Totem have taken the lead in tourism development, investing in first-class hotels, cruise ships, air taxis, and passenger-ferry sightseeing boats. Huna Totem corporation owns the *Alaskan Southeaster*, a magazine about the region. In Juneau, Goldbelt owns and operates the tram to the top of Mount Roberts, a modern hotel, and Glacier Bay Cruiseline. Sealaska Heritage Foundation, the nonprofit arm of Sealaska, another Juneau-based Native corporation, supports scholarly work, publishing videos, language learning materials, and such books as *Haa Shuka, Our Ancestors: Tlingit Oral Narratives*, by poet Nora Marks Dauenhauer, written in both Tlingit and English. Even small corporations, such as the Organized Village of Kake, have built lovely little hotels for visitors, overlooking beautiful vistas of seacoast and snow-covered mountains.

Alaska Natives run their corporations in some of Juneau's finest office buildings, dressed in business suits, and don ceremonial regalia (robes decorated with clan insignia and magnificent, carved headdresses inlaid with abalone shell) only during private and public celebrations. (The largest of these, called simply **Celebration,** is held in Juneau every 2 years for 4 days in June, with clans gathering from throughout Southeast Alaska to celebrate their cultural heritage and perform traditional dances.)

Having said this, there are many aspects of Native hospitality and colorful heritage for you to enjoy in Southeast Alaska. Distinctive Tlingit, Haida, and Tsimshian **totemic art** is prevalent and sets the region completely apart from other places in the world. In Ketchikan, for example, there are more than 70 standing **totem poles,** and a museum dedicated entirely to the oldest poles collected from abandoned Tlingit villages. There are also two traditional **clan houses,** reminiscent of dozens of large houses that lined the waterfront in the last century, constructed from hand-hewn cedar and adorned with carved house posts and decorated house screens. Both are open to the public. You can also observe Native carvers working on commissioned masks, canoes, and totem poles at places such as **Saxman Village,** 3 miles south of Ketchikan, and in private studios. Many of these artists, such as carvers Amos Wallace and Nathan Jackson, and Chilkat blanket weavers such as Delores Churchill, have their work in private and museum collections throughout the world.

Most towns in Southeast Alaska have fascinating museums filled with artifacts and traditional art. Those with the largest collections are the **Alaska State Museum** in Juneau and the **Sheldon Jackson Museum** in Sitka, but smaller museums shouldn't be missed.

Raven and **Eagle** clan symbols, representing the two major clan divisions to which every Haida, Tsimshian, and Tlingit Native belongs, adorn everything from bags of fresh-roasted coffee to beach blankets and T-shirts. However, don't be misled by souvenirs into thinking these are just pleasing designs. These clan symbols, which include other totem figures such as salmon, killer whales, frogs, and bears, define the strong family ties that reach back far into the past and bind contemporary Native people in this region. Rather than describe complicated clan lineage systems to you here, I suggest you learn firsthand about the clans from Native tour guides and at Native-based shore excursions designed especially for the time frame of cruise-ship passengers—such as at **Saxman Village** in Ketchikan, at **Metlakatla's** tour and salmon bake, or on one of **Sitka Tribal Tours'** bus or walking tours of the old Russian/Tlingit capital of Alaska.

When I researched my guidebook to the Native peoples of Alaska, I stayed at Native-owned hotels, visited with artists (one of the best places to meet carvers, weavers, painters, silversmiths, and bead-workers while they work is at the Southeast Alaska Indian Cultural Center in Sitka), gazed in wonder at museum collections, saw the old Chilkat and Ravenstail woven robes come out from behind the glass windows to be worn, and "danced" to the resonant beat of box drums at Celebration. I watched the walls of the **Sheet'ka Kwaan Naa Kahidi Community House,** a gorgeous new hall modeled after the old clan houses, go up in Sitka. I listened as Native guides explained how each totem pole tells a unique family story or honors a fallen clan member. I went fishing with Natives on their charter boats and toured canneries, fish-processing plants, and salmon hatcheries owned by Natives. (One had a standing totem pole right in the center of the creek, with an opportunistic eagle perched on top, eyeing the spawning salmon below.) In **Metlakatla,** I scaled Yellow Hill on the boardwalk and stairs that Terry Booth, a Tsimshian, built for his wife years ago, and watched the sun bathe the village in first morning light. It was all an unforgettable experience. I hope it will be for you as well.

2 From Gold Rush to Oil Boom: A Short History

Somewhere in that great U.S. State Department in the sky, a man named William Seward must be especially pleased with how the vast area of Alaska—all 586,000 square miles of it—has turned out. It was he who, in 1867, as secretary of state under President Andrew Johnson, prevailed upon Congress to buy the mostly wilderness, hugely underpopulated territory from the Russians. The tab? Just $7.2 million—about 2¢ an acre. Was that a bargain, or what?

And yet, at the time, Seward was ridiculed mercilessly—in fact, the purchase only made it through Congress by a single vote. Many Americans, led by those in the national legislature who opposed the deal, mocked him for buying a pig in a poke. They laughed at the place the Native peoples called Alyeska (loosely translated as "The Great Land," but more specifically an Aleut word meaning "Where the Sea Breaks Its Back"). It was widely derided as "Seward's Folly" and "Seward's Icebox."

The naysayers offered a variety of criticisms of the Alaska purchase. The place, some said, had no strategic value—although a part of Seward's argument for buying it had been that it would provide the United States with a northern military bastion. Others clucked that nothing and nobody could live there. Many others scoffed that the new U.S. possession had no mineral wealth.

Could they have been more wrong?

Gold in commercial quantities was discovered in 1880 by drifter/prospector Joe Juneau in the Gastineau Channel, near the city that came to bear his name. (It was originally known as Harrisburg after Juneau's one-time partner, Richard Harris.) Major gold strikes also occurred at Circle City in 1893, at Nome in 1898, and at Fairbanks in 1902. In 1896, of course, the mother of all gold finds was made in the frigid waters of the Klondike's Bonanza Creek in Canada's Yukon Territory and triggered the great gold rush 2 years later. (It took that long for the news to filter down to the then-45 states of the Union.) That gold, although Canadian, had an enormous impact on Alaska, as the nearest point of entry to the Klondike was Skagway, at the head of the Lynn Canal.

Tens of thousands of hitherto stable, unadventurous Americans—bankers, farmers, shopkeepers, accountants, schoolteachers, people from every conceivable walk of life—flocked to Skagway to start their difficult trek over the Chilkoot Pass or White Pass into the Canadian interior in search of riches. They came by ship, some from the eastern states by way of Cape Horn, some crossing by land to join ships in Los Angeles, San Francisco, Portland, and Seattle. Once arrived, their numbers transformed Skagway from a collection of tents and huts into a bustling small town whose colorful history contributes so much to the visitor's experience even today.

Some of the prospectors hit pay dirt (literally), though the vast majority didn't. Although some moved to other areas, still hoping for a big strike, many of them settled in Southeast Alaska, marrying, opening businesses, and generally breathing new life into the wilderness.

The stampede of 1898 forever and inextricably linked Alaska and the Klondike. And the route the stampeders took has become an especially popular tourist itinerary: Take a ship to Skagway, then go over the White Pass (not on foot, but in comfy motor coaches or on a train), and continue by riverboat or road to Dawson City.

After the gold finds in Alaska, of course, there were copper and silver. And then an oil strike at Katalla, near Cordova, all the way back in 1902, which yielded fuel for local use for 30 years or more. Oil was also found on the Kenai Peninsula in 1957 and then at Prudhoe Bay in 1968, 9 years after Alaska became a state. At the time, the Prudhoe Bay fields were estimated as containing a quarter of the known deposits in the United States.

No folly for Mr. Seward, who surely has had the last laugh.

3 Whale-Watching 101

Imagine standing on deck, looking out onto the calm, silver waters of an Alaskan bay. Suddenly, the surface of the water pulls back and an immense yet graceful creature appears, moving silently, the curve of its back visible for a moment before the water again closes over it. You wait for it to reappear. And wait. And wait. Then, just as you're beginning to think it's gone forever, the creature leaps straight out of the water, twisting around in midair before falling back with a gigantic *kersploosh!* that's followed a half second later by an equally distinctive sound: That of 1,000 cruise ship passengers saying "Oooh!," "Aaah!," and "Marty! Marty! Did you see *that?!*"

On most large cruise ships, the captain or officer on watch will make an announcement when he or she spots a whale, but due to its strict schedule the ship probably won't be able to stop and linger. A few lines, though (mostly the small-ship lines), feature whale-watching as a major part of their focus, so their ships will visit areas favored by whales—for instance, waters near Petersburg or Sitka, near Gustavus and Glacier Bay National Park, and near Seward and Kenai Fjords National Park—and spend time waiting there for an encounter, or will monitor marine-traffic radio broadcasts and deviate from course to go where whale sightings have been reported. Most ships, both large and small, will offer lectures about whales at some point during each cruise.

To get you ready for your whale encounter, we've prepared the following little whale primer. Study up so you'll know what you're looking at.

THE HUMPBACK WHALE   These migratory whales spend their summer in Alaska feeding, then swim to Mexican or Hawaiian waters for the winter, where they give birth to their young and then fast until going north again in spring. The cold northern waters produce more of the small fish and other tiny creatures humpbacks filter through their baleen—the strips of stiff, fibrous material that humpbacks have instead of teeth. A humpback is easy to recognize by its huge, mottled tail; by the hump on its back, just forward of its dorsal fin; and by its arm-like flippers, which can grow to be 14 feet long. Most humpback sightings are of the whales' humped backs as they cruise along the surface, resting, and of the flukes of the tail as they dive.

Humpbacks know how to weave nets of bubbles around their prey, then swim upward through the schooled fish, mouths wide open, to eat them in a single swoop, sometimes finishing with a frothy lunge through the surface. Feeding dives can last a long time and often mean you won't see that particular whale again, but if you're lucky the whale may be just dipping down for a few minutes to get ready to leap completely out of the water, a practice called **breaching.** No one knows for sure why they do this; it may simply be play. For viewers, it's thrilling and, if you happen to be in a small boat or kayak, a little scary, even if safe. (Paddlers should group their boats and tap the decks to let the whales know where they are.) Humpbacks are highly sensitive to noise, so keep quiet to see longer displays.

The Humpback Whale. Maximum length: 53 ft.

Humpbacks tend to congregate to feed, making certain spots with rich supplies of food reliable places to watch them. In Southeast Alaska, the best spots include the waters of **Icy Strait,** just outside Glacier Bay, **Frederick Sound** outside Petersburg, and **Sitka Sound.** In Southcentral Alaska, **Resurrection Bay,** outside Seward near Kenai Fjords National Park, has the most reliable sightings.

THE ORCA (KILLER WHALE)   The starkly defined black-and-white patches of the orca, the ocean's top predator, recall the sharp, graphic look of the Native American art of the Pacific Northwest and Southeast Alaska. Moving like wolves in highly structured family groups called pods, and swimming at up to 25 knots (about 29 mph), orcas hunt salmon, porpoises, seals, sea lions, and even juvenile whales, but there's never been a report of one attacking a human being. Like dolphins, orcas often pop above the surface in a flashing, graceful arc when they travel, giving viewers a glance at their sleek shape, markings, and tall dorsal fin.

Unlike humpbacks and other whales that rely on a predictable food supply, orcas' hunting patterns mean it's not easy to say exactly where you might find them—you need to be where their prey is that day. **Resurrection Bay** and **Prince William Sound** both have pods often sighted in the summer, and we saw a pod of orcas from the beach in Gustavus, but they could show up anywhere in Southeast Alaska waters. For cruisers coming to Alaska from Vancouver, a top spot to see orcas is **Robson Bight,** an area in Johnstone Strait (between Vancouver Island and mainland British Columbia).

The Orca, or Killer Whale. Maximum length: 30 ft.

THE BELUGA WHALE   This small, white whale with the cute rounded beak is one of only three types that spend all their lives in cold water rather than heading south for the winter. (The other two are the narwhale and bowhead.) More likely to be confused for a dolphin than any other whale, belugas are larger and fatter than a dolphin and lack the dolphin's dorsal fin. Adults are all white, while juveniles are gray. Belugas swim in large packs that can number in the dozens. The beluga is the only whale that can turn its head and one of the few with good eyesight.

Belugas feed on salmon, making the mouths of rivers with salmon runs the best places to see them. Occasionally, a group will strand itself chasing salmon on a falling tide, swimming away when the water returns. The Cook Inlet group of belugas is the most often seen: If you're in Anchorage after your cruise, head out the Seward Highway, just south of town, and keep your eyes on the waters of **Turnagain Arm,** or watch from the beach near the mouth of the **Kenai River** in Kenai.

The Beluga Whale. Maximum length: 16 ft.

THE MINKE WHALE   The smallest of the baleen whales, the minke is generally under 26 feet long and has a blackish-gray body with a white stomach, a narrow, triangular head, and white bands on its flippers. Along with the humpback and (occasionally) the gray whale, it is the only baleen commonly seen in Alaskan waters.

When breaching, minkes leap something like dolphins, gracefully reentering the water headfirst—unlike humpbacks, for instance, which smash down on their sides. Also unlike the humpbacks, they don't raise their flukes clear of the water when they dive. Minkes are easy to confuse with dolphins: Watch for the dark skin color for differentiation.

The Minke Whale. Maximum length: 26 ft.

THE GRAY WHALE   Here's one you'll probably see only if you take a shoulder-season cruise (in May or very late Sept), and then only if you're lucky. The grays spend their winter months off the coast of California and in the Sea of Cortez (between Baja and mainland Mexico) and their summer months off northern Alaska, meaning that the only chance cruise passengers sailing in the Inside Passage and Gulf of Alaska have of spotting one is while it's on its migration.

Like the humpback, grays are baleen whales. They're also about the same size as the humpback, though they lack the humpback's huge flippers. Their heads are pointed, and they lack a dorsal fin. Grays will often smack the water with their flukes, and are very friendly—it's not uncommon for them to swim right up to a small boat and allow their heads to be patted.

The Gray Whale. Maximum length: 45 ft.

4 Alaska Wildlife

Large mammals other than mankind still rule most of Alaska—even in the urban areas, there sometimes remains a question of who's in charge. In this section, we'll go through some of the more common ones. For visitors, the chances of seeing the animals described below are excellent.

BALD EAGLE   Now making a comeback all over the United States, the bald eagle has always been extremely common in Alaska: In most coastal towns, a pigeon would be more unusual. Eagles even soar over the high-rise buildings of downtown Anchorage, and every fishing town is swarming with them. Only adult eagles have the familiar white head and tail; juveniles of a few years or less have mottled brown plumage and can be hard to tell from a hawk. Eagles most often are seen soaring on rising air over ocean or river waters, where they are likely looking for fish to swoop down and snatch, but you also can often see them perched on beach driftwood or in large trees. **Haines** is a prime eagle-spotting area, where thousands congregate in the fall; **Sitka** and Ketchikan both have raptor centers where you can see eagles in enclosures.

The eagle represents one of the two main kinship groupings in the matrilineal Tlingit culture (the other is the raven), so eagles frequently appear on totem poles and in other Southeast Native art.

Bald Eagle

Raven

RAVEN   A member of the Corvidae family, which includes jays, crows, and magpies, the raven is found throughout the northern hemisphere and is extremely common in Southeast Alaska. You can tell a raven from a crow by its larger size, heavy bill, shaggy throat feathers, and unmistakable voice, a deep and mysteriously evocative "kaw" that provides a constant soundtrack to the misty forests of Southeast Alaska. The raven figures importantly in Southeast Alaska Native stories and in the creation myths of many other Native American peoples, where its personality is of a wily and resourceful protagonist with great magical powers, an understandable match for this highly impressive and intelligent scavenger.

BLACK BEAR   Black bears live in forests all over Alaska, feeding on fish, berries, insects, and vegetation. In Southeast Alaska, they can be so common as to be a pest, and many communities have adjusted their handling of garbage to keep the bears out of town. Although not typically dangerous, blackies still deserve caution and respect: They stand about a yard tall at the shoulders and measure 5 or 6 feet from nose to tail. Black bears are usually black, but they can also be brown, blond, or even blue—color is not the best way to tell a black bear from a brown bear. Instead, look at the smaller size, the blunt face, and the shape of the back, which is straight and lacks the brown bear's large shoulder hump.

Black Bear

Brown Bear

BROWN BEAR   Also known as grizzly bears, brown bears are among the largest and most ferocious of all land mammals. Size depends on the bear's food source. In coastal areas where salmon are plentiful, such as Southeast Alaska or Katmai National Park, brown bears can grow to be well over 1,000 pounds and even approach the 1-ton mark. The largest of all are found on salmon-rich Kodiak Island. Inland, at Denali National Park and on similar tundra landscape (where they feed on rodents, berries, insects, and the like), brown bears top out closer to 500 pounds. They can also take larger prey, but that's less common. You can recognize a brown bear by the prominent shoulder hump, long face, and large size; color can range from almost black to blond. Among the best places to see brown bears are **Pack Creek,** on Admiralty Island near Juneau, at **Denali and Katmai national parks,** or on bear-viewing floatplane excursions from **Homer.** Of these, Denali is the only inexpensive option.

MOOSE   In winter, when they move to the lowlands, moose can be an absolute pest, blocking roadways and eating expensive shrubbery. In the summer, they're a little more elusive, most often seen standing in forest ponds, eating the weeds from the bottom or pruning streamside willows—but even then, gardeners can often be heard cursing these animals, which despite their immense size, can oh-so-delicately and neatly chomp the blossom off each tulip in a flower bed. The largest member of the deer family, with males reaching 1,200 to 1,600 pounds, moose are found primarily in the boreal forest that covers Interior and Southcentral Alaska, so you'll be much more likely to see one if you're on a pre- or post-cruise land package such as the Anchorage–Denali–Fairbanks route. They are unmistakable. As big as a large horse, with bristly, ragged brown hair, a long, bulbous nose, and huge, mournful eyes, moose seem to crave pity—though they get little from the wolves and people who hunt them or from the trains and cars that run them down, and they give little to anyone in their way when they're on the move. Males grow large antlers, which they shed after battling for a mate every fall. Females lack antlers and are smaller, having one to three calves each year.

Moose

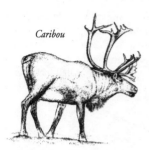
Caribou

CARIBOU   Alaska's barren-ground caribou are genetically identical to reindeer but were never domesticated as reindeer were in Europe. For Inupiat and Athabascan people, they were an essential source of food and hides, and the hunt remains a cultural mainstay. Both males and females have antlers that they shed annually. Reindeer travel the arctic tundra and Interior foothills in herds of up to hundreds of thousands of animals, a stunning sight witnessed by only a lucky few, as the migration routes lie in remote regions. You can, however, often see caribou in smaller groups of a few dozen at Denali National Park, along the Dalton and Denali highways, and on other northern rural roads above treeline. They're skittish, so the best technique is to stop and let them approach you.

SITKA BLACK-TAILED DEER   The Sitka black-tailed deer is a relatively small deer found in the coastal rain forests of Alaska. Males typically weigh in at around 120 pounds and show similarly small antlers. Both males and females sport a reddish-brown coat in summer. They can be found throughout the Southeast, in Prince William Sound, and on Kodiak Island.

*Sitka
Black-Tailed
Deer*

Dall Sheep

DALL SHEEP   Dall sheep resemble the more familiar bighorn but are smaller, weighing up to 300 pounds for males and 150 for females. Like the bighorn, males have the same curling horns, which they butt against each other to establish dominance for mating. Their habitat is the high, rocky places, where their incredible agility makes them safe from predators. Except in a few exceptional spots, such as on the cliffs above the Seward Highway just south of Anchorage on Turnagain Arm, you almost always need strong binoculars to see sheep. **Denali National Park** is a good place to see them in the usual way: from a great distance. Scanning the mountains, pick out white spots, then focus in on them. Often, the sheep move in herds of a dozen or more.

MOUNTAIN GOAT   Another animal that you won't see unless you bring your binoculars, the mountain goat inhabits the same craggy mountain habitat as the Dall sheep, including the prime viewing area on Turnagain Arm. From a distance, it's easy to confuse mountain goats with female Dall sheep, but mountain goats are shaggier; have short, straight black horns (which appear in both the male and female); have the typical goat beard; and have a much more pronounced hump at the shoulders.

Mountain Goat

Sea Otter

SEA OTTER   Possibly number one in Alaska's "cute critter" category, the sea otter is a member of the weasel family (as are minks and river otters) and spends almost all of its life in the water. Extensively hunted for its rich coat from the mid–18th century (when Russian explorer Vitus Bering brought back pelts from his voyage of discovery and initiated extensive Russian settlement of Alaska) until the early 20th, the sea otter was almost driven to extinction—in 1911, there were probably fewer than 2,000 of them left in Alaska, but by the mid-1970s that number had risen above 150,000. Adult males weigh between 70 and 100 pounds, while females average 40 to 60 pounds. Adults average 4½ feet in length. Their fur is generally brown to black, often with a silvery or gray tinge, particularly in older animals. You typically see sea otters floating on their backs, sometimes cradling a rock on their stomachs (which they use to crack open shellfish), sometimes just watching the cruise ships float by.

SEA LION   You'll hear 'em—and smell 'em—before you see 'em. An argumentative honking, like cars stalled in traffic, mixes with a low undertone that sounds like elephants with sinus problems. Then the smell hits you: fishy beyond belief. Still, when you get close enough to know what you're smelling, you won't mind because it's some sight: Sea lions typically haul out in the hundreds onto small islands, where they loll in the sun, argue, occasionally fight, go fishing, and breed—meaning that, in this sense at least, they're just like people on vacation. Their bodies are huge, blubbery, tubular affairs that are perfect for the cold northern waters but appear impossibly ungainly on land, over which they bounce and bound on perfectly inadequate-looking front flippers. Still, even on land you wouldn't want to mess with one: The average adult male weighs approximately 1,250 pounds and measures 10½ feet long, while adult females average 580 pounds and are 8½ feet long. Most adult females are brownish yellow, while males typically are a bit darker, some with a reddish coat.

Sea Lion

5 Glaciers: An Intro to the Ice

Along with whales, glaciers are the big drawing card on Alaska cruises, and with good reason: They're truly awesome. To see one spread between the comparatively insignificant bulk of massive mountains, flowing down into the sea, is to quite literally see how our world as we know it came to be. As the naturalist John Muir wrote while standing near an Alaskan glacier in the late 19th century, "Standing here with facts so fresh and telling and held up so vividly before us . . . one learns that the world, though made, is yet being made; that this is still the morning of creation."

If you want to explore glaciers further, the National Snow and Ice Data Center has a great glacier website, with many photos, a glossary, and other data, at http://nsidc.org/glaciers/.

HOW GLACIERS FORM   Glaciers form when snow accumulates over time at high altitudes. Successive snowfalls add more and more weight, compacting the snow underneath into an extremely dense type of ice known as **glacial ice.** As the accumulation assumes mass, forming what is known as an **ice field,** gravity takes over and the ice field begins to seek the lowest altitude, flowing very slowly downhill through the lowest, easiest passage. As glaciers flow, their enormous mass sculpts the landscape below, grinding the shale and other rock and pushing rubble and silt ahead and to the sides. This sediment is known as **moraine.** Terminal moraine is the accumulation of rubble at the front of a glacier; lateral moraine lines the sides of glaciers. A dark area in a glacier's center—seen when two glaciers flow together, pushing their ice and crushed rubble together—is median moraine.

TYPES OF GLACIERS   Glaciers come in several different varieties. **Tidewater glaciers** are the kind most often seen in postcards; they spill down out of the mountains and run all the way to the sea. **Piedmont glaciers** are two glaciers that have run together into one. When seen from above, piedmonts resemble a highway interchange, edged by road slush, with the median moraine looking like lane dividers. **Hanging glaciers** are just that—glaciers hanging in the mountains, over rounded hillsides. There are also **mountain glaciers** (also known as alpine glaciers), which are confined by surrounding mountain terrain; **valley glaciers,** which are mountain glaciers confined by valley walls; and **cirque glaciers,** which sit in basins near ridge crests and are usually circular (as opposed to the typical river shape).

GLACIAL BEHAVIOR   Glaciers are essentially rivers of ice that flow continually downhill. When they reach the sea, the effects of water and gravity cause

ing, a phenomenon where large chunks of ice break off from the mass and crash into the sea, forming **icebergs.** Calvings are always a high point on a cruise. At the South Sawyer Glacier in Tracy Arm, we once saw a piece of ice 150 feet long calve off with a sound like thunder. The wave it caused sent the whole ship rocking.

Depending on temperature and the rate of precipitation, glaciers may either **advance** or **retreat.** Think of glaciers as human bodies and snowfall as calories—when the accumulation of snowfall (and resultant glacial ice) is greater than the amount of ice lost to melting and calving, the glacier grows, which is known as advancing. When the opposite occurs—when melting and calving outpace new buildup of ice—the glacier is said to be retreating. (The Mendenhall Glacier in Juneau, for instance, is retreating at the rate of about 30 ft. a year.) Glaciers can also be in a state of equilibrium, where the amount of snowfall roughly equals the amount of melt-off. Even where this is the case, though, the glacier is still a slow-moving river, always flowing downhill—it's just that its total length remains the same, with new ice replacing old at a more or less constant rate.

Some glaciers may **gallop,** surging either forward or backward as much as 10 to 150 feet a day, and some may recede or retreat at the same rate. Hubbard Glacier became a galloping glacier for a brief time in 1986, moving forward rapidly and blocking in Yakutat Bay for several months.

By the way, glacial ice isn't blue. It may look blue—and a startling, electric blue at that—but it's really a trick of the light. The ice absorbs all colors of the spectrum *except* blue, which is then reflected away, making the ice itself appear to be blue.

AN ICEBERG BY ANY OTHER NAME   When a glacier calves, the icebergs formed are classified differently depending on their size, a system that allows one ship's captain to warn another of the relative ice hazard. Very large chunks are officially called **icebergs;** pieces of moderate size (usually 7–15 ft. across) are known as **bergy bits; growlers** are slightly smaller still, at less than 7 feet across, with less than 3 feet showing above water; and **brash ice** is any random smaller chunks. And remember the old adage: What you're seeing is only the tip—most of the berg is below the water.

FAMOUS GLACIERS   Some of the most visited glaciers on the various cruise itineraries include **Glacier Bay National Park and Preserve** and its 16 tidewater glaciers (see p. 181), **Hubbard Glacier** in Yakutat Bay (p. 191), **Mendenhall Glacier** outside Juneau (p. 180), **North and South Sawyer Glaciers** in Tracy Arm (p. 171), and the many glaciers of **College Fjord** (p. 195).

Choosing Your Ideal Cruise

Just like clothes, cars, and gourmet coffee, Alaska cruises come in all different styles to suit all different tastes, so the first step in assuring that you have the best possible vacation is to match your expectations to the appropriate itinerary and ship.

In this chapter, we explore the advantages of the two main Alaska itineraries, examine the differences between big-ship cruising and small-ship cruising, pose some questions you should ask yourself to determine which is the right cruise for you, and give you the skinny on cruisetours, which combine a cruise with a land tour that gets you into the Alaskan Interior.

1 The Alaska Cruise Season

Alaska is a seasonal, as opposed to year-round, cruise destination, with the season generally running from May through September, although some smaller ships start up in April. May and September are considered the shoulder seasons, and lower brochure rates are offered during these months (and more aggressive discounts, as well). We particularly like cruising in May, before the crowds arrive, when we've generally found locals to be friendlier than they are later in the season, when they're pretty much ready to see the tourists go home for the winter. There is also the statistical fact that May in the Inside Passage ports is the driest month in the season. Late September, though, also offers the advantage of fewer fellow tourists clogging the ports. The warmest months are June, July, and August, with temperatures generally around 50°F to 80°F during the day, and cooler at night. You may not need a parka, but you will need to bring along some outerwear. June 21 is the longest day of the year, with the sky light virtually all night. June tends to be drier than July and August. (We have experienced trips in July when it rained nearly every day.) April and May are drier than September, although in early May you may encounter freezing rain and other vestiges of winter. If you are considering traveling in a shoulder month, keep in mind that some shops don't open until Memorial Day, and the visitor season is generally considered over on Labor Day (although cruise lines operate well into Sept).

2 The Inside Passage or the Gulf of Alaska?

For the purposes of cruising, Alaska comprises essentially two separate and distinct areas, known generically as "The Inside Passage" and "The Gulf."

THE INSIDE PASSAGE

The Inside Passage runs through the area of Alaska known as Southeast (which the locals also call "the Panhandle"), that narrow strip of the state—islands, mainland coastal communities, and mountains—that runs from the Canadian border in the south to the start of the Gulf in the north, just above the

Shore Excursions: The What, When & Why

Shore excursions offered by the cruise lines provide a chance for you to get off the ship and explore the sights close up, taking in the history and culture of the region, including the gold-rush times and Native Alaskan traditions, such as totem carving.

Some excursions are of the walking-tour or bus-tour variety, but many others are activity-oriented: Cruise passengers have the opportunity to go sea kayaking, mountain biking, horseback riding, and salmon fishing and to see the sights by seaplane or helicopter—maybe even to land on a glacier and go for a walk. Occasionally, with some of the smaller lines, you'll find quirky excursions, such as a visit with local artists in their studios. Some lines even offer scuba diving and snorkeling, and most also make it easy for you to see some of inland Alaska by offering **cruisetours** that combine a cruise with a pre- or post-cruise trip over land by motor coach or train.

With some lines, shore excursions are included in your cruise fare, but with most lines they are an added (though very worthwhile) expense. See chapters 9 and 10 for details on the excursions available at the various ports. For more information, see "Cruisetours: The Best of Land & Sea" (p. 33) and chapter 11.

Juneau/Haines/Skagway area. The islands on the western side of the area afford cruise ships a welcome degree of protection from the sea and its attendant rough waters (hence the name Inside Passage). Because of that shelter, such ports as Ketchikan, Wrangell, Petersburg, and others are reachable with less rocking and rolling and thus less risk of seasickness. Sitka is not on the Inside Passage (it's on the ocean side of Baranof Island) but is included in most cruise itineraries in that area.

Southeast encompasses the capital city, **Juneau,** and townships reflective of the days of Russian influence (**Sitka,** for instance), the Tlingit and Haida Native cultures (**Ketchikan**), and the great gold rush of 1898 (**Skagway**). It is a land of rain forests, mountains, inlets, and glaciers (including Margerie, John Hopkins, Muir, and the others contained within the boundaries of **Glacier Bay National Park**). The region is rich in wildlife, especially of the marine variety, and is a scenic delight. But then, what part of Alaska isn't?

THE GULF OF ALASKA

The other major cruising area is the **Southcentral** region's Gulf of Alaska, usually referred to by the cruise lines as the "Glacier Discovery Route," or the "Voyage of the Glaciers," or some such catchy title. "Gulf of Alaska," after all, sounds pretty bland.

The coastline of the Gulf is that arc of land from just north of Glacier Bay to the Kenai Peninsula. Southcentral also takes in **Prince William Sound;** the **Cook Inlet,** on the northern side of the peninsula; **Anchorage,** Alaska's biggest city; the year-round **Alyeska Resort** at Girdwood, 40 miles from Anchorage; the **Matanuska** and **Susitna Valleys** (the "Mat/Su"), a fertile agricultural region renowned for the record size of some of its produce; and part of the Alaska Mountain Range.

The principal Southcentral ports of call are **Valdez, Seward,** and **Anchorage** (though few ships actually head for Anchorage, instead disembarking passengers in Seward and taking them to Anchorage by motor coach). Going on a Gulf cruise does not mean that you get no Inside Passage, though. The big difference is that, whereas the more popular Inside Passage cruise itineraries run round-trip from Vancouver, the Gulf routing is one-way—from Vancouver to Anchorage/Seward or the reverse—so a typical Gulf itinerary also visits such Inside Passage ports as **Ketchikan, Juneau, Sitka,** and/or **Skagway.**

The Gulf's glaciers are quite dazzling and every bit as spectacular as their counterparts to the south. **College Fjord,** for instance, is lined with glaciers—16 of them, each one grander than the last. Our favorite part of a Gulf cruise, though, is not necessarily College Fjord. It's the visit to the gigantic **Hubbard Glacier**—at 6 miles, Alaska's longest—at the head of **Yakutat Bay.** A few years back we saw the ice face at its best on a bright, sunny day during a *Crystal Harmony* cruise. As we stood on the deck in shirt-sleeves, the glacier was hyperactive, popping and cracking and shedding tons of ice into the bay. The ship got so close to the face that passengers began speculating about just how near we might be. One awestruck golf enthusiast assured all within hearing, "It's not more than a nine-iron shot away." Now that's close!

We should mention, however, that on a recent visit, we couldn't even get into the Bay because another ship was blocking our path (and hogging the optimum views). Our fear is with all the new ships in Alaska, glacier-viewing could become a blood sport.

WHICH ITINERARY IS BETTER?

It's a matter of personal taste. Some people don't like open-jaw flights (flying into one city and out of another)—which can add to the ticket price—and prefer the round-trip Inside Passage route. Others don't mind the extra flying and enjoy the additional glacier visits of the Gulf cruise itineraries. It's entirely up to you.

It wasn't so long ago that you wouldn't have had a choice. A few years back, there were practically no Gulf crossings. Then Princess Cruises and its touroperating affiliate decided to accelerate the development of its land infrastructure (lodges, railcars, motor coaches, and so on), particularly in the Kenai Peninsula and Denali National Park areas, for which Anchorage is a logical springboard. To feed these land services with cruisetour passengers, Princess beefed up the number of Gulf sailings it offered. In 2002, it will deploy four of its six Alaska ships on that route—including the massive 109,000-ton, 2,600-passenger *Star Princess*—with two on Inside Passage duty. The other cruisetour giant, Holland America Line, will have four vessels in the Inside Passage and two across the Gulf. Each deployment is designed to complement the lines' areas of cruisetour expertise as much as anything else.

3 Big Ship or Small Ship?

Picking the right ship is really the most important factor in ensuring you get the vacation you're looking for. Cruise ships in Alaska range from **small, adventure-type vessels** to really **big, resort-like megaships,** with the cruise experience varying widely depending on the type of ship you select. There are casual cruises and luxury cruises; educational cruises where you attend lectures and cruises where you attend musical reviews; adventure-oriented cruises where hiking,

SIZE COMPARISON CHART

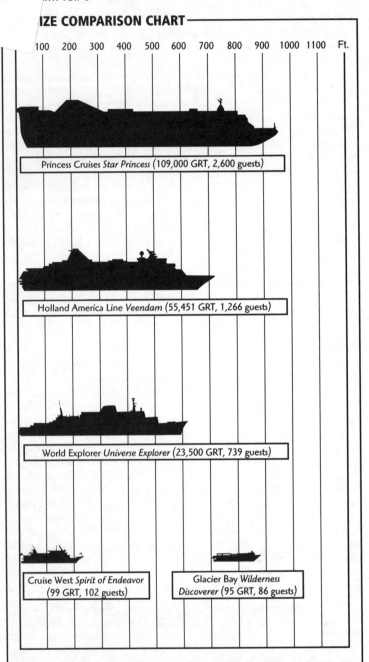

| 100 | 200 | 300 | 400 | 500 | 600 | 700 | 800 | 900 | 1000 | 1100 | Ft. |

Princess Cruises *Star Princess* (109,000 GRT, 2,600 guests)

Holland America Line *Veendam* (55,451 GRT, 1,266 guests)

World Explorer *Universe Explorer* (23,500 GRT, 739 guests)

Cruise West *Spirit of Endeavor*
(99 GRT, 102 guests)

Glacier Bay *Wilderness
Discoverer* (95 GRT, 86 guests)

Ships in this chart represent the various size vessels sailing in Alaska. See ship reviews in chapters 5 and 6 for comparative size of ships not shown here. (GRT = gross register tons, a measure of interior space on ships.)

kayaking, and exploring remote areas are the main activities; and resort-like cruises where aquatherapy and mud baths are the order of the day.

You'll need to decide what overall cruise experience you want. Itinerary and type of cruise are even more important than price. After all, what kind of bargain is a party cruise if what you're looking for is a quiet time? Your fantasy vacation may be someone else's nightmare, and vice versa.

Unlike the Caribbean, which generally attracts people looking to relax in the sun, people who want to spend all their time scuba diving and snorkeling, and people who want to party till the cows come home, visitors to Alaska usually have a different goal: They want to experience Alaska's glaciers, forests, wildlife, and other natural wonders. The cruise lines all recognize this, so almost any option you choose will allow you opportunities to see what you've come for. The main question, then, is how you want to see those sights. Do you want to be down at the waterline, seeing them from the deck of an adventure vessel, or do you want to see them from a warm lounge or, even better, from your own private veranda?

In this section, we'll run through the pros and cons of the big ships and the small and alternative ships.

THE BIG SHIPS

Big ships operating in Alaska vary in size and scope and include everything from a classic cruise ship to really, really big and really new megaships and even, new in 2002, one of the biggest ships in the world. (The *Star Princess,* at 109,000 tons, is part of a class second only to Royal Caribbean's Voyager-class ships which are not deployed in the Alaska market.) They all offer a comfortable cruising experience, with virtual armies of service employees overseeing your well-being and ship stabilizers assuring smooth sailing.

The size of these ships may keep Alaska's wildlife at a distance (you'll probably need binoculars to see the whales), but they offer plenty of deck space and comfy lounge chairs to sit in as you take in the gorgeous mountain and glacier views and sip a cup of coffee or cocoa. Due to their deeper drafts (the amount of ship below the waterline), the big ships can't get as close to the sights as the smaller ships, and they can't visit the more pristine fjords, inlets, and narrows. However, the more powerful engines on these ships do allow them to visit more ports during each trip—generally popular ports where your ship may be one of several, and where shopping for souvenirs is a main attraction. Some of the less massive ships in this category may also visit alternative ports, away from the typical tourist crowds.

Regardless of the port's size, the big-ship cruise lines put a lot of emphasis on **shore excursions,** which often take you beyond the port city to explore different aspects of Alaska—nature, Native culture, and so on. (See shore excursion listings in chapters 9 and 10 for more information.) Dispersing passengers to different locales on these shore trips is a must. When 2,000 passengers disembark on a small Alaska town, much of the ambience goes out the window—on particularly busy days, when several ships are in port, there may actually be more cruise passengers on the ground than locals. Due to the number of people involved, disembarkation can be a lengthy process.

The big ships in the Alaska market fall generally into two categories: midsize ships and megaships.

Carrying as many as 2,600 passengers, the **megaships** look and feel like floating resorts. Big on glitz, they offer loads of activities, attract many families and (especially in Alaska) seniors, offer many public rooms (including fancy casinos and fully equipped gyms), and provide a wide variety of meal and entertainment options. And though they usually feature 1 or 2 formal nights per trip, the ambience is generally casual. The Alaska vessels of the Carnival, Celebrity, Princess, and Royal Caribbean fleets all fit in this category, as does Norwegian Cruise Line's *Norwegian Sky.*

Midsize ships in Alaska for 2002 fall into three segments: the ultra-luxury ships of the Crystal and Radisson Seven Seas fleets and the considerably smaller but still very post *Seabourn Spirit;* the modern midsize *Veendam, Ryndam, Volendam, Amsterdam, Zaandam,* and *Statendam* of Holland America Line and Norwegian Wind of Norwegian Cruise Line; and the older, education-oriented *Universe Explorer* of World Explorer Cruises. In general, the size of these ships is less significant than the general onboard atmosphere of the company that runs them: Holland America's midsize ships all have a similarly calm, adult-oriented feel, while Norwegian's vessels all share the same ultra-casual, activities-oriented feel. Crystal's, Seabourne's, and Radisson Seven Seas' vessels are luxurious all the way (though Radisson's is more casually luxurious), and World Explorer's ship provides a pretty humble yet comfortable way to explore a fantastic range of ports.

Both the midsize ships and the megaships have a great range of **facilities** for passengers. There are swimming pools, health clubs, spas (of various sizes), nightclubs, movie theaters, shops, casinos, bars, and special kids' playrooms. In some cases, especially on the megaships, you'll also find sports decks, virtual golf, computer rooms, and cigar clubs, as well as quiet spaces where you can get away from it all. There are so many rooms that you more than likely won't feel claustrophobic. **Cabins** range from cubbyholes to large suites, depending on the ship and the type of cabin you book. Most offer TVs and telephones, and some have minibars, picture windows, and private verandas.

These ships have big dining rooms and buffet areas and serve a tremendous variety of **cuisine** throughout the day, including at midnight. There may also be additional eating venues, such as pizzerias, hamburger grills, ice-cream parlors, alternative restaurants, wine bars, champagne bars, caviar bars, and patisseries.

In most cases, these ships have lots of **onboard activities** to keep you occupied when you're not whale- or glacier-watching, including games, contests, and classes and lectures (sometimes by naturalists, park rangers, or wildlife experts; sometimes on topics such as line dancing and napkin folding). These ships also offer a variety of entertainment options that may even include celebrity headline acts and usually include stage-show productions, some very extravagant. (Those of Princess come to mind.) These ships carry a lot of people and, as such, can at times feel crowded—there may be lines at the buffets and in other public areas, and it may take a while to disembark in port.

THE SMALL & ALTERNATIVE SHIPS

Just as big cruise ships are mostly for people who want every resort amenity, small or alternative ships are best suited for people who prefer a casual, crowd-free cruise experience that gives passengers a chance to get up close and personal with Alaska's **natural surroundings** and **wildlife.**

Thanks to their smaller size, these ships, carrying fewer than 150 passengers (American Safari Cruises' *Safari Spirit* carries only 12), can go places that larger ships can't, such as narrow fjords, uninhabited islands, and smaller ports that cater mostly to small fishing vessels. Due to their shallow draft, they can nose right up to sheer cliff faces, bird rookeries, bobbing icebergs, and cascading waterfalls that you can literally reach out and touch. Also, sea animals are not as intimidated by these ships, so you may find yourself having a rather close encounter with a humpback whale, or watching other sea mammals bobbing in the ship's wake. The decks on these ships are closer to the waterline, too, giving passengers a more intimate view than from the high decks of the large cruise ships. Some of these ships stop at ports on a daily basis like the larger ships, and some avoid ports almost entirely, exploring natural areas instead. They also have the flexibility to change their itineraries as opportunities arise—say, to go where whales have been sighted and to linger a while once a sighting's been made.

The alternative ship experience comes with a sense of adventure (although it's usually adventure of a soft rather than a rugged sort) and offers a generally casual cruise experience: There are no dress-up nights, the food may be rather simply prepared, and because there are so few public areas to choose from—usually only one or two small lounges—camaraderie tends to develop more quickly between passengers on these ships than aboard larger vessels, which can be as anonymous as a big city. **Cabins** on these ships don't usually offer TVs or telephones and tend to be very small and, in some cases, downright spartan. Meals are generally served in a single open seating (meaning seats are not assigned), and dress codes are usually nonexistent.

None of these ships offer exercise or spa facilities such as those you'll find on the big ships—your best exercise bet is usually a brisk walk around the deck after dinner—but may compensate by offering **more active off-ship opportunities,** such as hiking or kayaking. (On three of Glacier Bay Cruiseline' ships, stern launch platforms actually allow you to kayak right from the ship.) The alternative ships are also more likely to feature **expert lectures** on Alaska-specific topics, such as marine biology, history, Native culture, and other intellectual pursuits.

There are no stabilizers on most of these smaller ships, and the ride can be bumpy in open water—which isn't much of a problem on Inside Passage itineraries, since most of the cruising area is protected from sea waves. They are also difficult for travelers with disabilities, as only three (Cruise West's *Spirit of '98* and *Spirit of Oceanus* and Clipper's *Clipper Odyssey*) have elevators. And the alternative ship lines do not offer specific activities or facilities for children, although you will find a few families on some of these vessels.

4 Cruisetours: The Best of Land & Sea

Most folks who go to the trouble of getting to a place as far off the beaten path as Alaska try to stick around for a while once they're there rather than jet home as soon as they hop off the boat. Knowing this, the cruise lines have set themselves up in the land-tour business as well, offering a number of great land-based excursions that can be tacked on to your cruise experience.

We're not just talking about an overnight stay in, say, Anchorage or Juneau before or after your cruise—any cruise line will arrange an extra night's hotel accommodation for you, but enjoyable as that may be, it doesn't begin to hint at the real opportunities available in Alaska. No, the subject here is **cruisetours,** a total package with a cruise and a structured, prearranged, multiple-day land itinerary already programmed in—for instance, a 7-day cruise with a 5-day land package. There are any number of combinations between 9 and 21 days in length.

In this section, we'll discuss the various cruisetour itineraries that are available through the lines. See chapter 11 for details on the various cruisetour destinations.

CRUISETOUR ITINERARIES

Many parts of inland Alaska can be visited on cruisetour programs—Denali National Park, Fairbanks, Wrangell–St. Elias, Nome, and Kotzebue included. If you've a mind to, you can even go all the way to the oil fields of the North Slope of Prudhoe Bay, hundreds of miles north of the Arctic Circle.

Three tour destination areas are combinable with your Inside Passage or Gulf of Alaska cruise—two major ones, which we'll call the **Anchorage/Denali/Fairbanks** corridor and the **Yukon Territory,** and one less-traveled route that we'll call the **Canadian Rockies Route,** which is an option due to Vancouver's position as an Alaska cruise hub.

ANCHORAGE/DENALI/FAIRBANKS CRUISETOUR

A typical Anchorage/Denali/Fairbanks cruisetour package (we'll use Princess as an example, since it is heavily involved in the Denali sector) might include a 7-day Vancouver–Anchorage cruise, followed by 2 nights in Anchorage, and a scenic ride in a private railcar into **Denali National Park** for 2 more nights at Princess's Denali Lodge or Mt. McKinley Lodge (or 1 night at each). On a clear day, the McKinley property, now in its fourth year, affords a panoramic view of the Alaska Mountain Range and its centerpiece, **Mount McKinley,** which at 20,320 feet, is North America's highest peak.

A full day in the park allows guests to explore the staggeringly beautiful wilderness expanse and its wildlife before reboarding the train and heading into the Interior of Alaska, to **Fairbanks,** for 2 more nights. Fairbanks itself isn't much to look at, but the activities available in outlying areas are fantastic, the Riverboat Discovery paddle-wheeler day cruise on the Chena and Tanana rivers and an excursion to a gold mine being highlights. Passengers on that particular cruisetour fly home from Fairbanks.

A shorter variation of that itinerary might be a cruise combined with an overnight (or 2-night) stay in Anchorage along with the Denali portion, perhaps with rail transportation into the park and motor coach back to Anchorage, skipping Fairbanks. In 2002, Princess will offer new cruisetours that include a hitherto largely inaccessible area, **Wrangell–St. Elias National Park,** where it has built the Cooper River Princess Wilderness Lodge, the fifth in the company's hotel network. Construction of the 85-room property was expected to end in the spring of 2002—in plenty of time for the start of the high season.

YUKON TERRITORY CRUISETOUR

Another popular land itinerary offered along with Alaska cruises is the one that typically involves a 3- or 4-day cruise between Vancouver and Juneau/Skagway (you either join a 7-day sailing late or get off early), combined with a land program into the **Klondike,** in Canada's Yukon Territory, then through the Interior of Alaska to Anchorage. En route, passengers experience a variety of transportation modes, which may include rail, riverboat, motor coach, and possibly air. There are a number of variations.

The Yukon, although located in Canada, is nevertheless an integral part of the overall Alaska cruisetour picture, due to its intimate ties to Alaska's gold-rush history. The overnight stops are **Whitehorse,** the territorial capital, and **Dawson City,** a remote, picture-perfect gold-rush town near where the gold was found. And if it's wilderness scenery you want, you'll be hard pressed to find any more awesome.

After heading north through the Yukon, cruisetour passengers cross the Alaska border near Beaver Creek, travel thence to **Fairbanks,** and from there go through **Denali** to **Anchorage.** Again, the tour can be taken in either direction and on a pre- or post-cruise basis.

CANADIAN ROCKIES CRUISETOURS

A Canadian Rockies tour is easily combinable with a Vancouver-originating (or terminating) Inside Passage or Gulf cruise. In 5-, 6-, or 7-day chunks, you can visit such scenic wonders as **Banff, Lake Louise,** and **Jasper National Park** in conjunction with an Alaska sailing.

The Canadian Rockies offer some of the finest **mountain scenery** on earth. It's not just that the glacier-carved mountains are astonishingly dramatic and beautiful; it's also that there are hundreds and hundreds of miles of this wonderful wilderness high country. Between them, **Banff National Park** and **Jasper National Park** preserve much of this mountain beauty. Other national and provincial parks make accessible other vast and equally spectacular regions of the Rockies, as well as portions of the nearby Columbia and Selkirk mountain ranges. The beautiful **Lake Louise,** colored deep green from its mineral content, is located 35 miles north of Banff.

BEFORE OR AFTER?

Though the land portion of both the Denali and the Yukon itineraries can be taken either before or after the cruise, we feel that it's better to take the land portion pre-cruise rather than post-cruise. Why? After several days of traveling around in the wilderness, it's nice to be able to get aboard a ship to relax and be pampered for a while.

That, at any rate, is the conventional wisdom, and there's more of a demand for pre-cruise land packages than for post-cruise. Since the lines obviously can't always accommodate everybody on a land itinerary *before* the cruise (they're hoping to even out the traffic flow by having a like number of requests to go touring after the voyage), it's smart to get your bid in early.

BATTLE OF THE TOP PLAYERS

If we talk in this section more about **Princess** and **Holland America** than we do about other lines, it's because they, by dint of investing tens of millions of dollars in land tourism, have become the 800-pound gorillas duking it out for dominance in Alaska. Other lines offer some of the same cruisetours as these two, but many of them buy at least some of their cruisetour components from Princess and/or Holland America's land operations. It may seem odd to have companies buying from (or selling to) competitors, but with tourism in Alaska, there's practically no other way. As recently as the 1980s, when Holland America–Westours owned the bulk of the land-tour components, Princess, its number-one rival, was also its number-one customer! Hey, a 4-month season makes for strange bedfellows.

It was to carve out a niche for itself and to lessen its reliance on the services of a competitor that Princess plunged heavily into the lodging and transportation sectors. Princess is arguably stronger in the Denali corridor than any other line, while Holland America clearly has the upper hand in the Yukon/Klondike market. But each line offers both tour areas in its portfolio.

Princess owns railcars (called the *Midnight Sun Express*) in the Denali corridor. Holland America also owns railcars there; it calls them the *McKinley Explorer*. Both, incidentally, rely on the Alaska Railroad to pull them. Princess owns wilderness lodges; Holland America owns city hotels. Princess has a fleet of motor coaches; so does Holland America, including a number of wonderfully comfortable, double-length Alaska Yukon Explorer flexi-vehicles with a cozy lounge at the rear for snacking and schmoozing.

The fast-growing baby gorilla is **Royal Caribbean.** With its Royal Caribbean International and Celebrity Cruises brands, Royal Caribbean is on its way to becoming a major player in its own right. The company will have three Royal Caribbean ships and two Celebrity ships in the 49th State this summer. To support cruisetour demand, the company has formed **Royal Celebrity Tours** to operate its land packages. Its first investment was in luxury motor coaches and truly state-of-the-art domed rail carriages for the Denali Park run. The first of the carriages (the *Wilderness Express*) debuted last year in competition with those of Holland America and Princess. This year, Royal Celebrity will have three of the wagons in service. The cars have comfortable, airline-style leather seats at least on a par with the business-class seating of most major airlines, huge expanses of glass which makes viewing a treat, a fine kitchen on the lower level (lunch, say, $6.95–$12.95; dinner $17.95–$21.95) and a friendly, knowledgeable staff. Plus, the carriages are more handicapped-accessible than Princess's or Holland America's. (Each of Royal Caribbean's is equipped with a mechanical lift that can carry two wheelchairs at a time to the second level from the station platform.) With buses and railcars in hand, it may not be long before Royal Caribbean begins buying or building lodging, just like Holland America and Princess. Stay tuned!

5 Questions to Ask When Choosing Your Cruise

After you've decided which itinerary and what kind of ship appeal to you, we suggest you ask yourself some questions about the kind of experience you want, then read through the cruise-line and ship reviews in chapters 5 and 6 to see which ones match your vision of the perfect Alaska cruise vessel.

When looking at the attributes of the various ships to make your choice, some determining factors will be no-brainers. For instance, if you're traveling with kids, you'll want a ship with a good kids' program. If you're a foodie, you'll want a ship with gourmet cuisine. If you're used to staying at a Ritz-Carlton hotel when you travel, you'll probably want to cruise on a luxury ship. Conversely, if you usually stay at a B&B, you'll probably prefer one of the small ships.

Also, ask yourself whether you require resort-like amenities, such as a heated swimming pool, spa, casino, aerobics classes, and state-of-the-art gym. Or do you care more about having an adventure or an enriching and educational experience? If you want the former, choose a large cruise ship; if your prefer the latter, a small ship may be more your speed.

Here are some more pertinent questions to help you narrow the field:

How much does it cost and what's not included?   Here's the number-one important rule to remember: *Don't let the rates in cruise-line brochures scare you off.* Very rarely does anyone actually pay the brochure price, which is the highest rate the line charges for the cruise; discounts are calculated off that rate. Virtually all the lines (with the exception of some of the small-ship lines) offer early-booking discounts. The numbers and dates may vary, but the formula is fairly standard: You get about 25% off if you book by mid- to late February and 20% off if you book by mid-April. For the past couple of years, thanks to the introduction of additional ships, there has been more space in the Alaska market than the cruise lines can fill at top dollar, and that has resulted in some really deep discounts both of the last-minute and early-bird variety. Savings (involving a limited number of cabin types) have reached 60% and more. Bigger ships (with more passenger capacity) coming into the market in 2002 make it likely that the trend will continue.

Cruise fares cover onboard accommodations, meals, entertainment, and activities. There are, however, a number of expenses not covered in the typical cruise package, and you should factor these in when planning your vacation budget. Airfare to and from your port of embarkation and debarkation is usually extra (though cruise lines offer reduced rates), as are any necessary hotel stays before or after the cruise. Gratuities, taxes, and trip insurance are typically extra, as well. Shore excursions are rarely included in the cruise fare, and if you opt for pricey ones, such as flightseeing, you can easily add $500 to $1,000 to your total. Alcoholic beverages and soda are typically extra also, as are such incidentals as laundry, telephone calls from the ship, beauty and spa services, photos (taken by ship photographers), and babysitting.

Because travel agents keep constantly abreast of the latest bargains, they are best equipped to advise you on the best Alaska cruise deals. Most cruise lines encourage passengers to book through agents, so much so that some refuse to accept direct bookings.

How far in advance do I need to book?   Many itineraries used to sell out 6 months or more before sailing, but lines have detected a closer-in booking pattern in the last few years. It's not clear whether that will continue, but just to be sure, once you've selected the cruise that's right for you, check to see how much space is available. And plan to book your cabin of choice 3 to 6 months in advance, or be prepared to accept whatever cabin category remains available—if any are available at all.

How much time is spent in port and how much at sea?   Generally, ships on 7-night itineraries make port 3 days and sail in wild areas like Glacier Bay, College Fjord, or Wrangell–St. Elias National Park during the other three.

Coming into port, ships generally dock right after breakfast, allowing you the morning and afternoon to take a shore excursion or explore on your own. They usually depart in the early evening, giving you an hour or two to rest up before dinner.

On days at sea, the emphasis will be on exploring the natural areas, viewing the glaciers, and scanning for wildlife. Big ships stick to prearranged schedules on these days, but on small-ship soft-adventure-type cruises, days at sea can be very unstructured, with the captain choosing a destination based on reports of whale sightings, for example. Some itineraries (notably those sailed by some of Glacier Bay Cruiseline's ships) visit almost no ports, sticking instead to isolated natural areas that passengers explore by kayak, by Zodiac boat, or on foot.

Is the cruise formal or casual?   If you don't care to get dressed up, select a less formal cruise typical of the small ships and also offered on the *Universe Explorer*, on Radisson's luxurious but country-club casual *Seven Seas Navigator*, and on the Norwegian Cruise Line ships, which do not have formal nights. If, on the other hand, having the chance to put on your finery appeals to you, select one of the more elegant ships, such as the ultra-luxury *Crystal Harmony*, or premium lines, such as Celebrity or Holland America (and, to a lesser extent, mass-market lines, such as Royal Caribbean, Princess, and Carnival). These ships will offer casual, semiformal, and formal nights, meaning women can show off everything from a sundress to an evening gown over the course of a week, and men will go from shirt-sleeves one night to jacket-and-tie the next to full-on tuxedo (or dark suit) the next.

What are the other passengers usually like?　Each ship attracts a fairly predictable type of passenger. On small ships, you'll find a more physically active bunch that's highly interested in nature, but you'll find fewer families and single travelers. Larger ships cater to a more diverse group—singles, newlyweds, families, and couples over 55. We've included information on typical passengers in all the cruise-line reviews in chapters 5 and 6.

I'll be traveling alone. Will I have fun? And does it cost more?　A nice thing about cruises is that you needn't worry about dining alone because you'll be seated with other guests. (If you don't want to be, seek a ship with alternative dining options.) You also needn't worry much about finding people to talk to because the general atmosphere on nearly all ships is very congenial and allows you to easily find conversation, especially during group activities. And the ship may even host a party to give singles a chance to get to know one another and/or offer social hosts as dance partners.

The downside is that you may have to pay more for the cruise experience than do passengers sharing a cabin. Because their rates are based on two people per cabin, some lines charge a "single supplement" rate (aka an extra charge) that ranges from 110% to an outrageous 200% of the per-person, double-occupancy fare. As a single person, you have two choices: Find a line with a reasonable single supplement rate (World Explorer and Radisson are good bets) or ask if the line has a cabin-share program, under which the line will pair you with another single so you can get a lower fare. Some lines also offer a single-guarantee program, which means if they can't find you a roommate, they'll book you in a cabin alone but still honor the shared rate. Singles seeking real savings have the option on some ships of cramming into a shared quad (a room for four). Some older ships and a few small ships have special cabins designed for singles, but these tend to sell out fast and are not necessarily offered at bargain prices.

Is shipboard life heavily scheduled?　That depends to a certain extent on you and the ship you choose. Meals are generally served during set hours only, though on larger ships you'll have plenty of alternative options if those hours don't agree with you. (On smaller ships, you may just be out of luck until the next meal—unless you can charm the cook.) On both large and small ships, times for disembarking and reboarding at the ports are strict—if you miss the boat, you miss the boat. (See chapter 7 for tips on what to do in this situation.) Other than these two considerations, the only schedule you'll have to follow onboard is your own. It all depends on how busy you want to be.

What are the cabins like?　Cabins come in all sizes and configurations. See "Choosing Your Cabin" in chapter 4 for a detailed discussion.

What are meals like?　Meals are a big part of the cruise experience, and the larger the ship, the more choices you'll find. When booking your cruise on a larger vessel, you'll be asked ahead of time to schedule your preferred dinner hour since most large ships feature two seatings each evening, with tables assigned. Norwegian, Princess, and Radisson ships are exceptions offering open, restaurant-style seating, meaning that you can dine when and with whom you like. (On Princess ships, you choose in advance of your cruise whether to dine traditional- or restaurant-style, while the other ships offer open seating at all times.) On smaller ships, dining is also usually open seating. In the reviews in chapters 5 and 6, we discuss dining options for each line.

If you have any **special dietary requirements** (vegetarian, kosher, low salt, low fat), be sure the line is informed well in advance—preferably at the time you book your cruise. Some ships have vegetarian and healthful spa options available at every meal, and even most of those that don't can usually meet your needs with some advance warning.

What activities and entertainment does the ship offer?   On small ships, activities are limited by the available public space but often include recent-release videos, group-oriented games (bingo, poker, and the like), and perhaps an informal evening dance party or social hour. The small ships typically offer a lecture series dealing with the flora, fauna, and geography of Alaska, usually conducted by a trained naturalist. These lectures are also becoming more popular on the larger ships.

The big ships also offer activities such as fitness, personal finance, photography, or art classes; Ping-Pong tournaments; and singles or newlywed gatherings. Glitzy floor shows at night are almost de rigueur. (See the big ship and small ship summations earlier in this chapter for more information.)

Does the ship have a children's program?   More parents are taking their kids with them on vacation, and cruises to Alaska are no exception. The lines are responding by adding youth counselors and supervised programs, fancy playrooms, teen centers, and even video-game rooms to keep the kids entertained while their parents relax. Some lines even offer special shore excursions for kids, and most ships offer babysitting (for an extra charge).

It's important to ask whether a supervised program will be offered when you plan to cruise, as sometimes the programs are only in operation if there are a certain number of kids onboard. Some lines offer reduced rates for kids. Most lines discourage people from bringing infants. If your kids are TV addicts, you may want to make sure that your cabin will have a TV and VCR. Even if it does, though, channel selection will be very limited.

I have a disability. Will I have any trouble taking a cruise?   It's important to let the cruise line know your special needs when you make your booking. If you use a wheelchair, you'll need to know if wheelchair-accessible cabins are available (and how they're equipped), as well as whether public rooms are accessible and can be reached by elevator and whether the cruise line has any special policy regarding travelers with disabilities—for instance, some require that you be accompanied by a fully mobile companion. We've noted all this information in the cabin sections of the ship reviews in chapters 5 and 6. Note that newer ships tend to have the largest number of wheelchair-accessible cabins, and that of the small ships in Alaska, only Cruise West's *Spirit of '98* and *Spirit of Oceanus* and Clipper's *Clipper Odyssey* are even moderately wheelchair-friendly.

Travelers with disabilities should inquire when they're booking whether the ship docks at ports or uses tenders (small boats) to go ashore. Tenders cannot always accommodate passengers with wheelchairs—you can't wheel yourself onboard but, rather, will need crew assistance. (Holland America uses an industry-first lift system to accomplish this task without passengers with wheelchairs having to leave their chairs.) Also, once onboard the ship, travelers with disabilities will want to seek the advice of the tour staff before choosing shore excursions, as not all will be wheelchair-friendly.

If you have a chronic health problem, we advise you to check with your doctor before booking the cruise and, if you have any specific needs, to notify the cruise line in advance. This will ensure that the medical team on the ship is properly prepared to offer assistance.

What if I want to honeymoon on the cruise? One-week Alaska cruises start on Saturdays and Sundays, but also on Mondays, Thursdays, and Fridays, which should help you find an appropriate departure date so that you don't have to run out of your wedding reception to catch a plane. You will want to make sure that the ship you choose offers double, queen-, or king-size beds; and you may want to also request a cabin with a tub or Jacuzzi. Rooms with private verandas are particularly romantic. You can take in the sights in privacy and even enjoy a private meal, assuming that the veranda is big enough for a table and chairs (some are not) and that the weather doesn't turn chilly. If you want to dine alone each night, make sure the dining room offers tables for two and/or that the ship offers room service. (Your travel agent can fill you in on these matters.) You may also want to inquire as to the likelihood that there will be other honeymooners your age on the ship. Some ships—among them those of Princess, Royal Caribbean, Carnival, Celebrity, and Holland America—offer special honeymoon packages, and there may even be honeymoon suites. Most lines offer special perks, such as champagne and chocolates, if you let them know in advance that you will be celebrating your special event on the ship.

Can I get married onboard? The answer is yes. On Princess' *Star Princess,* you can get married at sea in the chapel, with the nuptials conducted by the ship's captain. And your friends at home can even watch the ceremony on the Internet, thanks to a special Wedding Cam. You can also get married at sea on the *Carnival Spirit,* which also boasts a nice wedding chapel. The ceremony is conducted by a designated crew member (not the captain) who is a notary.

Will I get seasick? On Inside Passage itineraries, most of your time will be spent in protected waters where there are islands between you and the open sea, thus making for generally smooth sailing. However, there are certain points, such as around Sitka and at the entrance to Queen Charlotte Strait, where there's nothing between you and Japan but a lot of wind, water, and choppy seas. Ships' sailing itineraries on the Gulf of Alaska and those sailing from San Francisco will of necessity spend more time in rough, open waters, and though ships that ply these routes tend to be very stable, you'll probably notice some rocking and rolling.

Unless you're particularly prone to seasickness, you probably don't need to worry much. But if you are, there are medications that can help, including Dramamine, Bonine, and Marezine, which are available over the counter and also stocked by most ships—the purser's office may even give them out for free. Another option is the Transderm patch, available by prescription only, which goes behind your ear and time-releases medication. The patch can be worn for up to 3 days but comes with a slew of side-effect warnings. Some people have also had success in curbing seasickness by using ginger capsules available at health-food stores or the acupressure wristbands available at most pharmacies.

4

Booking Your Cruise & Getting the Best Price

After you've thought about what type of cruise vacation experience you're looking for, when and for how long you'd like to travel, and what sort of itinerary you may be interested in, and after you've read through our ship reviews and narrowed your focus to a couple of cruise lines that appeal to you, it's time to get down to brass tacks and make your booking.

1 Booking a Cruise: The Short Explanation

Every cruise line has a brochure, or sometimes many different brochures, full of beautiful glossy photos of beautiful glossy people enjoying beautiful glossy vacations. They're colorful! They're gorgeous! They're enticing! But they're also about as believable as a cow in lederhosen, particularly when it comes to prices.

But that doesn't mean what you think it does. Instead of publishing rates that say something like "from $500" when, in fact, most of the cabins sell for much more, cruise lines actually publish rates that are *higher* than almost anyone will ever pay. What these published rates are, are the cruise line's pie-in-the-sky wish for how much they'd like to sell the cruise for in an ideal world. In reality, especially as a sailing gets close and it looks as if they'll get stuck with unsold space, cruise lines are almost universally willing to sell their cruises for much, much less. (In 2001, cruises in Alaska were, in some cases, discounted 60% or more.)

Here's the rule to follow: With the exception of some of the small, specialized lines (especially Clipper and Lindblad expeditions), you should **forget the brochure prices**—you'll almost always pay less. Overcapacity and fierce competition have ushered in the age of the discounted fare, and rates continue to stay relatively low. There are last-minute deals, early-booking deals, and all sorts of other bargains.

So how do you find them? Traditionally (meaning over the past 30 years or so) people have booked their cruises through **travel agents.** But, you may be wondering, hasn't the traditional travel agent been replaced by the **Internet** and gone the way of typewriters and 8-track tapes? Not exactly. Travel agents are alive and kicking, though the Internet has indeed staked its claim alongside them and knocked some out of business. Some traditional agencies have also created their own websites to try and keep pace.

So which is the better way to book a cruise these days? Good question. The answer can be "both." If you're computer-savvy, have a good handle on all the elements that go into a cruise, and have narrowed the choices to a few cruise lines that appeal to you, websites are a great way to trawl the seas at your own pace and check out last-minute deals, which can be dramatic. On the other hand, you'll barely get a stitch of personalized service searching for and booking a cruise online. If something goes wrong or you need help getting a refund or arranging special meals or other matters, you're on your own.

However you arrange to buy your cruise, what you basically have in hand at the end is a contract for transportation, lodging, dining, entertainment, housekeeping, and assorted other miscellaneous services that will be provided to you over the course of your vacation. That's a lot of services, involving a lot of people. It's complex, and like any complex thing, it pays (and saves) to study up. That's why it's important that you read the rest of this chapter.

2 Booking Through a Travel Agent

The large majority of cruise passengers book through agents. The cruise lines are happy with the system, have only small reservations staffs themselves (unlike the airlines), and actually discourage direct sales. Even if you do try to call a cruise line to book yourself, you may be advised by the line to contact an agent in your area. (The cruise line may even offer you a name from its list of preferred agencies.)

A good travel agent can save you both time and money. If you're reluctant to use an agent, consider this: Would you represent yourself in court? Perform surgery on your own abdomen? Tackle complicated IRS forms without seeking help? You may be the rare type that doesn't need a travel agent, but most of us are better off working with one.

A good agent can offer you expert advice, save you time, and (best of all) usually work for you for free—the bulk of their fees are paid by the cruise lines. In addition to advising you about the ships, the agent will also help you make decisions on the type of cabin you will need, your dining-room seating preference, any special airfare offerings from the cruise lines, pre- and post-cruise land offerings, and travel insurance.

Most Internet bargains are offered by agents rather than the cruise lines themselves. In cases where the lines do post Web specials, the same deals are usually also available through travel agents. (The lines don't want to upset their travel agent partners and generally try not to compete against them.)

It's important to realize that not all agents represent all cruise lines. In order to be experts on what they sell, and to maximize the commissions the lines pay them (they're paid more based on volume of sales), some agents may limit their product to, say, one luxury line, one mid-priced line, one mass-market line, and so on. If you have your sights set on a particular line or have it narrowed to a couple, you'll have to find an agent who handles your choices. (As we mentioned above, you can call the lines themselves to get the name of an agent near you.)

EXTRA-SPECIAL DEALS

Agents, especially those who specialize in cruises, are in frequent contact with the cruise lines and are continually alerted by the lines about the latest and best deals and special offers. The cruise lines tend to communicate such deals and offers to their top agents first, before the general public, and some of them will never appear in your local newspaper.

Experienced agents know how to play the cruise lines' game and get you the best deals. As an example, the lines run promotions where you can book a category of cabin, rather than a specific cabin, and are guaranteed that category or better. A smart agent will not only know about these offers, but may be able to direct you to a category on a specific ship where there are few cabins available, thus increasing your chances of an upgrade. The cruise lines will also sometimes upgrade passengers as a favor to their top-producing agents or agencies.

To keep their clients alert to specials, agencies may offer newsletters or have other means of communication, such as postcards, e-mail, or posting the specials on their websites. And depending on the agency you choose, you may run across various incentives for booking through an agent.

- **Group rates:** Some agencies buy big blocks of space on a ship in advance and offer it to their clients at a group price only available through that agency. These are called group rates, although "group" in this case means savings, not that you have to hang around with the other people booking through the agency.
- **Match the price:** Some agencies are willing to negotiate, especially if you've found a better deal somewhere else. It never hurts to ask.
- **Back-office systems:** Once you make a booking, some agencies have systems that check deals as they come in to make sure the rate you got is the best rate. (If not, the agency will contact the cruise line to make adjustments accordingly.)
- **Rebates and incentives:** Some agencies are willing to give back to the client a portion of their commissions from the cruise line in order to close a sale. This percent may be monetary, or it might take the form of a perk such as a free bottle of champagne (hardly a reason to book in itself, but a nice perk).

FINDING A GREAT AGENT

If you don't know a good travel agent already, try to find one through your friends, preferably those who have cruised before. For the most personal service, look for an agent in your local area, and for the most knowledgeable service, look for an agent who has cruised him- or herself. It's perfectly okay to ask an agent questions about his experience, such as whether he has ever cruised in Alaska or with one of the lines you're considering. The easiest way to be sure the agent is experienced in booking cruises is to work with an agent at a **cruise-only agency** (meaning that the whole agency specializes in cruises) or to find an agent who is a **cruise specialist** (meaning the agent him- or herself specializes in cruises). If you are calling a full-service travel agency, ask for the **cruise desk,** which is where you'll find these specialists.

A good and easy rule of thumb to assure you find an agent who has cruise experience and who won't rip you off is to book cruises with agencies that are members of the **Cruise Lines International Association (CLIA)** (✆ 212/921-0066; www.cruising.org) or the **National Association of Cruise Oriented Agencies (NACOA)** (✆ 305/663-5626; www.nacoaonline.com). Members of both groups are cruise specialists. Membership in the **American Society of Travel Agents (ASTA)** (✆ 800/275-2782; www.astanet.com) assures the agency is monitored for ethical practices, although it does not in itself designate cruise experience.

You may also run across cruise specialists with the **Certified Travel Counselor (CTC)** designation. This means they have completed a professional-skills course offered by the Institute of Certified Travel Agents (www.icta.com) and is another guarantor of in-depth knowledge of the travel industry.

You can tap into the Internet sites of these organizations for easy access to agents in your area.

BOOKING A SMALL-SHIP CRUISE

The small-ship companies in Alaska—Alaska's Glacier Bay Cruiseline, American Safari Cruises, Clipper, Cruise West, and Lindblad Expeditions—all offer real niche-oriented cruise experiences, attracting passengers who have a very good idea of the kind of experience they want (usually educational and/or adventurous, and always casual and small-scale). In many cases, a large percentage of passengers on any given cruise will have sailed with the line before. Because of all this, and because the passenger capacity of these small ships is so low (12–138), in general you're not going to find the kind of deep discounts you do with the large ships. Still, for the most part these lines rely on agents to handle their bookings, taking very few reservations directly. (Clipper is the exception to this rule, taking most of its Alaska bookings directly, rather than through agents.) All of the lines have a list of agents with whom they do considerable business and can hook you up with one or another of them if you call (or e-mail) and ask for an agent near you.

A NOTE ON DISCOUNTERS

Keep in mind that discounters, who specialize in great-sounding, last-minute types of offers (usually without airfare), and whose ads you can find in Sunday papers and all over the Internet, don't necessarily offer service that matches their prices: Their staffs are more likely to be order-takers than advice-givers. Go to these companies to compare prices only when you are really sure what it is you want.

WATCH OUT FOR SCAMS

The travel business tends to attract more than its share of scam operators trying to lure consumers with incredible come-ons. If you get a solicitation by phone, fax, mail, or e-mail that just doesn't sound right, or if you are uneasy about an agent you are dealing with, call your state consumer protection agency or the local office of the Better Business Bureau. Or you can check with the cruise line to see whether it has heard of the agency in question. Be wary of working with any company, be it on the phone or Internet, that won't give you its street address. You can find more advice on how to avoid scams at the **ASTA** site, **www.astanet.com**.

3 Cruising on the Web

For those who know exactly what they want (we don't recommend this for first-timers), there are deals to be had on the Web. Those selling cruises include top online travel agencies (travelocity.com, expedia.com), agencies that specialize in cruises (icruise.com, uniglobe.com, cruise.com, cruise411.com), travel discounters (bestfares.com, 1travel.com, lowestfare.com), and auction sites (all cruiseauction.com, onsale.com).

There are also some good sites on the Web that specialize in providing cruise information rather than selling cruises. Nearly all the cruise lines have their own sites chock-full of information—some even offer virtual tours of specific ships—and you will find the site addresses in our cruise reviews in chapters 5 and 6. One terrific site that's dedicated to cruising in general (rather than linked with one line) is Cruisemates.com. There are reviews by professional writers as well as ratings by cruise passengers, useful tips, frequent chat opportunities, and message boards.

4 Cruise Costs

In chapters 5 and 6, we've included the brochure rates for every ship reviewed, but as noted above, these are generally only hints at the prices rather than hard and fast amounts, and are constantly fluctuating based on any special deals the cruise lines (and the travel agents) are running. The prices we've noted are for the following three basic types of accommodations: inside cabins (for example, without windows), outside cabins (for example, with windows), and suites. Remember that cruise ships generally have several different categories of cabins within each of these three basic divisions, all priced differently. That's why we give a range. See "Choosing Your Cabin," below, for more information.

The price you pay for your cabin represents the bulk of your cruise vacation's cost, but there are other costs to consider, and whether you're working with an agent or booking online, be sure that you really understand what's included in the fare you're being quoted. Are you getting a price that includes the cruise fare, port charges, taxes, fees, and insurance, or are you getting a cruise-only fare? Are airfare and airport transfers included, or do you have to book them separately (either as an add-on to the cruise fare or on your own)? One agent might break down the charges in a price quote, while another might bundle them all together. Make sure you're comparing apples with apples when making price comparisons. Especially when checking a Web offer, make sure that there are no shipping and handling charges. Read the fine print!

It's also important when figuring out what your cruise will cost to remember what extras are not included in your cruise fare. For instance, the items discussed in this section are not included and will add to the cost of your trip.

SHORE EXCURSIONS

The priciest additions to your cruise fare, particularly in Alaska, will likely be shore excursions. Ranging from about $20 for a walking tour to $184 and up (sometimes as high as $350) for a helicopter or seaplane flightseeing excursion, these sightseeing tours are designed to help cruise passengers make the most of their time at the ports the ship visits, but they can add a hefty sum to your vacation costs. See chapter 7 for more info.

TIPPING

You'll want to add to your calculations tips for the ship's crew, who are usually paid low base wages with the expectation that they'll make up the difference in gratuities. Of course, tipping is at your own discretion—Holland America even makes a point of this, with its "no tipping required" policy—but with the cruise lines being so forthcoming with their tipping advice (they even have special envelopes and cheat sheets prepared to help you out), you'll feel like a crumb for not obliging. An exception is Radisson, which is the only line in Alaska that includes tips in the cruise fare (but you can still leave a few bucks for your favorite crew members if you want to).

Tips are given at the end of the cruise, and passengers should reserve at least $9 per passenger, per day ($63 per passenger for the week) for tips for the room steward, waiter, and busperson. (In practice, we find that most people tend to give a little more.) Additional tips to other personnel, such as the headwaiter or maitre d', are at your discretion. If you have a fancy room with a butler, slip him or her about $2 a day. Most lines automatically add 15% to bar bills, so you don't have to tip your bartender.

Most lines suggest you tip in cash, but some also have a means to allow you to tip via your shipboard account. On small ships, tips are typically pooled among the crew: You hand over a lump sum, and they divide it up. Since tipping on small ships varies, we include information on tipping specifics in chapter 6.

Because some people find the whole tipping process confusing, in 2001 some lines began automatically adding tips to guests' shipboard accounts. Carnival, for instance, adds a standard tip of $9.75 per passenger, per day. Norwegian Cruise Line automatically adds tips of $10 per person, per day. In both cases, you are free to adjust the amount up or down as you see fit based on the service you received.

BOOZE

Most ships charge extra for alcoholic beverages (including wine at dinner) and for soda. Non-bubbly soft drinks, such as lemonade and iced tea, are included in your cruise fare. Soda will cost $1.50 to $2, beer $2.95 and up, and mixed drinks $3.25 and up. A bottle of wine with dinner will run anywhere from $10 to upwards of $300.

PORT CHARGES, TAXES & FEES

Port charges, taxes, and other fees are sometimes included in your cruise fare, but not always, and these charges can add as much as $210 per person onto the price of a 7-day Alaska cruise. Make sure you know whether these are included in the cruise fare when you are comparing rates. We've included information on port charges in the ship reviews in chapters 5 and 6.

5 Money-Saving Strategies

The best way to save on an Alaska cruise is to **book in advance.** Typically, lines offer early-bird rates, usually 25% or more off the brochure rate, to those who book their Alaska cruise by mid- to late February of the year of the cruise. If the cabins do not fill up by the cutoff date, the early-bird rate may be extended, but it may be slightly lower—say, a 15% or 20% savings. If the cabins are still not full as the season begins, the cruise line may start marketing special deals, usually through its top-producing travel agents. It used to be rare to find last-minute deals on Alaska cruises due to their popularity. But over the past couple of years, with bigger capacity ships in the Alaska market, discounts have proliferated, and the trend is likely to continue in 2002. Keep in mind, though, that these deals are usually for a very limited selection of cabins. Planning your Alaska cruise well in advance and taking advantage of early-booking discounts is still the best way to go.

You can also save by booking a cruise in the **shoulder months of May or September,** when cruise pricing is lower than during the high summer months. Typically, Alaska cruises are divided into budget, low, economy, value, standard, and peak seasons, but since these overlap quite a bit from cruise line to cruise line, we can lump them into three basic periods:

1. **Budget/Low/Economy Season:** May and September
2. **Value/Standard Season:** early June and late August
3. **Peak Season:** late June, July, and early to mid-August

The lines also tend to offer cut rates when they are introducing a new ship or moving into a new market. So it pays to keep track of what's happening in the industry—or to have your agent do so—when you're looking for a deal.

DISCOUNTS FOR THIRD & FOURTH PASSENGERS

Most ships offer highly discounted rates for third and fourth passengers sharing a cabin with two full-fare passengers, even if those two have booked at a discounted rate. You can add the four rates together and then divide by four to get your per-person rate. This is a good option for families (or friends) on a budget, but remember that it'll be a tight fit, since most cabins aren't very large. Some lines also offer **special rates for kids,** usually on a seasonal or select-sailing basis, that may include free or discounted airfare.

GETTING TOGETHER A GROUP

One of the best ways to get a cruise deal is to book as a group, so you may want to gather family together for a family reunion or convince your friends or colleagues they need a vacation, too. A "group," as defined by the cruise lines, is generally at least 16 people in at least eight cabins. The savings include not only a discounted rate, but also at least the cruise portion of the 16th ticket will be free. (On some upscale ships you can negotiate a free ticket for groups of eight or more.) The gang can split the proceeds from the free ticket or hold a drawing for the ticket, maybe at a cocktail party on the first night. If your group is large enough, you may even be able to get that cocktail party for free, and perhaps some other onboard perks as well.

SENIOR-CITIZEN DISCOUNTS

Senior citizens may be able to get extra savings on their cruise. Some lines will take 5% off the top for those 55 and up, and the senior rate applies even if the second person in the cabin is younger. Membership in groups such as AARP is not required, but such membership may bring additional savings. (World Explorer cruises offer AARP discounts of 20%.)

OTHER DEALS

Some of the more upscale lines will reward customers willing to pay their full fare in advance (thus giving the cruise line cash in hand). The discounts—sometimes as much as 10%—are significant enough that it might pay to go this route rather than putting your vacation money in a CD.

If you like your Alaska cruise so much you decide you want to vacation here again, consider booking your next cruise on the spot. Cruise lines have gotten smart about the fact that when you're on a ship you're a captive audience, so they may pitch you to make your future vacation plans onboard. *Before you sign on the dotted line, though, make sure the on-the-spot discount can be combined with other offers you might find later.* Keep in mind that, if you do choose to book onboard, you can still do the reconfirmation and ticketing through your travel agent by giving the cruise line his or her name.

6 Airfares, Cruisetours & Hotel Offerings

AIR ADD-ONS

Unless you live within driving distance of your port of embarkation, you'll probably be flying to Vancouver, Anchorage, or one of the other ports to join your ship. Your cruise package may include airfare, but if not, you'll have to make other arrangements. You can book air separately, but remember that those attractive sale fares you see in the newspapers may not apply, especially if your cruise departs on the peak travel days of Friday or Saturday. A better option is usually to take advantage of the cruise lines' air **add-ons.** Why? First of all, as big customers of the airlines, the cruise lines tend to get decent (if not the best) discounted airfare rates, which they pass on to their customers. Secondly, booking air with the cruise line also allows the line to keep track of you. If your plane is late, for instance, they may even hold the boat. Most cruise lines include **transfers** from the airport to the ship, saving you the hassle of getting a cab. (If you do book on your own, you may still be able to get the transfers separately—ask your agent about this.) Be aware that once the air ticket is issued by the cruise line, you usually aren't allowed to make changes.

The only time it may pay to book your own air transportation is if you are using frequent-flyer miles and can get the air for free, or if you are fussy about which carrier you fly or route you take. You are more or less at the mercy of the cruise line to make these choices if you take their air offers, and you may even end up on chartered aircraft. Some lines offer special **deviation programs** that allow you to request specific airlines and routing for an extra fee. The deadline for these requests is usually 60 days before the sailing date or the day your cruise reservation is made if you book later.

If you choose not to book your air transportation with the cruise line, and airfare is part of the cruise deal, you will be refunded the air portion of the fare.

CRUISETOURS & ADD-ONS
All sorts of add-on programs are offered by the cruise lines in Alaska, and are typically booked at the same time you book your cruise to create what's known as a **cruisetour offering,** which can total 9 to 21 days, including the 7-day cruise and excursions to Denali National Park and Mount McKinley, Nome, Fairbanks, Wrangell–St. Elias National Park, the Kenai Peninsula, and, in Canada, the Canadian Rockies and Yukon Territory.

Princess and Holland America have practically cornered the market on Alaska cruisetours, owning their own hotels and ground transportation operations, including deluxe motor coaches and luxury railroad cars with viewing domes. Last year, Royal Caribbean also introduced its own ground operation for passengers on Royal Caribbean and Celebrity ships.

PRE- & POST-CRUISE HOTEL OFFERINGS
Even if you don't take a cruisetour, you may want to consider spending a day or two in the port city either before or after your cruise. (See details on exploring the port cities in chapters 9 and 10.) But just as with airfare, you need to decide whether you want to buy your hotel stay from the cruise line or make arrangements on your own.

As with air add-ons, the cruise lines negotiate **special deals with hotels** at port cities. An advantage to coming in a day or two early is that you don't have to worry if your flight is running late. (Plus, Vancouver and Anchorage, into which most passengers fly, happen to be great cities to explore.)

When evaluating a cruise line's hotel package, make sure that you review it carefully to see what's included. See whether the line offers a transfer from the airport to the hotel and from the hotel to the cruise ship; make sure that the line offers a hotel that you will be happy with in terms of type of property and location; and inquire if any escorted tours, car-rental deals, or meals are included. You'll also want to compare the price of booking on your own. (See chapter 8 for port information.) Keep in mind that cruise lines usually list rates for hotels on a per-person basis, whereas hotels post their rates on a per-room basis.

7 Choosing Your Cabin

Once you've looked at the ship descriptions later in the book, talked over your options with your travel agent, and selected an itinerary, a big decision you're going to have to make is choosing your cabin. The cruise lines have improved things a bit since Charles Dickens referred to his stateroom as reminding him of a coffin, but cramped, windowless spaces can still be found. On the other hand, so can penthouse-size suites with expansive verandas, Jacuzzis, and butler service. Most cabins on cruise ships today have twin beds that are convertible to queen-size (you can request which configuration you want), plus a private bathroom with a shower. Some cabins have bunk beds, which are obviously not convertible. Most ships also offer cabins designed for three or four people that will include bunks. In some, it is possible to put in a fifth, portable bed. Some lines offer special cabins designed for families. Families may also be able to book connecting cabins (although they'll have to pay for two cabins to do so).

Most cabins, but not all, have televisions. Some also have extra amenities, such as safes, minifridges, VCRs, bathrobes, and hair dryers. A bathtub is considered a luxury on ships and will usually only be offered in more expensive rooms.

CABIN TYPES

What kind of cabin is right for you? Price will likely be a big factor here, but so should the vacation style you prefer. The typical ship offers several types of cabin, as outlined by floor plans in the cruise line's brochure. The cabins are usually described by price (highest to lowest), category (suite, deluxe, superior, standard, economy, and others), and furniture configuration ("sitting area with two lower beds," for example). The cabins will also be described as being **inside** or **outside.** Simply put, inside cabins do not have windows (or even portholes) and outside cabins do. On the big ships, the more deluxe outside cabins may also come with **verandas** that give you private outdoor space to enjoy sea breezes. Diagrams of the various cabin types are typically included.

Noise can be a factor that may influence your cabin choice. Consider that, if you take a cabin on a lower deck, you may hear engine noises; in the front of the ship, anchor noises; and in the back of the ship, thruster noises. A cabin near an elevator may bring door-opening and -closing sounds. And a cabin above or below the disco may pulse until all hours of the night. If noise is a problem for you, make your cabin choice accordingly.

If you plan to spend a lot of quiet time in your cabin, you should probably consider booking the biggest room you can afford, and you should also consider taking a cabin with a picture window or a private veranda. If, conversely, you plan to be off on tours or on deck checking out the glaciers and wildlife and will only be using your cabin to change clothes and collapse in at the end of the day, you may be just as happy with a smaller (and cheaper) cabin. Usually, the higher on the ship (by deck) the cabin is located, the more expensive and nicer the cabin is. This is true even if there are cabins of the same size on lower decks. (These are usually decorated differently.) **Luxury suites** are usually on upper decks, but a quirky thing about cabin pricing is that the most stable cabins during rough seas are those in the middle and lower parts of the ship. Still, you'll get lots of space to stretch out, with the top suites on some ships actually apartment-size.

Bear in mind that some views from some outside cabins may be obstructed— usually by a lifeboat—or look out onto a public area, which will be an issue if you crave privacy; an experienced travel agent should be able to advise you on these matters. With few exceptions, veranda cabins will not be obstructed, but the thing to remember is that the verandas themselves vary in size, so if you're looking to do more than stand on your balcony, make sure the outdoor space is big enough to accommodate deck chairs, a table, or whatever else you require. Also, keep in mind that these verandas tend to be more semiprivate than private. (Your neighbors may be able to see you.)

On the small ships, cabins can run to the truly tiny and spartan, though some can also give the big-ship cabins a run for their money. Generally, the difference lies in the orientation of the cruise line: Those promising a real adventure experience tend to feature somewhat utilitarian cabins.

Aboard both large and small ships, keep in mind that the most expensive and least expensive cabins tend to sell out fast. Also keep in mind that, just as with real estate, it's sometimes better to take a smaller cabin in a nicer neighborhood (in this case, nicer "ship") than a bigger cabin in a lesser neighborhood.

CABIN SIZES

The size of a cabin is described in terms of square feet. This number may not mean a lot unless you want to mark it out on your floor at home. But to give you an idea: 120 square feet and under is low-end and cramped, 180 square feet is midrange (and the minimum for people with claustrophobia), and 250 square feet and up is suite-size.

8 Choosing Your Dining Options

Smaller ships usually serve dinner in one sitting, at an open seating, allowing you to sit at any table you want, so if you plan to sail one of these lines, you don't have to read this section at all. But because most dining rooms on **larger ships** are not large enough to accommodate all passengers at once, these ships typically offer two seatings (exceptions are noted in the "Open Seating" section, below) especially for dinner. All table space, in these cases, is on a reserved basis and is generally arranged ahead of time, when you book your cruise.

MEAL TIMES

If you are on a ship with set dinner times, early or main seating is typically at 6pm. Late seating is at 8:30pm. There are advantages and disadvantages to both times, and it basically comes down to personal choice. **Early seating** is usually less crowded and the preferred time for families and seniors. The dining experience can be a bit more rushed (the staff needs to make way for the next wave), but food items may be fresher. You can see a show right after dinner and have first dibs on other nighttime venues as well. And you just may be hungry again in time for the **midnight buffet.**

Late seating, on the other hand, allows you time for a good long nap or late spa appointments before dining. Dinner is not rushed at all. You can sit as long as you want enjoying after-dinner drinks—unless, that is, you choose to go catch the show, which will start at 10 or 10:15pm.

If you choose to also eat **breakfast** and **lunch** in the dining room as opposed to at the more casual venues on the ship, theoretically you are supposed to eat at assigned times as well—typical meal times for breakfast are 7 or 8am for the early seating and 8:30 or 9am for the late; for lunch, it's usually noon for the early seating and 1:30pm or so for the late. We've found, though, that most ships aren't hard and fast on this. Crowds in the dining room are typically only an issue at dinner. If you show up other than at your assigned time for breakfast or lunch and your assigned table is full, the staff will probably just seat you elsewhere.

Most large ships today also offer **alternative dining options.** They have a casual, buffet-style cafe restaurant, usually located on the Lido Deck, with indoor and outdoor poolside seating and an extensive spread of both hot and cold food items at breakfast, lunch, and dinner. Some ships also have **reservations-only restaurants,** seating fewer than 100, where—except on the luxury ships of Crystal and Radisson—a fee is charged.

TABLE SIZES

Do you mind sitting with strangers? Are you looking to make new friends? Your dinner companions can make or break your cruise experience. Most ships offer tables configured for 2 to 12 people. For singles or couples who want to socialize, generally a table of eight seats allows enough variety so that you don't get bored, and also allows you the ability to steer clear of any one individual you don't particularly care for. (Tables are assigned, not seats.) Couples may choose to sit on their own, but singles may find it hard to secure a table for one. A family of four may want to choose a table for four, or request to sit with another family at a table for eight.

You need to state your preference in advance, unless you are on a ship with an open-seating policy, but don't worry if you change your mind once you're onboard. You'll probably be able to move around. Just tell the dining room maitre d', and he'll review the seating charts for an opening. (Greasing his palm will probably help.)

OPEN SEATING

Put off by all this formality? Want guaranteed casual all the way? Norwegian Cruise Line now serves all meals on an open-seating basis—dine when you want and sit with whom you want (within the restaurants' open hours). Princess Cruises has its own version of this system (introduced last year), allowing guests to choose before the cruise the traditional early or late seating or open, restaurant-style seating. A $6.50-a-day gratuity is automatically added to your bill for this restaurant service, but that's evened out to some extent by the fact that you won't be tipping your waiter at the end of the cruise. Radisson's *Seven Seas Navigator* also offers dining on an open-seating basis.

SPECIAL MENU REQUESTS

The cruise line should be informed at the time you make your reservations about any special dietary requests you have. Some lines offer kosher menus, and all will have vegetarian, low-fat, low-salt, and sugar-free options available.

SMOKE-FREE DINING

Many ships now feature smoke-free dining rooms, but if smoking is a particular concern to you, check this out with your travel agent. If the room isn't no-smoking, you can request a no-smoking table. Vice versa for smokers.

9 Deposits & Cancellation Policies

You'll be asked by your travel agent to make a **deposit,** either of a fixed amount or at some percentage of your total cruise cost. You later will receive a receipt in the mail from the cruise line. You'll be asked to pay the remaining fare usually no later than 2 months before your departure date.

Cruise lines have varying policies regarding **cancellations,** and it's important to look at the fine print in the line's brochure to make sure you understand the policy. Most lines allow you to cancel for a full refund on your deposit and payment anytime up to 76 days before the sailing, after which you have to pay a penalty. If you cancel at the last minute, you will typically be refunded only 75% of what you've paid.

10 Travel Insurance

There are three kinds of travel insurance: trip-cancellation, medical, and lost-luggage coverage. **Trip-cancellation insurance** is a good idea if you have paid a large portion of your vacation expenses upfront—as is the case with cruises. It offers protection if, for some reason, you're not able to take your cruise or your trip is interrupted. The other two types of insurance, however, don't make sense for most travelers. Rule number one: Check your existing policies before you buy any additional coverage.

Your existing health insurance should cover you if you get sick while on vacation (though if you belong to an HMO, you should check to see whether you are fully covered when away from home). For independent travel health-insurance providers, see below. Your homeowner's insurance should cover stolen luggage if you have off-premises theft protection. Check your existing policies before you buy any additional coverage. The airlines are responsible for $2,500 on domestic flights if they lose your luggage (and $9.07 per lb., or up to $640, on international flights); if you plan to carry anything more valuable than that, keep it in your carry-on bag. Some credit cards (American Express and certain gold and platinum Visa and MasterCards, for example) offer automatic flight insurance against death or dismemberment in case of an airplane crash. If you feel you need additional insurance, try one of the companies listed below. But don't pay for more than you need. For example, if you need only trip-cancellation insurance, don't purchase coverage for lost or stolen property. Trip-cancellation insurance costs approximately 6% to 8% of the total value of your vacation.

Among the reputable issuers of travel insurance are:

- **Access America,** 6600 W. Broad St., Richmond, VA 23230; ☎ **800/284-8300;** www.accessamerica.com.
- **Travel Guard International,** 1145 Clark St., Stevens Point, WI 54481; ☎ **800/826-1300;** www.travelguard.com.
- **Travel Insured International, Inc.** P.O. Box 280568, 52-S Oakland Ave., East Hartford, CT 06128-0568; ☎ **800/243-3174;** www.travelinsured.com.
- **Travelex Insurance Services,** 11717 Burt St., Ste. 202, Omaha, NE 68154; ☎ **800/228-9792;** www.travelexinsurance.com.

 FAST FACTS: **Alaska**

Area Code All of Alaska is in area code **907.** In the Yukon Territory, the area code is **867.** When placing a toll call within the state, you must dial 1, the area code, and the number. See "Telephone," below, for important tips.

Banks & ATMs There are banks and automated teller machines in all but the tiniest towns.

Business Hours In the larger cities, major grocery stores are open 24 hours a day and carry a wide range of products (even fishing gear) in addition to food. At a minimum, **stores** are open Monday through Friday from 10am to 6pm, are open Saturday afternoon, and are closed Sunday, but many are open much longer hours, especially in summer. **Banks** may close an hour earlier; if they're open on Saturday, they're only open in the morning. Under state law, **bars** don't have to close until 5am, but many communities have an earlier closing, generally around 2am.

Cellular Phone Coverage Most of the populated portion of the state has cellular coverage. Your cellphone provider should be able to give you a brochure detailing roaming charges, which can be steep.

Emergencies Generally, you can call ℭ **911** for medical, police, or fire emergencies. On remote highways, there sometimes are gaps in 911 coverage, but dialing 0 will generally get an operator, who can connect you to emergency services. Citizens Band channels 9 and 11 are monitored for emergencies on most highways, as are channels 14 and 19 in some areas.

Holidays Besides the normal national holidays, banks and state and local government offices close on two state holidays: Seward's Day (the last Mon in Mar) and Alaska Day (Oct 18, or the nearest Fri or Mon if it falls on a weekend). See chapter 3 for a listing of national holidays.

Liquor Laws The minimum drinking age in Alaska is 21. Most restaurants sell beer and wine, while a minority have full bars that serve hard liquor as well. Packaged alcohol, beer, and wine are sold only in licensed stores (not grocery stores), but these are common and are open long hours every day. More than 100 rural communities have laws prohibiting the importation and possession of alcohol (known as being "dry") or only the sale but not possession of alcohol (known as being "damp"). With a few exceptions, these are tiny Bush communities off the road network; urban areas are all "wet." Before flying into a Native village with alcohol, ask about the law — bootlegging is a serious crime (and serious bad manners) — or check a list on the Alcoholic Beverage Control Board website, www.abc.revenue.state.ak.us/localopt.htm.

Maps For the most popular areas, I recommend the excellent trail maps published by **Trails Illustrated** (ℭ **800/962-1643**; www.trailsillustrated.com). They're sold in park visitor centers, too. The maps are printed on plastic so that they don't get spoiled by rain; however, they don't cover the whole state. Buy **official topographic maps** from the U.S. Geological Survey in person or by order at USGS–ESIC, 4230 University Dr., Anchorage, AK 99508 (ℭ **907/786-7011**), open Monday to Friday, 8:30am to 4:30pm.

Newspapers The state's dominant newspaper is the *Anchorage Daily News* (www.adn.com); it's available everywhere but is not always easy to find in Southeast Alaska. Seattle newspapers and *USA Today* are often available, and in Anchorage, you can get virtually any newspaper.

Taxes There is no state sales tax, but most local governments have a sales tax and a bed tax on accommodations.

Telephone I am assured that all major calling cards will work in Alaska, but this certainly hasn't been the case in the past. To make sure, contact your long-distance company or buy a by-the-minute card.

Time Zone Although the state naturally spans five time zones, in the 1980s, Alaska's middle time zone was stretched so that almost the entire state would lie all in one zone that is known as Alaska time. It's 1 hour earlier than the U.S. West Coast's Pacific time. Crossing over the border from Alaska to Canada adds an hour and puts you at the same time as the West Coast. As with almost everywhere else in the United States, daylight saving time is in effect from 1am on the first Sunday in April (turn your clocks ahead 1 hr.) until 2am on the last Sunday in October (turn clocks back again).

5

The Cruise Lines, Part 1: The Big Ships

Here's where the rudder hits the road: It's time to choose the ship that'll be your home away from home for the duration of your Alaska cruise.

As we said earlier, your biggest decision is whether you want to sail on a big ship or a small ship. So that you can more easily compare like with like, in this chapter we'll deal only with the big ships; in chapter 6, we'll discuss the small ships.

The ships in Alaska are bigger than ever. Case in point: Princess's *Star Princess*, at 109,000 tons and carrying 2,600 passengers, is the biggest ever to sail in this market. And although it may be the 49th state's heavyweight champ of 2002, the *Star Princess* is by no means alone among new megaships there. There is, for instance, the *Summit*, of Celebrity Cruises, which weighs in at 91,000 tons and carries 1,950 souls, making its Alaska debut, and its returning similarly dimensioned sister ship *Infinity*. There's Royal Caribbean's *Radiance of the Seas*, also a first-timer in Alaska at 88,000 tons (2,100 berths), and the returning *Carnival Spirit* at 86,000 tons (capacity: 2,124).

The beauty of these latter-day megaships, though, is that they are designed so that it doesn't seem as though you're always sharing your vacation with thousands of others. The architectural state of the art allows for lots of nooks and crannies in which to relax and hide yourself far from the madding crowd, so to speak.

The ships featured in this chapter vary in size, age, and offerings, but share the common thread of having scads of activities and entertainment offerings. You will not be roughing it. On these ships, you'll find swimming pools, health clubs, spas, nightclubs, movie theaters, shops, casinos, multiple restaurants, bars, and special kids' playrooms, and in some cases sports decks, virtual golf, computer rooms, martini bars, and cigar clubs, as well as the aforementioned quiet spaces where you can get away from it all. Onboard activities generally include games, contests, classes, and lectures, plus a variety of entertainment options and show productions, some very sophisticated. An array of shore excursions are offered, for which you pay extra. Cabins vary in size and amenities but are usually roomy enough for the time you'll be spending aboard. And with all the public rooms, you won't be spending much time there anyway.

STRUCTURE OF THE CRUISE LINE REVIEWS

Each cruise line's review begins with a quick word about the line in general and a short summation of the kind of cruise experience you can expect to have aboard that line. The text that follows fleshes out the review, providing all the details you need to get a feel for what kind of vacation the cruise line will give you.

RATING THE INDIVIDUAL SHIPS

The individual ship reviews that follow the general cruise line description get down into the nitty-gritty, giving you all the details on the ships' accommodations, facilities, amenities, comfort level, and upkeep.

People feel very strongly about ships. For centuries, mariners have imbued their vessels with human personalities, and usually referred to them as "her." In fact, an old (really old) seafaring superstition holds that women should never be allowed aboard a ship because the ship, being a woman herself, will get jealous. Be that as it may, it's a fact that people bond with the ships they sail aboard. They find themselves in the gift shop, loading up on T-shirts with the ship's name emblazoned on the front. They get to port, and the first question they ask other cruisers they meet is "Which ship are you sailing on?" and then engage in a friendly comparison, each walking away knowing in his heart that his ship is the best. We know people who have sailed the same ship a dozen times or more and feel as warmly about it as though it were their own summer cottage. That's why, when looking at the reviews, you want to look for a ship that says "you." We've listed some of the ships' **vital statistics**—ship size, year built and most recently refurbished, number of cabins, number of crew—to help you compare. Size is listed in tons. Note that these are not actual measures of weight but gross register tons (GRTs), which is a measure of the interior space used to produce revenue on a ship. One GRT equals 100 cubic feet of enclosed, revenue-generating space.

Among the crew/officers statistics, an important one is the **passenger/crew ratio,** which tells you, in theory, how many passengers each crew member is expected to serve and, thus, how much personal service you can expect.

ITINERARIES

Each cruise line review includes a chart showing itineraries for each ship the line has assigned to Alaska itineraries for 2002. Often, a single ship sails on alternating itineraries—for instance, sailing from Anchorage/Seward to Vancouver one week and doing the same route backwards (Vancouver to Anchorage/Seward) the next. When this is the case, we've listed both and noted that they alternate. These itineraries are subject to change. Consult your travel agent for exact sailing dates.

We've also listed the **cruisetours and add-ons** you can book with your cruise, and we've provided brochure prices for these as well.

PRICES

We've listed the prices for cabins and suites. Note that all the prices listed are in the line's **brochure rates,** so depending on how early you book and on any special deals the lines are offering, you may get a rate substantially below what we've listed. (Discounts can run up to 60%, and sometimes more.) Rates are for a 7-night cruise, per person, and are based on double occupancy. If the ship does not do 7-night itineraries, we've noted that and offer rates for the itineraries the ship does do. Our rates are based on the basic types of accommodations:

- Inside cabin (for example, one without windows)
- Outside cabin (for example, one with windows)
- Suite

Remember that cruise ships generally have several different categories of cabins within each of these three basic divisions, all priced differently, which is why on some ships you'll see a rather broad range in each category.

1 Carnival Cruise Lines

SHIP   Carnival Spirit

3655 NW 87th Ave., Miami, FL 33178-2428. ✆ **800/CARNIVAL.** Fax 305/471-4740. www.carnival.com.

Almost the definition of mass market, Carnival is the Big Kahuna of the industry, boasting a modern fleet of big ships that are the boldest, most innovative, and most successful on the seas. Why? Like the line's now-famous ad campaign says, the experience of being on the ships is "fun"—as in fun, Fun, FUN! Like Kathie Lee Gifford used to sing, "In the morning, in the evening" you'll find fun on Carnival ships, and parties, and party-hearty fellow passengers, too.

THE EXPERIENCE   The decor on Carnival's ships is eclectic and definitely glitzy, offering an ambience that's akin to a theme park. Translating the line's warm-weather experience to Alaska has meant combining the "24-hour orgy of good times" philosophy to include the natural wonders, so you may find yourself bellying up to the rail with a multicolored party drink to gawk at a glacier. Drinking and off-color jokes are part of the scene, as are "hairy chest contests" and the like. This is either a plus or a minus, depending on your taste. In its Alaska brochure, the line says you may find yourself shouting "Eureka"—not at a gold-rush site but in the ship's casino.

Pros

- **Entertainment.** Carnival's entertainment is among the industry's best, with each ship boasting a dozen dancers, 10-piece orchestras, comedians, jugglers, and numerous live bands, as well as a big casino.
- **Children's program.** Carnival attracts a slew of families, and its children's program does an expert job of keeping them occupied, with some Alaska-specific activities thrown into the mix. The line offers a special series of shore excursions designed for teens.

Cons

- **Service.** The international crew doesn't provide terribly refined service, but then that's not the point here.
- **Loud public announcements.** All the Carnival ships are well-run and maintained, but there are minor annoyances like lines and frequent loud public announcements—factors that come with the mass-market experience.

THE FLEET   Carnival beefed up its presence in Alaska in 2001, positioning its big, brand-new, 2,124-passenger megaship *Carnival Spirit* in the market. (Previously, the line had one of its smallest and oldest vessels here.) And the vessel returns to Alaska in 2002. The *Spirit* offers almost innumerable activities, great pool and hot-tub spaces (some covered for use in chillier weather), a big oceanview gym and spa, and more dining options than your doctor would say is advisable.

PASSENGER PROFILE   Overall, Carnival has some of the youngest demographics in the industry: mostly under 50, including couples, singles, and a good share of **families.** (The line carries some 300,000 kids a year.) It's the same middle-America crowd that can be found in Las Vegas and Atlantic City and at Florida's megaresorts. Even though passengers on the Alaska sailings may be older than on Caribbean sailings, they tend to be young at heart. They are not a sedate, bird-watching crowd. They may want to see whales and icebergs, but

Carnival Fleet Itineraries

Ship	Itinerary
Carnival Spirit	**7-night northbound:** From Vancouver to Seward/Anchorage, visiting Ketchikan, Juneau, Skagway, and Sitka, and cruising Prince William Sound (to view College Fjord and the Columbia Glacier), and Endicott Arm. **7-night southbound:** From Seward to Vancouver, visiting Valdez, Juneau, Skagway, and Ketchikan, and cruising Yakutat Bay (to view Hubbard Glacier) and Prince William Sound (to view College Fjord and the Columbia Glacier). **7-night Glacier Bay:** Sails round-trip from Vancouver (offered only in May and Sept) visiting Juneau, Skagway, Ketchikan, the Inside Passage, and Glacier Bay.

they will also dance the Macarena on cue. If you are the type who wants to sit on deck, binoculars around your neck, waiting for a humpback whale to breach or a bald eagle to circle overhead, you may be happier aboard one of the more sedate lines, like Holland America. **Singles** take note: Carnival officials estimate that their ships attract more of you than any other line.

DINING   Food is bountiful, geared toward a middle-American audience: Red meat is popular on these ships. Recent improvements have led to some surprisingly good preparations in the dining room, including old favorites, such as beef Wellington and duck a l'orange, and new dishes, such as broiled Chilean sea bass with truffle butter and smoked turkey tenderloin with asparagus tips. Broiled lobster is featured one night on each cruise. Spa, pasta, and vegetarian options are offered nightly. And the casual dining buffets include Chinese and deli kiosks, with nearby pizza stations as well. Carnival bans smoking in its dining rooms. The *Spirit* also adds the special treat of a reservations-only supper club, where for a fee of $20 per person, you can dine on a great steak and Joe's Stone Crab while being entertained by a singer and keyboardist.

ACTIVITIES   "Nonstop" is the key description here. If Atlantic City and Las Vegas appeal to you, Carnival will, too. What you'll get aboard a Fun Ship is fun—lots of it, professionally and insistently delivered and spangled with glitter. Cocktails inevitably begin to flow before lunch. Singles and newlywed parties are frequent. You can learn to country line dance or ballroom dance, take cooking lessons, learn to play bridge, watch first-run movies, practice your golf swing by smashing balls into a net, or join in a knobby-knee contest. Plus, there are always the onboard staples of eating, drinking, and shopping, and the Alaska-specific naturalist lectures that are delivered daily. Once in port, Carnival lives up to its "more is more" ethos by offering **nearly 100 shore excursions in Alaska.** These are divided into categories of easy, moderate, and adventure. Internet cafes offer Internet access for 75¢ a minute.

CHILDREN'S PROGRAM   For kids, the line offers Camp Carnival, an expertly run children's and teen's program with a plethora of kid-pleasing activities designed to keep kids occupied so that parents can enjoy some downtime. (On the *Spirit,* parents of little kids can even request beepers so that they can keep in touch.) In Alaska, these activities include everything from Native American arts-and-crafts sessions to lectures conducted by wildlife experts, and there are special shore excursions for teens.

ENTERTAINMENT   Carnival consistently offers the most lavish entertainment extravaganzas afloat, spending millions on stage sets, choreography, and acoustical equipment that leave many other floating theaters in the dust. Carnival megaships each carry flamboyantly costumed dancers and singers (on the *Spirit*, there's a cast of 18), and a 10-piece orchestra, plus comedians, jugglers, acrobats, rock 'n' roll bands, country-western bands, classical string trios, pianists, and big bands.

SERVICE   As we said above, it ain't exactly what you call "refined," but it is professional. All in all, a Carnival ship is a well-oiled machine, and you'll certainly get what you need—but not much more. When you board the ship, for instance, you're welcomed by a polite staff at the gangway, given a diagram of the ship's layout, and then pointed in the right direction to find your cabin on your own, carry-on luggage in tow. Introduced on the *Spirit* was a new Carnival program that has your tips ($9.75 per passenger, per day) automatically charged to your shipboard account.

There is a **laundry service** onboard (for washing and pressing only) that charges by the piece, as well as a handful of **self-service laundry rooms** with irons and coin-operated washing machines and dryers. Dry cleaning is not available.

CRUISETOUR & ADD-ON PROGRAMS   Three- and four-night land extensions can be added to form a 10- or 11-night cruisetour. Land packages are provided by sister company Holland America–Westours to Anchorage, Fairbanks, and Denali National Park; 3-night is $910 per person, based on double occupancy, and 4-night is $1,100 (both plus cruise fare). Pre- or post-cruise hotel packages in Seattle, Vancouver, and Anchorage are also available, for $120 in Seattle, $140 in Vancouver, and $185 in Anchorage, based on double occupancy.

Carnival Spirit

Size (in tons)	84,000	Officers	Italian
Number of Cabins	1,062	Crew	920 (Int'l)
Number of Outside Cabins	849	Passenger/Crew Ratio	2.3 to 1
Cabins with Verandas	682	Year Built	2001
Number of Passengers	2,124	Last Major Refurbishment	n/a

The *Spirit* is big, new, and certainly impressive, although some may find the interior a bit over the top. Rooms reflect a purposeful mismatch of styles including Art Nouveau, Art Deco, Empire, Gothic, and Egyptian, with the decor done up with expensive materials, such as burled wood, marble, leather, copper, and even gold gild. (Legendary Carnival designer Joe Farcus showed little restraint.) Love it or not, you'll certainly be wowed.

The ship represents a new class for Carnival and offers the best features of the line's earlier ships, including an expansive outdoor area with four swimming pools (there is a retractable dome over the main pool so that you can take a dip no matter what the weather), four whirlpools, and a water slide; a high-tech children's play center with computers and a video wall; a multilevel oceanview fitness facility; numerous clubs and lounges; and a variety of eating and entertainment options. New features include a unique reservations-only Supper Club (for dinner with entertainment) and the line's first wedding chapel, as well as a mostly outdoor promenade. (If you are doing a full circle around the ship, you have to take a few steps inside.) The ship also has modified engines and new waste treatment and disposal systems to make it more environmentally friendly. And the *Spirit* offers more space per passenger than do most ships in the Alaska market.

CABINS Some 80% of the cabins on this ship boast ocean views, and of those, 80% boast private balconies, a big plus in a market like Alaska where views are the main draw. Cabins are larger than those you'll find offered by other lines in the same price category, and they are mostly furnished with twin beds that can be converted to king-size. (A few have upper and lower berths that cannot be converted.) All cabins come with a TV, wall safe, and telephone; oceanview cabins also come with bathrobes and coral-colored leather couches to sit on (with nifty storage drawers underneath). There are connecting cabins available for families or groups traveling together. Suites are offered at several different levels, and each boasts a separate sleeping, sitting, and dressing area; double sinks; a bathtub; and a large balcony. Sixteen cabins are wheelchair-accessible.

Cabins & Rates

Cabins	Brochure Rates	Bathtub	Fridge	Hair Dryer	Sitting Area	TV
Inside	$1,579–$2,129	no	yes	yes	no	yes
Outside	$1,879–$2,869	no	yes	yes	yes	yes
Suite	$2,929–$3,669	yes	yes	yes	yes	yes

PUBLIC AREAS The ship's soaring atrium spans 11 decks and is topped with a red stained-glass dome that is part of the Nouveau Supper Club, a reservations-only steakhouse-type restaurant (a fee of $20 per person is charged), with fine dining and live entertainment. A lobby bar (one of a dozen bar/lounges, including a piano bar, a sports bar, and a jazz club) offers live music and a chance to take in the vast space. A particularly fun room is the two-level Jackson Pollock–inspired disco, with paint-splattered walls. There is a two-level main dining room done up in Napoleonic splendor and a bevy of other food service offerings (including a 24-hr. pizzeria) to keep the gourmandistic side of your cruise personality happy and full.

The hundreds of onboard activities for which Carnival is famous, including Vegas-style shows and casino action (the ship's Louis XIV casino is one of the largest at sea), keep passengers on the *Spirit* on the fast track to that famous and oft-mentioned fun. It's up to you to find time to stop and catch the scenery, which you can do both from the generous open-deck spaces and from some (but not a lot) of indoor spaces as well. For kids, there's a children's playroom, children's pool, and video arcade. The Spirit's library doubles as an Internet cafe, and the clicking of the computers may be annoying to those who want to read a book there. Shoppers will find plenty of enticements at the ship's shopping arcade (including Fendi and Tommy Hilfiger).

POOL, SPA & FITNESS FACILITIES The ship boasts three pools, including one with a retractable dome, as well as a children's splash pool and a free-standing water slide on the top deck. The gym offers an interesting tiered design and more than 50 exercise machines, as well as a spacious aerobics studio and windows so you don't miss the scenery. The spa has a dozen treatment rooms and an indoor sunning area with a whirlpool. The ship also offers three additional whirlpools and a jogging/walking track (15 laps = 1 mile).

2 Celebrity Cruises
SHIPS   Infinity • Mercury • Summit

1050 Caribbean Way, Miami, FL 33132. ℂ **800/437-3111** or 305/262-8322. Fax 800/437-5111. www.celebritycruises.com.

With a premium fleet that's among the youngest and best-designed in the cruise industry, Celebrity Cruises offers a great combination: a classy, tasteful, and luxurious cruise experience at a moderate price.

THE EXPERIENCE   Each of Celebrity's ships is spacious, glamorous, and comfortable, mixing sleekly modern and vaguely Art Deco styles and throwing in an astoundingly cutting-edge art collection to boot. Their genteel service is exceptional: Staff members are exceedingly polite and professional, and contribute greatly to the elegant mood. Dining-wise, Celebrity shines, offering innovative cuisine that's a cut above what's offered by all the other mainstream lines.

Celebrity gets the "best of" nod in a lot of categories: The AquaSpas on the line's megaships are the best at sea, the art collections fleetwide the most compelling, the cigar bars the most plush, and the onboard activities among the most varied. Like all the big-ship lines, Celebrity offers lots for its passengers to do, but its focus on mellower pursuits and innovative programming sets it apart.

Pros

- **Spectacular spas and gyms.** Beautiful to look at and well-stocked, the spas and gyms on the *Infinity, Mercury,* and *Summit* (and Celebrity's other non-Alaska megaships) are the best at sea today.
- **Fabulous food.** High-rated cuisine is tops among mainstream cruise lines.
- **Innovative everything.** Celebrity's entertainment, art, cigar bars, service, spas, and cuisine are some of the most innovative in the industry.

Cons

- **Occasional crowding.** Pack a couple thousand people onto a ship (pretty much any ship), and you'll get crowds sometimes, such as at buffets and when debarking.

THE FLEET   Celebrity has two of its newest ships, the *Infinity* (91,000 tons, 1,950 passengers) and the similarly dimensioned *Summit,* in Alaska this summer, along with the stunning and only slightly older *Mercury,* which was to be in Europe but was moved back to Alaska following the September 11, 2001, tragedies. All are designed with crisp attention to detail and real decorative panache, and offer just the right combination of elegance, artfulness, excitement, and fun.

PASSENGER PROFILE   The typical Celebrity guest is one who prefers to pursue his or her R&R at a relatively relaxed pace, with a minimum of aggressively promoted group activities. The overall impression leans more toward sophistication and less to the kind of orgiastic Technicolor whoopee that you'll find, say, aboard a Carnival ship. Celebrity passengers are the type that prefers wine with dinner, though they can kick up their heels just fine if the occasion warrants. Most give the impression of being prosperous but not obscenely rich, congenial but not obsessively proper, animated and fun but not wearing a lampshade for a hat. You'll find everyone from kids to retirees.

Celebrity Fleet Itineraries

Ship	Itinerary
Infinity	**7-night Inside Passage:** Round-trip cruises from Vancouver visit Juneau, Skagway, Hubbard Glacier, and Ketchikan.
Mercury	**7-night Inside Passage:** Round-trip cruises from Vancouver visit Ketchikan, Hubbard Glacier, Sitka, and Juneau.
Summit	**7-night northbound Gulf of Alaska:** Sails from Vancouver to Anchorage/Seward, visiting Ketchikan, Juneau, Skagway, Hubbard Glacier, Valdez, and College Fjord. **7-night southbound Gulf of Alaska:** Sails from Anchorage/Seward to Vancouver, visiting Hubbard Glacier, Juneau, Skagway, Sitka, and Ketchikan.

DINING   Celebrity's cuisine is extra special and, due to the influence of executive chef Michel Roux, one of Britain's top French chefs, tends to lean toward the French (which also means it's not generally low-fat, although healthy alternatives are always available). The food offerings are plentiful and served with style.

Alaska cruises offer an array of **Pacific Northwest regional specialties,** and vegetarian dishes are offered at both lunch and dinner. If three meals a day in both informal and formal settings is not enough for you, Celebrity offers one of the most extensive 24-hour room-service menus in the industry, plus a late-night buffet or gourmet snacks offered by waiters who rove all the public areas with trays of goodies. Meals in the alternative dining rooms on the *Infinity* and *Summit,* offered on a reservations-only basis, show Roux at his finest and are worth the rather steep $25 admission charge.

ACTIVITIES   The line offers a variety of different activities, although many passengers prefer to go it on their own, enjoying the passing landscape or the company of friends. A typical day might offer bridge, darts, a culinary art demonstration, a trapshooting competition, a fitness fashion show, an art auction, or a volleyball tournament. **Lectures** on the various ports of call, the Alaska environment, glaciers, and Alaska culture are given by resident experts, who also provide commentary from the bridge as the ships arrive in port and, at other times, are available for one-on-one discussions with passengers. Cybercafes offer e-mail access for 95¢ a minute.

CHILDREN'S PROGRAM   For children, Celebrity ships employ a group of counselors who direct and supervise a camp-style children's program with activities geared toward different age groups. There's an impressive kids' play area and a separate lounge area for teens. Private and group babysitting are both available.

ENTERTAINMENT   Although entertainment is not generally cited as a reason to sail with Celebrity, the line's **stage shows** are none too shabby. You won't find any big-name entertainers, but neither will you find any obvious has-beens either—just a lot of singin' and dancin'. If you tire of the glitter, you can always find a cozy lounge or piano bar to curl up in, and if you tire of that, the disco and casino stay open late.

SERVICE   In the cabins, service is efficient and so discreet and unobtrusive you might never see your steward except at the beginning and end of your cruise. In the dining rooms, service is polite, accurate, professional, and cheerful. Five-star service can be had at the onboard beauty parlor or barbershop, and massages can be scheduled at any hour of the day. **Laundry, dry-cleaning,** and **valet services** are fast and accurate.

CRUISETOUR & ADD-ON PROGRAMS   Celebrity offers two 13-night cruisetours in conjunction with the *Infinity*'s schedule—both in the Canadian Rockies out of Vancouver (pre- or post-cruise). The packages are priced between $3,189 and $11,569, depending on date and shipboard accommodations. Celebrity has additional packages in conjunction with the cruises of the *Summit*, ranging in length from 9 to 13 nights (including the 7-night cruise), some of them involving transportation through Denali National Park on the Royal Celebrity Tours Wilderness Explorer domed rail cars, and others by motor coach. A 9-night package, with a visit to the year-round resort at Alyeska (the only itinerary that does not include Denali) is priced from $1,699 per person including the cruise fare. A 13-night Great Land Expedition that includes Anchorage, Talkeetna, Denali, and Fairbanks is priced from $2,599 per person. Pre- and post-cruise hotel packages are also offered in Anchorage (from $209 per person, per night) and Vancouver (from $89 per person, per night).

Infinity • Summit (preview)

Size (in tons)	91,000	Officers	Greek
Number of Cabins	975	Crew	997 (Int'l)
Number of Outside Cabins	785	Passenger/Crew Ratio	1.96 to 1
Cabins with Verandas	582	Year Built	2001
Number of Passengers	950	Last Major Refurbishment	n/a

When Celebrity's *Millennium* debuted a new class for the line in 2000, it was hailed as one of the most spectacular ships afloat; guests were equally struck by its sister ship, *Infinity,* and will presumably be amazed by the *Summit* (due at press time) as well. We're talking the finest materials, first-class artwork, and expert design, including lots of glass through which to view the Alaska vistas.

CABINS   There's not a bad cabin on these ships. Even the smallest inside cabins are 170 square feet and boast a minibar, sitting area with a sofa, and entertainment tower with a TV. Premium oceanview cabins are a very generous 191 square feet, and large oceanview cabins with verandas are just that—271 square feet, with floor-to-ceiling sliding-glass doors leading outside. Suites come in several sizes and offer such accoutrements as whirlpool tubs, VCRs, and walk-in closets. The fanciest also have whirlpools on the veranda. The two apartment-size penthouse suites (1,432 sq. ft. each), designed to be reminiscent of Park Avenue apartments, offer all of the above plus separate living and dining rooms, a foyer, a grand piano, a butler's pantry, a bedroom, exercise equipment, outbound fax, and—sure to be a favorite accessory—motorized drapes. Twenty-six cabins are wheelchair-accessible.

Cabins & Rates

Cabins	Brochure Rates	Bathtub	Fridge	Hair Dryer	Sitting Area	TV
Inside	$1,729–$2,339	no	yes	yes	yes	yes
Outside	$2,399–$3,079	no	yes	yes	yes	yes
Suite	$4,949–$10,429	yes	yes	yes	yes	yes

PUBLIC AREAS   Highlights on the *Infinity* and *Summit* include the botanical conservatories located on top of each ship. Pull up a rattan chair, sit under a ceiling fan, and enjoy a drink. You won't miss the Alaska views from this oasis thanks to two-story-high windows. If you want, you can also take a class here in flower arranging.

The ships also each boast a dramatic two-story dining room that features live music by a pianist or a quartet. And they also offer a gourmet dining experience in an intimate alternative restaurant: the SS United States on the *Infinity* and Normandie Room on the *Summit*. (A fee of $25 is charged to dine in these classy escapes, and reservations are required.) It's after dinner that Michael's Club, decorated like the parlor of a London men's club and devoted to the pleasures of fine cigars and cognac, comes into its own. Each ship also offers a coffee bar that provides a caffeinated alternative, and if you're looking to spend the evening socializing with friends, there are various other bars tucked into nooks and crannies throughout the ship.

Want more? How about a music library, shopping center, pizzeria, casino, coffee bar, champagne bar, martini bar, cigar lounge, cinema, theater, sports bar (with live ESPN), beauty salon, medical center, library, cybercafe, children's center, teen room, and arcade?

POOL, SPA & FITNESS FACILITIES   Spa aficionados, get ready: The *Infinity* and *Summit* are your ships. The 25,000-square-foot AquaSpa complexes feature a range of esoteric hydrotherapy treatments; site-specific attractions, such as the Persian Garden (a suite of beautiful New Agey steam rooms and saunas); a huge free-of-charge thalassotherapy über-whirlpool; as well as the usual array of massage and beauty procedures (and some unusual ones, such as an Egyptian ginger and milk treatment, too). Next door to the spa there's a very large and well-equipped cardio room and a large aerobics floor. On the top decks are facilities for basketball, volleyball, quoits, and paddle tennis; a jogging track; a golf simulator; two pools, four whirlpools, and a multitiered sunning area. The swimming pool boasts a waterfall.

Mercury

Size (in tons)	77,713	Officers	Greek
Number of Cabins	948	Crew	900 (Int'l)
Number of Outside Cabins	639	Passenger/Crew Ratio	2 to 1
Cabins with Verandas	220	Year Built	1997
Number of Passengers	1,896	Last Major Refurbishment	n/a

It's difficult to say what's most striking about the *Mercury*. The elegant spa and its 15,000-gallon thalassotherapy pool? The twin three- and four-story atria with serpentine staircases that seem to float without supports and domed ceilings of painted glass? The distinguished Michael's Club cigar lounge with its leather wingbacks, velvet couches, and hand-rolled stogies? The two-story, old-world dining room set back in the stern, with grand, floor-to-ceiling windows allowing diners to espy the glow of the wake under moonlight? An absolutely intriguing modern-art collection unmatched in the industry (except aboard Celebrity's other megaships)? Take your pick: Any one points to a winner.

CABINS   Overall, there are no really bad cabins on this ship. Inside cabins are about par for the industry standard, but outside cabins are larger than usual, and suites, which come in five different categories, are particularly spacious. Some, such as the Penthouse Suites, offer more living space than you find in many private homes, and the Sky Suites offer verandas that, at 179 square feet, are among the biggest aboard any ship.

Cabins are accented with wood trim and outfitted with built-in vanities. Closets and drawer space are roomy, and all standard cabins have twin beds that are convertible to doubles. Bathrooms are sizable and stylish. Celebrity is fond of high-tech gizmos, and you can actually order food, gamble, or check your bill from the comfort of your cabin via your interactive TV.

Butler service is offered to suite passengers. Eight cabins are designed specifically for passengers with disabilities.

Cabins & Rates

Cabins	Brochure Rates	Bathtub	Fridge	Hair Dryer	Sitting Area	TV
Inside	$1,729–$2,339	no	yes	yes	no	yes
Outside	$2,399–$3,079	no	yes	yes	some	yes
Suite	$4,949–$10,429	yes	yes	yes	yes	yes

PUBLIC AREAS   The interior of this ship is the product of a collaboration between a dozen internationally acclaimed design firms, working together to create a stylistically diverse yet harmonious whole that provides just the right amount of drama without resorting to glitz. The result is impressive. Our favorite is the champagne bar with champagne bubbles etched into the wall.

Throughout the ship, elements of a multimillion-dollar, cutting-edge art collection sometimes greet you at unexpected moments. Read the tags, and you'll be impressed to find names such as Sol LeWitt, who designed a mural specifically for the vessel.

Meals are a standout feature on all Celebrity ships. Breakfast on the *Mercury* is offered either in the dining room or at a vast buffet on the Lido Deck that manages to accommodate everyone's preferred waking hour. Lunch is also offered in both formal and informal venues. Dinner is served in the main dining room, a two-story affair, in two seatings. For posh relaxation after dinner, there's Michael's Club, decorated like the parlor of a London men's club and devoted to the pleasures of fine cigars and cognac. A coffee bar provides a caffeinated alternative, and if you're looking to spend the evening socializing with friends, there are various other bars tucked into nooks and crannies throughout the ship.

There's a two-deck theater with an unobstructed view from every seat if you want to take in the show—and a cinema if you want film—but if you're looking for more interactive pleasures, there's always the disco and casino. For kids, there's a children's playroom, children's pool, teen center, and video arcade.

POOL, SPA & FITNESS FACILITIES   The *Mercury's* spa is not your average spa: It's an incredible AquaSpa that provides a world of sensual pleasure. It features a Moorish theme with ornate tile work and latticed wood. There's a large hydrotherapy pool, steam rooms, and saunas, plus sometimes-pricey Steiner of London health and beauty services. These include hairdressing, pedicures, manicures, massage, and various herbal treatments. We highly recommend the Rasul mud treatment for two. It's both relaxing and worth a laugh. The attached fitness area offers exceptionally large cardiovascular floors and a full complement of exercise machines. An 18-member fitness staff is on hand in the spa and gym area to assist. Prearranged spa packages (that you can book before your cruise) are available and are a wise idea, as some services (including Rasul) sell out fast.

The resort deck features a pair of good-size swimming areas rimmed with teak benches for sunning and relaxation. Even when the ship is full, these areas don't seem particularly crowded. A retractable dome covers one of the swimming pools during inclement weather. A basketball court, jogging/walking track, fitness center, golf simulator, and volleyball court fill out the offerings.

3 Crystal Cruises

SHIP Crystal Harmony

2049 Century Park E., Ste. 1400, Los Angeles, CA 90067. ℂ **800/446-6620** or 310/785-9300. Fax 310/785-3891. www.crystalcruises.com.

Crystal's brand of luxury cruising appeals to a discerning clientele. Everything is first class, with fine attention paid to detail and to making guests feel comfortable.

THE EXPERIENCE The luxurious *Crystal Harmony* (the line's representative in Alaska for the fourth consecutive year) and its sister ship, *Crystal Symphony*, operate on a formula of offering all the amenities of much bigger ships but in a more luxurious and intimate atmosphere, with only 940 passengers.

Japanese-owned and Los Angeles–based Crystal had the Great Land's luxury market to itself for the past few years. Radisson Seven Seas is now also on the scene, with a product that offers a slightly more casual definition of luxury. Crystal is proud of offering you the chance to dress up and act like a millionaire (even if you're not one really).

Pros

- **The best of everything.** Superb cuisine, elegant service, handsome public areas, sparkling entertainment, excellent guest quarters—this ship has it all. It's a six-star ship in a five-star field.
- **Great itinerary.** Another of the *Harmony*'s selling points is its itinerary: It will be the only ship to offer a schedule of Alaska cruises out of San Francisco.

Cons

- **Rigid dining schedule.** For many upscale travelers, the *Harmony*'s biggest failing is that, like all biggish ships, it has two seatings at dinner, locking passengers into 6:30 or 8:30pm appointments in the main dining room.
- **Lack of closet space.** One more quibble is that some of the cabins on the *Harmony*'s lower decks are not as generously equipped with closet space as they might be.

THE FLEET Plush, streamlined, extravagantly comfortable, and not as overwhelmingly large as the megaships being launched by less glamorous lines, the 940-passenger *Crystal Harmony* (1990) offers a broad choice of onboard diversions and distractions, more than you'd expect on a luxury vessel. In an industry first, the line recently brought Feng Shui to the high seas, renovating space on both its vessels in accordance with this ancient and now very hip practice of balance and harmony.

PASSENGER PROFILE Generally, the passengers aboard Crystal are people of some discernment—say, successful businesspeople who can afford to pay for the best. Item: On one Panama Canal cruise aboard the *Harmony* a couple of years ago, we heard of a 70-something couple, occupying one of the better suites, who visited the future-bookings desk in the lobby and signed up for about $200,000 worth of the next world cruise, scheduled for a few months later. If memory serves, they were unable to take the entire 99-day world cruise because of a family commitment, so they "settled"—and paid on the spot—for two-thirds of it! These people may not have been typical, but they weren't all that out of the ordinary, either.

Crystal Fleet Itineraries

Ship	Itinerary
Crystal Harmony	**12-night Inside Passage:** Round-trip from San Francisco, visiting Victoria, Vancouver, Sitka, Skagway, Juneau, Ketchikan, and either Glacier Bay or Hubbard Glacier.

Whereas, at one time, that couple might have been closer to the average age on an Alaska cruise, they no longer are. Probably thanks to Crystal's innovative shore-excursion program, its Caesars Palace–operated casino, and its entertainment package, the *Harmony* is attracting a younger breed of cruiser, many under 50. The average age is, in fact, dropping fast. (Those new 40- and 50-something millionaire types have to vacation somewhere.) Whatever their age, they tend to be people who like to dress up rather than down. Casual nights don't mean the same to Crystal guests as they do to some others.

DINING   Cuisine aboard the *Harmony* is superbly prepared and professionally served, with dinner in the main dining room offering a choice of at least four entrees, health-conscious vegetarian dishes, and a pasta offering nightly. The Lido Cafe, an indoor/outdoor area, puts on a lavish breakfast and lunch buffet daily, and the poolside Trident Grill serves up hot dogs, hamburgers, pizza, and sandwiches from lunchtime throughout the afternoon. There is also the new casual option, on select nights, of dining at an open-air grill. An alternative Italian restaurant and Asian restaurant are open on a reservations-only basis. (The former includes the option of a five-course Valentino dinner offered thanks to a special agreement between the famed Los Angeles restaurant and the cruise line.)

There's also an ice-cream and frozen-yogurt bar and 24-hour room service. The wine cellar features some 25,000 bottles of some 171 varieties.

ACTIVITIES   Crystal *Harmony* carries a battery of **Alaska naturalists,** environmentalists, and National Park Service rangers to educate and entertain passengers in the wilderness areas of the 49th state. Once again in 2002, it will repeat—albeit on a somewhat abbreviated scale—its **food-and-wine series.** Capitalizing on the ship's San Francisco–based itineraries, the line will carry one of the great chefs of that city on a couple of its cruises (departures of July 4 and Sept 14) to offer food preparation demonstrations and lectures on the art of cookery and, on one evening, to prepare for passengers a gala dinner.

As far as non-food-related activities, a **PGA-approved golf pro** accompanies practically every *Harmony* cruise, conducting clinics along the way. The *Harmony* also has a flourishing **computer room** onboard, with training for the uninitiated, and Internet access for a fee ($1.25 per min. with a 10-min. minimum and a $5 set-up fee; or you can alternatively send or receive e-mails via a shipboard account for $3 each plus a $5 set-up fee). There are few things as gratifying as the smile on the face of a hitherto computer-illiterate grandma after she's sent her first e-mail to her grandkids in Cincinnati.

CHILDREN'S PROGRAM   Crystal focuses its attention on adults, so it's generally not a line for kids. That said, the *Harmony*'s small but bright children's playroom does see some action in Alaska, when as many as 20 to 40 kids may be onboard on any given cruise. Counselors are on hand to supervise activities for several hours in the morning and in the afternoon, and babysitting can be arranged privately through the concierge.

ENTERTAINMENT   Although it's certainly not the high point of the cruise, Crystal's onboard entertainment is good and plentiful. Shows in the lounge encompass everything from classical concertos by accomplished pianists to comedy to a troupe of lip-synching dancers and a pair of lead singers doing a Vegas-style performance. After dinner each night, a second large, attractive lounge is the venue for ballroom-style dancing to a live band. (Gentlemen hosts are available to dance with single ladies.) There's also a small, separate (and usually empty) disco featuring karaoke a couple of nights per cruise, and a pianist plays popular show tunes and pop hits before and after dinner in the dark, paneled, and romantic Avenue Saloon. A movie theater shows first-run movies several times a day, and cabin TVs feature a wonderfully varied and full movie menu as well.

Gamblers will have no problem feeling at home in the roomy casino, which is supervised directly by Caesars Palace Casinos at Sea, offering the bonus (unusual on ships) of free drinks.

SERVICE   Service on the ship is nothing short of superb. Crystal has a corporate philosophy that its staff will exhibit what it calls "The Crystal Attitude." Catchy promotional slogan, huh? But it actually works. You can usually tell when service people are faking it: the plastic smiles, the look that's meant to say "I care" while the actions clearly demonstrate "I don't give a hoot." That doesn't happen on Crystal. From the officers to the dining room staff, through the cabin stewards and the reception-desk employees to the guys who swab the deck and paint the rails, these people are genuinely glad to welcome passengers and to accommodate them in every way possible. It's not obsequiousness. It's not overpowering. It's just the right attitude.

In addition to **laundry** and **dry-cleaning services, self-service laundry rooms** are available.

CRUISETOUR & ADD-ON PROGRAMS   The 3-night "Wine-Making Tradition in Napa Valley" package (available pre-cruise only) includes 1 night at the Fairmont Hotel in San Francisco and 2 nights in Napa Valley country inns, plus wine tasting and vineyard visits. It's priced at $2,170 per person, double occupancy. Overnight stays are available in San Francisco at the luxurious Ritz-Carlton, for $405 per person, double ($265 per person, double, for extra nights). There's also a 5-night Alaska Frontier program from Seward that features Anchorage, Denali Park, and Fairbanks, for $2,570 per person, double.

Crystal Harmony

Size (in tons)	49,400	Officers	Int'l
Number of Cabins	480	Crew	545 (Int'l)
Number of Outside Cabins	461	Passenger/Crew Ratio	1.7 to 1
Cabins with Verandas	260	Year Built	1990
Number of Passengers	960	Last Major Refurbishment	2000

A handsome ship by any standard, *Crystal Harmony* was designed by an international team from Scotland, England, Denmark, and Italy, led by one of the bright lights of the ship-architecture world, Sweden's Robert Tillberg. A multi-million-dollar refurbishment last year made a good thing better. The ship's dining room was gutted and rebuilt virtually from scratch, introducing a roomier space with softer decor and, in the process, improving the acoustics. The atrium reception area was also overhauled to considerable effect, and the top suites were totally done over.

The ship has one of the highest passenger-space ratios (an esoteric measurement of the amount of cubic space throughout the ship, public and private rooms, divided by the number of passengers) of any cruise ship. In industry parlance, that ratio is 52.6, a fact that may not mean much to the layperson, at least until he or she cruises on the ship. Then, the spaciousness becomes obvious.

CABINS   The cabins are large, well-appointed, and tastefully decorated with quality fittings in agreeable color tones. Almost half of them have private verandas. The one small criticism is that space to hang clothes is a little tight in some of the lower cabin categories.

The very smallest of the *Harmony*'s cabins is almost 200 square feet, while the upper-end guest quarters are huge, the biggest measuring 982 square feet. There are houses on land that don't go much bigger than that! There are four of these Crystal penthouses on the *Harmony*, each with a large sitting room, a wet bar, a big Jacuzzi with a view of the ocean (ah, bliss!), a dining area, a massive bedroom, two bathrooms, and walk-in closets.

The *Harmony*'s 26 penthouse suites are a little less than 500 square feet each and the 32 staterooms designated as penthouses are 370 square feet. All of these, like the Crystal Penthouses, come with butler service and verandas. (Be careful with the terminology when buying a cruise on *Harmony:* Crystal Penthouse, penthouse suite, and penthouse sound awfully similar, but they're all different categories.)

Four cabins are handicapped-accessible, two on the Penthouse Deck and two on the Promenade Deck.

Cabins & Rates

Cabins	Brochure Rates	Bathtub	Fridge	Hair Dryer	Sitting Area	TV
Inside	$4,050	yes	yes	yes	yes	yes
Outside	$4,515–$6,740	yes	yes	yes	yes	yes
Suite	$9,435–$17,370	yes	yes	yes	yes	yes

PUBLIC AREAS   Let's hear it for *Crystal Harmony*'s public areas. Like the rest of the ship, they're pure class. It's our opinion that Palm Court is the prettiest public space afloat. Bright, airy, with enticing and comfortable wicker furniture and natural greenery all around, it's the kind of room that reeks of that good old-fashioned "understated elegance." There's also the large, well-designed casino; the intimate midship bistro and piano bar; and the two-story lobby, the Crystal Atrium, its tinkling waterfall and classy hand-cut glass sculptures such a refreshing change from the garishness of some of the lobbies on the new ships entering service. The elegance carries over to the rest of the ship: Sip a glass of wine in the Crystal Cove, in the lobby alongside the atrium, or in the snug Avenue Saloon, one deck up, and you'll see what we mean.

The *Harmony*'s two **alternative restaurants,** Prego (Italian, mostly northern) and Kyoto (Asian/Japanese), introduce a variety to the dining experience not found on all ships. The meals there are included in the fare (except for the tip of $6 a head), and dining is by reservation only.

The dramatic Vista Lounge, with wall-to-ceiling windows, is perfect for wildlife and glacier viewing. And to occupy the kids while you're doing that, there's a playroom.

POOL, SPA & FITNESS FACILITIES   The *Harmony* offers a lot of outdoor activities and spacious areas in which to do them. There are two outdoor swimming pools separated by a bar, ice-cream bar, and sandwich grill, as well as two hot tubs. One of the pools is refreshingly oversized, stretching almost 40 feet across one of the sun decks; the other can be covered with a retractable glass roof and has a swim-up bar. The gym and separate aerobics area are positioned for a view over the sea, and the adjacent spa and beauty salon are sizable. There's also a pair of golf-driving nets, a putting green, a large paddle-tennis court, and Ping-Pong tables. For runners and walkers, just under four laps equals 1 mile on the broad, uninterrupted teak Promenade Deck.

4 Holland America Line

SHIPS   Amsterdam • Volendam • Zaandam • Ryndam • Statendam • Veendam

300 Elliott Ave. W., Seattle, WA 98119. ℂ **800/426-0327** or 206/281-3535. Fax 206/286-7110. www. hollandamerica.com.

More than any other line in Alaska, Holland America has managed to hang on to some of its seafaring history and tradition, offering a moderately priced, classic, casual yet refined ocean-liner-like cruise experience.

THE EXPERIENCE   In Alaska terms, everybody else is an upstart when it comes to the cruise and cruisetour business. The line calls itself Alaska's most experienced travel operator, and the key to that was HAL's 1971 acquisition of the tour company Westours, founded in 1947 by Charles B. "Chuck" ("Mr. Alaska") West, the man widely recognized as the absolute pioneer of Alaska tourism and founder of the small-ship line Cruise West. Holland America can't claim to have been operating Alaska cruises for half a century, but Westours has certainly been in the Alaska tour-packaging business that long.

Over the years, Holland America Line–Westours has picked up a lot of "stuff"—Holland America Tours (formerly Gray Line of Alaska), for instance, plus Gray Line of Seattle, Westmark Hotels, the *Yukon Queen II* river-/day boat that operates between Eagle and Dawson City on the Yukon River, the MV *Ptarmigan* (another day boat that visits Portage Glacier outside Anchorage), rail-cars, motor coaches, and a lot more besides. Its control of so many of the components of tour packaging gave the cruise company a position of preeminence in the Alaska market, though that's been challenged in the past decade by Princess Cruises, which is also now in the accommodations and ground-transportation business. There are great similarities between the two lines besides their land possessions. Both have large fleets of primarily late-model ships, both strive for (and achieve) consistency in the cruise product, and both are pursuing (and capturing) younger passengers and families.

Pros

- **The expertise that comes with tradition.** Its ships are young, but Holland America's experience shows through. You want to know what experience is? The company was formed way back in 1873 as the Netherlands-America Steamship Company. It figures that you get to know a little about operating ocean-going vessels in 128 years!
- **Freebies.** HAL includes a lot of little perks in its cruise fare—no extra charge, for instance, for a latte or cappuccino.

Cons

- **Confusing tipping policy.** HAL follows a "No Tipping Required" policy that can be confusing. Some people start off under the misapprehension that there's no tipping on the ship, period. It then comes as a bit of a shock when the cruise director in his disembarkation talk makes jokes about how much gratuities should be, and who should get them, while emphasizing that, of course, they're not required. Technically, there's no tipping required on any ship; by definition, that's a purely personal decision. HAL should make it a flat "No Tipping" (and pay its people a higher base pay) or drop the gimmick entirely.
- **Sleepy nightlife.** If you're big on late-night dancing and barhopping, you may find yourself partying mostly with the entertainment staff.
- **Homogenous passenger profile.** Although this is changing to a certain degree, passengers tend to be a pretty homogenous group of low-key, 55+, North American couples who aren't overly adventurous.

THE FLEET The company's 1,266-passenger *Statendam*-class ships—the *Statendam* (1993), *Ryndam* (1994), and *Veendam* (1996)—are carbon copies of the same attractive, well-crafted design (with a dash of glitz here and there). The 1,440-passenger *Volendam* officially debuted in November 1999 and the *Zaandam* in May 2000. Brighter and bolder than the earlier ships, the *Volendam* and *Zaandam* share many features of the *Statendam*-class ships, though they're slightly larger than the latter in size (63,000 tons, as opposed to 59,652) and carry more passengers (1,440, against the *Statendam* class's 1,266). The 1,380-passenger *Amsterdam* was scheduled to be in Europe for the summer of 2002 but was moved to Alaska following the September 11, 2001, terrorist attacks (in anticipation of a decline in European bookings). The *Amsterdam* is 61,000 tons and is one of two flagships in the fleet. (The other is the *Amsterdam*'s sister ship, the *Rotterdam*.)

PASSENGER PROFILE Holland America's passenger profile used to reflect a much older crowd. Now the average age is dropping, partly thanks to an increased emphasis on its Club HAL program for children and partly due to some updating of its onboard entertainment.

Still, HAL's passenger manifests in Alaska show a high volume of middle-aged-and-up vacationers (the same demographic as aboard many of its competitors' ships), but on any given cruise they're also likely to list a few dozen between the ages of, say, 5 and 16. This trend gathered its initial momentum a couple of years ago in Europe, a destination that, parents seem to think, has more kid appeal. It's spilled over into Alaska as well now, mainly thanks to the cruise line's added emphasis on generational travel and family reunion travel, a growing segment of the market.

The more mature among Holland America's passengers are likely to be repeat HAL passengers, often retirees, not Fortune-500 rich, looking for solid value for their money.

DINING Years ago, HAL's meals were about as traditional as its architecture and its itineraries. In the last few years, though, it's become a lot more adventurous in all three areas. The variety of dishes on the menu is as good as on any other premium line, and the quality of the food is generally high throughout the fleet. Don't look for lots of pastas; do look for excellent soups. Vegetarian options are available at every meal; they even have excellent veggie burgers at the on-deck grill.

HAL Fleet Itineraries

Ship	Itinerary
Amsterdam	**7-night Inside Passage:** Round-trip from Seattle, visiting Juneau, Hubbard Glacier, Sitka, Ketchikan, and Victoria (B.C.).
Volendam/ Zaandam/ Ryndam	**7-night Inside Passage:** Round-trip from Vancouver, visiting Juneau, Skagway, Ketchikan, and Glacier Bay.
Statendam/ Veendam	**7-night Gulf of Alaska:** North- and southbound between Vancouver and Anchorage/Seward, visiting Juneau, Ketchikan, Sitka, and either Glacier Bay or Hubbard Glacier.

The kids' menu usually features spaghetti, pizza, hamburgers, fries, and hot dogs, plus often a few variations of what's being offered to the adults at the table.

Buffets are offered at the Lido Restaurant as an alternative to the main dining room at breakfast and lunch, and HAL recently expanded its dinner options to offer a casual alternative to dinner up on Lido Deck as well. (It's offered on all nights except the final night of the cruise.) There are also intimate, reservations-required alternative Italian restaurants on the *Amsterdam, Volendam,* and *Zaandam* in the Alaska market. (HAL was evaluating at press time whether or not to start charging extra for this special dining experience.)

ACTIVITIES   Young swingers need not apply. Holland America's ships are heavy on more mature, less frenetic activities and light on boogie-till-the-cows-come-home swingers' pursuits. You'll find good bridge programs and music to dance (or just listen) to in the bars and lounges, plus health spas and the other amenities found on most large ships. All ships offer Internet access for 75¢ a minute, with a 5-minute minimum.

In 2002, the line will continue its **Artists in Residence Program,** arranged through the Alaska Native Heritage Center in Anchorage, with Alaska Native artists accompanying all 7-night cruises and demonstrating traditional art forms such as ivory and soapstone carving, basket weaving, and mask making. Also added was a Huna Interpretive Program, with a member of the Huna Totem joining National Park Service employees in providing commentary as the ship visits Glacier Bay. (The Huna tribe has called that area home for centuries.)

CHILDREN'S PROGRAM   Club HAL is more than just one of those half-hearted give-'em-a-video-arcade-and-hot-dogs-at-dinner efforts, offering expert supervisors, a fitness center, and dedicated kids' common rooms (adults keep out!) on the *Zaandam, Volendam,* and *Ryndam.* On the other ships, some of the meeting rooms and lounges—the Half Moon Lounge on the *Veendam,* for instance—are set aside for the younger set during the day and revert to their general-population purposes at night. It must be said that all these rooms, whether dedicated or not, are universally dull—just empty rooms for the most part, and not comparable to the bright, kid-friendly rooms aboard the Princess, Celebrity, and Royal Caribbean ships.

Kids' activities are arranged in three parts, by age—5 to 8, 9 to 12, and teens. The youngest group might have, say, singalongs, while the older kids will try their hand at karaoke. The middle group will compete in golf putting and the teens in fake Monte Carlo nights. (Don't worry, there's no real gambling involved!) The line also has a portfolio of **kids-only shore excursions** (floatplane rides, treasure hunts, hikes, and the like) on which parents can send their teens and preteens off before setting off for their own adventure.

ENTERTAINMENT   The line has improved its nightly show-lounge entertainment, which was once, frankly, not so hot. Again, the change to some extent reflects the younger passengers that are starting to book with HAL. Each week includes a crew talent show in which the Indonesian and Filipino staff members perform their countries' songs and dances.

SERVICE   The line employs primarily Filipino and Indonesian staff members, and from the welcome aboard by a white-gloved steward who guides you to your stateroom to the final gala dinner and everything in between, they are gracious and friendly without being cloying.

We once sailed on the old *Rotterdam V* alongside one of those passengers who must make service people cringe. Three times in 6 nights in the dining room he sent a dish back with a complaint—"Needs more paprika" was one of his more exotic gripes. Nobody else at the table had any problem with the food—just this obnoxious character. He never once wanted a meal as is. Whatever the menu said, it was always, "I'd like this on the side," or, "That instead of such and such," or, "Don't put any of those in it." In short, the guy was an absolute pain. But the waiters never once reacted negatively to this aggravating little man. No matter what, the staff (we include the table captain and the maitre d' as well as the waiters) treated him exactly as they did the others at the table—with courtesy and warmth. He always got an apology when he sent his food back, no matter how spurious his complaint.

The manner in which the dining-room staffers dealt with this difficult customer (even though they must have been seething inside) told us a great deal about their commitment to service.

Onboard services aboard every ship in the fleet include **laundry** and **dry cleaning.** Each ship also maintains several **self-service laundry rooms** with irons.

Amsterdam

Size (in tons)	61,000	Officers	Dutch
Number of Cabins	690	Crew	647 (Indonesian/ Filipino)
Number of Outside Cabins	557	Passenger/Crew Ratio	2.13 to 1
Cabins with Verandas	172	Year Built	2000
Number of Passengers	1,380	Last Major Refurbishment	n/a

The *Amsterdam* is one of a line of attractive, midsize ships in the Holland America fleet. It has just enough classic style and tradition combined with innovation to appeal to a broad range of cruise-goers.

The ship is, in fact, the third in the Holland America fleet to bear the *Amsterdam* name. It shares flagship status with its sister ship, the *Rotterdam.*

One thing you can never say about Holland America is that it uses a "cookie-cutter" approach to building ships. Its new builds have all been slightly different in size and capacity. The small discrepancies are not the result of hit-or-miss thinking. HAL plans everything very thoroughly and the impact of its construction orgy gives the company a very young, very versatile fleet.

CABINS   Don't look for a lot of frills and fripperies on the *Amsterdam*. Its accommodations are warm, comfortable, low-key—and totally functional. Its inside rooms go as big as 182 square feet—not huge but more than adequate by today's standards. Outside rooms range up to a very comfortable 197 square feet, while mini- and full suites are between 284 and 1,226 square feet.

All of the cabins (apart from the smallest insides) have tub/shower combinations. The others have showers only. The suites feature whirlpool tubs—the one in the penthouse is an oversize affair, quite big enough for two. Suite guests also get VCRs. (You can borrow tapes from the ship's video library.) The full suites include a dressing room, living room, minibar, and refrigerator. Passengers on the all-suite Navigation Deck enjoy concierge service and exclusive use of a small lounge, the Neptune Room, on that level.

Cabin decor is subdued, with lots of pastels and white wood trim—and the odd splurge of rich, deep maroons and dark oak. There's nothing garish here. Twenty-one cabins, on four decks, are wheelchair-accessible.

Cabins & Rates

Cabins	Brochure Rates	Bathtub	Fridge	Hair Dryer	Sitting Area	TV
Inside	$1,513–$1,663	no	no	yes	some	yes
Outside	$1,873–$2,233	yes	no	yes	yes	yes
Suites	$2,533–$5,833	yes	yes	yes	yes	yes

PUBLIC AREAS   The first thing to catch passengers' eyes is the centerpiece of the atrium: the enormous, elaborate Astrolabe in the foyer. What's an Astrolabe? It's an astronomical timepiece, a celestial clock, complete with a carillon (that chimes tunes at certain hours of the day) and a constantly changing map of the heavens as if seen from the city of Amsterdam, from which the ship takes its name. You don't have to know how it works to enjoy its looks.

Strategically located around the ship are depictions of bears—big, ol' Alaskan grizzly bears. British artist Susanna Holt, a world-renowned sculptor, spent weeks in the 49th state, studying these creatures and preparing to create the bronzes that now decorate some of the public areas of the *Amsterdam.*

The **La Fontaine Room,** the ship's main dining room, is a two-level facility in which the friendly Indonesian and Filipino wait staff serves food on Rosenthal china in an ambience of elegance and richness. The effect is heightened by an impressive stained-glass ceiling. An alternative dining room, **The Odyssey,** is located midship on Promenade Deck. Reservations for this classy eatery are a must.

The double-decker **Queen's Lounge,** the main showroom, is an excellent spot to view some of Holland America's improved, and improving, evening entertainment.

For after-hours (or, for that matter, daytime) relaxing and imbibing, we particularly like the elegant **Explorer's Lounge** or the less-formal **Crow's Nest.** Other public rooms include a casino, a library (intellectually named the Erasmus Library), additional lounges, and a coffee bar.

POOL, FITNESS & SPA FACILITIES   The ship has two pools (including one that can be covered in inclement weather), a jogging track, a well-equipped gymnasium, and two paddle-tennis courts. The oceanview spa offers the usual array of dual saunas, a loofah scrub room, massage specialists, steam rooms, and beauty and hair salons. It's not the most imaginative spa in the world, but it does cover all the bases.

Statendam • Ryndam • Veendam

Size (in tons)	55,451	Officers	Dutch
Number of Cabins	633	Crew	588 (Int'l)
Number of Outside Cabins	502	Passenger/Crew Ratio	2.2 to 1
Cabins with Verandas	150	Year Built	1993/1994/1996
Number of Passengers	1,266	Last Major Refurbishment	n/a

These three nearly identical vessels were built within a 3-year span and fall somewhere between midsize and megaships. They demonstrate an extremely good use of space that pays attention to traffic flows; interior components include leather, glass, cabinets, textiles, and furniture from around the world. Touches of marble, teakwood, polished brass, and around $2 million worth of artwork for each vessel evoke the era of the classic ocean liners. Decorative themes usually emphasize the Netherlands' seafaring traditions and the role of Holland America in opening commerce and trade between Holland and the rest of the world.

CABINS   All the cabins have a sitting area that can be closed off from the sleeping area with curtains, plus lots of closet and drawer space. The outside doubles have either picture windows or verandas. The least expensive inside cabins run almost 190 square feet (quite large by industry standards) and have many of the amenities of their higher-deck counterparts—sofa and chair, desk-cum-dresser, stool, hair dryer, safe, and coffee table. All cabins have TVs and telephones, and some have bathtubs (including some whirlpool tubs), VCRs, and minibars. Penthouses (one only on each ship) are huge—almost 1,200 square feet.

Six cabins on each ship are suitable for passengers with disabilities.

Cabins & Rates

Cabin	Brochure Rates	Bathtub	Fridge	Hair Dryer	Sitting Area	TV
Inside	$1,532–$1,692	no	no	yes	some	yes
Outside	$1,892–$2,372	yes	no	yes	yes	yes
Suites	$2,625–$6,039	yes	yes	yes	yes	yes

PUBLIC AREAS   The striking dining rooms and the two-tiered showrooms are among these ships' best features; the latter are comfortable and conducive to easy watching. It helps, of course, that Holland America has begun efforts to upgrade its entertainment package.

The lobby area on each ship has taken on added significance as not just a place to board the ship but a place to hang out as well. The *Statendam*'s lobby houses a magnificent three-story fountain, and the *Ryndam*'s is a smaller version of the same piece, while the *Veendam*'s has a huge glass sculpture called "Jacob's Ladder."

Other public rooms include a coffee bar, card room, casino, children's playroom, cinema, conference facilities, and library. We especially like the Crow's Nest forward bar and lounge up on the sports deck, an inviting place to while away an hour or three.

POOL, SPA & FITNESS FACILITIES   All three ships have a sprawling expanse of teak-covered aft deck surrounding a swimming pool. One deck above that is a second swimming pool plus a wading pool, spacious deck area, bar, and two hot tubs that can be sheltered from inclement weather with a sliding-glass "magrodome" roof. Both areas are well planned and wide open. There's a practice tennis court and (*Statendam* only) an unobstructed track on the Lower Promenade Deck for walking or jogging. The ships' roomy, windowed gyms have a couple dozen exercise machines, a large separate aerobics area, steam rooms, and saunas. The spas lack pizzazz but offer the typical menu of treatments.

Volendam • Zaandam

Size (in tons)	63,000	Officers	Dutch/Int'l
Number of Cabins	720	Crew	647 (Indonesian/ Filipino)
Number of Outside Cabins	581	Passenger/Crew Ratio	2.2 to 1
Cabins with Verandas	197	Year Built	1999
Number of Passengers	1,440	Last Major Refurbishment	n/a

Holland America has pulled out all the stops on these two new ships: The centerpiece of the striking triple-decked oval atrium on the *Volendam,* for instance, is a glass sculpture by Luciano Vistosi, one of Italy's leading practitioners of the art, and that's just part of the ship's $2 million art collection, which reflects a flower theme. On the *Zaandam,* the centerpiece is a 22-foot-tall pipe organ reflecting that ship's music theme, which is also enhanced by a collection of guitars signed by rock musicians including The Rolling Stones, Iggy Pop, David Bowie, and Queen (an attempt to attract a younger, baby boomer clientele?). Apart from the art treatments and overall themes, you don't need to spend too much time trying to identify differences between these two magnificent vessels: They really are virtually indistinguishable from one another. The *Zaandam* may look just the teeniest bit brighter than the *Volendam,* but hardly enough to make a major impact.

CABINS   The 197 suites and deluxe staterooms have private verandas, and the smallest of the remaining 523 is a comfortable 190 square feet. All staterooms come complete with sofa seating areas, hair dryers, telephones, and TVs. The suites and deluxe rooms also have VCRs, whirlpool baths, and minibars. Both ships have more balcony cabins than other HAL vessels.

Twenty-three of the cabins are equipped for passengers with disabilities.

Cabins & Rates

Cabins	Brochure Rates	Bathtub	Fridge	Hair Dryer	Sitting Area	TV
Inside	$1,665–1,825	no	no	yes	yes	yes
Outside	$2,025–$2,505	yes	no	yes	yes	yes
Suites	$2,625–$6,039	yes	yes	yes	yes	yes

PUBLIC AREAS   Each ship has five showrooms and lounges, with the main show lounge on two levels; another, called the Crow's Nest, is a combined nightclub and observation lounge and is a good place to watch the passing Alaska scenery during the day.

The *Volendam*'s alternative Marco Polo restaurant is designed as an artist's bistro and features drawings and etchings on the walls; the *Zaandam* features a collection of 17th-century still-life paintings the ship's interior designers happened upon and decided to display intact. Both serve Italian cuisine on a reservations-only basis. Each ship also has an Internet Center (where you can surf for 75¢ a min., with a 5-min. minimum), casino, children's playroom, cinema, library, and arcade.

POOL, SPA & FITNESS FACILITIES   On both ships, the gym is downright palatial, with dozens of state-of-the-art machines surrounded by floor-to-ceiling windows, and with an adjacent aerobics room. The spa and hair salon are not quite as striking. Three pools are on the Lido Deck, with a main one and a wading pool under a retractable glass roof that also encloses the cafe-like Dolphin Bar. A smaller and quieter aft pool is located on the other side of the Lido buffet restaurant. On the Sports Deck is a pair of paddle-tennis courts as well as shuffleboard. Joggers can use the uninterrupted Lower Promenade Deck for a good workout.

5 Norwegian Cruise Line

SHIPS   Norwegian Sky • Norwegian Wind

7665 Corporate Center Dr., Miami, FL 33126. ℂ **800/327-7030.** Fax 305/448-7936. www.ncl.com.

The very mass-market Norwegian Cruise Line offers an informal and upbeat onboard atmosphere on medium- to megasize ships, with its newest vessel, the *Norwegian Sky*, sailing round-trip cruises from Seattle.

THE EXPERIENCE   NCL excels at activities—if it offered any more, passengers would be exhausted. Recreational and fitness programs are among the best in the industry, including programs where attendance at fitness events earns you points that you can cash in for prizes. Also top-notch are the line's children's program and entertainment.

The company, under new management and a new owner, Star Cruises of Malaysia, has changed its program to what it calls "freestyle" cruising, which makes life a whole lot easier for passengers. The idea is that passengers can eat in their choice among a variety of restaurants pretty much any time between, say, 5:30 and 11pm or midnight, with no preset table assignment. Tips are automatically charged to room accounts, dress codes are more relaxed (resort casual) at all times, and at the end of the voyage passengers can remain in their cabins until their time comes to disembark rather than huddling in lounges or squatting on luggage in stairwells until their lucky color comes up. This so-called "freestyle" cruising is unique among lines operating in the U.S., but it's SOP (Standard Operating Procedure) for Star Cruises, Norwegian's new parent company.

Pros

- **Sports-orientation.** Sports fans will be happy to find that major weekend sports games are broadcast into passengers' cabins and at the sports bars.
- **Smoke-free zones.** Norwegian promotes a smoke-free environment for those who want it. At least half the cabins on its ships are no-smoking cabins, and on any ship with more than one dining room, one will be no-smoking. There are even blackjack tables in its casinos reserved for nonsmokers.
- **Flexible dining.** NCL's dining policy lets you sit where and with whom you want, dress as you want, and dine when you want (within certain hours).

Cons

- **Inflated self-opinion.** One thing to watch out for is that the line tends to promote itself as more luxurious than it really is.

NCL Fleet Itineraries

Ship	Itinerary
Norwegian Sky	**7-night Inside Passage:** Round-trip from Seattle, visiting Glacier Bay or Sawyer Glacier, Haines, Skagway, Juneau, and Vancouver. Some cruises include Ketchikan as well.
Norwegian Wind	**7-night Inside Passage:** Round-trip from Vancouver, visiting Skagway, Haines, Juneau, Ketchikan, and Glacier Bay or Sawyer Glacier.

- **Unmemorable food.** The food is plentiful and okay, but it's not the line's strongest point. An exception is the cuisine served in Le Bistro (see below).

THE FLEET　The brand-new, 2,000-passenger *Norwegian Sky* debuted in August of 1999, and the 1,750-passenger *Norwegian Wind* was built in 1993. Both ships have lots of windows for great viewing, but, though large and moderately large (respectively), with lots of public areas, their cabins (especially closet space) leave something to be desired, size-wise.

PASSENGER PROFILE　In Alaska, the demographic tends more toward retirees than on the line's warmer-climate sailings, but you'll find families as well, including grandparents bringing along the grandkids. You'll also find a good mix of first-timers and veteran cruisers (many who have cruised with this line before).

DINING　None of the NCL vessels is distinguished for its cuisine, but the way they handle the business of dining these days is pretty darn innovative. The *Sky* was the first in the NCL fleet to go "freestyle," making all of its five restaurants open-seating each and every evening, allowing you to dine when and with whom you like between about 5:30pm and midnight. (All must be seated by 10pm.) And you can dress however you like, too: Even jeans and T-shirts are acceptable. There is one optional formal night for those who want to dress up. (On this night, some of the dining outlets are formal and others remain casual.)

　In addition to the dining room, the ships also have a Le Bistro alternative venue serving very good French/Mediterranean food in a romantic setting. There's a recommended cover charge of $10 per person. The *Norwegian Sky* also offers two other specialty venues, Horizons, for Italian cuisine; and Ciao Chow, where the Pacific Rim/Asian menu includes sushi, sashimi, and Peking Duck pizza. (There is a $10 cover charge at both.) A chocolate midnight buffet, offered once during the cruise, has become an NCL standard.

ACTIVITIES　In Alaska, the line offers an Alaska lecturer, wine tastings, art auctions, trapshooting, cooking demonstrations, craft and dance classes, an incentive fitness program, daily quizzes, board games, lotto, and bingo, among other activities. Passengers also tend to spend time at sports activities, which include basketball. The *Sky* and the *Wind* both have an Internet cafe that costs 75¢ a minute.

CHILDREN'S PROGRAM　NCL ships tend to be very family-friendly: There's at least one full-time youth-activity coordinator, a kids' activity room, video games, an ice-cream bar, and guaranteed babysitting aboard, plus a Polar Bear Pajama Party and sessions with park rangers. In 1999, the line upgraded its kids' program to include escorted shore excursions for youngsters (an NCL youth counselor goes along), such as an Alaskan Bushplane Ride in Ketchikan, and a White Pass Train and Bicycle Tour in Skagway.

ENTERTAINMENT Entertainment is generally strong, with Vegas-style productions that are expensive, surprisingly lavish, and artistically ambitious. On some nights, the showrooms also feature comedians and juggling acts. The *Sky* boasts the NCL fleet's biggest and splashiest casino, and both ships have intimate lounges presenting pianists and cabaret acts. Music for dancing is popular aboard all the ships and takes place before or after shows, and each ship has a late-night disco.

SERVICE Personalized service is an increasing area of focus for the line. In the past, service has ranged from just okay to great—varied, in other words. Generally, room service and bar service fleetwide is speedy and efficient, and waiters are attentive and accommodating. Although service isn't bad aboard the *Wind,* it's better on the *Sky* because it's a new ship, and new ships are often staffed with the best in the fleet. With the line's new flexible dining program, additional crew members, mostly waiters and kitchen staff, have been added to each ship. On a recent *Sky* cruise, service in the buffet restaurant was especially efficient, even when the place got packed, as it often did at breakfast. To eliminate confusion as to tipping, the line automatically adds a charge of $10 per passenger, per day, to shipboard accounts. **Full-service laundry** and **dry cleaning** are available.

CRUISETOUR & ADD-ON PROGRAMS Five-night Canadian Rockies (*Norwegian Wind* only) from $1,129 per person, double occupancy; 3-night Vancouver and Victoria (*Norwegian Wind* only), from $479; 3-night Seattle and Victoria (*Norwegian Sky* only), from $599; 2-night Seattle (*Norwegian Sky* only), from $319. Also 2- and 3-night hotel packages in Seattle, and 1- and 2-night hotel packages in Vancouver.

Norwegian Sky

Size (in tons)	80,000	Officers	Norwegian
Number of Cabins	1,001	Crew	750 (Int'l)
Number of Outside Cabins	574	Passenger/Crew Ratio	2.7 to 1
Cabins with Verandas	252	Year Built	1999
Number of Passengers	2,002	Last Major Refurbishment	n/a

The *Norwegian Sky* is the newest and biggest ship in the NCL Alaska fleet and brings the line into the megaship age, offering a lot of wows including an Internet center and photographers snapping digital photos onboard that guests can e-mail home. Web access is also available from every cabin, for a fee.

Other fun extras include a sun deck that the line claims is the largest at sea, though we didn't pace it off to make sure. The deck even has a driver in a golf cart delivering drinks. A bar in the cabaret lounge is also billed as the largest at sea. Got a measuring tape?

CABINS Standard cabins average a small 154 square feet and come with queen beds convertible to twins, sitting areas, dressing tables, refrigerators, safes, and TVs. Cabins feel a bit cramped and have too little storage space. Outside cabins have large round portholes, and 258 cabins and 21 junior suites have private verandas. The ship's top 14 suites also come with butler service, and some have private outdoor Jacuzzis.

Six cabins are handicapped-accessible.

Cabins & Rates

Cabins	Brochure Rates	Bathtub	Fridge	Hair Dryer	Sitting Area	TV
Inside	$1,399–$1,799	no	yes	yes	yes	yes
Outside	$1,899–$2,799	no	yes	yes	yes	yes
Suite	$4,499–$6,049	some	yes	yes	yes	yes

PUBLIC AREAS   The ship feels spacious and features a contemporary design that includes a glass-domed atrium midship that rises impressively for seven decks and a nice arrangement of open and partially covered areas in the stern. There are five dining venues including two large (at 604 and 564 seats) dining rooms. We prefer the cozier Horizons, which serves Italian cuisine (for a cover charge of $10), and has just 88 seats and banquettes facing large picture windows. The Observation Lounge also has picture windows, as does the Roman-inspired spa, where you can watch the Alaska views even when you're getting a massage. Churchill's Cigar Bar and the Windjammer Bar are both dark, clubby spaces, while the sports bar, perched on a high deck, has a wide-open feel. Other public rooms include a card room, casino, conference facilities, disco, and library. The much-touted Internet cafe is not really a cafe, but an arrangement of computers stuck right in one of the wide public corridors. Hardly as cozy as the word "cafe" implies, but at least you won't have trouble finding it.

The children's center, all the way up in the bow of the ship, is a huge, cavernous room with a ceiling so high that small children will feel like they're in an airplane hangar. The teen center has a large movie screen, a pair of Foosball tables, and a video arcade, and there's a children's pool on deck.

POOL, SPA & FITNESS FACILITIES   The well-stocked gym may be on the small side for a ship of this size, but, like the large adjacent aerobics room, has floor-to-ceiling windows that make it a pleasure to work out in and a convenient location abutting the main pool deck. Nearby, the attractive spa and beauty salon are oceanview, too, with lovely gilded Buddha statuary dotting the area.

Out on deck, there is a pair of pools with a cluster of four hot tubs between them. There's a fifth hot tub and kids' wading pool sequestered at the aft end of the deck above, the Sports Deck. Up there, you'll find the combo basketball/ volleyball court, a pair of golf-driving nets, and shuffleboard.

Norwegian Wind

Size (in tons)	50,760	Officers	Norwegian
Number of Cabins	874	Crew	614 (Int'l)
Number of Outside Cabins	716	Passenger/Crew Ratio	2.8 to 1
Cabins with Verandas	48	Year Built	1993
Number of Passengers	1,748	Last Major Refurbishment	1998

The *Norwegian Wind,* formerly known as the *Windward,* went to a shipyard in Germany in 1998, where it was literally cut in two and then stitched back together with a new 130-foot section added to its middle. The addition increased its capacity by 500 berths and allowed for a sports bar and grill, an expanded health club, new meeting facilities, improved children's facilities, and new gift shops, lounges, and a cigar/cordial club.

CABINS   At 160 square feet, the outside deluxe staterooms are smaller than outside cabins on other mainstream ship lines, such as Holland America and Carnival. (Inside cabins on both are just over 180 sq. ft. for ships built post-1990.) About 85% of them are outside, and most have picture windows. Inside cabins are smaller than those outside, ranging from 130 to 150 square feet. Suites have floor-to-ceiling windows and refrigerators, and a number of them have private balconies. All are equipped with TVs, telephones, small dressing tables, soundproof doors, individual climate control, and sitting areas that are actually big enough to stretch out in. Closet and drawer space is quite limited, so pack lightly.

Four cabins are suitable for passengers with disabilities.

Cabins & Rates

Cabins	Brochure Rates	Bathtub	Fridge	Hair Dryer	Sitting Area	TV
Inside	$1,449–$1,749	no	no	yes	no	yes
Outside	$1,949–$2,274	no	no	yes	some	yes
Suite	$2,449–$4,799	yes	yes	yes	yes	yes

PUBLIC AREAS   Instead of one or two giant dining rooms, the *Wind* has three smaller, more intimate restaurants and a romantic specialty bistro (serving French/Mediterranean cuisine for a $10 cover charge), as well as the casual Sports Bar & Grill. Request a table in The Terraces or the Sun Terrace for panoramic sea views. Dinners follow a theme (which might include Viking, Northern Lights, Klondike, International, or the like), as do the extravagant late-night buffets. (Don't miss the unique "Galley Raid" for a chance to meet the chefs and watch ice-carving and cooking demonstrations as you pass through the galley, piling your plate high.) Miles of glass bring the outside in on this ship, and there are plenty of view lounges for relaxation. A card room, casino, cigar bar, conference facilities, disco, library, and show lounge round out the public room offerings, and for kids there's a children's playroom and a video arcade.

POOL, SPA & FITNESS FACILITIES   The *Wind* is well equipped for the sports-minded and active vacationer—in addition to the fitness center, there are two heated pools (one with a swim-up pool bar and two hot tubs), an unobstructed rubberized jogging/walking track, a sports bar with walls of TV screens tuned to ESPN, and a good selection of sports facilities, including Ping-Pong tables and a golf-driving range. Windscreens wrap around the Sports Deck, protecting it and the terraced Pool Deck, so these areas remain warm even when you're cruising next to glaciers.

For a ship carrying 1,700 passengers (double occupancy), the cramped gym is pretty inadequate. There are four treadmills, four stair-steppers, and five stationary bikes squished into a small room with little space to spare. On a recent cruise, passengers were waiting in line to use machines, and several were out of order the entire cruise. The gym and small spa are also right underneath the basketball/volleyball court, so expect some intense banging when a game is in progress. The spa offers a range of treatments as well as his and hers saunas.

6 Princess Cruises

SHIPS   Star • Dawn • Sun • Ocean • Sea • Regal

10100 Santa Monica Blvd., Los Angeles, CA 90067. © **800/LOVE-BOAT** (568-3262) or 310/553-1770. Fax 310/277-6175. www.princess.com.

Consistency is Princess's strength. With new premium ships joining its fleet like so many cars off a Detroit assembly line (all five of its ships in Alaska this year were built in the 1990s, and one—the 109,000-ton *Star Princess*—debuted early last year), you'd think that maintaining acceptable service standards could be a problem. All things considered, though, Princess accomplishes this rather well.

THE EXPERIENCE If you were to put Carnival, Royal Caribbean, Celebrity, and Holland America in a big bowl and mix them all together, you'd come up with the Princess's megas. The *Sea Princess, Sun Princess, Dawn Princess,* and *Star Princess* (the Grand-class ships) are less glitzy and frenzied than Carnival and Royal Caribbean; not quite as cutting-edge or witty as Celebrity's *Infinity* and *Summit;* and more exciting, youthful, and entertaining than Holland America's near-megas, appealing to a wider cross section of cruisers by offering lots of choice, activities, and touches of big-ship glamour, along with lots of private balconies and plenty of the quiet nooks and calm spaces of smaller, more intimate-size vessels. Aboard Princess, you get a lot of bang for your buck, attractively packaged and well-executed. The other Princess ship in this market this summer, the 77,000-ton *Regal Princess,* is a little more mature: It's all of 11 years old. As a result, it lacks some of the pizzazz of the newer vessels and doesn't have as many dining options, but it is, nevertheless, a fine representative for the Southern California–based line. The *Regal,* by the way, was not meant to be in Alaska this year; it was scheduled for Europe/Mediterranean service when demand for that area dipped after the September 11 attacks. So at short notice, the ship was redeployed to the icy waters of the northland, where it had been for several years previously.

Although its ships serve every corner of the globe, nowhere is the Princess presence more visible than in Alaska. Through its affiliate, Princess Tours, it owns wilderness lodges, motor coaches, and railcars in the 49th state, making it one of the two major players in the Alaska cruise market, alongside Holland America. This year Princess will unveil its fifth wilderness lodge—in Wrangell–St Elias National Park.

Pros

- **Good service.** The warm-hearted Italian, British, and Filipino service crew do a great job. On a Princess cruise a few years ago, one barman with a glorious Cockney accent (which we noted he could mute or emphasize at will) was a huge hit with our group, dispensing one-liners, simple magic tricks, and drinks with equal facility. We've met others on Princess ships with the same gift for making passengers feel welcome without being overly familiar.
- **Private verandas.** The *Sun Princess, Dawn Princess, Sea Princess,* and *Ocean Princess* have verandas in an amazing 411 out of 603 (630 on the *Sea Princess*) outside cabins, and even more amazing is that more than 75% of the outside cabins on the *Star Princess* have them, too. The *Regal Princess* has fewer—just 184 of a total of 614 outside cabins.

Cons

- **Average food.** The ships' cuisine is perfectly fine if you're not a gourmet, but if you are, you'll find it's pretty banquet-hall-like and not as good as Celebrity's, Carnival's, or Holland America's.

THE FLEET Princess's diverse fleet in Alaska includes four Grand-class megaships all launched since 1995—the megasisters **Ocean Princess** (2000), **Sea Princess** (1998), **Dawn Princess** (1997), and **Sun Princess** (1995)—and its newest and biggest, **Star Princess,** set to debut in March, after press time, and the **Regal Princess,** built in 1991. The ships are pretty but not stunning; glitzy but not gaudy; spacious but not overwhelmingly so; and decorated in a comfortable, restrained style that's a combo of classic and modern. They're a great choice when you want a step up from Carnival, Royal Caribbean, and NCL but aren't interested in the slightly more chic ambience of Celebrity.

PASSENGER PROFILE Typical Princess passengers are likely to be between, say, 50 and 65, and be experienced cruisers who know what they want and are prepared to pay for it. (Although they don't have to pay as much as they would on, say, Crystal.) The line's recent additional emphasis on its youth and children's facilities has begun to attract a bigger share of the **family market,** resulting in the passenger list becoming more active overall.

DINING Princess's meals in general are good if hardly gourmet, but give them points for at least trying to be flexible: At the end of 2001, Princess implemented a new fleetwide dining option known as Personal Choice. Basically, the plan allows passengers to sign up for the traditional first or second seating for dinner or for a come-as-you-please restaurant-style dining option. The latter allows you to eat dinner any time between 5:30pm and midnight each night. Passengers may request a cozy table for two or bring half a dozen shipmates with them, depending on your mood each evening. Because under this restaurant-style program you are likely to be seated at a different table each night with different service staff, a $6.50-a-day gratuity will be automatically added to your bill for the restaurant service. If you want to raise or lower that amount you should do so when you make your cruise reservation. (It will be harder to do it once you're onboard.) It's also possible to eat all your meals in the 24-hour Lido Deck cafe on all Princess ships in Alaska. If you don't go to the main dining room, though, you may miss one of Princess's best features: its pastas, prepared tableside several times during each cruise by your dining-room captain. The new *Star Princess* also offers two alternative dining restaurants, one Italian and the other Mexican, and it's our experience, based on cruises on the *Star Princess*'s sister ships, that meals at these restaurants are well worth the price of admission. (There is a $15 cover charge for the fancy Italian venue and an $8 cover charge for the more casual Mexican venue.)

ACTIVITIES Princess passengers can expect enough onboard activity to keep them going morning to night, if they've a mind to, and enough nooks and crannies to allow them to do absolutely nothing, if that's their thing. The line doesn't go out of its way to make passengers feel that they're spoilsports if they don't participate in the amateur-night tomfoolery, or putt for dough, or learn to fold napkins. These activities are usually there, along with the inevitable bingo, shuffleboard, and the rest, but they're low-key. Internet access is offered on all the ships for $30 an hour with a 15-minute ($7.50) minimum.

Specifically in Alaska, the line has naturalists and park rangers onboard to offer commentary. And last year, as part of what appears to be a trend of cruise lines trying to make their Alaska cruises more Alaskan, Princess featured Libby Riddles, the first woman to win the famous Iditarod dogsled race, who discussed not only dog mushing but also what it's like to live in a Native Inupiat village near Nome.

CHILDREN'S PROGRAM Supervised activities are offered year-round for ages 2 to 17, and are divided into two groups: "Princess Pelicans," ages 2 to 12, and teens, ages 13 to 17. All of the ships are well-equipped for children and are clearly intended to cater to families as Princess seeks to broaden its appeal and distance itself from its old image as a staid, adults-only line. Each ship has a spacious children's playroom and a sizable area of fenced-in outside deck for kids

Princess Fleet Itineraries

Ship	Itinerary
Star/Dawn/ Sun/Ocean Princess	**7-night Gulf of Alaska:** North- and southbound between Vancouver and Seward/Anchorage, visiting Ketchikan, Juneau, and Skagway, and cruising Glacier Bay and College Fjord.
Sea Princess	**7-night Inside Passage:** Round-trip from Vancouver, visiting Juneau, Skagway, Sitka, and Glacier Bay or Hubbard Glacier.
Regal Princess	**10-night Inside Passage:** Round-trip from San Francisco, visiting Juneau, Skagway (or Sitka, on some sailings), Ketchikan, Tracy Arm, and Victoria, B.C.

only, with a shallow pool and tricycles. Teen centers have computers, video games, and a sound system. Wisely, these areas are placed as separate as possible from the adult passengers.

ENTERTAINMENT   From glittering, well-conceived, and well-executed Vegas-style production shows to New York cabaret singers on the main stage, and from a wonderfully entertaining cabaret piano/vocalist in one of the lounges to a rocking disco, this line offers a terrific blend of musical delights, and you'll always find a cozy spot where some soft piano or jazz music is being performed. You'll also find entertainment like hypnotists, puppeteers, and comedians, plus karaoke for you audience-participation types, and, in the afternoons, a couple of sessions of that ubiquitous cruise favorite, the "Newlywed and Not-So-Newly-wed Game." Each of the ships also has a wine bar selling caviar by the ounce and vintage wine, champagne, and iced vodka by the glass. The Princess casinos are sprawling and exciting places, too, and are bound to keep gamblers entranced (hypnotized?) with their lights and action. Good-quality piano-bar music and strolling musicians, along with dance music in the lounge, are part of the pre- and post-dinner ritual.

Princess has for years had a connection to Hollywood—this is the Love Boat line after all. It's also the only line we know of where you can watch yesterday's and today's television shows on your in-room TV. Also shown are A&E Biography, E! Entertainment TV, Nickelodeon, Discovery Channel, BBC, and National Geographic productions, as well as recently released movies.

SERVICE   Throughout the fleet, the service in all areas—dining room, lounge, cabin maintenance, and so on—tends to be of consistently high quality. An area in which Princess particularly shines is the efficiency of its shore-excursion staffs. Getting 2,000 people off a ship and onto motor coaches, trains, and helicopters—all staples of any Alaska cruise program—isn't as easy as they make it look. And a real plus to the Princess shore-excursions program is that passengers are sent the options about 60 days before the sailing and can book their choices on an advanced-reservations basis, before the trip (tickets are issued onboard), either by mail or on the Internet at www.princesscruises.com. The program improves your chances of getting your first choice of tours before they sell out.

All of the Princess vessels in Alaska offer **laundry** and **dry-cleaning services** and have their own **self-service laundromats.**

CRUISETOUR & ADD-ON PROGRAMS   Princess offers a total of 46 dif-ferent cruisetour itineraries in Alaska in conjunction with its Gulf of Alaska and Inside Passage voyages (not to mention another 10 in the Canadian Rockies). Certain to attract a lot of passenger attention this year is the new Copper River

Princess Wilderness Lodge in Wrangell–St. Elias National Park, which the company is packaging as a 12-day cruisetour. The program features two nights at the new lodge, a train ride through Denali National Park, and a night in Fairbanks. It costs from $1,899 per person, double, depending on the date, ship, and accommodations chosen. The longest Princess cruisetour is an 18-day Heart of Alaska and Canadian Rockies package (with a 7-day cruise, 6 days of land tours in B.C., and 5 days of land tours in Alaska), starting at $3,529.

Dawn Princess • Sun Princess • Sea Princess • Ocean Princess

Size (in tons)	77,000	Officers	Italian
Number of Cabins	975	Crew	900 (Int'l)
Number of Outside Cabins	603	Passenger/Crew Ratio	2.2 to 1
Cabins with Verandas	410	Year Built	1995/1997/2000
Number of Passengers	1,950	Last Major Refurbishment	n/a

These four ships are virtually indistinguishable from one another except for cosmetics, and despite their size and passenger complement, you'll probably never feel crowded: There always seems to be lots of space on deck, in the buffet dining areas, and in the lounges.

CABINS   More than 400 of each ship's 975 cabins and suites have private balconies, including many in the midprice range, such as those on Baja Deck. All, including the 408 inside units, come equipped with minibars, TVs, and twin beds that are easily converted to queens. Closet space is at least adequate, although it's a little cramped in the lower-end cabins.

The smallest cabins are a spacious 175 square feet, and the six suites aft measure up at 754 square feet, offering a large living room, separate bedroom/dining area, stall shower and bathtub with whirlpool, two TVs, refrigerator, and safe. The 32 minisuites are somewhat less lavish, but still highly desirable accommodations.

All four of the ships have handicapped-accessible cabins located on several decks and in several different categories.

Cabins & Rates

Cabins	Brochure Rates	Bathtub	Fridge	Hair Dryer	Sitting Area	TV
Inside	$1,699–$1,969	no	yes	yes	no	yes
Outside	$2,029–$3,149	no	yes	yes	no	yes
Suite	$4,099–$5,079	yes	yes	yes	yes	yes

PUBLIC AREAS   These ships shine when it comes to communal areas. All have a decidedly unglitzy decor that relies on lavish amounts of wood, glass, and marble, and feature $2.5 million collections of original paintings and lithographs. The one-story showrooms offer unobstructed viewing from every seat, and several seats in the back are reserved for passengers with mobility problems. The smaller Vista Lounge also offers shows with good sight lines and comfortable cabaret-style seating. The pair of dining rooms on each ship are broken up by dividers topped with frosted glass. The elegant, nautical-motif Wheelhouse Bar is done in warm, dark-wood tones and features live entertainment; it's the perfect spot for pre- or post-dinner drinks. There's a dark and sensuous disco; a bright, spacious, enticing casino; a card room, cinema, and show lounge; and lots of little lounges for an intimate rendezvous, such as the Entre Nous and the Atrium Lounge (a real grabber, so popular with passengers that it's where the captain holds his opening cocktail party). Another striking feature on each of these ships is the library, with leather easy chairs equipped with built-in headphone sound systems. They absolutely cry out, "Sit here!"

If you're hungry, options besides the usual main dining rooms and the buffet include an all-night sit-down restaurant (you can get a full dinner until 4am) and Lago's Pizzeria, a sit-down restaurant open afternoons and nights. Sorry, no takeout or delivery. Pizza is also available by the slice in the Horizon Court between 4 and 7pm daily.

The ships have extensive children's playrooms with ball drop, castles, computer games, puppet theaters, and more.

POOL, SPA & FITNESS FACILITIES   There are four pools total (one of which is the kids' wading pool), and hot tubs scattered around the Riviera Deck. These ships boast some of the best-designed, most appealing health clubs of any of Princess's vessels. The spa offers all the requisite massage and spa treatments. The gym is on the small side for ships of this size. A teakwood deck encircles the ship for joggers, walkers, and shuffleboard players, and a computerized golf center called Princess Links simulates the trickiest aspects of some of the world's best and most legendary golf courses.

Fitness classes are available throughout the day in a very roomy aerobics room, where stretching and meditation classes are also offered.

Star Princess (Preview)

Size (in tons)	109,000	Officers	British/Italian
Number of Cabins	1,301	Crew	1,200 (Int'l)
Number of Outside Cabins	935	Passenger/Crew Ratio	2.1 to 1
Cabins with Verandas	711	Year Built	2002
Number of Passengers	2,600	Last Major Refurbishment	n/a

Star Princess is bound to get more than its share of attention this summer, if for no other reason than that it is the biggest ship ever to sail Alaskan waters—bigger by almost 20,000 tons and carrying some 500 more guests than any other vessel in the market. The ship is the third in its particular class in the Princess fleet, behind the *Golden Princess* and *Grand Princess,* neither of which has been deployed in the 49th state.

Based on the experience of these other virtually identical liners, you can expect a number of things from the *Star Princess*.

Like them, it has umpteen restaurants, including two for which a charge is made—Sabatini's Trattoria (Italian cuisine, as you may imagine from the name) and the Desert Rose, an elegant Southwestern-themed eatery. The charges are $15 per person and $8 per person, respectively, which includes the gratuity. Otherwise, the *Star Princess* offers any number of options—three main dining rooms, for instance, as well as the Horizon Court, a casual 24-hour restaurant; Prego, offering poolside pizza during the day; the Promenade Lounge Patisserie; and the Trident Grill for excellent hamburgers and hot dogs. All this, plus an ice-cream-sundae bar (open at strategic hours of the day) and 24-hour room service.

The ship has four pools and nine whirlpool spas dotted around the upper deck and a fitness center and spa, children's and teens' centers, a 9-hole putting green, and a basketball/paddle-tennis court. Internet facilities are available at $30 an hour, with a 15-minute minimum.

In keeping with an increasingly popular trend nowadays, the ship also boasts a wedding chapel. The captain will perform the marriage ceremony or you may bring your own clergy along on the trip if you wish. The wedding packages start at $1,400 per couple (plus the cruise fare).

CABINS 711 of the 935 outside staterooms—or 80% of them—are equipped with verandas. The smallest of these balcony rooms is 215 square feet, a sizeable footage. The next level up, the minisuites, are 325 square feet in size, with full suites ranging from 515 to 800 square feet. Inside rooms range from 160 to 210 square feet.

All rooms have refrigerators, spacious closets and TVs offering in-cabin films, CNN, ESPN, and Nickelodeon. Minisuites and suites have ample sitting areas. Twenty-eight of the rooms are wheelchair-accessible.

PUBLIC AREAS One of the most striking features of this class of ship is the futuristic nightclub/disco located 15 decks above the sea and reachable by a moving sidewalk. Throughout the ship, there are no fewer than 12 bars/lounges, more than enough to cater to the largish passenger complement without allowing any one of them to become unacceptably crowded.

As on the four ships mentioned above, one of the *Star Princess*'s classiest rooms is the library, fitted with comfy, inviting easy chairs with a selection of CDs and tapes (music or books) that can be listened to in complete privacy through the special ports in the arms of the chairs.

Cabins & Rates

Cabins	Brochure Rates	Bathtub	Fridge	Hair Dryer	Sitting Area	TV
Inside	$1,919–$2,129	no	yes	yes	no	yes
Outside	$2,549–$3,889	no	yes	yes	no	yes
Suites	$3,989–$5,809	yes	yes	yes	yes	yes

POOL, SPA & FITNESS FACILITIES The gym, in which guests can work out on the treadmill, stationary bicycle, rowing machines and weights, has large windows to the ocean, which we always feel makes it somewhat easier to stand the pain of aching muscles. The ship's enormous spa also has a view of the outside world.

The ship is equipped with four swimming pools (two under a retractable roof) and nine whirlpool spas dotted around. The *Star Princess* has a wraparound promenade deck (4 laps = 1 mile).

Regal Princess

Size (in tons)	70,000	Officers	British/Italian
Number of Cabins	795	Crew	696 (Int'l)
Number of Outside Cabins	614	Passenger/Crew Ratio	2.3 to 1
Cabins with Verandas	184	Year Built	1991
Number of Passengers	1,590	Last Major Refurbishment	1999

It seems like only yesterday that this ship, along with its twin, the *Crown Princess,* were the jewels in the cruise line's crown: its most modern, most dramatic, and most frequently photographed vessels. That was a decade ago, but the *Regal* has maintained its freshness and glamour. It's a winner.

THE EXPERIENCE The *Regal Princess*—which becomes Princess's sixth Alaska representative this year—will operate a pattern of 11 round-trip voyages of 10 days each. It will be one of only two ships home-ported in San Francisco in 2002, the other being the *Crystal Harmony* of Crystal Cruises.

Regal Princess designer Renzo Piano is the man responsible for such high-profile designs as Paris's Pompidou Center. To create the ships, he worked from "the silhouette of a dolphin." The result was a cutting-edge exterior design that some people may find just downright weird. But only in profile.

Inside, the ship is warm and inviting, although the layout is somewhat disjointed, and boasts a multimillion-dollar art collection, as well as all the amenities one would expect, including 24-hour casual dining in the Café del Sol, a good choice of bars, a coffee and pastry cafe, a wine and caviar bar, a pizzeria, cushy seating areas (including in the lobby), a decent casino, and a variety of shopping options.

The vessel's outdoor deck space is a disappointment because there's not enough of it. This means congestion at deck buffets and around swimming pools whenever the ship is full. There's also no uninterrupted Promenade Deck around the periphery of the ship, so for a bit of exercise, you'll have to walk back and forth along the ship's sides or get on a treadmill in the gym.

Cabins & Rates

Cabins	Brochure Rates	Bathtub	Fridge	Hair Dryer	Sitting Area	TV
Inside	$1,899–$2349	no	yes	yes	no	yes
Outside	$2,199–$3,334	no	yes	yes	no	yes
Suites	$3,449–$3,849	yes	ye	yes	yes	yes

CABINS   Of 795 total, 624 are outside cabins, and many have private verandas; in fact, two whole decks of cabins have them.

Standard cabins are quite spacious at 190 to 210 square feet, and suites with balconies are 587 square feet (including veranda). Decor includes comfortably upholstered chairs and sofas, framed artwork, and rectangular windows for easy wave-gazing. Bathrooms are compact but comfortable.

If you're booking a standard cabin, opt for one of the four classified as category GG on the Plaza Deck, if they're available. These outside doubles with queen-sized beds are the ship's most convenient and the best of the standard lot. Note that views from some cabins on the Dolphin Deck are partially obstructed by lifeboats.

The lowest priced outside cabins are category G on the Fiesta Deck, which have bunk beds and round portholes. These cabins are good buys, especially for budget-minded friends or families traveling together.

All cabins have safes, terry-cloth robes for use during the cruise, and TVs broadcasting CNN, ESPN, Nickelodeon, BBC programming, and TNT.

About 10 cabins are wheelchair-accessible.

PUBLIC AREAS   The elegant interiors, studded with artwork (and lots of pillars that wind up obstructing the flow of the rooms), feel as much like a hotel as a ship.

The three-story Plaza Atrium is an oval-shaped area with a reception desk, patisserie, wine and caviar bar, and shops. The overall effect is one of refined elegance. The Palm Court dining room boasts two-level terracing, and there's also a two-level International Show Lounge for nightly Vegas-style entertainment. If you want a drink and don't mind noise, there's The Dome lounge, set, as the name would suggest, in the Dolphin-shaped dome forward. It's located, unfortunately, just behind the casino, and the noise from the clinking slot machines, along with loud laughter and conversation, sort of takes away from what could be a very comfortable R&R area. The Stage Door lounge on D[ ] relatively calmer and more soothing.

The dome was meant to be the observation lounge, but it was[ ] too big for that purpose and was converted into the ship's casino and a bar. You can still use the space to view the passing scenery (an observation area is separated from the rest of the room by a glass partition), but don't expect much peace or serenity while you're doing it (unless you find jangling slots and ringing bells soothing). A better place to catch the views is on the Promenade Deck or Lido Deck aft.

The health club/spa is located very low in the ship, so there are no ocean views. But it is well-equipped and well-maintained. The spa offers massage and treatment rooms, as well as steam rooms and saunas.

7 Radisson Seven Seas Cruises

SHIP   Seven Seas Navigator

600 Corporate Dr., Ste. 410, Fort Lauderdale, FL 33334. © 800/285-1835. www.rssc.com.

Radisson carries passengers in style and extreme comfort. Its brand of luxury is casually elegant and subtle, and its cuisine among the best in the industry.

THE EXPERIENCE   A subsidiary of Radisson Hotels Worldwide, this line operates five upscale small to midsize ships and one expedition ship, geared toward taking affluent and worldly travelers to such locations as Europe, South America, Antarctica, and Tahiti. This year marks the line's third full season in Alaska, and the return of the all-suite *Seven Seas Navigator*, which cruised here in 2000.

The Radisson experience offers the best in food, service, and accommodations in an environment that's a little more casual than Crystal's more determined luxury. (Attire is country-club casual at all times.)

Pros

- **Overall excellence.** The line has a no-tipping policy, excellent food, open seating for meals, generally fine service, great accommodations, and creative shore excursions.
- **Great room service.** Room service is about the best we've found on a ship, the food served promptly, fresh, and course by course (rather than all at once).

Cons

- **Sedate nightlife.** Most passengers, exhausted after a full day in port, or perhaps wanting to watch a movie on their in-suite VCR, head back to their cabins after the show (or around 11pm), leaving only a few night owls in the disco and other lounges.

THE FLEET   For 2002, Radisson has returned to Alaska the all-suite *Seven Seas Navigator*. It's the second largest ship in the Radisson fleet and offers an elegant yet comfortable modern design and onboard atmosphere.

PASSENGER PROFILE   Radisson tends to attract passengers of an average age in the 50s, with a household income of more than $100,000, but who don't like to flaunt their wealth. The typical passenger is well-educated, well-traveled, and inquisitive.

DINING   Radisson's cuisine is among the best on the high seas, and would gain high marks even if it were on land. Service by professional waiters adds to

Radisson Fleet Itineraries

Ship	Itinerary
Seven Seas Navigator	Two slightly different itineraries (not counting position cruises before and after the season): (1) **7-night Inside Passage/Gulf cruises** from Vancouver to Seward, visit Misty Fjords, Ketchikan, Juneau, Skagway, Sitka, and Hubbard Glacier. (2) **7-night Gulf cruises** from Seward to Vancouver visit Hubbard Glacier, Sitka, Juneau, Tracy Arm, Skagway, and Ketchikan.

the experience, as do little touches such as fine china and fresh flowers on the tables. Complimentary wines are served at dinner. Complimentary, that is, unless you want a very expensive bottle of champagne, say, or Opus 1, but since the line serves Santa Margharita Pinot Grigio, Barton & Guestier Beaujolais Villages, or Kendall Jackson Reserve Chardonnay (as Radisson did on a couple of evenings on the *Navigator* last time we sailed on it), you're left with very little reason to trade up. The main dining room is open-seating. (You can eat when and with whom you like.) You can also dine at the lavish buffets offered for breakfast and lunch or in the alternative dining restaurant (Italian on the *Navigator*) open on a reservations-only basis. (Unlike on other ships, no fee is charged.) There is also an outdoor grill.

ACTIVITIES   The line assumes that, for the most part, passengers want to entertain themselves onboard, but that doesn't mean there isn't a full roster of activities including lectures by local experts, well-known authors, and the like, plus facilities for card and board games, blackjack and Ping Pong tournaments, bingo, big screen movies with popcorn, and instruction in the fine art of pom-pom making, juggling, and such. Bridge instructors are onboard on select sailings, and the ships offer facilities to send and receive e-mail.

CHILDREN'S PROGRAM   The line is adult-oriented, but a children's program is offered on Alaska cruises only, and you may find a dozen or so youngsters on any given sailing. Activities, held in borrowed spaces such as the nightclub or card room (there is no dedicated children's facility), include games, tournaments, Alaska-oriented crafts projects, storytelling, and a Sony PlayStation. There are also a limited number of special kids' shore excursions.

ENTERTAINMENT   Entertainment includes small-scale production shows, cabaret acts, headliners including comedians and magicians and sometimes (as on a 2001 Alaska cruise) members of the Florida Philharmonic Orchestra. The library stocks books and movies that guests can play on their in-cabin VCRs.

SERVICE   The dining room waiters generally have experience at fine hotels as well as on ships and provide service so good that you don't really notice it. Ditto for the excellent room stewards. The *Navigator* offers full-service and self-service **laundry** and **dry cleaning.**

The *Navigator* was the largest ship in the Radisson fleet (until the arrival of the *Seven Seas Mariner,* which was in Alaska in 2001) and features an eclectic modern design. Italian-designed and built, its officers are Italian and its crew international. The ship's Portofino Grill restaurant offers Italian cuisine.

CRUISE TOURS & ADD-ONS   Two- to four-night escorted tours are offered to destinations including Denali, from Seward, either pre- or post-cruise (depending on which direction you cruise). They range in price from $795 to $2,295 per person, plus the cruise fare. There are also some post-cruise offerings from Vancouver, including a 3-night plan that includes a visit to Whistler and is priced at $1,695 per person.

Seven Seas Navigator

Size (in tons)	30,000	Officers	Italian
Number of Cabins	250	Crew	313
Number of Outside Cabins	250	Passenger/Crew Ratio	1 to 1.56
Cabins with Verandas	214	Year Built	1999
Number of Passengers	490	Last Major Refurbishment	n/a

CABINS   The cabins are all oceanview suites, most with private verandas. (Those without verandas have windows.) The standard suite is a large 301 square feet, and the largest four suites are a whopping 1,173 square feet, two with full wraparound balconies. Some suites can interconnect if you want to book two for additional space. All offer separate living room areas, and top levels of suites have dining areas as well. All the suites come with queen-size beds that convert to twins, walk-in closets, marble-appointed bathrooms with full-size tubs and separate showers, TVs and VCRs, refrigerators stocked with complimentary bottled water and soft drinks, complimentary in-suite bar setups, safes, phones, and 24-hour room service. (You can order full meals from the dining room menu served in-suite.)

Cabins & Rates

Cabins	Brochure Rates	Bathtub	Fridge	Hair Dryer	Sitting Area	TV
Suites	$2,595–$7,895	yes	yes	yes	yes	yes

PUBLIC AREAS   An impressive atrium starts on Deck 4 and reaches to Deck 12. The show lounge is two-tiered, and designed to resemble a 1930s nightclub. There are two additional lounges and a Connoisseur Club, a cushy venue for pre-dinner drinks and after-dinner fine brandy and cigars. The casino offers blackjack, roulette, Caribbean stud poker, and slots. Shoppers can indulge in two small boutiques offering clothes, jewelry, and your usual array of logo items. The library offers books and videos and 10 computer terminals. (You can send and receive e-mail for about $1 per message.)

Meals are served in the pretty, windowed main dining room on an open-seating basis. Buffets are also offered at breakfast and lunch at the indoor/outdoor Portofino Grill. To create an intimate dining experience at night, they close part of the space. (Reservations are required at night.)

POOL, SPA & FITNESS FACILITIES   The ship's Judith Jackson spa offers treatments using a variety of herbal and water-based therapies, as well as a variety of beauty services. The seawater pool is flanked by two heated whirlpools and surrounded by lots of open deck space. Recreational facilities include a fitness center, golf-driving cages, Ping Pong, and shuffleboard.

8 Royal Caribbean International

SHIPS   Legend of the Seas • Vision of the Seas • Radiance of the Seas

1050 Caribbean Way, Miami, FL 33132. ✆ **800/327-6700** or 305/379-4731. www.rccl.com.

A bold, brash industry innovator second in size only to Carnival, Royal Caribbean introduced the concept of the megaship with its *Sovereign of the Seas* in 1988, and has continued to innovate, building (among other things) the two largest passenger ships in the world.

THE EXPERIENCE   The mass-market style of cruising Royal Caribbean sells aboard these megaships is reasonably priced and offers nearly every diversion imaginable. The ships are more informal than formal and are well run, with a veritable army of friendly service employees paying close attention to day-to-day details. Dress is generally casual but neat during the day and informal most evenings, with 2 semiformal or formal nights per 7-night cruise.

The contemporary decor on Royal Caribbean vessels doesn't bang you on the head with glitz like, say, Carnival. It's more subdued, classy, and witty, with lots of use of glass, greenery, and art. All the Royal Caribbean vessels feature the line's trademark Viking Crown Lounge, an observation area located in a circular glass structure on the upper deck (in some cases encircling the smokestack), which looks like a Martian spacecraft atop the vessels. Another popular trademark feature is the ships' nautically themed Schooner bars.

Pros

- **Great spas and recreation facilities.** Royal Caribbean's Alaska ships for 2002 all have elaborate health club and spa facilities, a covered swimming pool, and large, open sun-deck areas.
- **Great observation areas.** The Viking Crown Lounge and other glassed-in areas make excellent observation rooms to see the Alaska sights.
- **Quality entertainment.** Royal Caribbean spends big bucks on entertainment, which includes high-tech show productions. Headliners are often featured.

Cons

- **Crowds.** Big ships are more anonymous than small ships, and RCI's ships are very big. You almost need a map to get around, and you'll experience the inevitable lines for buffets, debarkation, and boarding of buses during shore excursions; you will sometimes have to wait a while for your drink when a bar or lounge is particularly crowded.

THE FLEET   Royal Caribbean is the owner of the current largest ships in the world, the 142,000-ton *Voyager of the Seas, Explorer of the Seas,* and new *Adventure of the Seas,* with more enormo-vessels on the way. Although those 3,000-plus-passenger ships—which introduced such cruise-ship design features as ice-skating rinks, rock-climbing walls, and cabins overlooking interior atrium areas—are not in the Alaska market, Royal Caribbean will bring into the market this year its new and very up-to-date 2,100-passenger *Radiance of the Seas,* representing a new category of ship for the line and offering further innovations, including a billiards room with self-leveling pool tables. The 2,000-passenger *Vision of the Seas* will continue its Alaska presence and will be joined this year by the 1,800-passenger *Legend of the Seas* (marking the second year Royal Caribbean has had three ships in the Alaska market).

PASSENGER PROFILE   The crowd on Royal Caribbean ships, like the decor, tends to be a notch down on the whoopee scale from what you find on Carnival. Passengers represent an age mix from 30 to 60, and a good number of families are attracted by the line's well-established and fine-tuned kids' programs.

In Alaska, Royal Caribbean is focusing more on international sales than the entrenched market leaders, Princess and Holland America, which has resulted in

Royal Caribbean Fleet Itineraries

Ship	Itinerary
Legend of the Seas	**7-night Gulf of Alaska:** North- and southbound between Vancouver and Seward, visiting Ketchikan, Juneau, Skagway, Hubbard Glacier, and Sitka. (Southbound cruises also cruise Misty Fjords.)
Vision of the Seas	**7-night Hubbard Glacier (Inside Passage):** Round-trip from Vancouver, visiting Hubbard Glacier, Skagway, Juneau, Ketchikan, and Misty Fjords.
Radiance of the Seas	**7-night Hubbard Glacier (Inside Passage):** Round-trip from Vancouver, visiting Juneau, Skagway, Hubbard Glacier, and Ketchikan.

sailings populated by a good many international passengers, including travelers from Canada, Asia, and Europe.

DINING   Food on Royal Caribbean has been upgraded, and although it's not a highlight of the cruise, you may actually encounter an occasional dish that knocks your socks off. Dining rooms feature two seatings with assigned tables at breakfast, lunch, and dinner. Every menu contains selections designed for low-fat, low-cholesterol, and low-salt dining, as well as vegetarian and children's dishes. On the *Radiance,* you also have the option of dining on a reservations-only basis at Chops, a classy steakhouse, or Portofino, an upscale Italian eatery. A rather stiff fee of $20 a head is charged at these venues, but in our experience, the food soars above what's offered in the dining room. Casual dining is offered as an alternative for those who don't want to sit in the dining room at night. In addition to the midnight buffet, sandwiches are served throughout the night in the public lounges, and a pretty routine menu is available from room service 24 hours a day. During normal dinner hours, however, a cabin steward can bring you anything being served that night. Royal Caribbean bans smoking in the dining rooms on all its vessels.

ACTIVITIES   On the activity front, Royal Caribbean offers plenty of the standard cruise line fare (craft classes, horse racing, bingo, shuffleboard, deck games, line-dancing lessons, wine-and-cheese tastings, cooking demonstrations, and art auctions), but if you want to take it easy and watch the world go by or scan for wildlife, no one will bother you or cajole you into joining an activity. Port lectures are offered on topics such as Alaska wildlife.

The ships also offer an extensive **fitness program** called ShipShape. You can e-mail home from **Internet cafe** areas for 50¢ a minute.

CHILDREN'S PROGRAM   Children's activities are some of the most extensive afloat and include a teen disco, children's play areas, and the Adventure Ocean program, which offers a full schedule of scavenger hunts, arts-and-crafts sessions, and science presentations—so many activities, in fact, that the kids get their own daily program delivered to their cabin.

ENTERTAINMENT   Practically no one does entertainment as well as Royal Caribbean, which incorporates sprawling, high-tech cabaret stages into each of its ships' showrooms, some with a wall of video monitors to augment live performances. Entertainment begins before dinner and continues late, late into the night. There are musical acts, comedy acts, sock hops, toga parties, talent shows, and that great cruise favorite, karaoke. The Vegas-style shows are filled with all the razzle-dazzle passengers have come to expect. Royal Caribbean uses 10-piece bands for its main showroom, and large-cast revues are among the best you'll find on a ship. Show bands and other lounge acts keep the music playing all over the ship; all are first-rate.

SERVICE   Overall, service in the restaurants and cabins is friendly, accommodating, and efficient. You're likely to be greeted with a smile by someone polishing the brass in a stairwell, a greeting that supervisors encourage on the part of even the lowest-ranking employees. That said, big, bustling ships like Royal Caribbean's are no strangers to crowds, lines, and harried servers not able to get to you exactly when you'd like them to. Considering the vast armies of personnel required to maintain a line as large as Royal Caribbean, it's a miracle that staffers appear as motivated and enthusiastic as they do.

Laundry and **dry-cleaning** services are available on all the ships, but none have self-service laundromats.

CRUISETOUR & ADD-ON PROGRAMS   Two- to six-night escorted land tours can be combined with 7-night cruises aboard *Legend.* Land portion visits such destinations as Girdwood's Alyeska Resort, Anchorage, Denali, Talkeetna, and Fairbanks. Four- and six-night Canadian Rockies (Banff, Lake Louise, and/or Jasper) packages are available pre- or post-cruise with sailings of the *Radiance* and *Vision,* priced from $3,449 (early-bird pricing also available), including the cruise fare. In addition, Royal Caribbean offers pre- and post-cruise hotel packages in Vancouver and Anchorage.

Legend of the Seas • Vision of the Seas

Size (in tons)	70,000/78,491	Officers	Norwegian/Int'l
Number of Cabins	1,000	Crew	834
Number of Outside Cabins	593	Passenger/Crew Ratio	2.4 to 1
Cabins with Verandas	231/229	Year Built	1995/1998
Number of Passengers	1,800/2,000	Last Major Refurbishment	2001/2000

The *Legend of the Seas* is the first ship in Royal Caribbean's *Vision* class, and the *Vision of the Seas* was the last in that class. Other megaships in the class include the *Grandeur, Rhapsody, Enchantment,* and *Splendour of the Seas.* The *Vision* is a little bigger than the *Legend,* but the layout is very similar, as is the passenger capacity. Both ships are true floating cities offering elegant trappings, from their multimillion-dollar art collections to their wide range of onboard facilities. Plenty of nice touches—sumptuous, big-windowed health clubs/spas with lots of health and beauty treatments, plus loads of fine shopping, dining, and entertainment options—give both the *Vision* and *Legend* the feel of a top-flight shore resort.

CABINS   Cabins are not large—inside cabins measure 138 square feet and outsides 153 square feet (compared to Carnival's 190 sq. ft. for standard cabins)—but do have small sitting areas. All cabins have TVs, telephones, and twin beds that convert to queen-size. They have ample storage space and well-lit, moderately sized bathrooms. TVs feature movies, news, and information channels. (Excursion and debarkation talks are rebroadcast in-room just in case you missed something.) Nearly a quarter of the cabins on these ships have private verandas, and about a third of the cabins are designed to accommodate third and fourth passengers. For big, check out the Royal Suite on the *Vision*—it measures a mammoth 1,150 square feet and even has a grand piano. Fourteen cabins on the *Vision* and 17 on the *Legend* are wheelchair-accessible.

Cabins & Rates

Cabins	Brochure Rates	Bathtub	Fridge	Hair Dryer	Sitting Area	TV
Inside	$1,579–$2,179	no	no	no	yes	yes
Outside	$2,179–$2,929	no	some	no	yes	yes
Suite	$3,229–$9,449	yes	yes	no	yes	yes

PUBLIC AREAS Both the *Vision* and *Legend* soar 10 stories above the water-line and feature seven-story glass-walled atriums with glass elevators (a la Hyatt) and winding brass-trimmed staircases. At the peak of each is the Viking Crown Lounge, which affords a 360° view of the passing scenery. You'll also appreciate the view through the glass walls of the bi-level dining room. Actually, other than in the windowless casino and show lounge, there are great views to be found virtually everywhere on these ships—perfect for scoping glaciers.

A playroom, teen center (on *Vision* only), and a video arcade provide plenty to keep the kids happily occupied while you relax, gamble, attend one of the many activities (there are around 200 to select from each week, including informative nature lectures), take in a show in the theater, or dance the night away in the disco or one of numerous lounges and bars, which include a champagne/caviar bar and piano bar. Other rooms include a card room, library, several shops, and a conference room.

Meals are served both in the windowed, two-story dining room and in the casual Windjammer Café (an indoor/outdoor venue), so there's freedom as to when you dine and choices as to what you'll eat. Pizza is served in the Solarium.

POOL, SPA & FITNESS FACILITIES The spas on these ships are some of the most attractive around and are truly soothing respites from the hubbub of ship life. They offer a wide selection of treatments, as well as the standard steam rooms and saunas. Adjacent to the spas are spacious Solariums, each with a pool, lounge chairs, floor-to-ceiling windows, and a retractable glass ceiling. These spots are a peaceful place to repose before or after a spa treatment, or any time at all. Surprisingly, the gyms are small for the ships' size—and in comparison to those on Carnival's, Holland America's, and Celebrity's megaliners—but they are well-equipped.

The main pool area has four whirlpools on the *Vision* (two on the *Legend*), and there are two more in the Solarium. Glass windbreaks out on deck shelter an observatory (complete with star-gazing equipment). Both ships offer cushioned jogging tracks, and the *Legend* boasts an 18-hole miniature golf course, complete with trees, sand traps, and water hazards. Both also have small basketball courts.

Radiance of the Seas

Size (in tons)	90,000	Officers	Norwegian/Int'l
Number of Cabins	1,050	Crew	859
Number of Outside Cabins	813	Passenger/Crew Ratio	2.4 to 1
Cabins with Verandas	577	Year Built	2001
Number of Passengers	2,100	Last Major Refurbishment	n/a

This ship is Royal Caribbean's first vessel of the 21st century, as well as being the first in a new class, and continues the line's tradition of being an innovator in the industry with such features as a billiards room with custom-made, self-leveling tables (in case there are big waves), and a revolving bar in the disco.

The ship is designed to remind guests they are at sea and, to that extent, features literally walls of glass through which to view the passing Alaska scenery. You won't even miss the views when you are in the 12-story lobby elevators because they, too, are made of glass and face the ocean—even the Internet cafe is oceanview.

This ship is slightly more upscale than the line's other vessels. (Royal Caribbean seems to have borrowed a page from sister company, Celebrity.) It features wood, marble, and lots of nice fabrics and artwork, adding up to a pretty, low-key decor that lets the views provide most of the drama.

CABINS Cabins on this vessel are larger than on the *Vision* and *Legend*—the smallest is 170 square feet—and more come with verandas than on the earlier vessels. All cabins are equipped with an interactive TV, telephone, computer jack, vanity table, refrigerator/minibar, and hair dryer. Suites also come with a veranda, a sitting area with a sofa bed, a dry bar, a stereo and VCR, and a bathtub and double sinks. The Royal Suite has a separate bedroom (with a king-size bed) and living room, a whirlpool bathtub, and a baby grand piano. Family cabins and suites can accommodate five. Fourteen cabins are wheelchair-accessible.

Cabins & Rates

Cabins	Brochure Rates	Bathtub	Fridge	Hair Dryer	Sitting Area	TV
Inside	$1,879–$2,249	no	yes	yes	no	yes
Outside	$2,479–$3,079	no	yes	yes	some	yes
Suite	$3,749–$9,749	yes	yes	yes	yes	yes

PUBLIC AREAS This ship is full of little surprises. There's a billiards room, and a card club where five tables are dedicated to poker. (The others are for bridge, chess, and so on.) You can, of course, also find more gaming options in the ship's massive French Art Nouveau–inspired Casino Royale. Bookworms will want to check out the ship's combo bookstore and coffee shop (a first at sea), and virtual worms will head for the Internet center.

The numerous cushy bars and lounges include a champagne bar and piano bar. If you get sick of oceanviews, you can view eight decks below into the atrium from a porthole-like window in the floor of the Crown and Anchor Lounge. The ship's Viking Crown Lounge holds the disco with its revolving bar, as well as an intimate cabaret area. The three-level theater is designed to recall the glacial landscapes of not Alaska but the North Pole. The elegant two-level main dining room features a grand staircase but is a rather noisy space. Casual meals are offered in both the buffet-style Windjammer Cafe and Seaview Cafe (where you order from a casual menu), and the ship also boasts two alternative, reservations-only restaurants: Chops Grill, featuring steaks and chops, and Portofino, featuring Italian cuisine. Pizza is served in the Solarium. Other public rooms include a show lounge, conference center, library, shopping mall, and business center. For kids, there's a children's center equipped with computer and crafts stations, and teens get their own hangout space. There's also a video arcade.

POOL, SPA & FITNESS FACILITIES For the active sort, there's a rock-climbing wall and 9-hole golf course (the latter themed on a baroque garden, of all things), a nice spa (including sauna and steam rooms), an oceanview fitness center with dozens of machines (including 18 Stairmaster treadmills), a jogging track, a sports court (including basketball), golf simulators (for those who like to play virtual golf), and three swimming pools—one outside, one enclosed (the indoor pool features an African theme complete with 17-ft.-high stone elephants and cascading waterfalls), and the third a teen/kiddie pool with slide. Whirlpools can be found in the Solarium and near the outdoor pool.

9 Seabourn Cruise Line

SHIP Seabourn Spirit

6100 Blue Lagoon Dr., Ste. 400, Miami, FL 33126. *C* **800/929-9595** or 305/463-3000. Fax 305/463-3010. www.seabourn.com.

Small and intimate, Seabourn's sleek modern *Spirit* is a floating pleasure palace, rewarding all onboard with extraordinary service and some of the finest cuisine at sea.

THE EXPERIENCE   Seabourn is a genuine aristocrat with perfect manners and a high degree of sophistication, and the *Spirit,* its representative in Alaska this year, reflects the company's philosophy. The small, super-luxurious ship has unprecedented amounts of onboard space and staff for each passenger, service worthy of the grand hotels of Europe, and the hushed, ever-so-polite ambience that appeals to prosperous, usually older passengers who appreciate the emphasis on their individual pleasures.

Pros

- **Top-shelf service.** The staff seems to be able to anticipate guests' every need—and there are more staff people per passenger than on most other lines. Not only are there a lot of them, but also they're uniformly professional, polished, and champing at the bit to please.
- **Excellent cuisine.** Rivaling the best land-based restaurants, Seabourn's cuisine is exquisite, with creative, flavorful, well-presented dishes complemented by an extensive wine list.
- **Large cabins.** The accommodations are not mere cabins but roomy suites, with cushy features, such as walk-in closets, bathtubs, quality bath amenities from Molton Brown of London, personalized stationery, and complimentary stocked minibars.
- **Free booze.** Liquor and wine are included in the price.

Cons

- **Limited activities.** If you need things to do around the clock, forget about it. The Seabourn ships have limited organized activities onboard (although those they do have are good). For the most part, guests are content with socializing over cocktails and catching up on their reading.
- **Shallow drafts, rocky seas.** If you happen to be sailing through rough water, you'll know it. These small ships get tossed around more than the megas. In the mostly protected waters of the Inside Passage, though, this is less likely to be a serious problem.
- **Few or no private verandas.** It's unfortunate that the Seabourn ships have only six private balconies apiece. (The line tried to correct the situation by adding narrow French balconies with sliding-glass doors onto 36 cabins on each ship, but it's not the same thing as having your own private outdoor space.)

THE FLEET   Although the Seabourn *Spirit* is the only ship in the fleet that will set sail in Alaska, it is every bit as classy and every bit as desirable as its fleetmates, *Pride* and *Legend.* Virtually identical, these three ships represent the very

Seabourn Fleet Itineraries

Ship	Itinerary
Seabourn Spirit	**10-day Gulf of Alaska between Vancouver and Seward:** Visiting College Fjord, Hubbard Glacier, Sitka, Skagway, Juneau, Ketchikan, and Misty Fjords. **10- and 11-day Inside Passage:** Round-trips from Vancouver, visiting Victoria, Misty Fjords, Wrangell, Tracy Arm, Juneau, Skagway, Ketchikan, and Sitka.

best of just about everything in cruising. They weigh 10,000 tons and carry 208 passengers.

PASSENGER PROFILE Most have more than comfortable household incomes, usually in excess of $250,000. Many are retired (or never worked to begin with), and many have net worths in the millions—and sometimes much higher. The majority of passengers are couples, but there is always a handful of singles as well, usually widows or widowers. Few seem to come aboard with children or grandchildren in tow.

In many ways, the passenger roster looks like the membership of a posh country club, where old money judges new money. Most passengers are North American and dress expensively, though not, of course, flashily. Many passengers are not excessively chatty, giddy, or outgoing. They are likely to have sailed aboard other luxury cruise lines and stayed in five-star hotels. Passengers expect to receive good service in an atmosphere of discreet gentility.

The line's history of repeaters is among the highest in the industry, sometimes as many as 50% aboard any given cruise.

DINING Cuisine is one of Seabourn's strongest points, matching what you'd find in a world-class European resort hotel. Meals are served in a manner that satisfies both the appetite and the expectation of high-class service. Dining is offered in a single seating, and the ships have an open-seating policy that allows guests to dine whenever they choose and with whomever they want, within a window of several hours at each mealtime. Dinner service is high-style and extremely formal. Men are expected to wear jackets and, on most evenings, neckties as well. There will be at least 2 formal nights on each Alaska cruise. At these, virtually every male present appears in a tuxedo. The dining room staff serves an elaborate, six-course meal.

If your mood doesn't call for the dining room, the ship has an **alternative dining option**—the Veranda Café—at no extra charge, of course. Here, they serve bountiful breakfasts every morning, with omelets made fresh to your specifications. At lunchtime, you'll find salads, sandwich makings, fresh pasta, and maybe jumbo shrimp, smoked salmon, and smoked oysters on the cold side and hot sliced roast beef, duck, and ham on the carving board.

Room service is available 24 hours a day. During normal lunch or dinner hours, your private meal can mirror the dining room service, right down to the silver, crystal, and porcelain. After hours, the menu is more limited, with burgers, salads, sandwiches, and pastas. And whenever a cruise itinerary calls for a full-day stopover on a remote island, a lavish beach barbecue might be whipped up at midday.

ACTIVITIES You won't find the bingo, karaoke, or the silly poolside contests featured by mass-market lines. The atmosphere is ever-tasteful and unobtrusive. Activities include card games and tournaments, trivia contests, tours of the ship's galley, visits to the cozy library, and watching movies in your cabin. You'll soon realize that many passengers are aboard to read or to quietly converse with their peers while being ushered from one stylish spot to the next.

That said, you don't have to be sedentary, either. The *Spirit* has a **retractable watersports marina** that unfolds from the stern, weather and sea conditions permitting. From the marina, passengers can enter the sea for water-skiing, windsurfing, sailing, snorkeling, and swimming. How much use the marina gets in Alaska depends very much on the weather.

Passengers may send e-mails to friends and loved ones through the Radio Officer for $5 per message. Or they can do it themselves by using onboard computers that also allow them to surf the Web. The cost: 95¢ a minute.

CHILDREN'S PROGRAM   The *Seabourn Spirit* is not geared to children, although they are permitted. You may occasionally see a younger child—probably a very bored child, as the line provides no special programs, no special menus, and no special concessions for children.

In a pinch, you may be able to arrange babysitting with an available crew member.

ENTERTAINMENT   Entertainment is not Seabourn's strong suit, but if you're happy with a singer, pianist, or duo doing most of the entertaining, you'll be pleased enough. On this ship, a resident dance band or music duo performs a roster of favorites, while the mellow piano bar is always a good option.

The ship has a small-scale, staid, and rather un-casino-like **casino** with a couple of blackjack tables and a handful of slots.

SERVICE   Seabourn maintains the finest service staff of any line afloat. Overall, they are charming, competent, sensitive, and discreet—among Seabourn's most valuable assets.

Cabin minibars are stocked with wine, liquor of the guest's choice, and soft drinks upon check-in. Fleetwide, complimentary wine is served with lunch and dinner. All drinks in public bars and lounges are complimentary. Seabourn's cruise prices, though high, are about as all-inclusive as you can get. Across the fleet, gratuities are officially included in the cruise fare, but staff is not prohibited from accepting additional tips, and some passengers do tip. **Laundry** and **dry cleaning** are available. There is also a self-service laundry room on the *Spirit.*

CRUISE TOUR & ADD-ON PROGRAMS   Seabourn offers Denali Park tours (Anchorage–Fairbanks) in conjunction with the Gulf of Alaska cruises of the *Spirit.* Full details of these programs were not known at press time.

Seabourn Spirit

Size (in tons)	10,000	Officers	Norwegian
Number of Cabins	100	Crew	140 (International)
Number of Outside Cabins	100	Passenger/Crew Ratio	1.5 to 1
Cabins with Verandas	6	Year Built	1989
Number of Passengers	208	Last Major Refurbishment	n/a

The *Seabourn Spirit's* understated, beautifully designed ship represents luxury cruising at its very best, going everywhere one would ever want to cruise. Passengers who like to be social and meet others with similar interests will find plenty of opportunities to do so at open-seating meals, in the intimate public rooms, and out on deck. On the other hand, if you want to get away from it all, you can also be completely private in your spacious suite, at a table for two in the restaurant, or in a quiet corner of the deck.

CABINS   The great majority of the accommodations are handsomely designed "Type A," 277-square-foot, one-room suites. (For comparison, an average cabin on, say, Carnival is 190 sq. ft.) The lounge area's coffee table rises to dining table height, and you can order hors d'oeuvres, such as caviar and smoked salmon, at no extra charge, making these suites ideal for entertaining. Closet space is more than adequate for hanging clothes, but drawer space is more limited.

The **Classic Suites** measure 400 square feet, and two pairs of Owner's Suites are 530 and 575 square feet. These have the only (small) verandas on the ship. French balconies with sliding-glass doors (read: no space for sitting or standing) are to be found in some of the suites (the 277-sq.-ft. Type A suites on the top two decks).

The **Owner's Suites** have dining rooms and guest powder rooms. As any cabin positioned near the bow of relatively small ships such as these, these forward-facing suites can be somewhat uncomfortable during rough seas. The dark-wood furnishings give the overall feeling of a hotel room more than a ship's suite. Regal Suites, at 554 square feet, are simply a combination of two 277-square-foot Seabourn suites, with one room given completely over to a lounge.

Everything about a Seabourn cabin has the impeccably maintained feel of an upscale Scandinavian hotel. Each unit contains a stocked bar; walk-in closet; safe; hair dryer; VCR and TV broadcasting CNN and ESPN, among other channels; crystal glasses for every kind of drink; terry-cloth robes; and fresh fruit daily. VHS movies are available from the ship's library, and the purser's office broadcasts films from the ship's own collection. Tasteful color schemes are either ice-blue- or champagne-colored, with lots of bleached oak or birch trim, as well as mirrors and a sophisticated bank of spotlights.

Owner's Suites 05 and 06 have obstructed views. There are four wheelchair-accessible suites.

Cabins & Rates

Cabins	Brochure Rates	Bathtub	Fridge	Hair Dryer	Sitting Area	TV
Suites	$6,659–$17,959*	yes	yes	yes	yes	yes

For 10-night Alaska cruise.

PUBLIC AREAS   An attractive double, open spiral staircase links the public areas, which are, to be frank, a bit duller than you'd expect on a ship of this caliber. For the most part, they're spare and almost ordinary looking. Art and ornamentation are conspicuous by their absence. It's almost as if, in the zeal to create conservative decors, management couldn't decide on the appropriate artwork and, so, omitted it completely.

The forward-facing observation lounge on Sky Deck offers an attractive, quiet venue all day long for reading, a drink before meals, cards, and afternoon tea. A chart and compass will help you find out where the ship is currently positioned, and a computerized wall map lets you track future cruises.

The Club lounge and bar, with an aft-facing position, is the ship's principal social center, with music, a small band, a singer and/or pianist, and fancy hot hors d'oeuvres before and after dinner. Next door, behind glass, is the ship's casino, with gaming tables and a separate small room for slot machines. The semicircular and tiered formal lounge on the deck below is the venue for lectures, pianists, and the captain's parties.

The formal restaurant, located on the lowest deck, is a large, low-ceilinged room with an open-seating policy. The Veranda Café, open for breakfast, lunch, and, except on formal nights, dinner, is an intimate, well-designed indoor/outdoor facility.

One of the best places for a romantic, moonlit moment is the isolated patch of deck at the far forward bow on the Magellan Deck.

POOL, RECREATION & FITNESS FACILITIES   The outdoor pool, not much used, is awkwardly situated in a shadowy location aft of the open Lido Deck, between the twin engine uptakes; it's flanked by lifeboats that hang from both sides of the ship. A pair of whirlpools are located just forward of the pool. There's a third hot tub perched on the far forward bow deck. It's isolated and a perfect spot (as is the whole patch of deck here) from which to watch the landscape or a port come into sight or fade away.

A retractable, wood-planked watersports marina opens out from the stern of the ship so passengers can hop into sea kayaks or go windsurfing, water-skiing, or snorkeling right from the ship. An attached steel-mesh net creates a saltwater pool when the marina is in use. The gym and Steiner-managed spa are roomy for ships this small and are located forward of the Lido. There is a separate aerobics area, plus two saunas, massage rooms, and a beauty salon.

10 World Explorer Cruises

SHIP   Universe Explorer

555 Montgomery St., San Francisco, CA 94111-2544. ☏ **800/854-3835** or 415/393-1565. Fax 415/391-1145. www.wecruise.com.

Among the large-ship lines in Alaska, World Explorer offers the only experience that we can honestly call one-of-a-kind. Education-oriented and port-intensive, it's almost closer to the small-ship experience, getting you close to the real Alaska, but also gives passengers numerous onboard options.

THE EXPERIENCE   World Explorer's education-oriented, 740-passenger *Universe Explorer* is not the biggest ship in the market, or the newest; it's not the most luxurious; and it maybe doesn't provide the same level of cuisine of some of its more upscale rivals. What it does give you, though, is an incredible itinerary, an educational lecture series, an atmosphere of friendly informality, and some truly high-caliber shore excursions. Options include bike-and-hike tours at every port for people who want to see the sites on an active basis.

World Explorer is the only major cruise ship that visits Kodiak, famous for its bear population, and the Tsimshian Indian village of Metlakatla, the only federal reservation in Alaska for indigenous people.

Glitzy, Broadway-style entertainment; a casino; a disco; formal nights: These are the things you won't find on the Universe Explorer. Opera and folk music, lectures by people who know their subject, art classes, singalongs, and more ports and lots of time in them: These are the things you will find.

Pros

- **Amazing itinerary.** The *Universe Explorer* specializes in 14-night round-trip cruises out of Vancouver—the only round-trips of that length out of the British Columbia gateway—that offer all of the popular ports of call along with a few less-visited ports for good measure.

- **Giant library.** Honorable mention in the Best Features department has to go to the ship's 15,000-volume library, with many volumes on nature and history.
- **Onboard lecture schedule.** Anthropologists, biologists, historians, Native American artists/storytellers, and others are onboard, educating passengers about their destinations.

Cons

- **Ship shows its wrinkles.** The line's one ship is aged (in ship terms), so if you're looking for a big, state-of-the-art glitz-machine, look elsewhere.
- **Few high-end accommodations.** The ship has only four suites and no cabins with verandas.
- **So-so service.** Service is warm and attentive but hardly as polished as in the finest ship dining rooms or the best hotels.

THE FLEET   The 739-passenger *Universe Explorer* is, shall we say, mature, having been built during the Eisenhower administration (1958, to be exact). World Explorer chartered the vessel from Commodore Cruises, in whose fleet it sailed as the *Enchanted Seas,* and spent a chunk of money on renovations after taking delivery, but there are only so many things you can do with a ship with that much mileage on it.

PASSENGER PROFILE   The *Universe Explorer* in the past tended to attract an older clientele (it caters to seniors by offering AARP discounts of up to 20%), though the average age is declining due to family-oriented offerings including the bike-and-hike/cruise options we mentioned above. It's not unusual for the ship to sail with between, say, 15 and 30 teens and preteens onboard. There is a youth program and a team of counselors to keep the kids out of mischief (and out of Mom and Dad's hair) while at sea. The line is also making a push for singles, offering fair single rates without a supplement in cabin categories D, E , F, and G. Passengers overall are attracted by price, the ship's casual atmosphere, and the opportunity to learn something about Alaska. Many arrive with binoculars and spend as much time as possible on the ample open deck areas searching for wildlife and calling other passengers over when they spot something.

DINING   The food is good and nobody leaves the table hungry, but the cuisine could never be mistaken for gourmet. Breakfast and luncheon buffets, on the promenade deck, lack variety when compared with those of the other ships in the Alaska market, but they're fine for anybody who just wants to nibble. The dining room offers a wider selection of dishes—generally a fish plate (including Dungeness crab one night), meat or chicken in some form, and vegetarian, pasta, and light options, with a salad and a choice of appetizers and dessert. There are also themed nights, including Chinese and Italian.

The best meals, however, are the fish grill and steak grill, offered outside on the pool deck on designated nights as an alternative to eating in the dining room. Also not to be missed are the afternoon teas, offering a plentiful array of snacks including themed offerings—dim sum one day, Mexican treats another.

This is not a ship where you dress up for dinner—there are no formal nights.

ACTIVITIES   Ecology and the cultures of Alaska are big on the ship's lecture-circuit log, with anthropologists, biologists, historians, Native American artists/storytellers, and others onboard. For the particularly studious, the line

World Explorer Fleet Itineraries

Ship	Itinerary
Universe Explorer	**14-night Inside Passage/Gulf of Alaska:** Round-trip from Vancouver, visiting Juneau, Skagway, Glacier Bay, Hubbard Glacier, Seward, Ketchikan, Sitka, Victoria, Valdez, and Wrangell, and on select voyages Metlakatla and Kodiak. **8-night Inside Passage:** Roundtrip from Vancouver, visiting Ketchikan, Sitka, Skagway, Juneau, Metlakatla, and Misty Fjords. **9-night Inside Passage:** Roundtrip from Vancouver, visiting Ketchikan, Juneau, Skagway, Glacier Bay, Sitka, Metlakatla, and Misty Fjords.

offers an optional Enhanced Education Program: For a fee of $180 to $240 per person, up to 40 participants get special attention from the lecture staff, including small classes and personally guided field trips with the experts. The ship also boasts a 150-seat cinema for movie-watching (free popcorn is offered, and you can buy a beer and take it in with you), as well as a 24-terminal computer learning center (you can take five classes on such topics as word processing, graphics, and the Internet at no cost). You can also send or receive e-mail from a shipboard account for 75¢ a minute. Fitness classes are offered on deck or in the main show lounge, and those attending get prizes at the end of the cruise. More group fun comes in the form of bingo and horse racing, shuffleboard, and bridge tournaments, a passenger talent show and costume parade, and silly contests.

CHILDREN'S PROGRAM   Kids are entertained with crafts, games, movies, and Nintendo, offered in a small, unadorned, converted meeting room, now dedicated to the youth program.

ENTERTAINMENT   One night it might be a string quartet, the next a folk-singing duo with guitar and dulcimer. A classical pianist may be the headliner on another occasion, and an operatic soprano may find her way into the program as well. There are performances by a cabaret singer, and the *Universe Explorer* Orchestra performs for your dancing pleasure. (There are gentlemen hosts onboard to keep unescorted ladies happy.) Late-night revelers, of which there may be few, can enjoy piano tunes and open-mike nights.

SERVICE   Service on the ship is very friendly and caring, and that's just fine given the ship's overall casual ambience. Don't expect French table service and white-gloved butlers.

   Laundry service (only $6 for a bag of laundry) and **dry cleaning** are available.

CRUISETOUR & ADD-ON PROGRAMS   New in 2002 is a Rocky Mountaineer Rail Tour, available pre- or post-cruise. The 3-night, pre-cruise tour is from Calgary to Vancouver and includes 1 night on the train, an overnight visit to Kamloops, and a night in Vancouver with a Vancouver City tour; it's priced at $778 per person, plus the cruise fare. The 5-night, post-cruise tour is from Vancouver to Calgary and includes an overnight on the train, an overnight in Kamloops, an overnight in Whistler, an overnight in Banff, and an overnight in Calgary; it's priced at $1,048 per person, plus the cruise fare. Add-on hotel stays are available in Vancouver. Rates start at about $90 per person in Vancouver, with an optional city tour.

Universe Explorer

Size (in tons)	23,500	Officers	Int'l
Number of Cabins	368	Crew	330
Number of Outside Cabins	290	Passenger/Crew Ratio	2.2 to 1
Cabins with Verandas	0	Year Built	1958
Number of Passengers	739	Last Major Refurbishment	1995

Mississippi-built for South American cruising, this ship, in its most recent previous life, was the *Enchanted Seas* of Commodore Cruises. World Explorer took over the vessel 6 years ago, renamed it *Universe Explorer*, and gave it an extensive cosmetic face-lift. The ship also got a safety upgrade that included the addition of a state-of-the-art sprinkler system.

The vessel sails in Alaska from May to August, and offers a couple of 18-day Panama Canal/Central America cruises, and the rest of the year is the floating campus for Semester at Sea, a college program affiliated with the University of Pittsburgh. Because of this connection, the ship has some rather quirky design features. For instance, what was once the casino is now a 15,000-volume research library (university-style, with metal bookcases) and a computer room. Throughout the ship, including in cabin areas, there are small lounge areas with TVs that are used for classes and student gathering places in the off-season, but also make nice quiet hideaways for cruise ship passengers as well. (Many boast windows.)

During the cruise season, World Explorer keeps the ship in good shape. (The artwork and better furniture are put away when the students are onboard.) The vessel has some comfortable but not spectacular public spaces and adequate if not palatial cabins. It's a good buy for those who don't want frills and frippery or too much dressing up and who don't expect the last word in pampering. It's not recommended for debutantes or Vegas-style high rollers.

CABINS　The bulk of the ship is taken up with double-occupancy rooms with twin beds (convertible to queen-size). Some also are capable of accommodating third passengers in foldaway sofa beds. The smallest are pretty darned small—starting at about 140 square feet, although many are 170 square feet. All the cabins have TVs and telephones, and outside cabins have either picture windows or portholes. (Some have views partially obstructed by lifeboats.) Bedspreads and curtains were recently updated, but don't look for any deluxe amenities. No Jacuzzis, no walk-in closets, and no private verandas. But more than 50 cabins come with bathtubs—a relative rarity on ships today. Cabins on Boat Deck overlook the Promenade (close your curtains if you don't want walkers and joggers peeping in), and if you're a late sleeper you may want to avoid the cabins under the metal sports court.

The cabins designated as superior all have sitting areas, refrigerators, TVs with VCRs, and showers, and two of them have bathtubs as well. Two cabins are wheelchair-accessible.

Cabins & Rates

Cabins	Brochure Rates	Bathtub	Fridge	Hair Dryer	Sitting Area	TV
Inside	$1,525–$2,995*	some	no	no	no	yes
Outside	$2,245–$3,995*	some	no	no	some	yes

For 14-night Alaska cruise.

PUBLIC AREAS By today's standards, the *Universe Explorer*'s public areas are fairly few and spartan in their decor. There's a comfortable main show lounge that serves as the hub of ship activity, with lectures and shows from this venue broadcast on in-cabin TV thanks to a fixed video camera.

The updated St. George's Watch lounge faces forward (it's above the bridge) and is the ship's nicest lounge; in the off-season, it doubles as the faculty lounge. There's a large piano bar, several small lounges and alcoves that offer quiet relaxation areas but do not offer drink service, and a card room and cinema. The updated dining room has the nifty coral displays in glass cases. There's a meeting room that doubles as a children's playroom for the kids.

POOL, SPA & FITNESS FACILITIES The small beauty salon and massage area offers massages for only $65 an hour. There's a gym, too, but it's located literally in a metal shack up on the top deck, with a stationary bike, a few treadmills, and a handful of weights.

6

The Cruise Lines, Part 2: The Small Ships

Whereas big ships allow you to see Alaska while immersed in a vibrant, resort-like atmosphere, small ships allow you to see it from the waterline, without distraction from anything un-Alaskan—no glitzy interiors, no big shows or loud music, no casinos, no spas, and no crowds, as the largest of these ships carries only 138 passengers. You're immersed in the 49th state from the minute you wake up to the minute you fall asleep, and for the most part, you're left alone to form your own opinions.

Small ships also allow you to visit more isolated parts of the coast. Thanks to their smaller size and shallow draft (the amount of hull below the waterline), these ships can go places larger ships can't, and they have the flexibility to change their itineraries as opportunities arise—say, to go where whales have been sighted. Depending on the itinerary, ports of call might include popular stops such as Sitka or Ketchikan, tiny towns such as Elfin Cove or Warm Springs Harbor, or a Tlingit Native village such as Kake, and all itineraries include **glacier- and whale-watching.** Most of them also build in time to explore the wilder parts of Alaska, ferrying passengers ashore for **hikes in wilderness areas** and, in some cases, carrying **sea kayaks** for passenger use. Rather than glitzy entertainment, you'll likely get **informal lectures** and, sometimes, video presentations on Alaskan wildlife, history, and Native culture. In most cases, at least some shore excursions are included in your cruise fare. (An exception is Clipper, which charges extra.) Meals are served in open seatings, so you can sit where and with whom you like, and time spent huddled on the outside decks scanning for whales fosters great camaraderie among passengers.

Cabins on these ships don't generally offer TVs or telephones and tend to be very small and sometimes spartan. (See the individual reviews for exceptions.) There are no stabilizers on most of these smaller ships, so the ride can be bumpy in rough seas.

Of the small ships, only Cruise West's *Spirit of '98* and *Spirit of Oceanus* and Clipper's *Clipper Odyssey* are even moderately wheelchair-friendly. Most do not have e-mail access of any kind. (The *Clipper Odyssey* does.) These small ships may not be the best choice for families with children, unless those kids are avid nature buffs and are able to keep themselves entertained without a lot of outside stimuli.

READING THE REVIEWS

See the explanation of itineraries, prices, and ship reviews at the beginning of chapter 5, which applies equally to this chapter. In this chapter, you'll also see the following terms used to describe the various small-ship experiences:

- **Soft Adventure:** These ships don't provide grandeur, organized activities, or entertainment but instead give you a really close-up Alaska experience. These ships often avoid large ports.
- **Active Adventure:** These ships function less like cruise ships than like base camps. Passengers use them only to sleep and eat, getting off the ship for hiking and kayaking excursions every day.
- **Port-to-Port:** These ships are for people who want to visit the popular Alaska ports (and some lesser-known ones) but also want the flexible schedules and maneuverability of a small ship and a more homey experience than aboard a glitzy big ship.

TIPPING

Tipping on small ships is a little different than on big ships. Tips on the following vessels are pooled among the crew. Below is a rundown of suggested tips. (You are free to move the numbers up or down as you see fit.)

Suggested tips, per passenger, for a 1-week cruise:

- **American Yacht Safari:** 5% to 10% of the cost of the cruise
- **Clipper:** $70 (or $10 per day), plus tips to bartenders at your discretion
- **Cruise West:** $70 (or $10 per day)
- **Glacier Bay Cruise Line:** $84 to $105 (or $12–$15 per day)
- **Lindblad Expeditions:** $56 to $70 (or $8–$10 per day)

Note: Rates in these reviews are brochure rates. Some discounts may apply, including early booking and last-minute offers, although small-ship lines do not discount their fares, traditionally, as much as bigger ship lines.

1 American Safari Cruises

SHIPS   Escape • Quest • Spirit

19101 36th Ave. W., Ste. 201, Lynnwood, WA 98036. ℭ **888/862-8881.** Fax 425/776-8889. www.american safaricruises.com.

Directed to the slightly jaded high-end traveler, American Safari Cruises sails luxury soft-adventure cruises aboard three full-fledged luxury yachts.

THE EXPERIENCE   American Safari Cruises promises an intimate, all-inclusive yacht cruise to some of the more out-of-the-way stretches of the Inside Passage. The price is considerable, as is the pampering. The company books only 12 to 22 people per cruise, guaranteeing unparalleled flexibility, intimacy, and privacy. Once passenger interests become apparent, the expedition leader shapes the cruise around them. Black-bear aficionados can chug off in a Zodiac boat for a better look; active adventurers can explore the shoreline in one of the yacht's four kayaks; and lazier travelers can relax aboard ship. A crew-to-passenger ratio of about one to two ensures that a cold drink, a clever meal, or a sharp eagle-spotting eye is always nearby on the line's comfortable 120-foot ships.

Pros

- **Almost private experience.** With only one or two dozen fellow passengers, it's like having a yacht to yourself.
- **Built-in shore excursions.** All off-ship excursions, including a flightseeing trip, are included in the cruise fare, as are drinks.
- **Night anchorages.** A great boon to light sleepers is that the route taken allows time for the vessels to overnight at anchor, making for quieter sleeping than aboard most ships, which travel through the night.

American Safari Cruises Fleet Itineraries

Ship	Itinerary
Safari Escape	**7-night Inside Passage:** North- and southbound between Juneau and Sitka, visiting Tracy Arm, Admiralty Island, Frederick Sound, Thomas Bay, Petersburg (with LeConte Glacier flightseeing trip included), the Native village of Kake, Red Bluff Bay on Baranof Island, Warm Springs Bay, Chatham Channel, and Schultz Bay.*
Safari Quest	**7-night Inside Passage:** North- and southbound between Juneau and Sitka, visiting Tracy Arm, Admiralty Island, Frederick Sound, Thomas Bay, Petersburg (with LeConte Glacier flightseeing trip included), the Native village of Kake, Red Bluff Bay on Baranof Island, Warm Springs Bay, Chatham Channel, and Schultz Bay.*
Safari Spirit	**7-night Inside Passage:** North- and southbound between Juneau and Prince Rupert (B.C.), visiting Foggy Cove (B.C.), Ketchikan, Misty Fjords, Traitors Cove, Meyers Chuck, Wrangell Narrows, Canoe Cove, Petersburg, Frederick Sound, and Tracy Arm; includes a picnic and nature hike on the Brothers Islands and black-bear-watching in Foggy Bay.

* In addition to the itineraries above, all three boats offer 10-night repositioning cruises between Vancouver and Juneau in spring (May 8 for Spirit, May 1 for Quest, May 22 for Escape) and Juneau and Vancouver in September (Sept 14 for Quest, Sept 7 for Spirit and Escape). Rates start at $3,695 (Quest), $5,795 (Spirit) and $6,195 (Escape). Note that the rates for these shoulder-season cruises are actually the same as the 7-night cruises on the Quest and Spirit, and the longer cruises are actually cheaper on the Escape.

Cons

- **The price.** Shore excursions and drinks are included, but even when you remove these costs, the price is still high. You pay for all that luxury.

THE FLEET The 22-passenger *Safari Quest* (1992), 12-passenger *Safari Spirit* (1981), and new-to-the-fleet 12-passenger *Safari Escape* (rebuilt 2001) are the closest things you'll find to private yachts in the Alaska cruise business. They're sleek, they're stylish, and they're as far as you can get from the megaship experience without owning your own boat.

PASSENGER PROFILE Passengers—almost always couples—tend to be more than comfortably wealthy and range from about 45 to 65 years of age. Most hope to get close to nature without sacrificing luxury. They've paid handsomely for food, drink, and service, all of which are sweetly close to overwhelming. Dress is always casual, with comfort being the prime goal.

An advantage of the ships' small size is that if you can round up enough friends, you can rent the ships as full charters, for which good discounts are available.

DINING A shipboard chef assails guests with multiple-course meals and clever snacks (wild-mushroom cups, rack of lamb, thyme-infused king salmon, amaretto cheesecake, fresh-baked bread), barters with nearby fishing boats for the catch of the day, and raids local markets for the freshest fruits and vegetables—say, strawberries the size of a cub's paw and potent strains of basil and cilantro. Between meals, snacks such as Gorgonzola and brie with pears, walnuts, and table crackers are set out. Guests may always serve themselves from the ludicrously well-stocked bar, which during our visit had two kinds of sherry and four brands of gin alone.

ACTIVITIES When passengers aren't eating or drinking, an expedition leader is rousing them into Zodiac boats or kayaks to investigate shoreline black bears or prancing river otters, or to navigate fjords packed with ice floes and lolling seals. Expeditions include trips to boardwalked cannery towns and Tlingit villages, where local people receive the yachts more personally and gracefully than they might a larger ship. Activities throughout the day are well spaced, with many opportunities to see wildlife.

From time to time, local bush pilots may swoop down for a landing beside the ships and take two or three passengers for a whirl over a glacier or a nearby fjord. Because these are private operations, they're not included in the cruise fare.

CHILDREN'S PROGRAM   None—these aren't ships for kids, unless you charter the whole thing and bring your extended family. (The ships are small enough that that's a realistic option for some, but it'll cost you in excess of $63,000 to take over one of them in the shoulder season, rising to a cool $130,000 or so in the peak period.)

ENTERTAINMENT   A big-screen TV in the main lounge forms a natural center for impromptu lectures during the day and movie-watching at night. Guests may choose from a library of 100-odd videotapes (guests in the Owner's and Captain's staterooms have TV/VCRs in their cabins) or opt for a casual game of cards or Scrabble in the public rooms upstairs.

At the beginning or end of a trip, the crew and passengers gather for an all-you-can-eat salmon bake and local saloon crawl, and from time to time, the ship docks at a town with a measure of nightlife—at the least, you'll get to shoot a game of pool and have a drink among the locals.

SERVICE   Crew members cosset the passengers cheerfully and discreetly, fussing over such details as the level of cilantro in lunchtime dishes or making elaborate cocktails from the fully stocked open bar. They've even been known to call ahead to upcoming anchorages to arrange for a passenger's favorite brand of beer to be brought aboard. Laundry service is not available onboard except in "emergency situations." (The company recommends, by the way, a crew gratuity of 5%–10% at the end of each voyage, a hefty sum when you're paying, say, $3,500–$7,500 or so for a cruise.)

CRUISETOURS & ADD-ON PROGRAMS   Anchorage/Talkeetna/Denali/Fairbanks tour includes two nights at the Denali Wilderness Lodge, billed as the world's most remote lodge, reachable only by bush plane. Available as a pre- or post-cruise add-on, it's priced at $4,695 per person, double, plus the cruise fare. There is also a pre- or post-cruise hotel program offering rooms in Prince Rupert (for $119), Juneau (for $175), and Sitka (for $119).

Safari Escape • Safari Quest • Safari Spirit

Size (in tons)	n/a*	Officers	American
Number of Cabins	6/11/6	Crew	6/9/7 (American)
Number of Outside Cabins	6/11/6	Passenger/Crew Ratio	2 to 1 (approx.)
Cabins with Verandas	0	Year Built	1983/1992/1981
Number of Passengers	12/22/12	Last Major Refurbishment	2001/2000/2000

* These ships' sizes were measured using a different scale than the others in this book, so comparison is not possible.

More private yachts than cruise ships, American Safari Cruise's vessels are an oddity in the cruise community: One old tar we met called them "Tupperware ships," a pretty accurate description for their exceedingly sleek, contoured, Ferrari-looking exteriors. Inside, there are very few areas out of bounds, lending to the feel that you're vacationing on an impossibly rich friend's space-age yacht.

CABINS   Sleeping quarters are comfortable and clean, with large, firm beds; adequate light; and art (of varying quality) on the walls. Bathrooms are roomy, even in the standard cabins. The showers shoot a steady but not spectacular stream of reliably hot water. The Owner's Stateroom has a large picture window, a small sitting area, and a 13-inch TV/VCR. Unless you plan to make frequent use of the sitting space in the Owner's Stateroom, the Captain's Stateroom—smaller but not at all cramped—is probably a better deal. Down below, deluxe rooms are tidy, filled with a surprising amount of natural light, and fairly spacious.

There are no special facilities for travelers with disabilities and no cabins designed specifically for single occupancy.

Cabins & Rates

Cabins	Brochure Rates	Bathtub	Fridge	Hair Dryer	Sitting Area	TV
Outside	$3,695–$7,995*	no	no	yes	some	yes

* The lowest fares are for Quest itineraries. Rates include all shore excursions.

PUBLIC AREAS   Sitting rooms are intimate and luxurious, almost as if they had been transported whole from a spacious suburban home. Four or five prime vantages for spotting wildlife (one is a hot tub!) ensure as little or as much privacy as you desire. All public rooms have generous panoramic views for cold or inclement weather. All three meals are served on a wooden table in a casual room, usually when the ship is at anchor. Expect paper napkins at lunch and cloth serviettes at dinner. There are 24-hour coffee/tea facilities, a fully stocked open bar, and a small library/video library.

POOL, SPA & FITNESS FACILITIES   There's a stair-stepper on *Safari Quest* and sea kayaks for passenger use (four on *Safari Spirit* and eight on *Safari Quest*); both ships have a hot tub on the top deck. The *Safari Escape* has a whirlpool tub and sea kayaks.

2 Clipper Cruise Line

SHIPS   Clipper Odyssey • Yorktown Clipper

7711 Bonhomme Ave., St. Louis, MO 63105. ℂ **800/325-0010** or 314/727-2929. Fax 314/727-6576. www.clippercruise.com.

Not your typical cruise, these down-to-earth, comfortable small ships focus on offbeat ports of call, learning, and mingling with your fellow passengers. It's the ideal small-ship cruise for people who've tried Holland America or Princess but want a more intimate cruise experience.

THE EXPERIENCE   Clipper caters to mature, seasoned, easygoing, relatively affluent, and well-traveled older passengers seeking a casual vacation experience. Being small ships, the ambience is intimate and conducive to easily making new friends. You won't find any glitter, glitz, or Las Vegas gambling here. On the downside, like many of the American-crewed small ships, cruise rates are not cheap.

The line is particularly strong in providing information on the nature, history, and culture of the ports visited, carrying one or more naturalists on every sailing. These experts also accompany some shore excursions. A cruise director helps organize the days, answers questions, and assists passengers.

Pros

- **Great learning opportunities.** Naturalists and educators sail with the ships, offering informal lectures onboard and accompanying guests on shore excursions.
- **Informal atmosphere.** No need to dress up here—everything's casual.
- **Young, enthusiastic American crew.** Although they may not be the most experienced, they're sweet, engaging, and hardworking, and add a homey feel to the trip.

Cons

- **No stabilizers.** If you hit some choppy waters and you're prone to seasickness, good luck.
- **Noisy engines on *Yorktown Clipper.*** If you can help it, don't book a cabin on the lowest deck (Main Deck), where noise from the engines can get quite loud.

THE FLEET The 138-passenger *Yorktown Clipper* (1988) is a spacious, comfortable small ship that's an ideal choice for someone who's sailed with a big-ship line, such as Holland America, and wants to try a small ship experience. In 1999, the line acquired the more luxurious 120-passenger *Clipper Odyssey*, which was built in 1989 and previously sailed as the *Oceanic Odyssey* from Spice Islands Cruises of Bali, Indonesia. This is its first year in Alaska.

PASSENGER PROFILE The majority of Clipper passengers are well-traveled, 50+ couples who are attracted by the casual intimacy of small ships and by the opportunities Clipper offers for actually learning something about the places its ships visit. Most are well-educated though not academic, casual though not sloppily so, and adventurous in the sense that they're up for a little hiking but are happy to be able to get back to their comfortable cabins or have a drink in the lounge afterwards. As a company spokesperson notes, "We provide a soft adventure for travelers who may shy away from roughing it, and we think of ourselves not as a cruise line, but as a travel company that just happens to have ships."

Clipper attracts a remarkably high number of repeat passengers: 40% to 45% on any given cruise have sailed with the line before, and many have also sailed with other small-ship lines such as Lindblad Expeditions and ACCL. On a recent Clipper cruise in the Caribbean, repeaters were thanked verbally at the captain's cocktail party, and the list went on for several minutes. Many, many passengers were onboard for their second Clipper cruise, and many more were taking their third or fourth, but the winner that day was one couple who were on their eighth. If that doesn't say something about customer satisfaction, I don't know what does.

DINING The fare is all-American, prepared by attendees of the Culinary Institute of America, and incorporates local ingredients whenever practicable. Although relatively simple in ingredients and presentation, the cuisine is easily the equal of all but the best served aboard mainstream megaships.

Breakfast is served in both the lounge and dining room, with cereals, fruit, toast, and pastries at the former and a full breakfast menu in the latter. Similarly, you can create your own sandwich in the lounge from an assortment of cold cuts or get a full lunch in the dining room. Set lunches offer a hot luncheon platter (perhaps crab cakes, baby-back ribs, or pasta primavera); a lighter, cold entree (Cobb salad, chicken Caesar salad, seafood salad, and more); and one or another kind of omelet, and there's always the option of a platter of fresh fruit and cottage cheese.

Clipper Fleet Itineraries

Ship	Itinerary
Clipper Odyssey	**14-night Alaska Coast/Russia Far East:** Sails from Petropavlovsk in the Russian Far East (Clipper gets guests there on a charter flight from Anchorage) to Anchorage, visiting Egg Island, Baby Island, Unga Island, Popof Island, Semidi Islands, Chirikof Island, Geographic Harbor, Kukak Bay, and Seward, plus several destinations in Russia. (Sailing June 7, 2002, only.) (There is also a comparable 14-night itinerary from Nome to Petropavlovsk with stops in remote Alaskan and Russian Far East ports on Aug 4, 2002, only).
	12-night Gulf of Alaska/Inside Passage/British Columbia: Sails from Anchorage to Prince Rupert, B.C., visiting Seward, Prince William Sound, Kayak Island, Lituya Bay, Haines, Juneau, Tracy Arm, Wrangell Narrows, Ketchikan, Prince of Wales Island, and Misty Fjords. (Sailing June 19, 2002, only.)
	8-night Inside Passage: Round-trip from Prince Rupert, B.C. (Clipper flies guests to Prince Rupert on a charter flight from Seattle), visiting Ketchikan, Juneau, Tracy Arm, Petersburg, Wrangell Narrow, and Misty Fjords. (Sailing July 1, 2002, only.)
Yorktown Clipper	**11-night Inside Passage/British Columbia:** Sails from Seattle to Juneau, visiting Victoria, Nanaimo, Telegraph Cove, Alert Bay, Hartley Bay, Misty Fjords, Ketchikan, Petersburg, Frederick Sound, Sawyer Glacier/Tracy Arm, Sitka, Taylor Bay, Inian Islands, George Island, Althorpe Rocks, and Elfin Cove. (Sailing May 14, 2002, only.)
	7-night Inside Passage: North- and southbound between Juneau and Ketchikan, visiting Tracy Arm (for Sawyer Glacier), Sitka, Glacier Bay, Chatham Straight, Petersburg, and Misty Fjords. (Departures on May 25, July 27, Aug 3, Aug 24, and Aug 31, 2002.)
	11-night Inside Passage: Sails from Juneau to Seattle, visiting Taylor Bay, Inian Islands, George Island, Elfin Cove, Sitka, Tracy Arm, Petersburg, Ketchikan, Misty Fjords, and Alter Bay. (Sailing Sept 7, 2002, only.)

Dinner is served in a single open seating in the dining room, at tables set up for four to six, and offers four courses with five main entree options: seafood (perhaps herb-marinated halibut, stuffed lobster tail, or Chilean sea bass), a meat entree (such as roast duck, veal marsala, or prime rib), a vegetarian entree (such as marinated grilled portobello mushroom, vegetarian lasagna, and 10-vegetable couscous), a pasta entree, and a "starch and vegetables" entree such as steamed vegetables over saffron rice.

Clipper can accommodate dietary preferences or restrictions if you give them ample warning.

Although the onboard dress code is casual at all times, most passengers tend to get a bit more gussied up at dinner, and men may even wear jackets at the captain's welcome-aboard and farewell parties (though you can get away with a nice shirt and slacks if you don't want to pack the fancies).

In the lounge you can get coffee, tea, iced tea, orange and cranberry juice, and lemonade 24 hours a day. Some kind of crunchy snack food (goldfish crackers, cashew nuts, rice crackers, and so on) is also on the bar during the day. The famous (and really delicious) "Clipper Chipper" cookies are set out here as well in the late afternoon, and hors d'oeuvres are served here before dinner. These may include mushroom caps stuffed with escargot or perhaps smoked salmon with petit toasts.

As aboard almost all small ships, there is no room service unless you're too ill to attend meals.

ACTIVITIES   By design, these ships don't offer much in the way of typical cruise-ship activities; instead, they offer activities designed to focus your attention on the area you're visiting, giving you the opportunity to return home from your vacation not only relaxed, but enriched. Throughout the cruise, onboard naturalists offer a series of informal lectures. Organized shore excursions are offered at each port (the tours cost extra), including flightseeing, sport-fishing, and city tours with commentary by local residents. E-mail access is offered on the *Clipper Odyssey* only: You can send and receive e-mail from a shipboard account (but you can't check your e-mail back home) for about $1 a page.

CHILDREN'S PROGRAM   None.

ENTERTAINMENT   As is true of the vast majority of small-ship companies, Clipper offers no casino, no dancing girls, no comedy and/or magic acts—nothing, in fact, that is usually standard-issue on one of the megas (except for the occasional second-run movie shown in the lounge). That said, the line does bring aboard local musicians and/or dancers, when possible, to perform in the evenings.

The *Yorktown Clipper* has an Observation Lounge, where you'll find a bar, a piano, and a small library well-stocked with books on Alaska history, culture, nature, and geography (as well as a smattering of bestsellers). The *Clipper Odyssey* also has an observation lounge with a piano, a second lounge, and a very small gym and separate library.

SERVICE   Service staff aboard Clipper's ships is basically collegiate or post-collegiate Americans having an adventure before getting on with whatever it is they're getting on with. In other words, these aren't the same folks you'll find serving at the Four Seasons. They're amateurs—fresh-faced, willing to work, and happy to help, but don't expect them to bow when you cross the threshold. Not that you'd want them to—which is, I think, the point. As Clipper's demographic base is generally couples over 50, we suspect a nefarious plot on the line's part to staff its ships with young men and women of approximately the same age as passengers' children and grandchildren, who (unlike those real offspring) *actually do what you tell them to.* What a refreshing change!

There is no room service, nor are there any laundry facilities or services. In a nod to water conservation and a more detergent-free environment, bathroom towels are changed on an as-needed basis only: If you want fresh towels, leave the old ones on the bathroom floor; if you don't, leave them hanging.

CRUISETOURS & ADD-ON PROGRAMS   Four-night Fairbanks/Denali/Anchorage package by motor coach and train: $1,550 per person, in addition to cruise fare. For May 14 and September 11, pre- and post-options in Seattle are available for $115 per person.

Clipper Odyssey

Size (in tons)	5,200	Officers	International
Number of Cabins	64	Crew	72 (American/Int'l)
Number of Outside Cabins	64	Passenger/Crew Ratio	1.8 to 1
Cabins with Verandas	9	Year Built	1989
Number of Passengers	128	Last Major Refurbishment	1999

Acquired by Clipper in 1999, the *Clipper Odyssey* has been sailing in the Far East ever since, which is a damned long way to go to check out a cruise ship, so we've not yet been able to inspect it in person. What we do know is that it's

Clipper's sleekest and most luxurious vessel, continuing a trend that they began a few years back when they bought and renovated the beautiful expedition ship *Clipper Adventurer*. Like that ship, the *Odyssey* sails a very limited number of beyond-the-norm Alaska itineraries (see above).

CABINS   Cabins are all outside, with twin lower beds that can be converted to queen-size. All have a small sitting area, and the two top levels have small private verandas—almost unheard of on a small ship, and completely unheard of on the other small ships sailing in Alaska.

This vessel is one of only three small ships in Alaska that has an elevator, making it a better bet than most for people with mobility problems. (The other two are Cruise West's *Spirit of Oceanus* and *Spirit of '98*.) All public rooms and one cabin are accessible, but the gangway is not.

Cabins & Rates

Cabins	Brochure Rates	Bathtub	Fridge	Hair Dryer	Sitting Area	TV
Outside	$4,520–$7,000	yes	yes	yes	yes	yes
Suite	$7,100	yes	yes	yes	yes	yes

For 12-night Alaska cruise.

PUBLIC AREAS   The *Odyssey* boasts more extensive public rooms than your average small ship, with the usual lounge/bar and dining room augmented by a second lounge, a library, and a beauty salon.

POOL, SPA & FITNESS FACILITIES   If these amenities are important to you, the *Odyssey* is just about the only small ship in Alaska that offers them. It's got a heated outdoor pool, a small gym, a Jacuzzi, and a dedicated jogging track.

Yorktown Clipper

Size (in tons)	2,354	Officers	American
Number of Cabins	69	Crew	40 (American/Int'l)
Number of Outside Cabins	69	Passenger/Crew Ratio	3.5 to 1
Cabins with Verandas	0	Year Built	1988
Number of Passengers	138	Last Major Refurbishment	n/a

The impression we kept coming back to when sitting in the spacious lounge of this ship, or in our cozy cabin, was that someone had taken one of the Holland America or Princess ships and shrunk it to one-tenth its normal size. Though not boasting the multifarious public rooms of those large ships, the four-deck *Yorktown Clipper* offers similar clean styling and easy-to-live-with colors, fabrics, and textures, while also offering a small ship's ability to take passengers into shallow-water ports and other out-of-the-way locations away from the megaship crowds.

The ship has no elevator, nor does it have any cabins designed for passengers with disabilities.

CABINS   Although smallish (average cabin size is 123–140 sq. ft.), cabins are very pleasantly styled, with blond-wood writing desk, chair, and bed frames; "not-really-there"-style paintings (better than a bare wall, I guess); and a goodly amount of closet space, plus additional storage under the beds. There are no phones or TVs, but each cabin does have music channels. There are no cabin safes as such, but two drawers in the closet can be locked.

Cabins come in six different categories, differentiated mostly by their location rather than their size. Each has two lower-level beds, permanently fixed in either an L-shaped corner configuration or as two units set parallel to one another (taller passengers—over 6 ft. 2 in.—would be better off with the L-shaped arrangement, as the others are abutted by wall and headboard and are not much longer than 6 ft. 4 in.). No cabins have beds that can be pushed together to form a king- or queen-size, so these ships are off the list for honeymooners or congenitally randy couples. Some cabins contain upper berths that unfold from the wall to accommodate a third person.

All cabins have picture windows except for a few Category 1 cabins on Main Deck, which have portholes. All cabins on the Promenade Deck and a handful at the stern on the Lounge Deck open onto the outdoors (rather than onto an interior corridor), and whereas we normally prefer this simply because it makes us feel closer to nature, here it doesn't seem to matter because the doors open out—meaning you can't really leave the door open to breezes without blocking the deck. It's worth noting that passengers in the Promenade Deck cabins should also be careful when opening their doors from the inside, lest you end up braining one of your poor fellow passengers out taking a walk around the promenade.

Cabin bathrooms are compact, though not nearly so tiny as aboard many of Cruise West's and all of Glacier Bay's ships. Toilets are wedged between the shower and sink area and may prove tight for heavier people. Bathrooms have showers but no tubs.

There are no special facilities aboard for travelers with disabilities and no cabins designed specifically for single occupancy.

Cabins & Rates

Cabins	Brochure Rates	Bathtub	Fridge	Hair Dryer	Sitting Area	TV
Outside	$2,310–$3,550	no	no	no	no	no

PUBLIC AREAS As aboard most small ships, there are only two public areas: the dining room and the Observation Lounge. The pleasant lounge has big windows, a bar, a small but informative library, a piano (that gets little use), and enough space to comfortably seat everyone onboard for lectures and meetings. It's the main hub of onboard activity. The dining room is spacious and comfortable. Other than that, there are no cozy hideaways onboard other than your cabin. There is, however, plenty of outdoor deck space for wildlife- and glacier-watching.

POOL, SPA & FITNESS FACILITIES For exercise, you can jog or walk around the deck (18 laps = 1 mile). Other than this, there are no exercise facilities.

3 Cruise West

SHIPS Spirit of '98 • Spirit of Alaska • Spirit of Columbia • Spirit of Discovery • Spirit of Endeavour • Spirit of Oceanus

2401 4th Ave., Ste. 700, Seattle, WA 98121. ☎ **800/426-7702** or 206/441-8687. Fax 206/441-4757. www.cruisewest.com.

Like all small ships, Cruise West's ships can navigate tight areas such as Misty Fjords and Desolation Sound, visit tiny ports such as Petersburg, and scoot up close to shore for wildlife-watching, but these are not adventure cruises—like

Like a Road Trip, but by Boat

In addition to the cruises profiled here, Cruise West offers what it calls **"Days Aboard: Nights Ashore"** series of 5, 10, and 14 nights aboard the 70-passenger motor yacht *Sheltered Seas,* a craft without sleeping accommodations, which cruises Alaska's waterways by day and deposits you at a hotel each night. Additional travel by rail or motor coach allows visits to Fairbanks and Denali National Park, and the timing of your arrival in ports—generally in the early evening—means you'll be hitting the town after the crowds from larger cruise ships have left. If you can't decide between cruising Alaska and seeing it by land, this is an option worth exploring. **Rates:** 5-night trips from $1,569, 10-night from $3,269, 14-night from $4,579. Prices include all shore accommodations, port charges, luggage handling, and meals aboard ship.

Clipper Cruise Line's itineraries, these trips are for people who want to visit Alaska's port towns and see its wilderness areas up close and in a relaxed, comfortable, small-scale environment without big-ship distractions; they're not for people who want to spend their days hiking and kayaking.

THE EXPERIENCE   The operative words here are casual, relaxed, and friendly. At sea, the lack of organized activities on the line's port-to-port itineraries leaves you free to scan for wildlife, peruse the natural sights, or read a book. In port—whether one of the large, popular ports or a less-visited one—the line arranges some novel, intimate shore excursions, such as a visit with local artists at their home outside Haines or an educational walking tour led by a Native guide in Ketchikan.

Pros

- **The staff.** The line's friendly, enthusiastic staffs are a big plus, making guests feel right at home.
- **Great shore excursions.** Cruise West's list includes some real gems.
- **Comfort.** A couple of the line's ships—the *Spirit of Endeavour,* a sleek, yacht-like vessel, and *Spirit of '98,* a re-creation of a late-19th-century coastal steamer—offer snazzier surroundings than most of their small-ship competitors. (The line's newest vessel, *Spirit of Oceanus,* which entered the fleet in Apr 2001, is its nicest ship yet.)

Cons

- **Wacky bathrooms on some ships.** Some of the line's ships have the kind of awkward, head-style bathrooms that are common to many small vessels.

THE FLEET   The 96-passenger *Spirit of '98* (1984) is the most distinctive small ship in Alaska, having been built as a replica of a 19th-century coastal steamer. (It was even featured as such in the Kevin Costner film *Wyatt Earp.*) The 102-passenger *Spirit of Endeavour* (1983) formerly sailed as the *Newport Clipper* of Clipper Cruise Line and has a similar design and the same kind of low-key, comfortable feel as that line's current *Yorktown Clipper.* The 78-passenger *Spirit of Alaska* (1980) and *Spirit of Columbia* (1979) and the 84-passenger

Cruise West Fleet Itineraries

Ship	Itinerary
Spirit of '98	**8-night Inside Passage*:** North- and southbound between Seattle and Juneau, visiting Misty Fjords, Ketchikan, Skagway, Haines, Glacier Bay, and Frederick Sound.
Spirit of Alaska	**8-night Inside Passage*:** North- and southbound between Juneau and Ketchikan, visiting Misty Fjords, Metlakatla, Petersburg, Frederick Sound, Sitka, Glacier Bay, Skagway, and Haines.
Spirit of Columbia	**3-night Prince William Sound:** Round-trip from Whittier/Anchorage, cruising College Fjord and visiting Valdez and Columbia Glacier. **4-night Prince William Sound:** Round-trip from Whittier/Anchorage, visiting College Fjord, Cordova, Valdez, and Columbia Glacier.
Spirit of Discovery	**8-night Inside Passage*:** Same as *Spirit of Alaska* itinerary, above.**
Spirit of Endeavour	**8-night Inside Passage*:** North- and southbound between Seattle and Juneau, visiting Misty Fjords, Skagway, Haines, Ketchikan, Glacier Bay, and Frederick Sound.**
Spirit of Oceanus	**11-night Gulf of Alaska*:** North- and southbound between Vancouver and Whittier/Anchorage, visiting Prince Rupert (B.C.), Misty Fjords, Metlakatla, Tracy Arm, Haines, Skagway, Frederick Sound, and Prince William Sound. **13-night Bering Sea*:** Cruise between Whittier/Anchorage and Nome, visiting Homer, Kodiak, Katmai National Park, Dutch Harbor, the Pribilof Islands, St. Lawrence, and Little Diomed.

* *Includes one pre- or post-cruise hotel overnight.*

** *Spirit of Alaska, Columbia, and Discovery each also sail a 10-night repositioning cruise between Seattle and Juneau in late April/early May and between Juneau and Seattle in late August/early September.*

Spirit of Discovery are all extremely similar ships, with less fancy decors than the *Endeavour* and *'98*. On the other hand, the line's new, 114-passenger **Spirit of Oceanus,** the former *Renaissance V* of Renaissance Cruises, is the line's most luxurious ship, able to sail more far-flung itineraries.

Note: A staple of the Cruise West fleet for many years—the *Spirit of Glacier Bay*—is being retired and will not be in the fleet this year.

PASSENGER PROFILE   Passengers with Cruise West tend to be older (typically around 60–75), financially stable, and well-educated and consider themselves adventuresome. When we sailed the first time, there were a good number of current or retired physicians and teachers aboard, a smattering of farmers and ranchers, a pair of behavioral psychologists, several computer specialists and other high-tech types, and a few 30-ish and 40-ish adults traveling with their single parents. On one cruise, the passenger list included a group of 30-odd Yale alumni, including one delightful, 80-something lady from New Haven (widow of a Yale professor) who didn't miss a thing—hiking, kayaking, the lot. Passengers such as these want to visit Alaska's ports and see its natural wonders in a relaxed, dress-down atmosphere—and on this count, Cruise West delivers.

DINING   Breakfast, lunch, and dinner are served at set times at one unassigned seating. An early riser's buffet is set out in the lounge before the set breakfast time, but if you're a late riser you'll miss breakfast entirely, as no room service is available. A late afternoon snack is provided every day to tide passengers over until dinner, and the chef will occasionally whip up a batch of cookies. At all meals the fare is primarily home-style American—not overly fancy, but tasty and varied. Chefs make a point of stocking up on fresh salmon and crabs while in port. The galley can accommodate special diets (vegetarian, kosher, low-salt, low-fat), but be sure to make special arrangements for this when you book your cruise. Service can sometimes be a little slow, as each wait person must cover several tables, though when we overslept coming into Skagway and thought we'd only have time for toast and coffee, our waiter assured us he could have scrambled eggs and hash browns out in 30 seconds—and by God, he did.

ACTIVITIES   As with other small ships, Cruise West vessels don't offer much in the way of diversions. What onboard activities there are may include post-dinner discussions of the port or region to be visited the next day, afternoon talks by expert guests while at sea, and perhaps a tour of the engine room or galley. Onboard fitness options are limited to the exercise bike and/or Stairmaster each ship carries. One shore excursion in each port is included in the cruise fare. (There are also additional options for an extra charge.)

A cheerful and knowledgeable **cruise coordinator** accompanies each trip to answer passengers' questions about Alaska's flora, fauna, geology, and history, and Forest Service rangers, local fishers, and Native Alaskans sometimes come aboard to teach about the culture and industry of the state. Binoculars are provided for onboard use. If you have your heart set on a port activity that the line doesn't offer—say, salmon-fishing in Sitka—the cruise coordinator will do his or her best to set something up for you.

CHILDREN'S PROGRAM   None.

ENTERTAINMENT   Videos are available on some ships for in-cabin use, and organized entertainment, such as it is, is sometimes provided by the crew or by your fellow passengers, perhaps in a humbly titled "No-Talent Night" or in a game of Truth or Dare.

SERVICE   The line strives for a family feeling, and toward this end, employs young, energetic crews (mostly college students) who radiate enthusiasm and cover all shipboard tasks, from waiting tables at breakfast to unloading baggage at journey's end. They may not be polished pros, but passengers tend to find them adorable. Just be sure you don't come aboard expecting luxury and white-glove service. Crew members once told us of being sent into crisis mode when the occupants of the ship's most deluxe suite went into spasms because they couldn't order room service. If you see yourself in that scenario, cruise elsewhere.

CRUISETOURS & ADD-ON PROGRAMS   Three to fourteen-night options, depending on the cruise itinerary, available at various rates. Anchorage/Denali/Fairbanks tours (with Prince William Sound added on longer tours) are available and (new this year) an Arctic tour involving bush plane flight from Fairbanks to the Brooks Mountain Range and thence by motor coach to the Prudhoe Bay oil fields. (Pricing for this was not available at press time.)

Spirit of '98

Size (in tons)	96	Officers	American
Number of Cabins	49	Crew	23 (American)
Number of Outside Cabins	49	Passenger/Crew Ratio	4.2 to 1
Cabins with Verandas	0	Year Built	1984
Number of Passengers	96	Last Major Refurbishment	1995

The *Spirit of '98* is a time machine. Built in 1984 as a replica of a 19th-century steamship and extensively refurbished in 1995, it carries its Victorian

Jugglers, dancers and an assortment of acrobats fill the street.

She shoots you a wide-eyed look as a seven-foot cartoon character approaches.

What brought you here was wanting the kids

to see something magical while they still believed in magic.

America Online Keyword: Travel

Travelocity.com
A Sabre Company
Go Virtually Anywhere.

With 700 airlines, 50,000 hotels and over 5,000 cruise and vaca-

tion getaways, you can now go places you've always dreamed of.

"WORLD'S LEADING TRAVEL WEB SITE, 5 YEARS IN A ROW." WORLD TRAVEL AWARDS

I HAVE TO CALL THE TRAVEL AGENCY AGAIN. DARN, OUT TO LUNCH. NOW I HAVE TO CALL THE AIRLINE. I HATE CALLING THE AIRLINES. I GOT PUT ON HOLD AGAIN. "INSTRUMENTAL TOP-40" ... LOVELY. I HATE GETTING PUT ON HOLD. TICKET PRICES ARE ALL OVER THE MAP. HOW DO I DIAL INTERNA-TIONALLY? OH SHOOT, FORGOT THE RENTAL CAR. I'M STILL ON HOLD. THIS MUSIC IS GIVING ME A HEADACHE. I WONDER IF SOMEONE ELSE HAS CHEAPER FLIGHTS. FORGET IT, CAN'T TAKE IT ANYMORE ... I'M HANGING UP

YAHOO! TRAVEL
100% MUZAK-FREE

Booking your trip online at Yahoo! Travel is simple. You compare the best prices. You click. You go have fun. Tickets, hotels, rental cars, cruises & more. Sorry, no muzak.

YAHOO!®
Travel
travel.yahoo.com

flavor so well that fully two-thirds of the people we've met onboard think the ship was a private yacht at the turn of the century.

If you use a wheelchair or otherwise have mobility problems, note that the '98 is one of only three small ships in Alaska that has an elevator. (The line's *Spirit of Oceanus* and Clipper's *Clipper Odyssey* are the others.)

If you want to get a look at this ship, rent Kevin Costner's *Wyatt Earp* at your local video store—one of the final scenes was filmed onboard. Also, Sue Henry's 1997 mystery novel *Death Takes Passage* is set entirely aboard the '98 and provides detailed descriptions of the ship.

CABINS   Cabins are comfortable and of decent size, continue the Victorian motif, and feature TV/VCR combos and either twin, convertible twin, or double beds with firm, comfortable mattresses. Deluxe cabins have a refrigerator, a seating area, and a trundle bed to accommodate a third passenger. One owner's suite provides a spacious living room with meeting area, large bathroom with whirlpool tub, king-size bed, stocked bar with refrigerator, TV/VCR, stereo, and enough windows to take in all of Alaska at one sitting. Bathrooms are larger than aboard most other small ships, though they lack any hint of Victorian frills.

Cabin 309, located on the upper deck right next to the elevator, is fully wheelchair-accessible. Two cabins (321 and 322, in the stern) are singles.

Cabins & Rates

Cabins	Brochure Rates	Bathtub	Fridge	Hair Dryer	Sitting Area	TV
Outside	$3,649–$4,699*	no	some	no	some	yes
Suite	$6,099*	yes	yes	no	yes	yes

* Rates include a pre- or post-cruise hotel stay and select shore excursions.

PUBLIC AREAS   The Grand Salon Lounge has the ship's main bar, a suitably plinky-sounding 19th-century-ish player piano, a 24-hour tea/coffee station, and a small video library. The Klondike Dining Room is beautifully decorated and large enough to seat all guests in booths and round center tables. (The booths seem to suffer less ambient noise than the round tables in the middle, so try to snag one of those if you can.) Both rooms carry the 19th-century theme with pressed-tin ceilings (aluminum actually, but why be picky?), balloon-back chairs, ruffled drapery, and plenty of polished woodwork and brass throughout. A small bar called Soapy's Parlour sits just aft of the dining room, though there's only a bartender at mealtime and it otherwise gets little use—meaning it's a good spot to sneak off and read.

Out in the air, passengers congregate in the large bow area, on the open top deck, or at the railing in front of the bridge, which is open for visitors except when the ship's passing through rough water.

Spirit of Endeavour

Size (in tons)	99	Officers	American
Number of Cabins	51	Crew	25 (American)
Number of Outside Cabins	51	Passenger/Crew Ratio	4 to 1
Cabins with Verandas	0	Year Built	1983
Number of Passengers	102	Last Major Refurbishment	1996

POOL, SPA & FITNESS FACILITIES·   There's a single exercise machine, but other than that, nada.

Formerly the Newport Clipper of Clipper Cruise Line, the *Endeavour* closely resembles that line's *Yorktown Clipper* in style and layout. Along with the Clipper ships, Cruise West's new *Spirit of Oceanus,* and Glacier Bay's *Executive Explorer,* it offers a higher level of comfort than most other small ships in the Alaska market.

CABINS   Well-appointed and with a writing desk and two large view windows in all but the lowest price category (which has portholes), all cabins have firm, comfortable twin beds (convertible to queen-size only in Deluxe cabins), TV/VCR, adequate closet space, and decent-size bathrooms. Deluxe cabins feature a refrigerator, and several in the top two categories have a Pullman berth to accommodate a third passenger. Six pairs of cabins have the option of being adjoined.

There are no special facilities aboard for travelers with disabilities and no cabins designed specifically for single occupancy.

Cabins & Rates

Cabins	Brochure Rates	Bathtub	Fridge	Hair Dryer	Sitting Area	TV
Outside	$2,899–$3,949	no	some	no	no	yes

* Rates include a pre- or post-cruise hotel stay and select shore excursions.

PUBLIC AREAS   As with almost all small ships, the *Endeavour* has two indoor public areas, the dining room—the largest room on the ship, lined with wide picture windows and round dinner tables—and the plush piano lounge/bar, decorated with considerable style. Up top, a large sun deck and stern deck (both of beautiful teakwood) and a bow viewing area just below the bridge allow plenty of space for wildlife and nature observation. There's a 24-hour tea/coffee station and a video library in the lounge.

POOL, SPA & FITNESS FACILITIES   There's a single exercise machine.

Spirit of Oceanus

Size (in tons)	126	Officers	International
Number of Cabins	57	Crew	59 (Int'l)
Number of Outside Cabins	57	Passenger/Crew Ratio	2 to 1
Cabins with Verandas	12	Year Built	1984
Number of Passengers	114	Last Major Refurbishment	2000/2001

Cruise West took delivery of the former *Renaissance V* in June 2002. The addition of the oceangoing vessel allows Cruise West to pursue itineraries outside its normal coastal cruising waters, such as Southeast Asia and the South Pacific. Launched in 1990, the newly renamed *Spirit of Oceanus* has 57 outside suites ranging in size from 215 to 353 square feet, each containing a walk-in closet or wardrobe, a marble-topped vanity, a lounge area separated from the bedroom by a curtain, an in-room safe, a minibar, and satellite telephone access. Twelve cabins have private teak balconies.

Cabins & Rates

Cabins	Brochure Rates	Bathtubs	Fridge	Hair Dryer	Sitting Area	TV
Suites	$6,719–$9,969*	no	no	no	yes	yes

* For 11-night itinerary. Rate includes pre- or post-cruise hotel stay and select shore excursions.

PUBLIC AREAS   Public rooms include two lounges, a library, a beauty salon, laundry, an outdoor dining terrace, a piano bar, and a small swimming pool. The vessel is one of the few small ships in Alaska with an elevator (the others are Cruise West's *Spirit of '98* and Clipper's *Clipper Odyssey*), making it a better choice for passengers with mobility problems.

Spirit of Alaska • Spirit of Columbia • Spirit of Discovery

Size (in tons)	97/97/94	Officers	American
Number of Cabins	39/39/43	Crew	21/21/21 (American)
Number of Outside Cabins	27/27/43	Passenger/Crew Ratio	3.7 to 1 (average)
Cabins with Verandas	0	Year Built	1980/1979/1976
Number of Passengers	78/78/84	Last Major Refurbishment	1995/1995/1992

Though of slightly dissimilar sizes and passenger capacities, the *Spirit of Alaska, Columbia,* and *Discovery* are extremely similar ships, all offering the friendly Cruise West experience, though in somewhat less fancy surroundings than the *Spirit of Endeavour, Oceanus,* and *'98* (reviewed above). Though they're older ships, all have been extensively refurbished.

Interestingly, the *Columbia* is like Glacier Bay Cruiseline ships *Wilderness Adventurer* and *Wilderness Discoverer,* both formerly of the American Canadian Caribbean Line, which seems to be supplying half the small-ship lines around with its patented shallow-draft expedition vessels. All of these ships share a problem common to all ACCL-built vessels: They're not good choices for very tall people, as ceilings throughout are set at about 6 feet, 4 inches; many beds are also too short for those 6 feet, 2 inches or over. On the other hand, the *Alaska* and *Columbia* have ACCL's patented bow ramp, which in combination with their shallow draft, allows the ships to basically beach themselves, disembarking passengers right onto shore in wild areas without ports.

CABINS   Cabins aboard all three ships are very snug (smaller than those on the *Spirit of '98* and *Endeavour*) but comfortable, with light, airy decor and lower twin or double beds. (Aboard the *Discovery,* one category has upper and lower bunks, and deluxe cabins have queen-size beds.) Storage space is ample, and outside cabins feature picture windows. Bathrooms aboard the *Discovery* and *Columbia* are slightly better than those aboard the *Alaska,* which has tight, head-style arrangements.

There are no special facilities aboard for travelers with disabilities. There are two single-occupancy cabins on the *Discovery,* and three (small) suites on *Spirit of Columbia.*

Cabins & Rates

Cabins	Brochure Rates	Bathtub	Fridge	Hair Dryer	Sitting Area	TV
Inside	$919–$5,649	no	no	no	no	no
Outside	$1,319–$7,839	no	some	no	some	some

* Lower rates are low-end prices for a 3-night Prince William Sound cruise on the Spirit of Columbia; higher are the high-end prices for 7-night Inside Passage cruise on the Spirit of Alaska or Spirit of Discovery and include a pre- or post-cruise hotel stay. Rates include select shore excursions.

PUBLIC AREAS   All three ships have a dining room and lounge with similar amenities (such as a bar, 24-hr. tea/coffee station, and video library), though a less fancy feel than those on the *Endeavour* and *'98*. (See reviews above.) Lounges are a little too small to accommodate all passengers when the ships are full.

POOL, SPA & FITNESS FACILITIES   There's a single exercise machine.

4 Glacier Bay Cruiseline

SHIPS   Executive Explorer • Wilderness Discoverer • Wilderness Adventurer • Wilderness Explorer

226 2nd Ave. W., Seattle, WA 98119. © **800/451-5952** or 206/623-2417. Fax 206/623-7809. www.glacier baycruiseline.com.

Glacier Bay Cruiseline—the only **Native-owned** cruise line in Alaska—offers three types of cruises: adventure (both soft and active) and port-to-port sailings, with the balance weighted far toward the adventure side. The adventure sailings are for a particular type of traveler, one interested in exploring Alaska's wilds rather than its towns.

THE EXPERIENCE   On this line's average soft-adventure cruise the focus is not on cities and towns where souvenir shopping is a key activity, but rather, it's on kayaking, hiking in remote regions, exploring the glaciers, and cruising the waterways looking for whales and other wildlife. Onboard, the atmosphere is casual and friendly, with the staff providing just enough attention while leaving you the space to enjoy your vacation however you want.

Pros

- **Kayaking!** The line's adventure ships carry a fleet of stable two-person sea kayaks, which are launched from dry platforms at the ships' sterns. A week-long sailing typically includes three kayak treks.
- **Informality.** It's casual all the way, and you and the crew will bond in no time.
- **Focus on environment and Native culture.** No casinos and showgirls here; instead, you'll actually learn something about Alaska with this line.
- **Built-in shore excursions.** All off-ship excursions on the adventure cruises are included in the cruise price.

Cons

- **Spartan accommodations.** Most accommodations are very basic except for those on the line's *Executive Explorer*, the line's only port-to-port ship, and the new suites on the *Wilderness Discoverer*. Otherwise, cabins are tiny, and bathrooms are minuscule head-style units. (The toilet and sink are in the shower stall.)

THE FLEET   Glacier Bay Cruiseline has four vessels. The 36-passenger *Wilderness Explorer* (1969) is the most basic, but it also sails the most adventurous itineraries, basically diving right into wilderness for 6 days and not emerging again until the 7th. The 74-passenger *Wilderness Adventurer* (1984) and 86-passenger *Wilderness Discoverer* (1992) are very similar ships and a notch up in comfort and spaciousness (especially the suites on the *Discoverer*), though still very basic. The *Adventurer* sails 7-night itineraries that pretty much avoid civilization, while the *Discoverer* mixes kayaking and hiking days with days in port. The 49-passenger *Executive Explorer* is the line's fanciest vessel, but don't expect luxury. It sails 7-night port-to-port itineraries, visiting several popular ports, such as Skagway and Haines.

Glacier Bay Fleet Itineraries

Ship	Itinerary
Executive Explorer	**7-night* Inside Passage:** North- and southbound between Juneau and Ketchikan, visiting Misty Fjords, Wrangell, Sitka, Baranof Island, Glacier Bay, Haines, Skagway, and Tracy Arm.
Wilderness Discoverer	**7-night* Inside Passage:** North- and southbound between Juneau and Sitka. Itinerary includes kayaking and shore walks in Tracy Arm, Glacier Bay, Icy Strait, and Baranof Island; an excursion on the White Pass and Yukon Route Railway in Skagway; and tours in Juneau and Sitka.
Wilderness Adventurer	**7-night* Inside Passage:** Round-trip from Juneau. Itinerary includes kayaking, shore walks, and wildlife-/glacier-watching in Glacier Bay, Point Adolphus, Icy Strait, Chichagof and Baranof Islands, Admiralty Island, and Tracy Arm.
Wilderness Explorer	**7-night* Glacier Bay:** Round-trip from Glacier Bay. Itinerary includes 4 full days of intensive kayaking, shore walks, and wildlife-/glacier-watching in Icy Strait and Glacier Bay.

*Cruises include a pre-cruise hotel night at the disembarkation port and 6 nights on the ship.

PASSENGER PROFILE   On the line's **adventure** vessels, passengers tend to be on the youngish side, with as many couples in their 40s and 50s as in their 60s and 70s, and a scattering of 30-somethings (and a few 80- or 90-somethings) filling out the list. Whatever their age, passengers tend to be active and interested in nature and wildlife. They're definitely not looking to spend their trip shopping in the ports of call, and they don't want to get dressed up for dinner. They're individuals, happy to get away from TV, highway traffic, and the day-to-day grind; happy with the unstructured and casual ambience aboard ship; and happy with the flexible itinerary, which allows the captain complete freedom to sail wherever the passengers will get the best Alaska experience that day, taking into account factors such as weather and wildlife sightings.

On the *Executive Explorer,* the line's upscale **port-to-port** ship, passengers tend to be older (60 and up) and less active and adventurous, though they still enjoy the same informality as aboard the line's other vessels.

DINING   Meals are pretty standard middle-American fare (plus the requisite Alaska salmon) and are served in single open seatings. One dinner per cruise is designated the captain's dinner, and here the cuisine is ratcheted up a notch, perhaps to lobster and free champagne.

Each ship has a single bar (near which pre-dinner snacks of the chicken-wing and nacho variety are served). Other than that, coffee, tea, the occasional bowl of chips, and the fresh cookies baked at midafternoon are the only snacks available between scheduled mealtimes.

Special diets (vegetarian, kosher, low-fat, low-salt) can be accommodated with some advance warning.

ACTIVITIES   Activities aboard the adventure vessels are the integral elements of the trip: kayaking, hiking, and wildlife-watching (for which the line provides binoculars, though you should bring your own if you have them since there may not be enough to go around). Naturalists sail with every cruise to point out natural features and lead off-ship expeditions. One naturalist we encountered was a Native Aleut who had taken it upon herself to learn a number of Tlingit legends, which she told to the passengers in a traditional manner. It was a big, big highlight of the trip.

CHILDREN'S PROGRAM   None.

ENTERTAINMENT Entertainment facilities are minimal: board games; a piano (aboard the *Wilderness Explorer* only); and a TV/VCR in the lounge of each ship, on which passengers can view tapes on wildlife, Alaska history, and Native culture, and a few feature films.

SERVICE One of the line's greatest strengths is the extreme informality of the passenger/crew dynamic—the two groups tend to become so friendly so fast that after a couple of days you'll find off-duty deckhands watching nature videos with passengers in the lounge and naturalists sitting with passengers on the top deck at night, watching the stars. Most crew members are from Alaska and the Pacific Northwest, and a number are Native Alaskans. (Some of these Native crew members are, in fact, stockholders in the line's parent company, Goldbelt, a fact that adds a noticeable pride of ownership to the way they comport themselves onboard.) As with most small-ship lines, members of the staff do double- and triple-duty, cleaning the cabins, serving meals, and loading and unloading your luggage.

CRUISETOURS & ADD-ON PROGRAMS Six-night Kenai/Denali tour visits Kenai National Wildlife Refuge, Talkeetna, and Denali National Park, ending in Anchorage; $2,995. A 7-night version of the tour adds Seward or Chugach National Forest; $3,595. Three-night Fairbanks/Denali/Anchorage; $875 to $975. Six-night Fairbanks/Denali/Anchorage; $1,395 to $1,495. Six-night Fairbanks (round-trip) tour visits Gates of the Arctic National Park, the Athabascan village of Evansville, and Bettles and includes a float trip on the Koyukak River; $2,385.

Executive Explorer

Size (in tons)	98	Officers	American
Number of Cabins	25	Crew	18 (American)
Number of Outside Cabins	25	Passenger/Crew Ratio	2.7 to 1
Cabins with Verandas	0	Year Built	1986
Number of Passengers	49	Last Major Refurbishment	n/a

The *Executive Explorer* is Glacier Bay's most luxurious ship, sailing port-to-port itineraries and featuring larger, cushier, and generally more welcoming cabins and public areas than the line's other vessels. It's odd-looking—a very wide, tall catamaran with three enclosed decks rising above the waterline, topped by an open viewing deck—but the ship is streamlined and powerful and able to get between ports faster than its competition. In Ketchikan in July 1999, we watched as the ship, tied up next to three megaships, prepared to leave port. The captain fired up the engines, the crew let loose the lines, and a few seconds later the ship zoomed away from the dock like a sports car. This baby can move.

CABINS The *Executive Explorer* offers by far the largest and most appealing cabins in the Glacier Bay fleet. All have large (very, very large) view windows, refrigerators, plentiful closet space, and TV/VCRs. As on the line's other ships, bathrooms are head-style units, meaning the toilet is in the shower stall. (Unlike the other vessels, the sinks here are at least in the cabins themselves—which is more of a blessing than it sounds.) Two Vista Deluxe rooms on the middle deck face out the front of the vessel and have queen-size beds, a sitting area, larger closets, and two solid walls of windows providing a 180° view that's the same as the captain gets on the bridge, one flight up. Beds in all but the Vista Deluxe and B-level cabins are twins that convert to queen-size. The sole B-level cabin is significantly smaller than all the others and has upper and lower berths (otherwise known as bunk beds).

There are no special facilities aboard for travelers with disabilities. One cabin is suggested for single occupancy, though it could hold two with its upper berth.

Cabins & Rates

Cabins	Brochure Rates	Bathtub	Fridge	Hair Dryer	Sitting Area	TV
Outside	$2,780–$3,780*	no	yes	no	some	yes

* Rates include a shore excursion in each port and a pre-cruise hotel stay in the port of embarkation.

PUBLIC AREAS   As with all the other vessels in the Glacier Bay fleet, the *Executive Explorer* really has only two public rooms, the dining room and Vista View Lounge, which, like the Vista cabins above it, features a full view out toward the bow and to the port and starboard. Both are pleasingly furnished and, like the other vessels in the fleet, are decorated with art that reflects the line's Native Alaskan ownership. The lounge has the vessel's only bar, a small library, a 24-hour tea/coffee station, and a selection of board games and videotapes for passenger use.

Unlike on the line's other ships, you cannot use the bow area for water-level wildlife-viewing. (Owing to the ship's catamaran design, there isn't really a bow; the Vista View Lounge extends almost to the very front.) An open top deck and covered deck one level down are the best viewing spots, plus a small area at the waterline in the stern.

POOL, SPA & FITNESS FACILITIES   None.

Wilderness Adventurer • Wilderness Discoverer

Size (in tons)	89/95	Officers	American
Number of Cabins	35/43	Crew	22/22 (American)
Number of Outside Cabins	34/37	Passenger/Crew Ratio	3.4 to 1/3.9 to 1
Cabins with Verandas	0	Year Built	1984/1992
Number of Passengers	74/86	Last Major Refurbishment	2000/2001

Both of these vessels were purchased from American Canadian Caribbean Line, where they sailed as the *Caribbean Prince* and *Mayan Prince,* respectively. Because of this heritage, these ships have all the innovative, exploratory features for which ACCL founder Luther Blount's ships are known. They're low-slung, maneuverable, and quiet; have an incredibly shallow draft; and are outfitted with Blount's patented bow ramp, which allows them to nose right up onto dockless shorelines so passengers can easily disembark and explore. In addition, Glacier Bay has outfitted both vessels with a fleet of stable sea kayaks and a dry-launch platform in the stern that allows passengers to take off right from the ship. (Some other small-ship operators offer kayaking in Alaska, but in every other instance you must first take a boat to shore, where you then launch your kayak.)

The downside to all this innovation? Former owner Blount has never been known for making fancy ships. These are spartan vessels for people who want adventure, not cushy comfort.

CABINS   *Basic* is the word to remember here. Most of the cabins on these ships are just big enough for two to maneuver in simultaneously, decor is on the drab side, and closet space is minimal (though there's more space under the beds). Twin beds (convertible to queen- or king-size) are simply thin (though comfortable) mattresses over wooden platforms. All AA- and A-class cabins (plus deluxe cabins and suites on the *Discoverer*) have picture windows, while cabins on the lower deck are smaller than the rest and have no closet, nightstand, or windows. Some AA cabins can accommodate a third person, albeit tightly.

Bathrooms are referred to as "marine heads," and what they are is one-piece, one-space units where the toilet faces the sink, from which projects the shower head on a hose. Your whole bathroom is, in effect, the shower stall. Luxury it ain't.

There are four suites on the *Wilderness Discoverer* that offer at least a little more legroom, doors that open to the Observation Deck, queen beds, and TVs with VCRs. (Tapes are available to borrow.)

There are no special facilities aboard for travelers with disabilities, and none designated for single travelers.

Cabins & Rates

Cabins	Brochure Rates	Bathtub	Fridge	Hair Dryer	Sitting Area	TV
Inside	$2,190–$2,495*	no	no	no	no	no
Outside	$2,380–$3,280*	no	no	no	no	no
Suite	$3,280–$3,580*/**	no	no	no	yes	yes

Rates include a shore excursion in each port and a pre-cruise hotel stay in the port of embarkation.
** *On the Discoverer only.*

PUBLIC AREAS   The public rooms on both ships—the forward lounge and adjacent dining room—are similarly bare-boned but are lined with windows, so even at mealtimes you can keep watch for natural wonders. The lounges have TV/VCR setups and a selection of tapes, plus a small library, board games, and a 24-hour tea/coffee station.

On both ships, prime outdoor viewing areas are in the bow and stern of the main deck and on the top deck (a portion of which is covered with a plastic tarp for viewing in rainy weather). These three spots are where passengers spend most of their time onboard, making any deficiencies in the interior decor pretty much a moot point.

POOL, SPA & FITNESS FACILITIES   The sea-kayak excursions that are integral to these ships' itineraries will provide all the exercise you'll need, but you can also walk all the way around each ship on the sun deck.

Wilderness Explorer

Size (in tons)	98	Officers	American
Number of Cabins	18	Crew	13 (American)
Number of Outside Cabins	18	Passenger/Crew Ratio	2.8 to 1
Cabins with Verandas	0	Year Built	1969
Number of Passengers	36	Last Major Refurbishment	n/a

The *Wilderness Explorer*, which the line refers to as its "cruising base camp," offers the most active cruise experience available in Alaska, with cruises structured so passengers are out exploring most of each day and only use the vessel to eat, sleep, and get from place to place. It's the line's most basic ship, having been built in 1969 by American Canadian Caribbean Line's Luther Blount—one of his first ships and still going strong.

CABINS   Tiny, tiny, tiny. All cabins feature upper and lower bunks, the same kind of head-style bathrooms as aboard the *Wilderness Adventurer* and

Discoverer, and minimal storage space. Tiny windows in A-class cabins let in light but aren't much good for seeing the sights. AA-class cabins are one deck up and have more space and actual windows, while one Deluxe Cabin is located right behind the wheelhouse and has more space and windows at both port and starboard.

There are no special facilities aboard for travelers with disabilities, and none are designated for single travelers.

Cabins & Rates

Cabins	Brochure Rates	Bathtub	Fridge	Hair Dryer	Sitting Area	TV
Outside	$1,680–$2,090*	no	no	no	no	no

* Rates include a shore excursion in each port and a pre-cruise hotel stay at Glacier Bay Lodge.

PUBLIC AREAS   As on all the line's other vessels, there's a lounge with bar, 24-hour tea/coffee station, library, and TV/VCR, plus a dining room and an observation deck, part of which is covered for inclement weather.

POOL, SPA & FITNESS FACILITIES   These cruises are based around active adventure via sea kayak and hiking. That's all the exercise you'll need.

5 Lindblad Expeditions

SHIPS   **Sea Bird • Sea Lion**

720 Fifth Ave., New York, NY 10019. ℂ 800/397-3348 or 212/765-7740. Fax 212/265-3770. www. expeditions.com.

In 1984, Sven-Olof Lindblad, son of adventure-travel pioneer Lars-Eric Lindblad, followed in his father's footsteps by forming Lindblad Expeditions, which specializes in providing environmentally sensitive soft-adventure/educational cruises to remote places in the world, with visits to a few large ports.

THE EXPERIENCE   Lindblad cruises are explorative and informal, designed to appeal to the intellectually curious traveler seeking a vacation that's educational as well as relaxing. Your time is spent learning about the outdoors (from high-caliber expedition leaders trained in botany, anthropology, biology, and geology) and observing the world around you either from the ship or on shore excursions, which are included in the cruise package. Lindblad Expeditions' crew and staff emphasize respect for the local ecosystem, and flexibility and spontaneity are keys to the experience, as the route may be altered at any time to follow a pod of whales or school of dolphins. Depending on weather and sea conditions, there are usually two or three excursions every day.

Pros

- **Great expedition feeling.** Lindblad's programs offer innovative, flexible itineraries, outstanding lecturers/guides, and a friendly, accommodating staff.
- **Built-in shore excursions.** Rather than rely on outside concessionaires for their shore excursions (which is the case with most other lines, big and small), Lindblad Expeditions runs its shore excursions as an integral part of its cruises and includes all excursion costs in the cruise fare.

Cons

- **Cost.** Cruise fares tend to be a little higher than the line's small-ship competition.

Lindblad Expeditions Fleet Itineraries

Ship	Itinerary
Sea Bird/ Sea Lion	**7-night Inside Passage:** North- and southbound between Juneau and Sitka, visiting Tracy Arm, Petersburg, Le Conte Bay, and Glacier Bay, and including wildlife-watching and exploring days in Frederick Sound, Chatham Strait, Point Adolphus, and elsewhere.*

* In addition to the itinerary above, both ships offer 9-night repositioning cruises between Seattle and Juneau (May 29 and 30) and Juneau and Seattle (Aug 31 and Sept 1). Rates start at $3,980.

THE FLEET   The 70-passenger *Sea Lion* and *Sea Bird* (built in 1981 and 1982, respectively) are nearly identical in every respect and are, in fact, very similar to many of the other small ships in the Alaska market, including Glacier Bay's *Wilderness Adventurer* and *Wilderness Discoverer* and Cruise West's *Spirit of Columbia, Spirit of Discovery,* and *Spirit of Alaska.* (As a matter of fact, the *Spirit of Alaska* and the two Special Expedition ships all sailed at one time for the now-defunct Exploration Cruise Lines.) All are basic vessels built to get you to beautiful spots and feature a minimum of public rooms and conveniences: one dining room, one bar/lounge, and lots of deck space for wildlife- and glacier-viewing.

PASSENGER PROFILE   Special Expeditions tends to attract well-traveled and well-educated, professional, 55+ couples who have "been there, done that" and are looking for something completely different in a cruise experience. The passenger mix may also include some singles and a smattering of younger couples. Although not necessarily frequent cruisers, many passengers are likely to have been on other Lindblad Expeditions programs, tend to share a common interest in wildlife (whale- and bird-watching), and are also intellectually curious about the culture and history of the region they're visiting.

DINING   Hearty buffet breakfasts and lunches and sit-down dinners feature a good choice of both hot and cold dishes with plenty of fresh fruits and vegetables. Many of the fresh ingredients are obtained from ports along the way, and meals may reflect regional tastes. Although far from haute cuisine, dinners are well prepared and presented and are served at single open seatings that allow passengers to get to know each other by moving around to different tables. Lecturers and other staff members dine with passengers.

ACTIVITIES   During the day, most activity takes place off the ship, aboard Zodiac boats and/or on land excursions. While onboard, passengers entertain themselves with the usual small-ship activities: wildlife-watching, staring off into the wilderness, reading, and engaging in conversation.

CHILDREN'S PROGRAM   There are no organized programs, as there are few children aboard.

ENTERTAINMENT   Lectures and slide presentations are scheduled throughout the cruise, and documentaries or movies may be screened in the evening in the main lounge. Books on Alaskan topics are available in each ship's small library.

SERVICE   Dining-room staff and room stewards are affable and efficient and seem to enjoy their work. As with other small ships, there's no room service unless you're ill and unable to make it to the dining room.

CRUISETOURS & ADD-ON PROGRAMS Weeklong Denali, Fairbanks, Talkeetna, Anchorage tour; about $3,300.

Sea Lion • Sea Bird

Size (in tons)	100	Officers	American
Number of Cabins	37	Crew	22
Number of Outside Cabins	37	Passenger/Crew Ratio	3.2 to 1
Cabins with Verandas	0	Year Built	1981/1982
Number of Passengers	70	Last Major Refurbishment	n/a

The shallow-draft *Sea Lion* and *Sea Bird* are identical twins, right down to their decor schemes and furniture. Un-fancy, with just two public rooms and utilitarian cabins, they're very similar to other expedition-style small ships, such as Glacier Bay's *Wilderness Adventurer* and Cruise West's *Spirit of Alaska*.

CABINS Postage-stamp cabins are tight and functional rather than fancy. No cabins are large enough to accommodate more than two, and each features twin or double beds, a closet (there are also drawers under the bed for extra storage), and a sink and mirror in the main room. Behind a folding door lies a Lilliputian bathroom with a head-style shower (toilet opposite the shower nozzle). All cabins are located outside and have picture windows that open to fresh breezes (except the lowest-price cabins, which have a small "portlight" that allows in light but provides no view).

Cabins & Rates

Cabins	Rates	Bathtub	Fridge	Hair Dryer	Sitting Area	TV
Outside	$3,690–$5,350	no	no	no	some	no

PUBLIC AREAS Public space is limited to the open sun-deck and bow areas, the dining room, and an observation lounge that serves as the nerve center for activities. In the lounge, you'll find a bar; a library of atlases and books on Alaska's culture, geology, history, plants, and wildlife; a gift shop tucked into a closet; and audiovisual aids for the many naturalists' presentations.

POOL, SPA & FITNESS FACILITIES As aboard the majority of small ships, there is no gym aboard either ship, nor are there any other onboard exercise facilities. However, Lindblad's style of soft-adventure travel means you'll be taking frequent walks/hikes in wilderness areas, accessed via Zodiac landing craft.

7

The Cruise Experience

Now that you've made most of the hard decisions you have to make—choosing and booking your cruise—the rest of your vacation planning should be relatively easy because the cruise lines take over much of the arranging work, particularly if you've booked a package that includes air travel.

You should carefully read the brochure of your chosen cruise line—make sure that your agent gives you one—because most lines' brochures include sections that address commonly asked questions. In this chapter, we'll add our own two cents on these matters, and provide some practical hints that'll help you get under way glitch-free and be prepared for all you'll find in the 49th state, both aboard ship and in the ports of call.

1 Preparing for the Weather

The sometimes extreme and always unpredictable Alaska weather will be a big factor in the success of your vacation. During your summertime cruise, you may see temperature variations from the 40s to the 90s. The days will be long, with the sun all but refusing to set, and people will be energized by the extra daylight hours. You'll likely encounter some rain, but there could also be weeks of sunny skies with no rain at all. You're less likely to encounter snow, but it is a possibility, especially in the spring.

WHAT TO PACK

Some people agonize over what to pack for a cruise vacation, but you don't have to. Except for the addition of a formal night or two, a cruise vacation is really no different from any resort vacation. And in some cases, it's much more casual.

Weather plays a factor in what you need to pack, with the must-haves on an Alaska cruise including a raincoat and umbrella and comfortable walking shoes that you don't mind getting wet or muddy. A swimsuit is also a must if your ship has a pool (sometimes covered, sometimes heated) or hot tubs.

ALASKA'S CLIMATE, BY MONTHS & REGIONS

	May	June	July	Aug	Sept
Anchorage: Southcentral Alaska					
Average high/low (°F)	54/39	62/47	65/52	63/50	55/42
Hours of light	17:45	19:30	18:15	15:30	12
Sunny days	11	10	9	9	9
Rainy days	7	8	11	13	14
Precipitation	0.7	1.1	1.7	2.4	2.7

Juneau: Southeast Alaska

Average high/low (°F)	55/39	61/45	64/48	63/47	56/43
Hours of light	17:00	18:15	17:30	15:30	12:30
Sunny days	8	8	8	9	6
Rainy days	17	15	17	17	20
Precipitation	3.4	3.1	4.2	5.3	6.7

Even in the summer, temperatures in Alaska may not go much higher than the 50s or 60s, although they also may go into the 70s, 80s, or 90s. Having **layers of clothing** that you can peel off if the weather is hot and add on if the weather is cold is the most convenient approach.

Don't feel you have to go out and buy "cruise wear": Sweatshirts, jeans, and jogging outfits are the norm during the day. Dinner is dress-up time on most ships (an exception being adventure-type ships and the vessels of Norwegian Cruise Line, which remain casual 24 hr. a day).

Generally, ships describe proper dinner attire as formal, informal, or casual. There are usually 2 formal nights and 2 informal (or semiformal) nights during a weeklong cruise, with the rest casual; check with your line for specifics. **Formal** means a tux or dark suit with tie for men, and a nice cocktail dress, long dress, gown, or dressy pantsuit for women. **Informal** is a jacket, tie, and dress slacks, or a light suit, for men (jeans are frowned upon), and a dress, skirt, and blouse, or pants outfit, for women. (The little black dress is appropriate here.) **Casual** at dinner means sports shirt or open-collar dress shirt with slacks for men (some will also wear a jacket), and a dress, pants outfit, or skirt and blouse for women. Recently, a new term—country-club casual—has developed; in our experience, this is pretty much the same as informal without the tie. (Dress as you would to go out to dinner at a midrange restaurant.)

Men who don't own a **tuxedo** may be able to rent one in advance through the cruise line's preferred supplier (who will deliver the tux right to the ship). In some cases, the ship will keep a limited supply onboard. But if you attend a formal evening wearing a dark business suit instead of a tuxedo, you won't be alone. In any dinner seating of, say, 500 people, at least 100 men will be tuxedo-less.

> ### Cleaned & Pressed
> Many ships offer dry-cleaning and laundry services (for a fee, of course), and some offer coin-operated laundry facilities. Check your line's brochures for details. Using these services can save you a lot of packing.

ESSENTIALS

What you choose to bring obviously involves a lot of personal choice, but here's a checklist of some items that everyone should bring along.

- A lightweight, waterproof coat or jacket
- Two sweaters or fleece pullovers, or substitute a warm vest for one
- A warm hat and gloves
- Two to four pairs of pants or jeans
- Two pairs walking shoes (preferably waterproof)
- Sunscreen (SPF 15 or higher)
- Bug spray (Alaska has 55 different kinds of mosquitoes)
- Sunglasses

- Binoculars (some small ships stock them for guest use, but none of the big ships do)
- A camera, preferably with a telephoto or zoom lens
- Film (bring more than you think you'll need)
- Formal wear (with accessories) if your ship has formal nights (not all do)
- Semi-dressy wear for informal nights
- Long underwear if you're on a shoulder-season cruise

2 Money Matters

There are few forms of travel that are as easy as a cruise, at least as far as money is concerned. That's because you've already paid the lion's share of your all-inclusive vacation by the time you board the ship.

When you check in at the cruise terminal, the cruise-line folks will ask for a major credit card to handle your onboard expenses. (On some ships, you must report to the purser's office once onboard to establish your onboard credit account.) You also have the option of paying your account with cash, traveler's checks, or, in some cases, a personal check. Check the cruise line's brochure for specific rules on this. You may be asked to leave a deposit if you are paying with cash, usually $250 for a 1-week sailing.

The staff at the check-in counter will give you a special **ship charge card** (sometimes called a "signature card") that you will use for the length of your cruise. From this point on, on most ships, your time aboard is virtually cashless, discounting any gambling you do in the casino. On many ships you can even put your crew tips on your credit card, though on some you're expected to use cash (more on tipping later).

On most small ships, things aren't so formal—since there are so few passengers, and since the only places to spend money aboard are at the bar and the small gift counters, staff will just mark down your purchases, and you'll settle your account at the end of the week.

You will need some cash on hand for when you stop at a port, in order to pay for cabs, make small purchases, buy sodas, tip your tour guides, and so on. Having bills smaller than $20s may be useful here. At all the ports described in this book (even the Canadian ones), U.S. dollars are accepted, along with major credit cards. If you prefer to deal in Canadian currency in Canada, however, there are exchange counters, banks, and ATMs at most places you will visit. Ships in Alaska do not usually offer currency-conversion services.

Some ships have their own ATMs aboard, most often located, not surprisingly, in the casino. These give out U.S. dollars.

It's recommended that you not leave large amounts of cash in your room. All ships have some sort of safes available, either in-room or at the purser's desk, and passengers are wise to use them. You should also store your plane ticket and passport or ID papers there.

BUDGETING

Before your trip you may want to make a tentative budget. You should usually set aside about $50 per person, per day, not including tips (which usually total about $70 per passenger for a weeklong cruise), and more for the more expensive shore excursions like flightseeing.

Areas that should be included in your planning are bar drinks, dry cleaning, phone calls, massage and other spa services, beauty-parlor services, babysitting, photos taken by the ship's photographer, wine at dinner, souvenirs, shore excursions, and costs for any other special splurges your particular ship might offer (items at the caviar bars or cigar bars, time on the golf simulator). Here are some rough prices for the more common incidentals.

Alternative dining (service charge)	$5–$20
Babysitting (per hr., for 2 children)	
Private	$10
Group	$6–$8
Beverages	
Beer (domestic)	$2.95
Beer (imported)	$3.95
Mineral water	$2
Mixed drinks	$3.25–$5 (more for fine liquors)
Soft drinks	$1.50
Wine with dinner	$10–$300 per bottle
Cruise-line logo souvenirs	$3–$50
Dry cleaning (per item)	$2.50–$7.50
E-mail (per min.)	50¢–$1.50
Haircuts	
Men's	$29
Women's	$52–$70
Massage (50 min.)	$89–$109
Phone calls (per min.)	$6.95–$16.95
Photos (5×7)	$6.95–$7.95

We suggest that you keep careful track of your onboard expenses to avoid an unpleasant surprise at the end of your cruise.

On big ships, a final bill will be slipped under your door on the last night of your cruise. If everything is okay and you're paying by credit card, you don't have to do anything but keep the copy. If there's a problem on the bill, or if you are paying by cash, traveler's checks, or personal check, you will have to go down to the purser's or guest-relations desk and wait in what will likely be a very long line. On small ships, you usually have to settle up directly with the purser on the last full day of the cruise.

3 Your Very Important Papers

About 1 month (and no later than 1 week) before your cruise, you should receive in the mail your **cruise documents,** including your airline tickets (if you purchased them from the cruise line), a boarding document with your cabin and dining choices on it, boarding forms to fill out, luggage tags, and your pre-arranged bus-transfer vouchers from the airport to the port (if applicable). Also included will likely be a description of shore excursions available for purchase (either onboard or, in a few cases, in advance), as well as additional material detailing things you need to know before you sail.

All this information is important. Read it carefully. Make sure that your cabin category and dining preference are as you requested and also check your airline tickets to make sure everything is okay in terms of flights and arrival times. Make sure that there is enough time so you can arrive at the port no later than half an hour before departure time, and preferably a lot earlier. Be sure to carry these documents in your carry-on rather than in your luggage, since you can't board without them.

PASSPORTS & CUSTOMS

If you are embarking or disembarking your Alaska cruise in Vancouver, you will be required to show either a **passport** or a photo ID and proof of citizenship (such as a birth certificate with a raised seal). A driver's license is not considered sufficient ID. If you are not a U.S. citizen but live in the United States, you will have to carry your alien registration card and passport. Ditto for non–U.S. citizens (visas may be required). For more information about passports, call **The National Passport Information Center,** operated by the Department of State (*©* **900/225-5674** for automated information at a charge of 35¢ per min., or *©* **888/362-8668** for information from a real live person at a charge of $1.05 per min.). You may also be able to get your questions answered online at http://travel.state.gov (at no charge).

4 Getting to the Ship & Checking In

Before you leave for the airport, put one of the luggage tags sent by the cruise line with your cruise documents on each of your bags. Make sure that you correctly fill in the tags with your departure date, port, cabin number, and so forth. You can find all this information in your cruise documents. Put a luggage tag on your carry-on as well. If you have booked your airfare through the cruise line, you should be able at your departure airport to check your properly IDed luggage through all the way to the ship, where it will be delivered straight to your cabin. If you have booked your own air travel, you will have to check in your bags at the airline and retrieve them in baggage claim as usual.

AIRPORT ARRIVAL

If you booked your air travel and/or transfers with the cruise line, you should see a **cruise line representative** holding a card with the name of the line, either when you get off the plane or at the baggage area. (If you're arriving on a flight from the United States to Vancouver, you will need to clear Customs and Immigration. Follow the appropriate signs. The cruise-line rep will be waiting to greet you after you've cleared.) Check in with this person. If you are on a pre-cruise package, the details of what to do at the airport will be described in the cruise line's brochure.

If your bags are checked through to the ship, you will be directed right to waiting transportation (mostly likely buses or vans) that will take you to the pier. If not, you will have to reclaim your luggage, and the cruise-line representative will direct you to the transportation area. Don't forget to put your cruise line's luggage tags on all your bags, properly filled out, as this is probably the last you'll see of your luggage until it arrives at your stateroom.

You will have to turn over the **transportation voucher** you received with your cruise documents to the bus driver, so you'll want to have it handy.

If you're flying on your own, claim your own luggage at the baggage area and proceed to the pier by cab or whatever arrangements you have made. And again, remember to put the luggage tags provided by the cruise lines on your bags at this point because when you get to the pier, your bags will be taken from you by a porter for loading onto the ship. Ditto if you are driving to the pier. The porter who takes your bags may expect a tip of $1 per bag. Some will be more aggressive than others in asking for it, while some will be real princes.

Where's My Luggage?!

Don't panic if your bags aren't in your cabin when you arrive: Getting all the bags onboard is a rather slow process—on big ships, some 4,000 bags need to be loaded and distributed. If it gets close to sailing time and you're concerned, call guest relations or the purser's office. They'll probably advise you that it's on the way. If your luggage really is lost rather than just late, the cruise line's customer-relations folks will track it down and arrange for it to be delivered to the ship's first port of call.

Also, if you're on your own, make sure you got to the right ship at the right pier. That may sound silly, but in cities with multiple piers, it can get confusing. And cab drivers don't always know their way around the docks.

WHAT TO DO IF YOUR FLIGHT IS DELAYED

First of all, tell the airline personnel at the airport that you are a cruise passenger and that you're sailing that day. They may be able to put you on a different flight. Second, have the airline folks call the cruise line to advise them of your delay. There should be an emergency number included in your cruise documents. Keep in mind you may not be the only person delayed, and the line just may hold the ship until your arrival.

WHAT TO DO IF YOU MISS THE BOAT

Don't panic. Go directly to the cruise line's port agent at the pier. You may be able to get to your ship via a chartered boat or tug. (That means, of course, transferring from the small boat to the ship at sea—not an exercise to be taken lightly!) Or you may be put up in a hotel for the night and flown or provided with other transportation to the next port the next day. If you booked your flight on your own, you will likely be charged for this service.

CHECKING IN

Most ships start embarkation in the early afternoon, and depart between 4 and 6pm. You will not be able to board the ship before the scheduled embarkation time, usually about 2 or 3 hours before sailing, and even then, it's likely you'll have to wait in line (unless you're sailing on a small ship carrying very few passengers). If you've booked a suite you may get priority boarding at a special desk. Special-needs passengers may also be processed separately. Ship personnel will check your boarding tickets and ID and collect any documents you've been sent to fill out in advance. Any unpaid port taxes or fees will also be collected at this point, and you will be given a boarding card and your cabin key. (On some lines, your key may be waiting in your cabin.)

You have up until a half hour (on some ships, it's 1 hr.) before departure to board, but there are some advantages to boarding earlier, like getting first dibs on spa treatment times. Plus, if you get on early enough, you can eat lunch on the ship.

Protocol for establishing your **dining-room table assignment** if one is required (some ships are open-seating) varies by ship. You may be given your assignment in advance of your sailing (on your tickets), you may be advised of your table number as you check in, or a card with your table number may be waiting for you in your stateroom. If you do not receive an assignment by the time you get to your stateroom, you will be directed to a maitre d's desk, set up in a convenient spot onboard. This is also the place to make any changes if your assignment does not meet with your approval.

5 Some Vital Statistics of the Typical Cruise Experience

Here's where the kind of ship you chose for your cruise, and the itinerary, comes into play. On a big ship, you will likely visit the popular ports of Skagway, Juneau, and Ketchikan (and possibly Sitka, Victoria, or Valdez, depending on your itinerary) and will have several days at sea to enjoy the glorious glaciers, fjords, and wildlife, as well as participate in shipboard activities and relax. On a smaller ship, you may also visit several smaller ports of call and head into wilderness areas that cannot accommodate larger vessels.

On **days in port,** you will want to have a plan of what you want to see on land—see "Visiting the Ports of Call," below, for more info. On **days at sea,** you will probably want to be out on deck much of the time looking for whales and listening to the commentary of wildlife and glacier experts. There will be plenty of activities offered, but these may be reduced at certain times—for instance, when the ship is scheduled to pass one of the famous glaciers.

Nearly every ship in Alaska has **naturalists and other Alaska experts** onboard to offer commentary on glaciers, geography, plant life, and wildlife. Sometimes, these experts are on for the entire cruise and offer lectures complete with slides or films. Other times, they are Forest Service rangers who come onboard at glacier sites (particularly in Glacier Bay) to offer commentary, usually over the ship's PA system. Depending on the ship, local fishermen, Native Alaskans, teachers, photographers, librarians, historians, or anthropologists may come onboard to teach about local history and culture.

MEDICAL SERVICES

Large ships usually have a fully equipped medical facility and staff (a doctor and a nurse or two) onboard to handle any emergency. They work from a medical center that typically offers set office hours but is also open on an emergency basis 24 hours a day. A fee (sometimes a steep one) is charged. They're equipped to do some surgery, but in cases of major medical emergencies, passengers are usually airlifted off the ship by helicopter to the nearest hospital.

Small ships may have someone on staff with nursing skills, though they rarely have a doctor, but such ships in Alaska never get so far from civilization that a plane couldn't be summoned by radio to airlift a sick passenger to a hospital.

RELIGIOUS SERVICES

Depending on the ship and the clergy onboard, some ships offer Catholic Mass every day. Most ships offer a nondenominational service on Sunday and a Friday-night Jewish Sabbath service, usually run by a passenger. On Jewish and Christian holidays, clergy are typically aboard on large ships to lead services. These services are usually held in the library or conference room.

MAILING POSTCARDS

If you want to send mail from the ship, you should be able to find both stamps and a mailbox at the purser's office. The purser's office should have the appropriate postage available.

GETTING THE NEWS & KEEPING IN TOUCH

Newshounds don't have to feel out of touch on a cruise ship. Most newer cruise ships offer CNN on in-room TVs, and nearly every ship will post the latest news from the wire services outside the purser's office. Some lines excerpt information from leading newspapers each day and deliver the news to your room.

Every ship will offer the opportunity to make satellite phone calls, but these can be exorbitantly expensive—usually anywhere from $6.95 to $16.95 per minute. A cheaper alternative is e-mail, offered by an increasing number of ships, including most of the large ships reviewed in this book. Rates range from 50¢ to $1.50 per minute. At present, only a few of the small ships offer e-mail access.

You may also be able to use your cellular phone in some of the more populated areas of Alaska. Check with your cellular provider for details.

6 Visiting the Ports of Call

Cruise lines carefully arrange their itineraries to visit places that offer a little something for everyone, whether your thing is nature, museum-hopping, barhopping, or no hopping at all. You can take in the location's ambience and natural beauty, learn a little something about the local culture and history, eat local foods, and enjoy sports activities. And you'll have the opportunity to shop to your heart's delight.

SHORE EXCURSIONS

When the ship gets into port, you'll have the choice of going on a shore excursion organized by the cruise line or going off on your own. The shore excursions are designed to help you make the most of your limited time at each port of call, to get you to the top natural or historical attractions, and to make sure you get back to the ship on time. But shore excursions are also a moneymaking area for the cruise line, and the offerings can add a hefty sum to your vacation costs. Whether or not you choose to take one of these prearranged sightseeing trips is a matter of both personal preference and pocketbook concerns; you should in no way feel you need to do an excursion in every port. Our picks of some of the best shore-excursion offerings in Alaska's Southeast and Southcentral, as well as in Vancouver and Victoria, are included with all the port listings in chapters 9 and 10, along with advice on exploring on your own.

In most Alaska ports, it's easy to explore the downtown area on your own, and exploring on foot may be the best way to see the sights anyway. Plus, this way you can at least try to steer clear of the crowds. But in some ports, there's not much within walking distance of the docks, and it's difficult to find a cab or other transportation. In these cases, the cruise line's excursion program may be your best and most cost-effective option. For instance, a typical $35 to $45 **historical tour** in Sitka will take in the Russian St. Michael's Cathedral in the downtown area plus two great sights a little ways out of downtown: Sitka National Historic Park, with its totem poles and forest trails, and the Alaska Raptor Rehabilitation Center, where injured bald eagles and other birds of prey are nursed back to health. (The tour may also include a Russian dance performance by the New Archangel Dancers.) Although you could visit the church on your own, it's a long walk to the park, and the bus is the best way to get to see the eagles.

There are plenty of shore excursions in Alaska for those who want to get active, such as **mountain-bike trips, fishing, snorkeling,** and **kayak voyages,** all of which get you close to nature and allow you to experience stunning views. These trips are generally worth taking. They usually involve small groups of passengers, and by booking your activity through the cruise line, you have the advantage of the vendors having been prescreened: Their prices may be slightly higher than those offered by vendors you'll find once you disembark at the port, but you can be assured the vendors the cruise lines work with are reputable.

For those who don't mind trips in small planes or helicopters and are willing to pay for the experience, **flightseeing trips,** offered as shore excursions at many of the ports of call, are another fascinating way to see the Alaska landscape—but they run on the pricey side. Again, the ship's offerings may be priced slightly higher than tours offered at the port, but by booking the ship's package you should be able to avoid touring with Reckless Mike and His Barely Flying Machine. The extra few bucks you pay will be worth it.

At most ports, the cruise lines offer **guided tours** to the top sights, usually by bus. The most worthwhile ones take you outside the downtown area, or include a meal, a dance or music performance, or a crafts demonstration (or sometimes all of the above). There's a guide on each bus, and the excursion price includes all incidental admission costs. The commentary is sometimes hokey, other times educational.

Per person, shore excursions usually range in price from about $20 for a city walking tour, or $35 for a bus tour, to $184 and up (sometimes as high as $350) for an elaborate offering such as helicopter sightseeing.

You may be in port long enough to book more than one option or to take an excursion and still have several hours to explore the port on your own. And you may very well find that you want to do a prearranged shore excursion at one port and go it on your own at the next.

The best way to decide what shore excursions you want to take is to do some research in advance of your trip. In addition to our descriptions in chapters 9 and 10, which detail the most common and popular excursions offered in the various ports, your cruise line will probably send you a booklet of its shore excursions with your cruise tickets. You can compare and contrast. Onboard your ship, a shore excursion order form should be either in your cabin or available at the purser's desk or shore-excursion desk, or at the shore-excursion lecture that will be offered the first day of your cruise. To make your reservation, check off the appropriate places on the shore-excursion order form, sign the form (make sure to include your cabin number), and drop it off as directed, probably at the ship's shore-excursion desk or purser's office. Your account will be automatically charged, and tickets will be sent to your cabin before your first scheduled tour. The tickets will include such information as where and when to meet for the tour. Carefully note the time. If you are not at the right place at the right time, the tour will probably leave without you.

Remember, the most popular excursions (such as flightseeing trips) sell out fast. For that reason, you're best off booking your shore excursions the first or second day of your cruise. Some lines, including Princess, Royal Caribbean, and Celebrity, offer the option of booking shore excursions in advance of your trip, which we recommend you do (again, to assure yourself a spot).

ARRIVING IN PORT

When the ship arrives at the port, it will either dock at the pier or anchor slightly offshore. You may think that, in the former case, you can walk right off the ship as soon as it arrives, but you can't. Before the gangway is open to the public, lots of papers must be signed, and local authorities must give their clearance, a process that can take as long as 2 hours. Don't bother going down to the gangplank until you hear an announcement saying the ship has been cleared.

If your ship anchors rather than docks (a rarity in Alaska), you will go ashore in a small boat called a **launch** or **tender,** which ties up next to your ship and shuttles passengers back and forth all day. Getting on the tender may require a helping hand from crew members, and the waves may keep the tender swaying, sometimes requiring passengers to literally jump to get aboard.

Whether the ship is docked or anchored, you are in no way required to get off at every port of call. The ship's restaurants will remain open, and there will be activities offered, though usually on a limited basis.

If you do get off, before you reboard you may want to use the phones at the docks to call home. It'll be much cheaper than making calls from the ship.

THE ESSENTIALS: DON'T LEAVE THE SHIP WITHOUT 'EM

You must bring your **ship boarding pass** (and/or shipboard ID) with you when you disembark or you will have trouble getting back onboard. And also don't forget to bring a little **cash**—although your ship operates on a cashless system, the ports do not. Many passengers get so used to carrying no cash or credit cards while aboard ship that they forget them when going ashore.

WATCH THE CLOCK

If you're going off on your own, whether on foot or on one of the alternate tours or transportation options we've listed, remember to be very careful about timing. Cruise lines are very strict about sailing times, which will be posted around the ship. You're generally required to be back at the dock at least a half hour before the ship's scheduled departure. (Passengers running late on one of the line's shore excursions needn't worry: If an excursion runs late, the ship accepts responsibility and won't leave without the late passengers.)

If you're on your own and do miss the boat, immediately contact the cruise-line representative at the port. You'll probably be able to catch your ship at the next port of call, but you'll have to pay your own way to get there.

7 Tipping, Packing & Other End-of-Cruise Concerns

Here are a few hints that should save you some time and aggravation at the end of your cruise.

TIPS ON TIPPING

Tipping is a subject that some people find confusing. First, let's establish that you are expected to tip the crew at the end of the cruise, in particular your cabin steward, server, and busperson; not to do so is bad form. The cruise line will give suggested amounts in the daily bulletin and in the cruise director's disembarkation briefing, but these are just suggestions—you can tip more or less, at your own discretion. Keep in mind these people are extremely underpaid, and that their salaries are largely dependent on tips. Some lines pay their room stewards less than $2 an hour base pay, and many of these crew members support families back home on their earnings.

We think the **minimum tip** you should consider for the folks mentioned above is $3.50 per adult passenger, per day (for your room steward and your server) and $2 per adult passenger, per day (for your busperson). That totals up to about $63 per passenger for a 7-night cruise. (You don't have to include disembarkation day.) Some lines recommend more, some a little less. Of course you can always tip more for good service or simply to round out the number. You'll also be encouraged to tip the dining room maitre d', headwaiter, and other better-salaried employees. Whether to tip these folks or not is your decision. If you have a cabin with butler service, tip the butler about $2 per person, per day. Most lines suggest that you tip in cash, but some also allow you to tip via your shipboard account. And recently, lines including Carnival and Norwegian Cruise Line have begun automatically adding tips of about $10 per passenger, per day, to your shipboard account. (You can move the amount up or down depending on your opinion of the service you received.) Bar bills automatically include a 15% tip, but if the dining-room wine steward, for instance, has served you exceptionally well, you can slip him or her a few bucks, too. The captain and his officers should not be tipped—it'd be like tipping your doctor.

Usually, when ships operate on a no-tipping-required basis (Holland America being a case in point), the staff will still accept a tip. Radisson Seven Seas Cruises includes tips in the cruise fare, although some people choose to tip key personnel anyway—it's really up to you.

If you have spa or beauty treatments, you can tip that person at the time of the service (just add it to your shipboard account), and you can hand a bartender a buck if you like, but otherwise tips are usually given on the last night of your cruise. On some ships (especially small ships) you may be asked to submit your tips in a single sum that the crew will divide among itself after the cruise, but generally you reward people individually, usually in little preprinted envelopes that the ship distributes.

If a staff member is particularly great, a written letter to a superior is always good form and may earn that person an employee-of-the-month honor, and maybe even a bonus.

SETTLING YOUR SHIPBOARD ACCOUNT

On big ships, your shipboard account will close just before the end of your cruise, but before that time you will receive a preliminary bill in your cabin. If you are using a credit card, just make sure the charges are correct. If there is a problem, you will have to go to the purser's office, where you will likely encounter long lines. If you're paying by cash or traveler's check, you'll be asked to settle your account during either the day or night before you leave the ship. This will also require you to go to the purser's office. A final invoice will be delivered to your room before departure.

On small ships, the procedure will be simpler. Often, you can just mosey over to the purser's desk on the last evening, check to see that the bill they give you looks right, and sign your name.

LUGGAGE PROCEDURES

With thousands of suitcases to deal with, big ships have established the routine of requiring guests to pack the night before departure. You will be asked to leave your bags in the hallway before you retire for the night (or usually by midnight). The bags will be picked up overnight and placed in the cruise terminal before passengers are allowed to disembark. It's important to make sure that your bags are tagged with the luggage tags given to you by the cruise line toward the end of your cruise. These are not the same tags you arrived with; rather, they're color-coded to indicate deck number and disembarkation order—the order in which they'll likely be arranged on the dock. If you need more tags, alert your cabin steward.

If you booked your air travel through the cruise line, you may be able to check in your luggage for your flight right at the cruise terminal. You will collect your bags—there should be porters to help—turn them over to an airline representative, and receive your claim checks. You may even be able to get your flight boarding passes at the cruise terminal. You will then proceed to a bus that will take you to the airport.

If you're on a **post-cruise tour,** special instructions will be given by the cruise line.

DISEMBARKATION

You won't be able to get off the ship until it is cleared by Customs and other authorities, a process that usually takes 90 minutes or more. In most cases, you'll be asked to vacate your cabin by 8am, and will disembark based on your departure number, which is assigned according to such variables as early flights. Passengers with mobility problems and those who booked suites will often be debarked early as well.

CUSTOMS & IMMIGRATION

If your cruise begins or ends in Canada, you'll have to clear Customs and Immigration, which usually means your name goes on a list that is reviewed by authorities. You may be required to show your passport or ID.

When disembarking in U.S. ports after starting out from Vancouver, non–U.S. citizens (including green-card holders) will be required to meet with U.S. Immigration authorities, usually in a lounge or theater, when the ship arrives at the port. You will have to bring your passport receipt with you, and all family members must attend.

If you're flying home from Vancouver, you'll have to pay an **airport tax** at the Vancouver Airport. The tax is $10 Canadian ($7 U.S.) and can be paid in Canadian or U.S. dollars.

8

The Ports of Embarkation

Most Alaska cruises operate either (a) round-trip from Vancouver, (b) northbound from Vancouver to Seward/ Anchorage, or (c) southbound from Seward/Anchorage to Vancouver. Most of the small adventure-type vessels sail from popular Alaska ports of call such as Juneau, Ketchikan, and Sitka; Crystal operates Alaska itineraries from San Francisco; and Norwegian sails from Seattle. In this chapter, we'll cover the most common of these home ports: Anchorage/Seward, Vancouver, and Juneau.

You may want to consider traveling to your city of embarkation at least a day or two ahead of your cruise departure date. This will give you time to check out local attractions, alleviate any fears you may have about your plane being delayed (worrying that you'll miss the boat is not fun), and, if you're traveling between coasts, give you time to overcome jet lag.

In addition to the port-city information provided here, you may want to refer to Frommer's guides for each particular city for more details, particularly if you're planning to spend a few days there.

1 Anchorage

Anchorage, which started as a tent camp for workers building the Alaska Railroad in 1915, stands between the Chugach Mountains, which you can see from the airport, and the waters of upper Cook Inlet. It was a remote, sleepy railroad town until World War II, when a couple of military bases were located here and livened things up a bit. Even with that, though, the city did not start becoming a city in earnest until the late 1950s, when oil was discovered on the Kenai Peninsula, south of here.

Fortunes came fast, and development was haphazard, but the city seems at this point to have settled into its success. It now boasts good restaurants, good museums, and a nice little zoo, as well as the most exciting new attraction to make the scene in many a year—the Alaska Native Heritage Center, a 26-acre re-creation of the villages of Alaska's five Native cultural groups. And always, of course, there is wilderness, so close that moose regularly annoy gardeners, and even bears occasionally show up in town.

Anchorage's downtown area is about 8-by-20 blocks near Ship Creek, but the rest of the city spreads some 5 miles east and 15 miles south. Most visitors, whether heading off on a cruise ship or not, spend a day or two in town before going somewhere more remote. The downtown area is pleasant, but we recommend you try to see more than just the streets of tourist-oriented shops. Check out the **coastal trail** and the **museums,** and if you have time, plan a day trip about 50 miles south along **Turnagain Arm** to explore the receding **Portage Glacier** and visit the mountains.

And don't forget **Alaska Native Heritage Center,** which is well worth a visit, even at about $20 a head. It gives visitors an introduction to the various Native groups in the state through storytelling, dance, music, a Native crafts workshop, a museum, and an outdoor area in which five traditional Native homes have been constructed. It's included in most lines' shore-excursion books this year.

GETTING TO ANCHORAGE & THE PORT

Cruise ships usually dock in Seward, about 125 miles from Anchorage, on the east coast of the Kenai Peninsula, so as to avoid the extra day that cruising all the way around the peninsula to Anchorage adds to itineraries. It's quicker to ferry passengers between the two in motor coaches or by train. Most visitors will use Anchorage as a hub because, thanks to the international airport, it's where Alaska links with the rest of the world. You can spend a day or two here before heading off on a cruise from Seward or on a land adventure.

BY PLANE   If you're arriving by plane before your cruise, you'll land at the **Anchorage International Airport,** located within the city limits, a 10- to 15-minute drive from downtown. Taxis run about $14 for the trip downtown, and the **Borealis Shuttle** (© 907/276-3600) and **Mom's Shuttle** (© 907/344-6667) each charge $6 per person.

BY CAR   By car, there is only one road into Anchorage from the rest of the world: the Glenn Highway. The other road out of town, the Seward Highway, leads to the Kenai Peninsula.

EXPLORING ANCHORAGE

INFORMATION   The **Anchorage Convention and Visitor Bureau** (© 907/276-4118) maintains five information centers, the main one of which is the **Log Cabin Visitor Information Center** at Fourth Avenue and F Street (© 907/274-3531). It's open daily from 7:30am to 7pm June through August, from 8am to 6pm May and September.

GETTING AROUND   Most car-rental companies operate at the airport. A midsize car costs about $55 a day, with unlimited mileage. Advanced bookings are recommended. You can rent a bicycle from **CycleSights** (© 907/344-1771 or 907/227-6109), right in Elderberry Park (see below), for $15 for a half day, $25 full day. Bike tours are also offered. Anchorage's bus system is an effective way of moving to and from the top attractions and activities. The buses operate between 6am and 10pm daily, and passage costs $1 for adults, 50¢ for those between the ages of 5 and 18. In the 20-block downtown area, Fifth and Sixth avenues between Denali and K streets, the bus operates as a free people mover.

ATTRACTIONS WITHIN WALKING DISTANCE

With its old-fashioned grid of streets, Anchorage's downtown area is pleasant, if a bit touristy. The 1936 **Old City Hall,** at Fourth Avenue and E Street, offers an interesting display of city history in its lobby, including dioramas of the early streetscape. For a better sense of what Alaska's all about, though, you'll want to check out the heritage museums or take a ride outside the city to the Chugach Mountains. You can also take a walk on the **Tony Knowles Coastal Trail,** which comes through downtown and runs along the water for about 12 miles, from the western end of Second Avenue to Kincaid Park. You can hop on the trail at several points, including via Elderberry Park, at the western end of Fifth Avenue.

Anchorage Museum of History and Art   121 W. Seventh Ave., between A and B sts. © 907/343-4326. www.ci.anchorage.ak.us. $6.50 for adults, suggested $2 donation for children under 18.

Downtown Anchorage

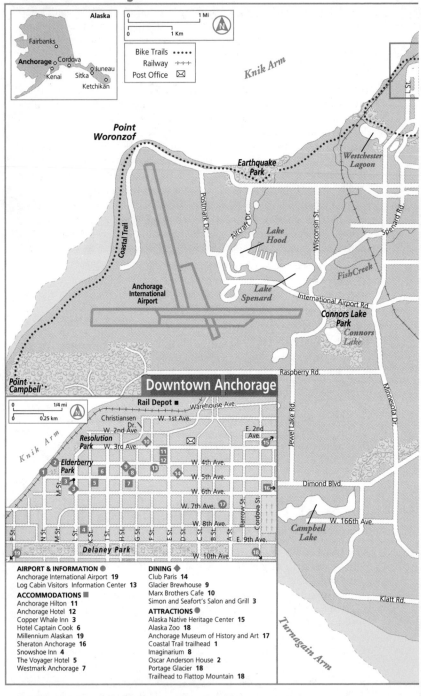

Alaska

Fairbanks
Anchorage
Cordova
Kenai
Sitka
Juneau
Ketchikan

Bike Trails •••••
Railway ┼┼┼
Post Office ✉

0 ___ 1 Mi
0 ___ 1 Km

Point Woronzof

Earthquake Park

Westchester Lagoon

Knik Arm

Postmark Dr.
Aircraft Dr.

Lake Hood

Wisconsin St.

Spenard Rd.

Coastal Trail

Anchorage International Airport

Lake Spenard

FishCreek

International Airport Rd.

Connors Lake Park

Connors Lake

Raspberry Rd.

Minnesota Dr.

Point Campbell

Downtown Anchorage

0 ___ 1/4 mi
0 ___ 0.25 km

Rail Depot ■
Warehouse Ave.

Christiansen Dr.
W. 1st Ave.
W. 2nd Ave.
E. 2nd Ave.

Resolution Park
W. 3rd Ave.

Knik Arm

Elderberry Park

M St.
N St.
M St.
L St.
K St.

H St.
G St.
F St.
E St.
D St.
C St.
B St.
A St.

Barrow St.
Cordova St.

W. 4th Ave.
W. 5th Ave.
W. 6th Ave.
W. 7th Ave.
W. 8th Ave.
E. 9th Ave.

Delaney Park
W. 10th Ave

Jewel Lake Rd.

Dimond Blvd.

Campbell Lake
W. 166th Ave.

Klatt Rd.

Turnagain Arm

AIRPORT & INFORMATION ●
Anchorage International Airport **19**
Log Cabin Visitors Information Center **13**

ACCOMMODATIONS ■
Anchorage Hilton **11**
Anchorage Hotel **12**
Copper Whale Inn **3**
Hotel Captain Cook **6**
Millennium Alaskan **19**
Sheraton Anchorage **16**
Snowshoe Inn **4**
The Voyager Hotel **5**
Westmark Anchorage **7**

DINING ◆
Club Paris **14**
Glacier Brewhouse **9**
Marx Brothers Cafe **10**
Simon and Seafort's Salon and Grill **3**

ATTRACTIONS ●
Alaska Native Heritage Center **15**
Alaska Zoo **18**
Anchorage Museum of History and Art **17**
Coastal Trail trailhead **1**
Imaginarium **8**
Oscar Anderson House **2**
Portage Glacier **18**
Trailhead to Flattop Mountain **18**

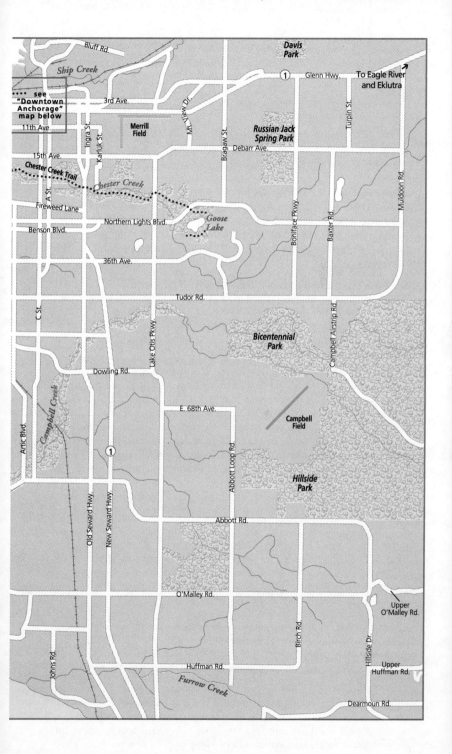

In the Alaska Gallery, you can enjoy an informative walk through the history and anthropology of the state, and in the art galleries, you can see what's happening in Alaska art today. The cafe serves excellent lunches, and Native dancers perform in the auditorium daily at 12:15, 1:15, and 2:15pm.

The Imaginarium   727 W. Fifth Ave., between G and H sts., Ste. 140. ✆ **907/276-3179.** $5 adults, $4.50 children 2–12 and seniors (65 and older).

This science museum is geared toward kids, with not many words and lots of fun learning experiences. There's a strong Alaska theme to many of the displays. The saltwater touch tank is like an indoor tide pool and one of the favorite places to visit.

The Oscar Anderson House   420 M St., in Elderberry Park. ✆ **907/274-2336.** $3 adults, $1 children 5–12.

This house museum shows how an early Swedish butcher lived. It's a quaint dwelling, surrounded by a lovely little garden, and the house tour provides a good explanation of the city's short history. Furnishings include a working 1909 player piano.

ATTRACTIONS OUTSIDE THE DOWNTOWN AREA

The Alaska Native Heritage Center   8800 Heritage Center Dr. (about 15 min. from downtown). ✆ **800/315-6608.** $19.95 adults, $14.95 children 7–16.

Years in the planning, this 26-acre center presents visitors with an introduction to the lives and cultures of the state's five major Alaska Native groupings: the Southeast (Inside Passage) region's Tlingits, Eyaks, Haida, and Tsimshians; the Athabascans of the Interior; the Inupiat and St. Lawrence Island Yupik Natives of the far north; the Aleuts and Alutiiqs of the Aleutian Islands; and the Yup'ik and Cup'ik tribes of the extreme west. A central "Welcome House" holds a small museum, a theater, a workshop where Native craftspeople demonstrate their techniques, and a rotunda where storytelling, dance, and music performances are presented throughout the day. Outside, spaced along a walking trail around a small lake, are five traditional dwellings representing the five regional Native groupings. Native staffers are on hand at each to provide information about the dwellings.

The Alaska Zoo   4731 O'Malley Rd. (about 8 miles from downtown). ✆ **907/346-3242.** $7 adults, $5 students 13–18, $4 children 3–12. To get there, take either the old or new Seward Hwy. south to O'Malley Rd., turn left, and travel for about 1.5 miles.

Don't expect a big city zoo. Still, it's a little Eden complete with Alaskan bears, seals, otters, musk oxen, mountain goats, moose, caribou, and waterfowl. There are also definitely non-Alaskan elephants and tigers and the like.

Flattop Mountain   In the Chugach Mountains. From the New Seward Hwy., drive east on O'Malley Rd., turn right on Hillside Dr. and left on Upper Huffman Rd., then right on the narrow, twisting Toilsome Hill Dr.

Rising right behind Anchorage, the mountains are a great and easy climb, and perfect for an afternoon hike. The parking area at Glen Alps, above the tree line, is a good starting point.

Portage Glacier   About 50 miles south of the city on the Seward Hwy. (toward Seward).

In 1985, the National Forest Service spent $8 million building a visitor center at Portage. Imagine its chagrin when the glacier then started receding, moving away from the center so fast that at this point you can't even see one from the other and must board a tour boat to get close to the glacier face. Portage is not the best glacier Alaska has to offer—it's relatively small—but if you haven't had enough of them after your cruise (or want a preview before your cruise), it might be worth a stop. The visitor center itself is still worth a visit; it's a sort of glacier museum and an excellent place to learn about the glaciers you'll be seeing on your cruise. Many bus tours are offered (your cruise line may offer one, too), including a 7-hour **Holland America Tours** (© **907/277-5581**) trip from Anchorage, which includes the boat ride to the glacier and a stop at the town of Girdwood. The cost is $59, and the trip is offered twice daily in the summer.

ORGANIZED TOURS

Anchorage Historic Properties 645 W. Third Ave. © 907/274-3600. Guided walking tour of historic downtown Anchorage June–Aug weekdays at 1pm, for a reasonable $5 per person, $1 for kids. You can also buy a combination ticket with the Oscar Anderson House (see above).

The 1-hour tour covers 2 miles, and the volunteer guides are both fun and knowledgeable. Meet at the lobby of old city hall, next door to the Log Cabin Visitor Information Center (see above).

ACCOMMODATIONS

Rooms can be hard to come by in Anchorage in the summer, so be sure to arrange lodging as far in advance of your trip as possible, whether through your cruise line or on your own. In addition to the listings below, you can try the luxurious **Anchorage Hilton,** Third Avenue and E Street (© **800/245-2527** or 907/272-7411; www.hilton.com); the **Westmark Anchorage,** 720 W. Fifth Ave. (© **800/544-0970** or 907/276-7676; www.westmarkhotels.com) which is owned by **Holland America Line;** the Sheraton Anchorage, 401 E. Sixth Ave. (© **800/325-3535** or 907/276-8700; www.sheraton.com); or the small and charming **Anchorage Hotel,** right next door to the Hilton on E Street (© **800/ 544-0988** or 907/272-4553). Expect all of these properties to charge rack rates of $200 a night or more and to accept all major credit cards.

Copper Whale Inn 440 L St., Anchorage, AK 99501. © 907/258-7999. Fax 888/WHALE-IN or 907/258-6213. www.copperwhale.com. 15 units, 9 with bathroom. TV TEL. $110 double with shared bathroom, $145 double with private bathroom. Additional person in room $10 extra. AE, DC, DISC, MC, V.

A pair of clapboard houses overlooks the water and Elderberry Park right on the coastal trail downtown, with charming rooms of every shape and size. There's a wonderfully casual feeling to the place. The rooms in the newer building, lower on the hill, are preferable, with cherry-wood furniture and high ceilings. All rooms are hooked up for TVs, phones, and voice mail, but you have to ask for the actual instrument to be connected. A limited number of bikes are available for loan, and a full breakfast is included in the price.

Hotel Captain Cook Fourth Ave. and K St. (P.O. Box 102280), Anchorage, AK 99510-2280. © 800/843-1950 or 907/276-6000. Fax 907/343-2298. www.captaincook.com. 642 units. TV TEL. $230–$260 double; $275–$1,500 suite. Additional person in room $10 extra. AE, DC, DISC, MC, V.

This is Alaska's great, grand hotel, where royalty and rock stars stay. Former governor Wally Hickel built the first of the three towers after the 1964 earthquake, and now the hotel fills a city block. Inside, the decor has a nautical theme, with art memorializing Cook's voyages and enough teak to build a square-rigger. The standard rooms are large, with great views from all sides; you don't pay more to be higher. The lobby contains 16 shops, and there's a concierge, tour desks, barbershop and beauty salon, and business center. The full-service health club in the basement has a decent-size pool and a racquetball court. It may not be easy to book a room, however, as packages and government and corporate clients tend to fill the hotel in the summer.

Millennium Alaskan 4800 Spenard Rd. ℂ **800/544-0553** or 907/243-2300. www.millennium hotels.com. AE, DISC, MC, V.

The hotel is ideally located near the airport and still just a few minutes' cab ride from downtown. It has a restaurant and comfy lounge bar, a health club, and 24-hour room service. The Millennium advertises itself as having "the feel of a world-class lodge"—which is pretty accurate.

Snowshoe Inn 826 K St., Anchorage, AK 99501. ℂ **907/258-SNOW** (907/258-7669). Fax 907/258-SHOE (907/258-7463). 17 units, 13 with bathroom. TV TEL. $89 double without bathroom, $99–$149 double with bathroom. Rates include continental breakfast. Additional person in room $10 extra. AE, DISC, MC, V.

This cheerful, family-run hotel on a quiet downtown street has comfortable, light, and attractively decorated rooms with bright fabrics, all perfectly clean. The six rooms with shared bathrooms are in pairs, and the bathrooms are close and secure. There's no better bargain downtown. Freezer and storage space and a coin-op laundry are available. No smoking.

The Voyager Hotel 501 K St., Anchorage, AK 99501. ℂ **800/247-9070** or 907/277-9501. Fax 907/274-0333. www.voyagerhotel.com. 38 units. TV TEL. $159 double. Additional person in room $10 extra. AE, DC, DISC, MC, V.

Thanks to an exacting proprietor, Stan Williams, The Voyager is just right. The size is small, the location central, the rooms large and light (all with kitchens), and the housekeeping exceptional. The desks have modem ports and extra electrical outlets, and the hospitality is warm yet highly professional. There's nothing ostentatious or outwardly remarkable about the hotel, yet the most experienced travelers rave about it the loudest. No smoking.

DINING

Club Paris STEAK/SEAFOOD 417 W. Fifth Ave. ℂ **907/277-6332**. Reservations recommended. Main courses $15–$44; lunch $5.75–$15. AE, DISC, MC, V. Daily 11:30am–2:30pm and 5–10pm; Fri–Sat 5–11pm; no lunch Sun.

Walking from a bright spring afternoon, under a neon Eiffel Tower into midnight darkness, past a smoke-enshrouded bar, and sitting down at a secretive booth for two, we felt as if we should be plotting a shady 1950s oil deal. And we would probably not have been the first. Smoky Club Paris may be too authentic for some, but it's the essence of old Anchorage boomtown years, when the streets were dusty and an oilman needed a class joint in which to do business. Beef, of course, is what to order, and it'll be done right. Full liquor license.

Glacier Brewhouse GRILL/SEAFOOD 737 W. Fifth Ave. ℂ **907/274-BREW**. Reservations recommended for dinner. Lunch $8–$13; dinner $9–$28. AE, MC, V. High season daily 11am–11pm.

A tasty, eclectic, and ever-changing menu is served in a large dining room with lodge decor, where the pleasant scent of the wood-fired grill hangs in the air. They brew five hearty beers behind a glass wall. It's noisy and active, with lots of agreeable if trendy touches, such as the bread—made from spent brewery grain—that's set out on the tables with olive oil. An advantage for travelers is the wide price range—a feta cheese, spinach, and artichoke pizza is under $10.

The Marx Brothers Cafe ECLECTIC/REGIONAL 627 W. Third Ave. ℂ **907/278-2133**. Reservations recommended. Main courses $17.50–$28.50. AE, DC, MC, V. Daily 6–9:30pm.

A restaurant that began as a hobby among three friends nearly 20 years ago is still a labor of love and has become a standard of excellence in the state. The cuisine is varied and creative, ranging from Asian to Italian, but everyone orders the Caesar salad made at the table. The decor and style are studied casual elegance. Beer and wine license.

Simon and Seafort's Saloon and Grill STEAK/SEAFOOD ℂ 907/274-3502. $21 and up. Reservations a must. AE, DISC, MC, V. Lunch Mon–Fri 11:15am–3:30pm; dinner Mon–Fri 5–10pm; no lunch on weekends, but dinner from 4:30pm.

One of the city's great dinner houses with a turn-of-the-century decor, a cheerful atmosphere, and fabulous sunset views of Cook Inlet. Prime rib and seafood are the specialties. Light meals are served in the bar.

2 Seward

Since Seward is the main northern embarkation and disembarkation port for cruise ships exploring the Inside Passage and Gulf of Alaska, cruise passengers can almost be forgiven if they sometimes think the correct name of this Resurrection Bay community is "Seward-the-port-for-Anchorage." Seven-day Gulf of Alaska cruises—which often appear in cruise ship advertising as "Vancouver to Anchorage" (or the reverse)—actually begin or end here and guests are carried by motor coach (or, most recently, by rail) to/from Anchorage. Why? Because Seward lies on the south side of the Kenai Peninsula, Anchorage on the north, and sailing around would add another day to the journey. So most lines prefer to ferry passengers the 125 miles overland.

This means that most people pass through Seward on their way to or from ships but never really see it. And that's a pity. Seward is an attractive little town rimmed by mountains and ocean, its streets lined with old wood-frame houses and new fishermen's residences. It's also home to the spectacular **Alaska SeaLife Center** (a marine-research, rehabilitation, and public-education center where visitors can watch scientists uncovering the secrets of nearby **Prince William Sound**). Seward is an ideal spot from which to make wildlife-watching day trips by boat into the Sound or a variety of road and rail trips through the **Kenai Peninsula,** one of Alaska's most beautiful expanses.

Seward was hit hard on Good Friday, 1964, when a massive earthquake rattled Anchorage, the peninsula, and everything in between. The villagers (there were only about 2,500 of them) watched the water in the harbor drain away after the shaking stopped and realized immediately what was about to happen: a tidal wave. Because they were smart enough to read the signs and run for high ground, loss of life was miraculously slight when the towering 100-foot wall of water struck. The town itself, however, was heavily damaged, so many of the buildings visitors see today are of a more recent vintage than might be expected.

GETTING TO SEWARD & THE PORT

Most cruise passengers will arrive at Seward either by ship (at the end of their cruise) or by bus from the nearest major airport, **Anchorage International Airport.** The bus trip takes about 3 hours, taking passengers through the beautiful Chugach National Forest. If you haven't made transportation arrangements through your cruise line, **Seward Bus Line** (ℂ 907/224-3608) offers one trip a day from Anchorage for $30 one-way. **Holland America Tours' Alaskan Express** (ℂ 800/544-2206) does the same for $40.

BY PLANE   Commuter air service is provided by **Era Aviation** (ℂ 800/866-8394) and **F. S. Air** (ℂ 907/248-9595) from Anchorage for about $75 one-way.

BY CAR   For those arriving by car, Seward and the Kenai Peninsula are served by a single major road, the Seward Highway.

BY TRAIN The **Alaska Railroad** (© **800/544-0552** or 907/265-2494; www.alaska.net/~akrr) offers extraordinarily scenic train service between Anchorage and Seward for $55 one-way ($82 round-trip).

EXPLORING SEWARD

INFORMATION The Seward Chamber of Commerce (© 907/224-8051) operates an information booth right on the cruise-ship dock; it's open from 8am to noon and 3 to 7pm daily. If you're going to have time to look beyond the boundaries of the village, drop in at the **Kenai Fjords National Park Visitor Center,** near the waterfront on Fourth Avenue (© **907/224-3175** or 907/224-2132), to pick up some literature, learn about what's new in the area, and pick up a list of hiking trails in Seward's environs.

GETTING AROUND You can easily cover downtown Seward on foot, although a little help is handy to get back and forth from the boat harbor. If it's not raining, a bike may be the best way. Seward **Mountain Bike Shop** (© **907/ 224-2448**), in a railcar near the depot at the harbor, rents high-performance mountain bikes and models good for just getting around town, plus accessory equipment. A cruiser is $12 half day, $19 full day. For motorized transport, the **Chamber of Commerce Trolley** runs every half hour from 10am to 7pm daily in summer; it goes south along Third Avenue and north on Ballaine Street, stopping at the railroad depot, the cruise-ship dock, the Alaska SeaLife Center, and the harbor visitor center. The fare is $2 per trip, or $4 to ride all day. **Independent Taxi** (© **907/224-5000**) is one of the local cab companies.

ATTRACTIONS WITHIN WALKING DISTANCE

The Alaska SeaLife Center 1000 Rail Way (right on the waterfront at mile 0 of the Seward Hwy.). © **800/224-2525** or 907/224-6300. Admission $12.50 adults, $10 for children 7–12. Daily 8am–8pm.

Opened in 1998, the center allows scientists to study, in their natural habitat, the Steller sea lions, porpoises, sea otters, harbor seals, fish, and other forms of marine life that abound in the area, as well as the umpteen species of local seabird—colorful rock puffins, cormorants, and more. The important thing, of course, is that you can study them, too—through windows that let you right into the undersea world. The center itself is something of a phoenix, rising from the metaphorical ashes of the 1989 *Exxon Valdez* disaster that so drastically affected the area's marine ecology and the creatures that inhabit the sound. Much of the $60 million needed to create the center came from an oil-spill reparation fund established by Exxon Corporation. It would be nice to record that the Center had been an unqualified financial success, but it hasn't. The planners way overestimated the potential visitation, and the facility, strapped for cash, is now looking for government grants. The failure of this great facility to turn a profit is a pity—and probably caused by the fact that visitors tend to land in Seward and almost immediately board trains and coaches for Anchorage, leaving very little time for touring and sightseeing. Nevertheless, the SeaLife Center will continue and should be on everybody's "must see" list.

The Seward Museum Corner of Third and Jefferson sts. © **907/224-3902.** $2 adults, 50¢ children.

The Seward Museum offers historical memorabilia, including a display about the Russian ships built here in the 18th century.

THE BEST SHORE EXCURSIONS

Anchorage City Tour (3–9 hr.; $29–$98): A restroom-equipped motor coach takes you on a 3-hour drive through the Chugach National Forest and along

AIRPORT & INFORMATION ●
Kenai Fjords National Park
   Visitor Center **5**
Seward Airport **1**

ACCOMMODATIONS ■
Best Western Hotel Seward/
   The New Seward Hotel **8**
Breeze Inn **4**
Seward Windsong Lodge **2**
VanGilder Hotel **7**

DINING ◆
Harbor Dinner Club **9**
Ray's Waterfront **3**

ATTRACTIONS ●
Alaska SeaLife Center **10**
The Seward Museum **6**

0   1/4 mi
0   0.25 km

▬ Cruise Ship Dock
⊠ Post Office

Turnagain Arm between Seward and Anchorage. Once you hit Anchorage, the bus makes a circuit through the downtown area, pointing out sights of interest, better shops, and popular restaurants. You'll then be free for a few hours to shop, eat, or visit the Museum of History and Art. The tour is either an all-day round-trip affair from Seward or a half-day trip that ends in Anchorage (either downtown at Egan Center or at the Anchorage Airport).

Exit Glacier (3 hr.; $45): This excursion includes a quick orientation trip through town before heading out the Resurrection River Valley to Exit Glacier. After a short hike along nature trails, you'll come to the glacier face. (*Note:* Chunks fall off the glacier regularly, so keep your distance—park rangers are on hand to see that you do.)

Mount McKinley Flightseeing (3 hr.; $297–$310): This tour is often canceled because of weather conditions, but if the skies are clear, you'll board a private plane at the Seward Airport and swoop over the dramatic valleys of the Kenai Peninsula to watch for wildlife before heading over Anchorage and up the Susitna Valley and Kahiltna River to towering Mount McKinley, the highest peak in North America. On the return flight, you'll pass over Prince William Sound for a different perspective.

Portage Glacier (2–8 hr.; $30–$96): This tour is typically done en route to Anchorage via motor coach, but it's also available as a daylong round-trip excursion from Seward. The MV *Ptarmigan,* an enclosed cruiser with an open top deck, sails up Portage Lake for an hour-long sojourn that sometimes brings you to within 300 yards of the glacier.

Resurrection Bay Wildlife Cruise (4–5 hr.; $77–$99): Board a 90-foot touring vessel for a 50-mile narrated tour into Resurrection Bay and the Kenai Fjords area. The highlight of this one is wildlife-watching; the region is teeming with birds and sea mammals, so chances are good that you'll see eagles, puffins, kittiwakes, cormorants, harbor seals, otters, sea lions, porpoises, and maybe even humpbacks.

ORGANIZED TOURS

Downtown Seward can be explored with the help of a **walking-tour map,** available from the chamber of commerce visitor centers at the docks and elsewhere. **Alaska Railroad** day tours are available for $50 per person on weekends by calling ✆ **800/544-0552** (better to do it in advance of arrival). The ride is as far as Portage and back, one of the state railway's most scenic segments. **Kenai Fjords Tours** (✆ **800/478-8068** or 907/224-8068) has a wide variety of land excursions and day cruises in Resurrection Bay and the Kenai Fjords National Park. A 3-hour Resurrection Bay cruise starts at $54 for adults and $27.50 for children under 12. A 6-hour cruise is priced at $109 for adults and $54 for children, while a 9½-hour, 150-mile cruise, including deli-style lunch, is priced at $139 for adults and $69 for children under 12. **Coastal Kayaking and Custom Adventures Worldwide** (✆ **800/288-2134** or 907/258-3866) offers kayaking day trips in Resurrection Bay for $95, as well as longer trips into Kenai Fjords National Park. **IditaRide dogsled tours,** Old Exit Glacier Road, 3.7 miles out the Seward Highway (✆ **800/478-3139** or 907/224-8607), offers dogsled demonstrations and rides on a wheeled dogsled.

In addition to these tours, fishing charters are available from various operators in the harbor.

ACCOMMODATIONS

Best Western Hotel Seward   217 Fifth Ave., Seward, AK 99664. ✆ **907/224-2378.** Fax 907/224-3112. www.bestwestern.com. 38 units. TV TEL. $176–$206 double. Additional person in room $10 extra. AE, MC, V.

The rooms are large, fresh, and attractively decorated; many have big bay windows, and all have VCRs, refrigerators, and coffeemakers. The view rooms on the front go for a premium. Avoid the south-facing rooms, which look out on the back of another hotel.

The New Seward Hotel (✆ **907/224-8001**) operates out of a connected lobby with the Best Western. The rooms are smaller and less expensive, ranging from $58 to $96 double. It's been called the "New Seward" since 1945, but some rooms have been recently remodeled with pleasant country decor.

The Breeze Inn   1306 Seward Hwy. (P.O. Box 2147), Seward, AK 99664-2147. ✆ **907/224-5237.** Fax 907/224-7024. www.seawardalaskahotel.com. 86 units. TV TEL. $109 single; $119–$160 double. Additional person in room $10 extra. AE, DC, DISC, MC, V.

Located right at the boat harbor, this large, three-story, motel-style building offers good standard accommodations with the most convenient location for a fishing or Kenai Fjords boat trip. Twenty new rooms, at the upper end of the price range, are especially nice. A restaurant and lounge are across the parking lot.

The Seward Windsong Lodge   ✆ **888/959-9590** or 907/224-7116. www.sewardwindsong. com. 12 units. TV TEL VCR. $99–$169 double. Additional person in the room $10. AE, MC, V.

The Windsong and the Best Western are in a league of their own among Seward hotels. The Windsong is the only lodge in Kenai Fjords National Park, and the views reflect that fact. Part of the excellent CIRI Native Indian corporation chain of hotels.

The VanGilder Hotel   308 Adams St. (P.O. Box 2), Seward, AK 99664. ✆ 907/224-3525. Fax 907/224-3689. 20 units. TV. $95 double; $165 suite. Additional person in room $10 extra. AE, DC, DISC, MC, V.

This charming if creaky old place was founded in 1916 and is listed on the National Register of Historic Places. Some rooms have a lot of charm, but authenticity means they tend to be small and unique, so choose carefully.

DINING

The Harbor Dinner Club   STEAK/SEAFOOD   220 Fifth Ave. ✆ 907/224-3012. Main courses $3–$40; lunch $5–$8.50. AE, DC, DISC, MC, V. Daily 11am–2:30pm and 5–11pm.

This old-fashioned family restaurant has been the same reliable place as long as anyone can remember. With white tablecloths and a menu that ranges from fine seafood to a $3 hamburger, you don't have to spend a lot of money to eat in a quiet, well-appointed dining room. Full liquor license.

Ray's Waterfront   STEAK/SEAFOOD   At the small-boat harbor. ✆ 907/224-5606. Main courses $14–$20; lunch $6–$10. AE, DC, DISC, MC, V. 15% gratuity added for parties of 6 or more. Daily 11am–11pm.

The lively, noisy dining room looks out from big windows across the small-boat harbor. This is where the locals will send you, and for good reason: The food is just right, and the atmosphere is fun. The specialty is salmon served on a cedar plank. To eat well and less expensively, order the delicious fish chowder and a small Caesar salad. Don't count on speedy seating or service. Full liquor license.

3 Vancouver

Vancouver is located in the extreme southwestern corner of British Columbia and has the good fortune to be surrounded by both mountains and ocean. The city has been expanding and growing rapidly, thanks to an influx of foreign money (especially from Hong Kong) and has undergone a major construction boom. But the development has not diminished the quality of life in Vancouver, which has a rich cultural heritage that includes northwest-coast Native tribes and a thriving Asian community. The city also has a thriving arts scene including numerous summertime festivals focusing on such topics as folk music, jazz, and comedy. Residents and visitors alike relish the proximity of opportunities to sailboard, rock climb, mountain bike, wilderness hike, kayak, and ski on a world-class mountain. You can do it all in the same day if you have the energy. For day-trippers, the city offers easily accessible attractions including the historic **Gastown district,** with its shops and cafes, and a thriving **Chinatown.** And with the U.S. dollar worth about 40% more here than at home (the exchange rate at press time was U.S.$1 = Can$1.54) a visit to the stores on Robson Street and **Granville Island** is practically a must.

You'll likely visit Vancouver at the beginning or end of your Alaska cruise, as it's the major southern transit point. Crystal—with its longer itinerary from San Francisco—also offers it as a port of call. We recommend that you try to come in at least a day before your cruise (or if you'll be here at the end of your cruise, plan to stay an extra day) so that you have time to explore.

Note: Rates below are calculated in U.S. dollars and could change based on the exchange rate at the time of your trip.

GETTING TO VANCOUVER & THE PORT

Most cruise ships dock at **Canada Place** (© **604/666-7200**) at the end of Burrard Street. The pier terminal is a landmark in the city, noted for its five-sail structure, which reaches into the harbor. It's located at the edge of the downtown district and is just a quick stroll from the **Gastown** area (see below), with its cafes, art and souvenir shops, and Robson Street, where trendy fashions can be found. Right near the pier are hotels, restaurants, and shops, as well as the **Tourism Vancouver Infocentre.** Ships also sometimes dock at the **Ballantyne** cruise terminal, a 5-minute cab ride away.

BY PLANE   Vancouver International Airport is located 8 miles south of downtown Vancouver. The average taxi fare from the airport to downtown is about $20. **Vancouver Airporter** (© **604/946-8866**) buses offer service one-way to the city for about $7 per person for adults (less for kids). **AirLimo** (© **604/273-1331**) offers flat-rate limousine service at $26 for up to six passengers. Car-rental agencies with local branches include Avis, Budget, Hertz Canada, and Thrifty.

EXPLORING VANCOUVER

INFORMATION   The **Vancouver Tourist InfoCentre,** 200 Burrard St. (© **604/683-2000**), is open May to Labor Day from 8am to 6pm, 8:30am to 5:30pm the rest of the year.

GETTING AROUND   You can easily walk the downtown area of Vancouver, but if you want transportation, you've got a few options. The **Translink system** (© **604/521-0400**) includes electric buses, ferries, and the magnetic-rail Sky-Train. Service on the main routes runs from 5am to 2am, and schedules are available at many hotels and online (www.cmbuslink.com). Taxis are available through **Black Top** (© **604/731-1111**), **Yellow Cab** (© **604/681-1111**), and **MacLure's** (© **604/731-9211**), and can be either called or found around the major hotels. You can rent a bicycle from Spokes and **Stanley Park Bicycle Rentals,** 1798 W. Georgia St. (© **604/688-5141**) from $2.50 per hour, $7.50 for a half day, and $10 for a full day. Helmets are required by law and, along with locks, are included in the rate. The city has several great bicycle runs, including Stanley Park and the Seawall Promenade, and Pacific Spirit Park.

ATTRACTIONS WITHIN WALKING DISTANCE

Chinatown   In the area bordered by E. Pender and Keefer sts. from Carrall St. to Gore Ave.

Vancouver's Chinatown is one of the largest in North America (though it doesn't hold a candle to those in New York and San Francisco), and like Gastown, it's also a historic district. Chinese architecture and the **Dr. Sun Yat-sen Garden** (578 Carrall St., © **604/689-7133;** admission is about $5 adults, $3 kids) are among the attractions, along with great food and shops selling Chinese wares. In addition to photogenic Chinese gates, bright-red buildings, and open-air markets, you'll find the amazing 6-foot-wide **Sam Kee Building,** at 8 W. Pender St.

Gastown   Located in the area bordered by Water and Alexander sts. from Richard St. east to Columbia St.

Gastown is named for "Gassy" Jack Deighton, who in 1867 built a saloon in Maple Tree Square (at the intersection of Water, Alexander, and Carrall) to serve the area's loggers and trappers. The Gastown of today offers cobblestone streets, historic buildings, gaslights, a steam-powered clock (near the corner of Water

Downtown Vancouver

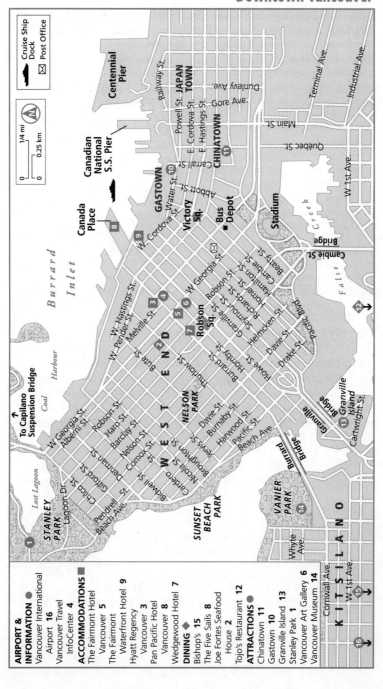

AIRPORT & INFORMATION
Vancouver International Airport **16**
Vancouver Travel InfoCenter **4**

ACCOMMODATIONS ■
The Fairmont Hotel Vancouver **5**
The Fairmont Waterfront Hotel **9**
Hyatt Regency Vancouver **3**
Pan Pacific Hotel Vancouver **8**
Wedgewood Hotel **7**

DINING ◆
Bishop's **15**
The Five Sails **8**
Joe Fortes Seafood House **2**
Tojo's Restaurant **12**

ATTRACTIONS ●
Chinatown **11**
Gastown **10**
Granville Island **13**
Stanley Park **1**
Vancouver Art Gallery **6**
Vancouver Museum **14**

155

and Cambie sts.), street musicians, and a touch of Bohemia. It's so close to the ship pier, it's a must-see. There are boutiques, antiques and art shops, and lots of touristy stuff, along with restaurants, clubs, and cafes.

Granville Island   Across False Creek. (It's a hearty walk from downtown, so depending on where you're staying, you may want to take a cab.)

Granville Island is Nirvana for shoppers. It has a vibrant daily market and streets lined with fine-art studios. Downtown, **Robson Street** is chockablock with boutiques, souvenir shops, coffeehouses, and bistros. The massive **Pacific Centre Mall** fills the city blocks between Robson, Dunsmuir, Howe, and Granville streets. It's within easy walking distance of the pier.

Stanley Park   Downtown Vancouver, northwest of the cruise ship terminal.

Safety Tip

In Vancouver, it's advised not to wander too far off the tourist path. Only a block or two from Gastown, one can encounter needle parks and other places tourists don't want to wander into.

Nestled in the heart of downtown Vancouver, Stanley Park's 1,000 acres contain rose gardens, totem poles, a yacht club, a kids' water park, miles of wooded hiking trails, great vantage points for views of Lions Gate Bridge, and the outstanding **Vancouver Aquarium Marine Science Center,** ✆ **604/659-FISH.** (Admission is $9.50 adults, $8 youth, $6 kids 4–12.)

Vancouver Art Gallery   750 Hornby St. ✆ **604/662-4700.** $6.50 adults (seniors half price Tues), $4 students, free for children under 12.

Located within easy walking distance of the pier, the gallery is housed in a building constructed in 1906 as the provincial courthouse and contains an impressive collection that includes works by British Columbia artist Emily Carr and the Canadian Group of Seven. Also on display are international and other regional paintings, sculptures, graphics, photography, and video ranging from classic to contemporary. The Annex Gallery features rotating educational exhibits geared to younger audiences.

Vancouver Museum   1100 Chestnut St. ✆ **604/736-4431.** $5 adults, $3.50 youth.

The museum offers a history of the city, from the Coast Salish Indian settlement to early pioneers, European settlement, and 20th-century expansion. The exhibit allows visitors to walk through the steerage deck of a 19th-century immigrant ship, peek into a Hudson's Bay Company trading post, and sit in an 1880s Canadian-Pacific passenger car. Re-creations of Victorian and Edwardian rooms show how early Vancouverites decorated their homes. The museum also offers rotating exhibits.

ATTRACTIONS OUTSIDE THE DOWNTOWN AREA

Capilano Suspension Bridge   3735 Capilano Rd., North Vancouver. ✆ **604/985-7474.** Admission is $8 adults, $5 students, $2 kids 6–12, kids 5 and under free.

Sure it's touristy, but it's still a kick to cross this narrow, historic, 450-foot walking bridge, located 230 feet above the Capilano River in North Vancouver (about a 10-min. drive, or about a $13 cab ride) from downtown. Even the towering evergreens below look tiny from that height. (This attraction is not for those with a fear of heights.) The adjacent park offers hiking trails, history and forestry exhibits, a carving center, and Native American dance performances (in the summer months only), as well as restaurants and a gift shop.

ORGANIZED TOURS

Stanley Park Horse-Drawn Tours (© 604/681-5115) has offered tours of the 1,000-acre Stanley Park by horse-drawn trolley for more than a century. The narrated, 1-hour tours depart from the Coal Harbour parking lot beside the Stanley Park information booth on Park Drive. Tickets are $12 adults, $11 students, $7 kids 3 to 12. **The Vancouver Trolley Company** (© 888/451-5581 or 604/801-5515) has old-fashioned (engine-powered) trolleys, offering narrated tours on a circuit that includes Gastown, Chinatown, Granville Island, Stanley Park, and other areas of interest. You can get off and on as you like. Stop #1 is in Gastown. Tickets are $16 adults, $8 kids.

THE BEST SHORE EXCURSIONS

City Tour (2½–3 hr.; $30–$34): This bus tour covers major sights like Gastown, Chinatown, Stanley Park, and high-end residential areas. You'll also visit Queen Elizabeth Park, located at the city's highest southern vantage point, and the Bloedell Conservatory, located in the park's environs and offering a commanding 360° city view as well as an enclosed tropical rain forest complete with free-flying birds.

   Note: This tour usually is offered after the cruise and is available only to passengers with late-afternoon or evening flights. At the end of the tour, you are dropped off at the airport for your flight home.

ACCOMMODATIONS

Virtually all of Vancouver's downtown hotels are within walking distance of shops, restaurants, and attractions, but for safety reasons you might want to avoid places around Hastings and Main after dark. Granville Street downtown is an area that has been "cleaned up" and is now home to some lower-end, boutique-type hotels. The area has clubs and an active nightlife that attracts a younger set—but also lots of panhandlers.

The Fairmont Hotel Vancouver   900 W. Georgia St., Vancouver, BC V6C 2W6. © 800/441-1414 (Fairmont Hotels & Resorts) or 604/684-3131. Fax 604/662-1929. www.fairmont.com. 544 units. A/C MINIBAR TV TEL. $168–$259 double; from $300 suite. AE, DC, DISC, MC, V. Parking $13.

With a $33 million renovation completed in 1996, the grande dame of Vancouver's hotels has been restored beyond its former glory. Designed on a generous scale, with a copper roof, marble interiors, and massive proportions, the hotel has a feeling of unparalleled luxury and spaciousness in its lobby and public areas. High tea is a proud tradition here. Guest rooms have marble bathrooms and mahogany furnishings and offer city, harbor, and mountain views.

The Fairmont Waterfront Hotel   900 Canada Place Way, Vancouver, BC V6C 3L5. © 800/828-7447 (Fairmont Hotels and Resorts) in the U.S., or 604/691-1991. Fax 604/691-1999. www.fairmont.com. 518 units. A/C MINIBAR TV TEL. $168–$246 double; from $298 suite. AE, DC, MC, V. Parking $14.

Twenty-three stories of blue reflective glass, this ultramodern 7-year-old hotel takes great advantage of its harborside location, offering spectacular waterfront and mountain views from 70% of the rooms. The rooms are filled with amenities, including two-line phones. A concourse links the hotel to the rest of Waterfront Centre, Canada Place, and the Alaska cruise-ship terminal.

Hyatt Regency Vancouver   655 Burrard St., Vancouver, BC V6C 2R7. © 800/233-1234 or 604/689-3707. Fax 604/643-5812. www.hyatt.com. 644 units. A/C MINIBAR TV TEL. From $175 double; $442 suite. AE, DC, DISC, MC, V. Parking $13.

The Hyatt is an ultramodern white tower built over the huge Royal Centre Mall, which contains 60 specialty shops. The very large guest rooms are tastefully decorated with understated yet comfortable furnishings. Corner rooms on the north and west sides have balconies with lovely views.

Pan Pacific Hotel Vancouver   300–999 Canada Place, Vancouver, BC V6C 3B5. ℂ 800/ 937-1515 or 604/662-8111. Fax 604/685-8690. www.pan-pac.com. 506 units. A/C MINIBAR TV TEL. $165– $318 double; from $379 suite. AE, DC, MC, V. Valet parking $15.

Apart from Vancouver's natural surroundings, the city's most distinctive landmark is Canada Place Pier, whose five gleaming white Teflon sails are reminiscent of a giant sailing vessel. The pier houses the Vancouver Trade and Convention Centre as well as the Alaska cruise-ship terminal. It also offers a splendid **IMAX theater** (ℂ **604/682-4629**) where, for about $7, cruise passengers can while away an hour or so studying the wonders of Alaska and other places, such as Mount Everest and the Galapagos Islands. Atop the terminal is the spectacular 23-story Pan Pacific Hotel Vancouver. This and the Waterfront Hotel are the closest accommodations to the cruise-ship dock. All of the guest rooms are modern, spacious, and comfortably furnished. Recently added were new amenities including coffeemakers, irons, and ironing boards. Try to book a harborside room so you can enjoy the view.

Wedgewood Hotel   845 Hornby St., Vancouver, BC V6Z 1V1. ℂ 800/663-0666 or 604/689-7777. Fax 604/608-5348. www.wedgewoodhotel.com. 89 units. A/C MINIBAR TV TEL. $143–$234 double; from $299 suite. AE, DC, MC, V. Parking $10.

This small, boutique property near the Robson Street shops offers individually furnished rooms filled with nice amenities. Penthouse suites also offer fireplaces, wet bars, Jacuzzis, and scenic garden terraces. Public rooms boast antiques and fresh flowers, and this hotel has one of the best waterholes in town, Bacchus, an upscale piano bar where you can sink into a plush chair or couch, enjoy an excellent martini, and take in the local scene. The Bacchus restaurant has also won awards for its fine cuisine.

DINING

Bishop's PACIFIC NORTHWEST   2183 W. Fourth Ave. ℂ **604/738-2025.** Reservations required. Main courses $18–$23. AE, DC, MC, V. Mon–Sat 5:30–11pm; Sun 5:30–10pm.

The atmosphere features candlelight, white linen, and soft jazz; the service is impeccable; and the food is even better. Owner John Bishop greets you personally, escorts you to your table, and introduces you to an extensive catalog of fine wines and a menu he describes as "contemporary home cooking"—which means dishes such as roast duck breast with sun-dried Okanagan Valley fruits and candied ginger glacé, steamed smoked black cod with new potatoes and horseradish sabayon, and marinated sirloin of lamb. If you have only one evening to dine out in Vancouver, spend it here.

The Five Sails WEST COAST/PACIFIC RIM/SEAFOOD   999 Canada Place Way, in the Pan Pacific Hotel. ℂ 604/891-2892. Reservations recommended. Main courses $17–$23. AE, DC, MC, V. Sun–Fri 6–10pm; Sat 6–11pm.

The Five Sails' view of Coal Harbour, the Lions Gate Bridge, and the Coast Mountains is spectacular (request a table near the window when you make reservations) and so is the food, an eclectic mix of Thai, Mongolian, Japanese, Vietnamese, and nouvelle influences.

Joe Fortes Seafood House SEAFOOD   777 Thurlow St. ℂ 604/669-1940. Reservations recommended. Most main courses $11–$17 ($25 for a veal chop). AE, DC, DISC, MC, V. Sun–Thurs 11:30am– 11pm; Fri–Sat 11:30am–midnight.

This two-story, dark-wood restaurant with an immensely popular bar is always filled with Vancouver's young and successful crowd. The decor and atmosphere are reminiscent of an oyster bar, and the spacious, covered and heated roof garden (where cigar smokers gather) is pure Vancouver. Pan-roasted oysters are a menu staple. A daily selection of up to a dozen types of oysters is offered raw or cooked in a variety of ways, along with fresh fish and Dungeness crab and live lobsters (at market prices). The wine list has earned well-deserved awards 8 years and running.

Tojo's Restaurant JAPANESE 777 W. Broadway. ✆ 604/872-8050. Reservations required for sushi bar. Main dishes from $11; complete sushi dinners from $34. AE, DC, MC, V. Mon–Sat 5–11pm.

Located above an A&W burger joint, this restaurant has an unimpressive decor but nice city views if you can snag a window seat. And Hidekazu Tojo's sushi is Vancouver's best, attracting Japanese businessmen, Hollywood celebrities, and anyone else who's willing to pay for the best. Tell Tojo how much you want to spend, and he'll prepare an incredible meal to fit your budget.

4 Juneau

Since Juneau is also a major port of call, we refer you to the Juneau section in chapter 9, "Ports & Wilderness Areas Along the Inside Passage," for a map and information on attractions and tours.

GETTING TO JUNEAU & THE PORT

BY PLANE Juneau is served by Alaska Airlines (✆ **800/426-0333** or 907/789-9791), with daily nonstop flights from Seattle and Anchorage. Because weather can wreak havoc with landing conditions, it's especially advisable if you're flying to Juneau to plan on getting there a day or two before your cruise embarkation date.

A cab from the airport to downtown will cost about $20. The Island Waterways van (✆ **907/780-4977**) charges $8 per person to major hotels. The Capital Transit city bus (✆ **907/789-6901**) offers hourly service for $1.25, but your luggage has to sit at your feet. Major car-rental companies have offices at the airport.

INFORMATION

The Davis Log Cabin Visitor Center, 134 Third Ave., at Seward Street (✆ **907/586-2201**), is open daily from 9am to 5pm mid-May through September, Monday through Friday the rest of the year. The visitor center at the cruise ship dock is open from 8:30am to 6pm mid-May to mid-September.

ACCOMMODATIONS

Goldbelt Hotel Juneau 51 W. Egan Dr., Juneau, AK 99801. ✆ 888/478-6909 or 907/586-6900. Fax 907/463-3567. www.goldbelttours.com. 105 units. TV TEL. $169 double, mountain side; $179 double, water side. Additional person in room $15 extra. AE, DC, DISC, MC, V.

This is a recently renovated hotel with large, nicely appointed rooms favored by business travelers. The rooms on the front have good views of the Gastineau Channel. The atmosphere is quiet and almost hermetic. There's a Mediterranean-theme restaurant off the lobby.

Inn at the Waterfront 455 S. Franklin, Juneau, AK 99801. ✆ 907/586-2050. Fax 907/586-2999. 21 units, 12 with private bathroom. TEL. $77 double, $60–$72 double with shared bathroom; $101 suite. Additional person in room $9 extra. AE, DC, DISC, MC, V.

This charming little inn across from the cruise-ship dock feels like a small European hotel, with its narrow stairs, oddly shaped rooms, and understated elegance. The proprietors make the most of the building's gold-rush history as a semilegal brothel, but the place is better than the typical Victorian kitsch. The Summit, one of Juneau's most sophisticated restaurants, is downstairs.

Prospector Hotel 375 Whittier St., Juneau, AK 99801-1781. ℂ **800/331-2711** or 907/586-3737. Fax 907/586-1204. 58 units. TV TEL. $100 double, $125–$135 double with kitchenette. AE, DC, DISC, MC, V.

The Prospector is a comfortable hotel right on the waterfront, with large, standard rooms in attractive pastel colors. More than two dozen rooms have kitchenettes, and some of the more expensive ones are like nice furnished apartments. Those facing the channel have good views. The lower level, called the first floor, is half-basement and somewhat dark.

Westmark Baranof Hotel 127 N. Franklin St., Juneau, AK 99801. ℂ **800/544-0970** or 907/586-2660. Fax 907/586-8315. www.westmarkhotels.com. 193 units. TV TEL. $49–$159 double. AE, DC, DISC, MC, V.

In winter, the venerable old Baranof acts like a branch of the state capitol building for conferring legislators and lobbyists; in the summer, it's like a branch of the package-tour companies. The nine-story concrete building, built in 1939, has the feel of a grand hotel, although some rooms are on the small side. The upper-floor rooms are modern and have great views on the water. There are many room configurations, so make sure you get what you want. Kitchenettes are available.

DINING

The Fiddlehead Restaurant and Bakery SEAFOOD/ECLECTIC 429 W. Willoughby Ave. ℂ **907/586-3150.** Reservations recommended for the Fireweed Room. Main courses $8.25–$22; lunch $7–$15. 15% gratuity added for parties of 6 or more. AE, MC, V. Daily 6:30am–10pm.

In 1978, the Fiddlehead was the first restaurant of its quality in the region, serving cuisine that tends toward natural ingredients, vegetarian dishes, and occasional experimentation. It's sometimes inspired and sometimes less than perfect. The upstairs Fireweed Room, open from 5 to 9pm Thursday through Saturday, offers a more expensive and formal experience with huge picture windows and live music. Downstairs is quite reasonably priced, with a cafe atmosphere amid wood and stained glass. Full liquor license.

Red Dog Saloon SALOON FOOD 728 S. Franklin. ℂ **907/463-3777.** AE, MC, V.

Not by any means an elegant eatery; more of an experience. The Red Dog is a Juneau landmark, and its restaurant serves good, wholesome food in a frontier atmosphere. Try the world's biggest hamburger (a justifiable claim) for $12. Just don't go looking for speedy or particularly distinguished service.

9

Ports & Wilderness Areas Along the Inside Passage

The Inside Passage runs through the area of Alaska known as **Southeast.** It's that narrow strip of the state—islands, mainland coastal communities, and mountains—that stretches from the Canadian border in the south to the start of the Gulf in the north, just above Glacier Bay National Park. Since the typical cruise itinerary begins or ends in Vancouver, British Columbia (which we've covered in chapter 8, "The Ports of Embarkation"), we've arranged the ports chapters geographically, moving from Vancouver northward.

For ports and wilderness areas in the Gulf of Alaska, see chapter 10.

1 Victoria, British Columbia

We know it's in Canada, not Alaska, but cruises that start in Seattle or San Francisco typically include Victoria (on Vancouver Island) as a port of call on the way up to Alaska. This lovely city, the capital of British Columbia, offers Victorian architecture and a very proper British atmosphere—some say it's more British than Britain itself—with high tea and a visit to **Butchart Gardens** among the main attractions.

A former British outpost, Victoria claims a history filled with maritime lore: Whalers and trade ships once docked in the city's harbors, transporting the island's rich bounty of coal, lumber, and furs throughout the world. More recently (as historical events go), John Wayne summered here, and the Nixons honeymooned here.

Take a tour around the island and you'll see gorgeous homes and gardens and views that include the snowcapped mountains of Washington State. Or head downtown for shopping bargains.

COMING ASHORE   Cruise ships dock at the Ogden Point cruise ship terminal on Juan De Fuca Strait. Take the shuttle to the **Inner Harbour,** where flower baskets, milling crowds, and street performers liven the scene under the watchful eye of the grand **Empress Hotel,** famed setting for English-style high tea.

INFORMATION   You can pick up a map of the city at the Visitors Information Center (© **250/382-2127**), on the waterfront at 812 Wharf St. It's open daily from 9am to 8pm in May and June, 9am to 9pm in July and August, and 9am to 5pm the rest of the year.

SHORE EXCURSIONS

City Tour & Butchart Gardens (3½–4 hr.; $44 and $55): After an abbreviated tour of the sights in Victoria, the bus makes the 13-mile trip out the Saanich

Southeast Alaska

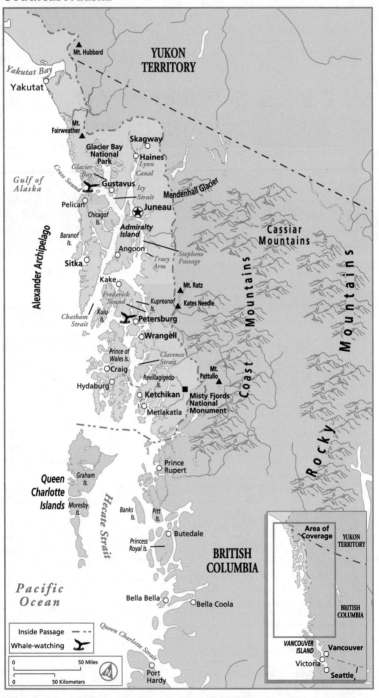

Peninsula to world-renowned Butchart Gardens in Brentwood Bay, where you'll have 2 hours or so to explore the 130-acre grounds. Expanded trips include high tea at the gardens (4 hr., $62).

City Tour with High Tea or Castle Visit (2½–4 hr.; $35 and $74): This guided excursion aboard a double-decker bus takes you by the major sights of the Inner Harbour, downtown, and residential areas; the variation comes with a stop for afternoon high tea or a visit to Craigdarroch Castle. (*Note:* Buses cannot park right at the castle, so some walking is required.)

TOURING THROUGH LOCAL OPERATORS

Several local operators greet passengers right at the pier, offering rides into the city and longer tours using various modes of transportation. **Heritage Tours and Daimler Limousine Service** (© 250/474-4332) does tours using stretch limos, Rolls Royces, and Daimlers. Fares are about $45 an hour for a six-passenger Daimler, the same for an 11-passenger van. Other luxury cars in the fleet go as high as $75 an hour. On a similar concept, a new firm, **Classic Car Tours** (© 250/883-8747), offers tours in classic convertibles (perfect on a sunny day), along with commentary we found colorful and delightful. Fares are $45 an hour; the cars seat up to four guests. The bicycle rickshaws operated by **Kabuki Kabs** (© 250/385-4243) and competing firms offer an unusual way to get into the city for about $40 an hour (for two people). For those seeking a more traditional bus tour, **Gray Line of Victoria** (© 250/388-5248) offers tours of Victoria and Butchart Gardens, leaving from near the Empress Hotel. The 1½-hour Grand City Tour costs $12 for adults and $6 for children; the 3-hour tour including the gardens is $26 adults, $13 kids.

ON YOUR OWN: WITHIN WALKING DISTANCE

The Fairmont Empress Hotel   721 Government St. © 250/384-8111.

Located right by the Inner Harbour, this ivy-covered 1908 landmark has a commanding view of the harbor and an opulent lobby and is the place to go for your British-style high tea. Call ahead for reservations and ask about the dress code. (No shorts, no tank tops.) Tea with pastries, scones, sandwiches, and all the trimmings runs about $30 a person. Around back of the hotel you'll find the **Miniature World** museum (© 250/385-9731), with quirky displays that include big dollhouses, the world's smallest working sawmill, and a model of London in 1670. Admission is $6 adults, $4.50 kids.

The Pacific Wilderness Railway   206–1208 Wharf St. © 800/267-0610 or 250/206-1208. Tickets $22 adults, $13 children 6–12, $6.50 children 5 and under in the deluxe air-conditioned coaches. Prices in the heritage coaches (no A/C, but the windows can be opened) are $3 cheaper all around.

The terminus of this attraction, now in its third year, is about 8 blocks from the Empress Hotel. It offers passengers a 20-mile, 2½-hour ride into the wilderness in vintage railcars, with narration along the way. It's an ecological adventure rather than a sightseeing spectacular, but it's well worth doing. However much fun the railway outing is, it doesn't seem to have captured as many visitors' hearts and minds as it might have. In 2001, operators ended the season early—in July—citing "low ridership." Nevertheless, the train is expected to roll again this year. Just check to be sure when you arrive in Victoria.

Royal British Columbia Museum and National Geographic IMAX Theatre   675 Belleville St. © 888/447-7977 or 250/387-3701. Museum admission $6 adults, $4 youth (6–18), family admission $16, children 5 and under free; IMAX admission $6.50 adults, $4.25 youth, $2 children 5 and under.

Victoria, British Columbia

Butchart Gardens **1**
Craigdarroch Castle **5**
The Fairmont
Empress Hotel **3**
Miniature World **3**
Pacific Wilderness
Railway **2**
Royal British Columbia
Museum/National
Geographic
IMAX Theatre **4**

Cruise Ship Dock

ⓘ Information

Outside the entrance to this modern, three-story concrete-and-glass museum is a glass-enclosed display of towering totem poles and other large sculptural works by Northwest Native artists. Inside, exhibits highlight the natural history of the province and Victoria's recent past, and another exhibit demonstrates how archaeologists study ancient cultures, using artifacts from numerous local tribes. There's also an IMAX theater showing features on nonlocal places like the Amazon. (The shows change every few months.) Behind the museum is **Thunderbird Park,** with Native totem poles and a ceremonial house. **Helmecken House,** 10 Elliot St., next to the park, is one of the oldest houses in British Columbia; it was the home of a pioneer doctor, and there are lots of torturous-looking medical tools to shudder over.

ON YOUR OWN: BEYOND WALKING DISTANCE

Butchart Gardens   800 Benevenuto Ave., in Brentwood Bay. ✆ 250/652-5256. Admission $12 adults, $6 youth 13–17, $1.30 kids 5–12, 4 and under free.

A ride by cab, public bus, or other transportation (see "Touring Through Local Operators," below) and several free hours will be required for a visit to these world-famous gardens. Well worth visiting, they lie 13 miles north of downtown Victoria on a 130-acre estate featuring English, Italian, and Japanese gardens, water gardens, and rose gardens. There are also restaurants and a gift shop on site. (*Note:* You can catch a public bus from downtown Victoria for only $1.60 [each way], or Gray Line offers a shuttle from near the Empress Hotel for $2.60. A cab will cost you about $25 each way.)

Craigdarroch Castle   1050 Joan Crescent. ✆ 250/592-5323. Admission $3.50 adults, $1.40 children.

You have to take a cab to see Craigdarroch Castle, the elaborate home of millionaire Scottish coal-mining magnate Robert Dunsmuir, who built the place in the 1880s. The four-story, 39-room Highland-style castle is topped with stone turrets and furnished in opulent Victoria splendor.

2 Canada's Inside Passage

Canada's Inside Passage is simply the part of an Inside Passage cruise that lies in British Columbia, south of the Alaskan border and running to Vancouver. On big ships, the first day out of Vancouver (or the last day going south) is usually a day at sea, a day to enjoy seeing the coastal beauties of the British Columbia mainland to the east and Vancouver Island to the west, including some truly beautiful scenery in Princess Louisa Inlet and Desolation Sound.

In most cases, that's all the ships do, though: go past. In their haste to get to Ketchikan, the first stop in Alaska, they invariably sail right past much of the Canadian Inside Passage. That may be a blessing in disguise. **Prince Rupert,** the only sizable community on that stretch and the only one capable of handling largish influxes of visitors, isn't much of a draw.

One of the Canadian Inside Passage's loveliest stretches is **Seymour Narrows,** 5 or 6 hours north of Vancouver, just after the mouth of the Campbell River. It's so narrow that it can only be passed at certain hours of the day, when the tide is right. Again, cruise visitors are often denied its full beauty because ships tend to reach it late in the day or in the wee small hours. On the long days of summer, it is often possible to enjoy Seymour Narrows if you're prepared to stay up late.

The U.S./Canadian border lies just off the tip of the Misty Fjords National Monument, 43 sailing miles from Ketchikan (and 403 miles from Glacier Bay, for those who are keeping count).

Shopping for Native Art

If you're interested in Native Alaskan art, you need to be aware that there is a large market in fakes. There have been noted cases of shopkeepers' assistants being spotted removing "Made in Taiwan" stickers from supposedly Native art objects with razor blades.

Before you buy a piece of Native art, ask the art dealer for a biography of the artist and ask whether the artist actually carved the piece (rather than just lending his or her name for knockoffs). Most dealers will tell you where a work really comes from, but you have to ask.

Price should also be a tip-off to fakes, as real Native art is pricey. An elaborate mask, for instance, should be priced at $3,000, not $300. Be particularly wary of soapstone carvings, as most are not made in Alaska.

There are two marks used for Alaska products: a Made-in-Alaska **polar bear sticker,** which means the item was at least mostly made in the state, and a **silver hand sticker,** which indicates authentic Native art. An absence of the label, however, does not mean the item is not authentic; it may just mean the artist doesn't like labels.

3 Ketchikan

Ketchikan is the southernmost port of call in Southeast Alaska, and its residents sometimes refer to it as "the first city." That's not because they seriously believe that it's the most important to the region's economy, or that it's the biggest, or even that it was literally the first built. It's just that it's the first city visited by cruise ships on the Inside Passage run northbound out of Vancouver or Seattle.

Just about the first thing that greets arriving cruise passengers on the dock at Ketchikan is a "Liquid Sunshine Gauge" put up by the city several years ago, on which is marked the cumulative rainfall, day by day. We once checked and saw that the mark showed over 36 inches—and it was only June. Even at that, the gauge had a long way to go. The average annual rainfall is about 160 inches (more than 13 ft.!) and has topped 200 inches in its worst years.

But here's a strange thing. Through the years, we've been in Ketchikan at least once in every month of the season, and we can recall only two real downpours. Go figure.

Maybe it's because the weather gods have been kind to us that we have a soft spot for the place. But it's not the only reason. Climate notwithstanding, this really is a fun port to visit, a glorified fishing village with quaint architecture, history, salmon, the great scenery that is to be found in just about every Inside Passage community, and **totem poles**—lots and lots of totem poles.

Ketchikan is a vigorous center of the Tlingit, Tsimshian, and Haida cultures. These proud Southeast Alaska Native peoples have preserved their traditions and their icons intact over the centuries and have re-created **clan houses** and made replicas of totem poles irretrievably damaged by decades of exposure to the elements. The tall, hand-carved poles are everywhere—in parks, in the lobbies of buildings, in the street. It should be no surprise to anyone that there are more totems in Ketchikan than in any city in the world.

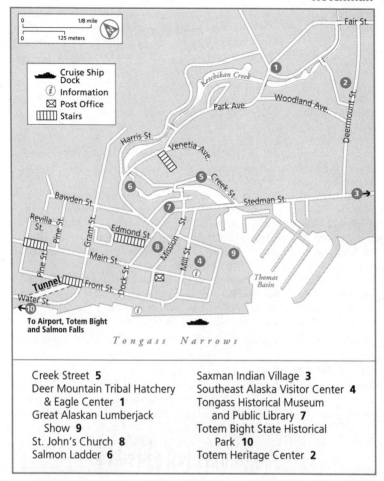

A word of caution about that: Unless you're really, really interested in the origins and the meaning of totem poles, choose your shore excursion very carefully. It was a cold day the last time we did the **Totem Bight State Historical Park** tour, but the guide, oblivious to the group's discomfort, seemed intent on sharing with us every fact he'd ever learned about Alaska Native cultures and relating, in infinite detail, the story behind pole after pole after pole. (They're not merely decorative, you see: Each tells a story of an incident in a tribe's life, a battle, a birth, and so on.) The first half dozen were fine, but then, frankly, the time began to drag. We're as curious as anyone else about other cultures, but by the time we climbed back on the coach more than 2 hours later to return to the ship, our teeth were chattering and our eyes were glassy from information overload.

The centerpiece of downtown Ketchikan is **Creek Street,** a row of buildings on pilings over a stream up which the salmon swim in their spawning season. Today, the narrow, wood-sidewalk street is filled mainly with boutiques (Soho Coho, for example, an art gallery specializing in offbeat pieces by local artists) and funky restaurants, such as the Creek Street Cafe. But it's what used to be there that gives Creek Street its special cachet. Once, in the early 1900s, this was Ketchikan's red-light district, with more than 30 brothels lining the waterway. It was, according to the little historical sign at the head of the street, the place where both the fishermen and the fish went up the stream to spawn. For reasons that don't seem to be entirely clear to anybody, the most famous of the courtesans (or at least the most enduring) was a woman who went by the name of Dolly Arthur. (Her real name was Thelma Copeland.) She wasn't necessarily the most financially successful of the ladies of the night, and if her pictures are any indication, she probably wasn't the prettiest. But somehow, her name outlived the rest. Most people can tell you who Dolly Arthur was, but it's doubtful if many could name another Creek Street madam. **Dolly's House** is now a small museum. Like the houses' old clientele, you have to pay to get inside. We don't know what they used to pay, but it'll cost you $4.

One of our favorite things to do in Ketchikan is to walk the short distance from the ship, by way of Creek Street, and take the **funicular railway to the Westmark Cape Fox Lodge** for lunch. The lunch is nourishing (if hardly gourmet), and the Alaskan Amber Beer is refreshing, but it's the views of the city—of the Tongass Narrows and of Deer Mountain, both from the funicular and from parts of the lodge and its grounds—that make the trip worthwhile.

It's also an easy walk from here to the **Deer Mountain Tribal Hatchery & Eagle Center,** at 1158 Salmon Rd. (admission is $6.95), a Native-run operation where you can learn where salmon come from and also see some rescued and healing eagles. Also nearby is the Totem Heritage Center (see below).

COMING ASHORE   Ships dock right at the pier in Ketchikan's downtown area.

INFORMATION   The first two places we usually drop into upon arrival in Ketchikan are the **Visitors Bureau Information Center** (© **907/225-6166**) on Front Street, right on the dock, to pick up literature and information on what's new in town (and discount coupons for attractions), and the **Southeast Alaska Visitor Center** (© **907/228-6214**) on nearby Main Street, one of the four Alaska Public Lands Information facilities in the state. The latter is more than a mere dispenser of information; it also houses a museum in which a number of exhibits and dioramas depict both the Native Alaskan cultures and the more modern business development of Ketchikan. Admission to the exhibits is $4.

SHORE EXCURSIONS

Misty Fjords Flightseeing (2 hr.; $184–$195): Everyone gets a window seat aboard the floatplanes that run these quick flightseeing jaunts over Misty Fjords National Monument. No ice fields and glaciers on this trip, but Misty Fjords has another kind of majesty: You'll see sparkling fjords, cascading waterfalls, thick forests, and rugged mountains dotted with wildlife, then come in for a landing on a serene wilderness lake.

Saxman Native Village Tour (2–2½ hr.; $42–$47): This modern-day Native village, situated about 2½ miles outside Ketchikan, is home to hundreds of Tlingit, Tsimshian, and Haida and is a center for the revival of Native arts and culture. The tour includes either a Native legend or a performance by the Cape Fox dancers in the park theater and a guided walk through the grounds to see the totem poles and learn their stories. Craftspeople are sometimes on hand in the working sheds to demonstrate totem-pole carving.

Sport-fishing (4–6 hr.; $160–$179): If catching salmon is your goal, Ketchikan is a good spot to do it. Chartered fishing boats come with tackle, bait, fishing gear, and crew to help you strike king and coho around the end of June or pink, chum, and silver from July to mid-September. (*Note:* $10 fishing license and $10 king-salmon tag are extra.)

Totem Bight Historical Park and City Tour (2–2½ hr.; $31–$36): This tour takes you by bus around Ketchikan and through the Tongass National Forest to see the historic Native fish camp where a ceremonial clan house and totem poles sit amid the rain forest. There's a fair amount of walking involved, making the tour a poor choice for anyone with mobility problems.

Tatoosh Island Sea Kayaking (4 hr.; $110–$125): There are typically two kayaking excursions offered in Ketchikan: this one (which requires you to take a van and motorized boat to the islands before starting your 90-min. paddle) and a trip that starts from right beside the cruise-ship docks. Of the two, this one is far more enjoyable, getting you out into a wilder area rather than just sticking to the busy port waters. The scenery is incredible, and you have a good chance of spotting bald eagles, seals (whether swimming around your boat or basking on the rocks), and leaping salmon.

Mountain Point Snorkeling Adventure (3 hr.; $79): Believe it or not, you can snorkel around Ketchikan, where the climate is warm for Alaska. Still, it's not the Caribbean, and insulating wetsuits are provided on this excursion, as well as hot beverages for when you get out of the water. Undersea are fish, starfish, sea urchins, sea cucumbers, and more.

TOURING THROUGH LOCAL OPERATORS

A bevy of tour operators sell their offerings at the **Ketchikan Visitors Bureau Information Center** (© **907/225-6166**) on Front Street, right at the dock. For a fun private tour, **Classic Tours** (© **907/225-3091**) offers 2-hour downtown sightseeing excursions in a 1955 Chevy for $75 for one or two people, $100 for three, $125 for four, and so on.

ON YOUR OWN: WITHIN WALKING DISTANCE

Creek Street   Off Stedman St., along Ketchikan Creek.

Ketchikan's former red-light district is now its number-one tourist attraction. The view of Creek Street from the bridge over the stream on Stedman Street (the main thoroughfare) is said to be the most photographed in Alaska. It may well be. (See introduction above for more lore and legend.)

The Great Alaskan Lumberjack Show   Behind Salmon Landing, just a few hundred yards from the cruise terminal. © **888/320-9049.** Admission $29 adults, $14.50 kids 6–12, kids 5 and under free.

In just 2 years, this show has become a popular attraction. It features logrolling, speed climbing, tree topping, chain-saw carving, and all of the other skills that real, honest-to-goodness lumberjacks possess. The amphitheater has covered grandstands to keep you from getting soggy.

The Salmon Ladder   Off Park Ave., in Ketchikan Creek.

We could spend hours on the observation deck at the artificial salmon ladder just off Park Avenue watching these determined fish make their way from the sea up to the spawning grounds at the top of Ketchikan Creek. How these creatures can keep throwing their exhausted bodies up the ladder at the end of their long journey from the ocean, never giving up though they fail in three out of four leaps, is one of those mysteries of nature that we will never understand—and never tire of observing.

St. John's Church　On Bawden St., at Mission.

St. John's Church is the oldest place of worship in town. Both the church (Episcopal, by the way) and its adjacent Seaman's Center—built in 1904 as a hospital and now a commercial building—are interesting examples of local early 1900s architecture.

Tongass Historical Museum and Public Library　In the Centennial Building at 629 Dock St. ✆ 907/225-5600. Admission is $2.

This museum offers Indian cultural displays and a fine exhibit outlining how Ketchikan earned its reputation as the Salmon Capital of the World. It also contains one of the city's grizzlier relics: the bullet-riddled skull of Old Groaner, a brown bear that took to molesting humans and was shot for its troubles.

Totem Heritage Center　601 Deermount St. ✆ 907/225-5900. Admission $4, kids 12 and under free. If you're also planning to visit the nearby Deer Mountain Tribal Hatchery (see above), buy a combo ticket for $9.95 and save a buck.

The Totem Heritage Center, built by the city of Ketchikan in 1976, has the virtue of being indoors, so weather isn't a factor. The museum houses a fine collection of 33 original totem poles from the 19th century, retrieved from the Tlingit Indian villages of Tongass and Village Islands and the Haida village of Old Kasaan. The Tsimshian people are also represented in some exhibits. There's a nice nature path outdoors. Be aware it's a long walk to the museum unless you take the funicular (see above), which at least lets you avoid some of the uphill hike.

ON YOUR OWN: BEYOND WALKING DISTANCE

Saxman Indian Village　2½ miles south of town on the S. Tongass Hwy. ✆ 907/225-4846. Admission $30 adults, $15 kids 12 and under. The village is mostly sold as a shore excursion for cruise passengers, at about $45 a head. If you want to do it independently (frankly, we don't advise it), you can take a cab from the ship for about $12 or $13.

This modern Native village is a center for the revival of Native arts and culture. There's a totem pole park (and artists at work on new poles) and a theater that showcases Native dance, and the 2-hour tours are timed to coincide with cruise ship arrivals.

Totem Bight State Historical Park　On the edge of Tongass Narrows, 10 miles outside town.

See introduction, above, for details. Visits to the facility are available from **Ketchikan City Tours** (✆ **800/652-8687** or 907/225-9465) for $29 adults, $12.50 for kids. We do not recommend taking a cab to Totem Bight State Park. It's a long way out, and the fare is hefty.

4 Misty Fjords National Monument

The 2.3-million-acre, Connecticut-size area of Misty Fjords starts at the Canadian border in the south and runs on the eastern side of the Behm Canal, which has Revillagigedo Island on the other side. (Ketchikan is on the western coast of Revillagigedo.) It is topography, not wildlife, that makes a visit here worthwhile. Among the prime features of Misty Fjords are New Eddystone Rock, jutting 237 feet out of the canal, and the Walker Cove/Rudyerd Bay area, a prime viewing spot for marine life, eagles, and other wildlife. Volcanic cliffs (up to 3,150 ft. high), coves (some as deep as 900 ft.), and peace and serenity are the stock-in-trade of the place.

Only passengers on small ships will see Misty Fjords close up, as its waterway is too narrow in most places for big ships. The bigger ships pass the southern tip of the Misty Fjords National Monument and then veer away northwest to dock at Ketchikan. Unfortunately, this means they miss one of the least spoiled of all wilderness areas.

By the way, the name Misty Fjords comes from the climatic conditions. Precipitation tends to leave the place looking as though it was under a steady mist much of the time. It was named a protected national treasure by U.S. President Jimmy Carter in 1978.

5 Admiralty Island National Monument

Situated about 15 miles due west of Juneau (see below), this monument comprises almost a million acres and covers about 90% of Admiralty Island. It's another of those Alaska areas that cruise passengers on the bigger ships will never set foot on, but whose villages, some of them Native, have recently begun to gain the interest of some small-ship operators. The Tlingit village of Angoon, for example, welcomes small groups of visitors off ships. Small ships (such as those operated by Alaska's Glacier Bay Cruiseline) may also ferry passengers ashore in a more remote area of the island for a hike. Admiralty Island is said to have the highest concentration of bears on earth.

6 Tracy Arm & Endicott Arm

Located about 50 miles due south of Juneau, these long, deep, and almost claustrophobically narrow fjords are a striking feature of a pristine forest and mountain expanse with a sinister name: **Tracy Arm–Ford's Terror Wilderness.** The place gets its name from the 1889 incident in which a crewman from a U.S. naval vessel (name: Ford; rank: unknown) rowed into an inlet off Endicott Arm and found himself trapped for 6 hours in a heaving sea as huge ice floes bumped and ground around and against his flimsy craft. He survived, but the finger of water in which he endured his ordeal was forever after known as Ford's Terror.

The Tracy and Endicott arms, which reach back from Stephens Passage into the Coastal Mountain Range, are steep-sided waterways, each with an active glacier at its head—the **Sawyer Glacier** in Tracy Arm and **Dawes Glacier** in Endicott. These calve constantly, sometimes discarding ice blocks of such size that they clog the narrow fjord passages, making navigation difficult. When the passage is not clogged, ships can get close enough for amazing viewing and hearing. (The sound of white thunder is amazing!) And on a Radisson ship last year, we were thrilled to find the captain ordering out the tenders at Sawyer Glacier to provide lucky passengers optimum viewing and a great photo op.

A passage up either fjord offers eye-catching views of high, cascading waterfalls, tree- and snow-covered mountain valleys, and wildlife that might include **Sitka black-tailed deer, bald eagles,** and possibly even the odd **black bear.** Around the ship, the animals you're most likely to see are whales, sea lions, and harbor seals.

7 Baranof Island

Named after the Russian trader Alexander Baranof, Russian America's first appointed honcho, the island's main claim to fame is **Sitka,** on the western coast, the center of Russian-era culture and the seat of the Russian Orthodox Church in Alaska. (The island name, by the way, is often spelled Baranov, which some people contend is the way Alexander himself spelled it.) **Peril Straits,** off the northern end of the island, separating Baranof from Chichagof Island, is a scenic passageway too narrow for big cruise ships. Some of the smaller ones can manage the passage.

8 Sitka

Sitka differs from most ports of call in Inside Passage cruises in that, geographically speaking, it's not on the Inside Passage at all. Rather, it stands on the outside (or western) coast of Baranof Island. Its name, in fact, comes from the Tlingit Indian Shee Atika, which means "People on the outside." For the relatively short time it takes ships to get to Sitka, they must leave the protected waters of the passage and sail with nothing between them and Japan but the sometimes turbulent Pacific Ocean. If you're going to run into heavy seas at any point on an Inside Passage cruise, chances are you'll find them here. And this is one of the few ports in Alaska where you'll likely tender to shore (in small ships) rather than dock at the harbor. Be that as it may, the idea of missing this delightful port of call is unthinkable to many people, the two of us included.

Step off your cruise ship here, and you step into Russian Alaska, the Alaska of 200 years ago. This is where, in 1799, trader Alexander Baranof established a fort in what became known as New Archangel. Today, Sitka has two attractions that, more than any others, reflect its Russian heritage. **St. Michael's Cathedral,** with its striking onion-shaped dome and its ornate gilt interior, is one. Located on Lincoln Street, at the focal point of the downtown thoroughfare, it's the official seat of the Russian Orthodox church in Alaska. The other is the **New Archangel Dancers,** who perform during the cruise season in **Harrigan Centennial Hall,** just a stone's throw from the pier. The colorfully costumed, 30-strong troupe performs a program of energetic Russian folk dances daily—several times a day, in fact. Once a week, the **New Archangel Dancers** get together with a Tlingit dance troupe in a joint performance in the Sheet'ka Kwaan Naa Kahidi Community House on Katlian Street. (See "On Your Own: Within Walking Distance," below, for more information.)

Most attractions in Sitka are within walking distance of the passenger docks. The **Sitka National Historical Park,** a must-do attraction with its impressive (mostly reproduction) totem poles and excellent views is about a 15-minute walk from the passenger docks. One attraction that is too far to walk to but ought not to be missed is the **Alaska Raptor Rehabilitation Center.** A nonprofit venture supported by tour companies, cruise lines, and public donations, the center was opened in 1980 to treat sick or injured birds of prey (primarily eagles) and to provide an educational experience for visitors. We don't mind admitting that the sight of our majestic national bird close up, with its snowy white head and curved beak, gives us goose bumps. We often wonder what they're thinking about when they fix you with that unblinking, disdainful eye. You almost get the feeling that they're asking, "What do you think you're gaping at, Buster?"

If you get the munchies while in town, stop at the Sitka Bowling Center (no, we're not kidding), where you'll find good burgers and shakes. Next door, at the **Shee Atika Lodge,** you can get a fancier restaurant meal. Highliner Coffee (behind the Subway shop, which is behind the lodge) offers lattes and other coffee drinks and excellent baked goods (try the giant oatmeal cookies) and has computers you can use (for a fee) to e-mail your friends back home.

Sitka

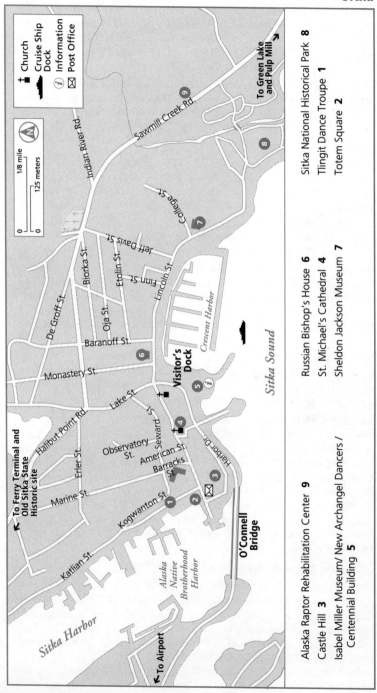

Legend:
- ✝ Church
- Cruise Ship Dock
- ⓘ Information
- ⊠ Post Office

Alaska Raptor Rehabilitation Center **9**
Castle Hill **3**
Isabel Miller Museum/ New Archangel Dancers / Centennial Building **5**

Russian Bishop's House **6**
St. Michael's Cathedral **4**
Sheldon Jackson Museum **7**

Sitka National Historical Park **8**
Tlingit Dance Troupe **1**
Totem Square **2**

COMING ASHORE Most passengers will arrive in Sitka by tender because the harbor is too small to accommodate large ships. Tenders drop you right by the downtown area, but shuttle buses are also available to ferry you to local sights ($7 for an all-day pass, or $3 for a one-way pass). They meet arrivals at the docks. Cabs are also available for a $3 ride downtown.

INFORMATION Pick up a map at the **Sitka Convention and Visitor Center** in the Centennial Building at the Visitors Dock (which also houses the Isabel Miller Museum and the auditorium where the New Archangel Dancers perform). Or call the Visitors Bureau at ✆ **907/747-5940.**

SHORE EXCURSIONS

Sea Otter & Wildlife Quest (3 hr.; $95–$106): A naturalist accompanies passengers on this jet-boat tour to point out the various animals you'll encounter and explain the delicate balance of the region's marine ecosystem. They're so sure you'll see a whale, bear, or otter that they offer a partial cash refund if you don't.

Silver Bay Nature Cruise (2 hr.; $34–$42): An excursion vessel takes you through beautiful Silver Bay to view wildlife, scenery, the ruins of the Liberty Prospect Gold Mine, and a salmon hatchery.

Sitka Historical Tour (3 hr.; $40–$45): This bus excursion hits all the historic sights, including St. Michael's Cathedral, the Russian Cemetery, Castle Hill, and Sitka's National Historic Park with its totem poles and forest trails. This tour is often combined with a performance by the New Archangel Dancers and/or a visit to the Alaska Raptor Rehabilitation Center. (Tours including either or both of the latter cost $45–$55.)

Sport-fishing (4 hr.; $145–$170): An experienced captain will guide your fully equipped boat to a good spot for halibut and salmon; the rest is up to you. Your catch can be frozen or smoked and shipped to your home, if you wish. (*Note:* A $10 fishing license and a $10 king-salmon tag are extra.)

TOURING THROUGH LOCAL OPERATORS

Tribal Tours (✆ **907/747-7290**), owned by the Sitka Tribe of Alaska, offers a cultural tour program giving the history of Sitka with an emphasis on Native history and culture. Tickets can be purchased at the Sheet'ka Kwaan Naa Kahidi Community House at 200 Katlian St. (near the tender docks). A 1-hour city tour is $10 a person. A 2½-hour comprehensive tour, priced at $29, includes a 45-minute narrative drive, a half-hour stop at the Sheldon Jackson Museum, a stop at the Sitka National Historical Park, and a performance by the Tlingit Indian Dance Troupe. (For $39, you also get to visit the Alaska Raptor Rehabilitation Center.)

ON YOUR OWN: WITHIN WALKING DISTANCE

Castle Hill Climb stairs near intersection of Lincoln and Katlian sts.

At first, we found the prospect of the climb up to the top of the hill—by way of a lengthy flight of stairs from the western end of Lincoln Street—a little daunting, but after climbing to the top, we have two words of advice: Do it. The reward is panoramic views of downtown Sitka. This is where the first post–Alaska purchase U.S. flag was raised, in 1867.

Isabel Miller Museum Also in the Harrigan Centennial Building. Admission is free, but donations are accepted.

Sharing a building with the above dance troupe, this museum, operated by the Sitka Historical Society, outlines the city's history with art and artifacts. There's also a large diorama of Sitka as it was in 1867 when land was transferred from Russia to the U.S.

New Archangel Dancers   Performances (on most days that a cruise ship is in port) are held in the Harrigan Centennial Building, 330 Harbor Dr., near the tender docks. ✆ 907/747-5516. Admission is $6, and tickets must be purchased at least ½ hour before the show.

The dancers are all women—they even play the men's parts, complete with false beards if the action requires it—and the way they throw themselves around the stage makes us tired just watching. Where do they get the energy? When the troupe was organized in 1969, the men of the town pooh-poohed the idea. It'll never work, they said. Later, when the original handful of women proved that it could work, some of the men expressed that they might not mind joining in. Too late, guys. The founders decided to keep the show all female.

The Russian Bishop's House   A few blocks past the cathedral, at Lincoln and Monastery sts. ✆ 907/747-6281. Admission is $3 for upstairs tour. (You need to have exact change.)

The house was built in 1842 and is owned and operated by the National Parks Service. Ranger-led tours include the Bishop's furnished quarters and an impressive chapel. Exhibits downstairs trace the development of New Archangel into Sitka.

The Sheldon Jackson Museum   104 College Dr. (at Lincoln St.). ✆ 907/747-8981. Admission $4, under 18 free.

Located on the grounds of the college founded by the Presbyterian missionary of that name as a vocational school for young Tlingits (founded in 1878, it was the first educational institution in Alaska), the museum now contains a fine collection of Native artifacts—not just those of the Tlingits, but also those of the Aleut, Athabascan, Haida, and Tsimshian peoples, as well as the Native peoples of the Arctic. The museum also has a decent gift shop.

Sitka National Historical Park   106 Metlakatla St. (about a 15-min. walk from the tender pier). ✆ 907/747-6281.

At just 107 acres, it's the smallest national park in Alaska, but don't let that discourage you, because the place fairly reeks of history. This is where the Russians and the Tlingits fought a fierce battle in 1804. Within the park are a beautiful totem-pole trail (which you can tour on a ranger-led tour or on your own) and a newly renovated visitor center where Native artisans from the Southeast Alaska Indian Cultural Center create totems, jewelry, and Native drums.

St. Michael's Cathedral   Located at Lincoln and Cathedral sts. ✆ 907/747-8120. Admission $2.

Even if you're not a fan of religious shrines, you'll probably be impressed by the architecture and the finery of this rather small place of worship. One of the 49th state's most striking and photogenic structures, the current church is actually a replica; the original burned to the ground one night in 1966. So revered was the cathedral that Sitkans, whether Russian Orthodox or not, formed a human chain and carried many of the cathedral's precious icons, paintings, vestments, and jeweled crowns from the flames. Later, with contributions of cash and labor from throughout the land, St. Michael's was lovingly re-created on the same site and rededicated in 1976. It still contains those religious symbols that the citizens worked so hard to rescue from the inferno.

Tlingit Indian Dance Troupe   At the Sheet'ka Kwaan Naa Kahidi Community House at 200 Katlian St., just 100 yds. or so from the tender dock. ✆ 907/747-7290. Tickets $6.

This troupe puts on a show that encapsulates Sitka's history. It goes like this: The Tlingits were there first; then the Russians came; the two sides fought wars; and finally they learned to live together in harmony.

Totem Square Katlian St., at the west end of Lincoln St. ℭ **907/747-6671**.

This area was originally under water. It was the Russian shipyard, which was reclaimed from the sea in 1940–41 and now contains Russian cannons, huge anchors believed to have come from ships lost in Sitka Harbor in the 1700s, and other historical memorabilia.

ON YOUR OWN: BEYOND WALKING DISTANCE
Alaska Raptor Rehabilitation Center 1101 Sawmill Creek Rd. (milepost 0.9), just across Indian River. ℭ **907/747-8662**. Admission $10 adults, $5 children under 12. (Proceeds help heal the birds.)

Local informational literature claims that the center is 20 minutes on foot from town, but these must be some kind of special chamber-of-commerce minutes because it seems to take that long by bus. However you get there, though (and every cruise line offers it as a shore excursion), the center is well worth seeing. It's not a performing-animal show, with stunts and flying action, but rather a place where injured raptors (birds of prey) are brought and, with luck, healed to the point where they can be returned to the wild. Some eventually can; those that cannot are housed permanently at the center or sent to zoos. The tour through the center and surrounding rain forest takes about an hour.

9 Juneau

Quick quiz: Can you name a state capital that cannot be reached by road from anywhere else in the state? The answer is Juneau, of course. Fronted by the bustling Gastineau Channel and backed by Mount Juneau (elevation 3,819 ft.) and Mount Roberts (elevation 3,576 ft.), the city is on the mainland of Alaska but is cut off by the Juneau Icefield to the east and wilderness to the north and south. To be sure, there are roads—150 miles of them, in fact—but they all dead-end against an impenetrable forest.

The nature of its isolation makes Juneau one of those win-a-beer-in-a-bar trivia questions. It also means that not all Alaskans believe Juneau is the right and logical place for a legislative center. Its inaccessibility, some argue, disenfranchises many voters, and every few years somebody puts a "move the capital" initiative on the ballot. Like all the rest (so far), the most recent such proposal was defeated, which is good news for Juneau's 12,500 civil servants. In Juneau, government is the city's biggest industry. However, tourism is not far behind: Besides the thousands of independent visitors who arrive by air and ferry, many thousands more come ashore during the 450-plus passenger-ship port calls made here each summer.

On any given day, four or five cruise ships may be in port, ranging from the biggest in the fleets of Princess, Celebrity, Holland America, to the small ships of Cruise West, Glacier Bay Cruiseline, Clipper, and others. The small ships and most of the large ships usually find a dock, but depending on how many large ships are in port that day, some might have to anchor in the channel and tender their guests ashore.

It surprises some people to think that a city so dependent on the revenue generated by tourism, and cruises in particular, should think of imposing additional taxes on visitors, but that's just what Juneau did 2 years ago. Some movers and shakers there decided that they didn't like having their turf invaded by so many outsiders, and so imposed a $5 head tax on each arriving cruise passenger, ostensibly to cover the cost of the vital services they use—roads, police, sewers, and so on. As tourism-minded as we are, it's easier to grasp the residents' unhappiness when you figure numbers. We were recently in Juneau on a day when three

Downtown Juneau

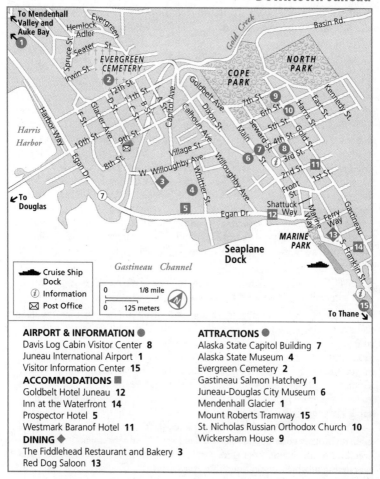

large ships were docked and another was anchored in the channel. That meant that more than 6,000 visitors—counting crews—might be coming ashore that day, equal to almost one-sixth of the total population of Juneau!

Juneau is a product of Alaska's golden past. It was no more than a fishing outpost for local Tlingit Indians until 1880, when gold was discovered in a creek off the Gastineau Channel by two prospectors, Joe Juneau and Richard (Dick) Harris. To be absolutely accurate, the gold was discovered first by Chief Kowee of the Auk Tlingit clan who, in return for 100 warm blankets (more important to him than gold), passed the information on to a German engineer named George Pilz. Pilz, then surveying sites around the Inside Passage for mineral deposits, gave the hitherto unsuccessful Juneau and Harris directions to the spot described by Chief Kowee—and they couldn't find it! Only when Kowee accompanied them on a second expedition did they succeed in pinpointing the source of the precious metal. And the rush was on.

Mines sprang up on both sides of the channel. So rich was the area's gold yield that mines continued to open for the next 3 decades, including the most successful of them all, the **Alaska-Juneau Mine,** known locally simply as the A-J, which produced a whopping 3.5 million ounces of gold before it closed in 1944.

Today, Juneau is arguably the most handsome of the 50 state capitals, despite a glut of souvenir shops near the pier (where you can buy anything from "I Love Alaska" backscratchers to fur coats), and runs with a mix of quiet business efficiency and easygoing informality. It has a good deal more sophistication to it than any city in Alaska outside of Anchorage, and yet it also has the frontier-style **Red Dog Saloon,** a sawdust-floored, swing-door, memorabilia-filled pub (offering food and drink) whose old-time raucousness may be tempered by its pursuit of the tourist buck (and by its location—adjacent to the Juneau Police headquarters) but whose appeal is undeniable. (Another place to enjoy a not-so-quiet drink is the bar of the **Alaskan Hotel,** nearby on South Franklin St., built in 1913. On the National Register of Historic Sites, the Alaskan is Juneau's oldest operating hotel.)

For those who can tear themselves away from that cool drink, Juneau offers another major attraction: the **Mendenhall Glacier,** at the head of a valley a dozen miles away and one of Alaska's most accessible and most photographed ice faces.

COMING ASHORE   Unless you arrive on one of the busiest days of the year, your ship will dock right in the downtown area, along Marine Way.

INFORMATION   Midway down the cruise-ship wharf is a blue building housing the visitor information center; stop in to pick up a walking tour map and visitors' guide before striking out to see the sights. The pier is directly adjacent to the downtown area, but there is also shuttle bus service available that travels back and forth along the waterfront road. The **Davis Log Cabin Visitor Center** (© 907/586-2201), located on Third Street and Seward, is another spot to pick up maps, suggested walking itineraries, and Juneau literature. It's a replica of Juneau's first school.

While you're at the dockside visitor center, look down the dock a bit for the oversize bronze statue of Patsy Ann, a beady-eyed bull terrier who in the 1930s was dubbed "the official boat greeter of Juneau" because she never failed to meet all arriving boats. Consider yourself greeted.

SHORE EXCURSIONS

Gold History Tour (1½ hr.; $36–$40): Juneau's gold-rush history comes to life (especially for kids) as you pan for gold near the ruins of a mine while a guide in prospector garb recounts colorful tales of the gold rush.

Glacier Helicopter Tour (2–4 hr.; $176–$310): Here's your chance to walk on the face of a glacier. The price differential depends on whether you actually land on the glacier, and for how long, or simply overfly the ice surface for sightseeing purposes. After transferring to the airport by bus, guests board helicopters bound for Mendenhall, Norris Glacier, or other glacier areas. (The more expensive trips involve the pilot choosing his preferred route, which will likely go farther afield than the standard tour.) The tours may include one or two stops on a glacier and soaring over the jagged peaks carved by the massive Juneau Icefield. If special equipment (boots, rain slickers, and so on) is required, they will be provided. As if this isn't already a once-in-a-lifetime experience, there are also more elaborate helicopter-travel offerings, such as a fantastic **Glacier Dog Sled Expedition** that combines a flight over the Juneau Icefield with a visit to a dog-mushing camp (3 hr.; $310–$365).

Mendenhall Glacier & City Highlights Tour (2½–4 hr.; $30–$75): Twelve miles long and 1½ miles wide, Mendenhall is the most visited glacier in the world and the most popular sight in Juneau. This trip will take you by bus to the U.S. Forest Service Observatory, from which you can walk up a trail to within half a mile of the glacier (which feels a lot closer) or take one of the nature trails if time allows. After this, you will visit Juneau's historic highlights and you may, on some tours, also visit the Gastineau Salmon Hatchery, the Alaska State Museum, and other local attractions.

Mendenhall Glacier Float Trip (3½ hr.; $85–$105): On the shore of Mendenhall Lake, you'll board 10-person rafts, and an experienced oarsman will guide you out past icebergs and into the Mendenhall River. You'll encounter moderate rapids and stunning views, and be treated to a snack of smoked salmon and reindeer sausage somewhere along the way.

Rain Forest Nature Walk (3 hr.; $60–$64): Explore the world's largest temperate rain forest on this easy hike along trails made of wooden planks. You'll see lush vegetation, tall trees, bogs, and babbling brooks, as well as beaches and excellent views of Glacier Bay, and there's a good chance you'll spot wildlife, including an eagle or two.

Wilderness Lodge Flightseeing Adventure (3 hr.; $184–$210): This trip combines flightseeing over glaciers and an ice field with a stop at the Taku Glacier Lodge for a traditional all-you-can-eat salmon bake. After a hearty lunch, you can hike the nature trails around the wilderness lodge before reboarding the floatplane for the flight back to Juneau.

TOURING THROUGH LOCAL OPERATORS

The Juneau Trolley Car Company (℃ 907/789-4342) provides narrated tours around the downtown area. (Pickup is at the Tram Center at the pier.) You can get off and on as you like at sites including the Alaska State Capital. Fares are $12.60 adults, $8.95 kids. Also at the pier, you'll find booths operated by various independent tour operators selling city and glacier tours starting at about $15 to $20 a head.

ON YOUR OWN: WITHIN WALKING DISTANCE

The Alaska State Capitol Building   Fourth St., between Main and Seward.

We've often wondered how so lovely a capital city could come up with such an unprepossessing legislative home. The interior is worth a visit, though. Tours leave the reception desk every half hour.

The Alaska State Museum   Whittier St., right up the hill from the seaplane dock. ℃ 907/456-2901. Tickets $4, free for kids.

This place opened as a territorial museum in 1900 and has a wildlife exhibit, a first-class collection of artifacts reflecting the state's Russian history and Native cultures, and reminders of the city's mining and fisheries heritage.

The Evergreen Cemetery   12th St., just west of the downtown area.

Here, you can view the gravesites of Joe Juneau, Richard Harris, and a lot of other pioneers.

The Juneau-Douglas City Museum   Corner of Fourth and Main sts. ℃ 907/586-3572. Admission $3, free for kids.

This museum highlights the development of the city from its golden beginnings to statehood. The facility specializes in programs and displays geared toward youngsters.

Mount Roberts Tramway   At the cruise-ship docks. (888/461-TRAM or 907/463-3412. Open 9am–9pm.

The best place to take in Juneau's lovely position on the Gastineau Channel is from high up on Mount Roberts, the ascent of which used to entail a strenuous hike but is now an easy 6-minute ride away in the comfortable, 60-passenger cars of the Mount Roberts Tramway. Operated by Goldbelt, a Tlingit corporation that also owns Alaska's Glacier Bay Cruiseline (see chapter 6), the tramway rises from a base alongside the cruise-ship docks and whisks sightseers 2,000 feet up to a center with restaurant/bar, gift shop, museum, cultural film shows, a series of nature trails (bring mosquito repellent!), and a fabulous panorama. Don't miss it, but on the other hand, don't bother if the day is overcast: Many's the visitor who's paid his or her $20 ($10.50 for kids) for an all-day pass, gotten to the top, and been faced with a solid wall of white mist.

The Red Dog Saloon   Located on Franklin St. and Marine Way, right by the cruise-ship docks.

This is the place to go for a taste of frontier Alaska—and of the scrumptious locally brewed Alaskan Amber ale. Look up on the wall behind the bar, where, among other things (many other things), they've got one of Wyatt Earp's pistols. Also look on the walls, where you'll see scrawled messages from legions of cruise-ship passengers that came before you.

St. Nicholas Russian Orthodox Church   Fifth and Gold sts.

This tiny, ornate, octagonal structure is altogether captivating. It was built in 1893 by local Tlingits who, under pressure from the government to convert to Christianity, chose the only faith that allowed them to keep their language. (Father Ivan Veniaminov had translated the Bible into Tlingit 50 years earlier, when the Russians were still in Sitka.) Open daily through the season. A donation of $2 is requested.

The Wickersham House   Seventh St. (907/586-9001.

The house was built in 1899 and bought in 1928 by Judge James Wickersham, who did much to shape the face of Alaska. (He was the first territorial delegate to the U.S. Congress, was in the vanguard of the fight for statehood, and founded the University of Alaska.) (*Note for walkers:* The house is at the top of a very steep hill.)

ON YOUR OWN: BEYOND WALKING DISTANCE
The Gastineau Salmon Hatchery   2697 Channel Dr., about 3 miles from downtown.

From the well-designed outdoor decks at this hatchery, visitors can watch the whole process of harvesting and fertilizing salmon eggs. The Capital Transit bus stops at the hatchery on its way from downtown to the airport. Pick up a route map and schedule at the visitor information center at the cruise-ship dock.

Mendenhall Glacier   Off Mendenhall Loop Rd.

Mendenhall is the easiest glacier to get to in Alaska and the most visited glacier in the world. Its U.S. Forest Service visitor center has glacier exhibits, a video, and rangers who can answer questions, and there are several trails that'll take you closer to the glacier, the easiest being a half-mile nature trail. Mendenhall is located about 13 miles from downtown, but taxis and local bus services are readily available in town (the bus costs $1.25 each way; taxis about $15) for those who want to visit independent of a tour. (If you take a taxi out, make arrangements with the driver to also pick you up—and negotiate a round-trip price before you leave.)

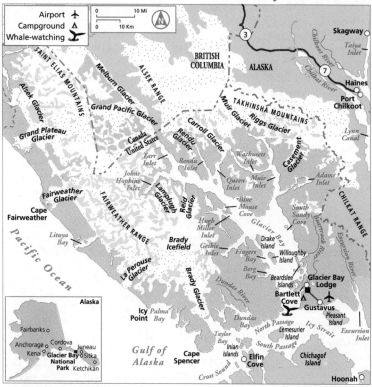

Legend:
- Airport ✈
- Campground ⛺
- Whale-watching 🐋

0   10 Mi
0   10 Km

BRITISH COLUMBIA — ALASKA

Skagway
Taiya Inlet
Chilkoot River
Chilkat River
Haines
Port Chilkoot
Lynn Canal

SAINT ELIAS MOUNTAINS
Melburn Glacier
ALSEK RANGE
TAKHINSHA MOUNTAINS
Muir Glacier
Riggs Glacier
Alsek Glacier
Grand Pacific Glacier
Carroll Glacier
Rendu Glacier
Wachusett Inlet
Casement Glacier
Adams Inlet
CHILKAT RANGE
Grand Plateau Glacier
Canada United States
Tarr Inlet
Rendu Inlet
Queen Inlet
Muir Inlet
South Sandy Cove
Excursion River
Fairweather Glacier
Johns Hopkins Inlet
Lamplugh Glacier
Reid Glacier
Blue Mouse Cove
Glacier Bay
Cape Fairweather
FAIRWEATHER RANGE
Hugh Miller Inlet
Drake Island
Willoughby Island
Lituya Bay
Brady Icefield
Geikie Inlet
Fingers Bay
Berg Bay
Beardslee Islands
Glacier Bay Lodge
Pacific Ocean
La Perouse Glacier
Brady Glacier
Dundas River
Bartlett Cove
Gustavus
Pleasant Island
Icy Point
Palma Bay
Dundas Bay
North Passage
Lemesurier Island
Icy Strait
Excursion Inlet
Taylor Bay
South Passage
Inian Islands
Elfin Cove
Chichagof Island
Gulf of Alaska
Cape Spencer
Cross Sound
Hoonah

Alaska
Fairbanks
Anchorage Cordova Juneau
Kenai Glacier Bay Sitka
National Ketchikan
Park

10 Icy Strait, Point Adolphus & Gustavus

The strait, the promontory, and the town all lie at or near the mouth of Glacier Bay, in prime **whale-watching** waters. The whales, who migrate to the bay each year to feed in preparation for their winter breeding in Mexico, must pass through the strait to get in or out. Passengers aboard large ships may well be fortunate enough to see them on their journey, and those in small ships will likely have an even better chance—they have the luxury of going places the bigger vessels can't, and their size and maneuverability make it possible for them to get closer than the others.

The big ships don't visit **Gustavus,** which isn't too much of a town anyway (it has just 400 residents) and is interesting more as an anthropological exercise ("What on earth makes people live here?") than anything else.

11 Glacier Bay National Park & Preserve

There are about 5,000 glaciers in Alaska, so what's all the fuss about Glacier Bay? Everybody has a theory about that, of course. Some think it's the wildlife, which includes humpback whales, bears, Dall sheep, seals, and more. Some people think it's the history of the place, which was frozen behind a mile-wide wall of ice until about 1870 and, a mere 55 years later, was designated along with its 3.3 million surrounding acres as a national park. Those with an interest in geology and glaciology might argue it's the receding ice faces at the ends of Glacier Bay's various inlets, which are thought to be the fastest moving in the world, receding at some 1½ inches a year. Whatever the reason, Glacier Bay has taken on an allure unachieved by other glacier areas.

The first white man to enter the vast (60-plus miles) Glacier Bay inlet was naturalist **John Muir** in 1879; just 100 years or so before Muir, when Capt. James Cook and, later, George Vancouver sailed there, the mouth was a wall of ice. Today, all that ice has receded, leaving behind a series of glaciers and inlets (**Margerie, Johns Hopkins, Muir,** and others) whose calving activity provides the entertainment for hundreds of cruisers lining the rails as their ships sit, becalmed, for several hours. Watching massive slabs of ice break away and crash with a roar into the ice-strewn waters is one of our favorite experiences.

Each ship that enters the bay takes aboard a park ranger who provides commentary over the ship's PA throughout the day about glaciers, wildlife, and the bay's history. On large ships, they may also give a presentation about conservation in the show lounge; on small ships, they'll often be on deck throughout the day and available for questions.

12 Haines

This pretty and laid-back port is an example of Alaska the way you probably thought it would be. It's a scenic, small-town place with wilderness at its doorstep. If you are not on one of the few ships that regularly visit Haines (pop. 2,250), you can easily reach the port on a day excursion from **Skagway.** (The two communities lie at the northern end of the Lynn Canal, just a stone's throw apart.) The trip is worth the $35 round-trip water-taxi fare, especially for those who have "done" Skagway before.

The thing that's immediately striking about Haines is its setting, arguably one of the prettiest in Alaska. The village lies in the shadow of the Fairweather Mountain Range, about 80 or so miles north of Juneau and on the same line of latitude as the lower reaches of Norway. Framed as it is by high hills, it is more protected from the elements than many other Inside Passage ports. Ketchikan, for instance, gets up to 200 inches of rain in a bad year, Haines a mere 60 inches. That's positively arid by some Southeast Alaska standards!

Haines was established in 1879 by Presbyterian missionary S. Hall Young and naturalist John Muir as a place to convert the Chilkoot and Chilkat Tlingit tribes to Christianity. They named it for Mrs. F. E. Haines, secretary of the Presbyterian National Committee, who raised the funds for the exploration. The natives called it *Da-Shu,* the Tlingit word for "End of the Trail." Traders knew the place as Chilkoot. The military, who came later and built a fort here in 1903, knew it as Fort Seward or Chilkoot Barracks. In 1897–98, the town became one of the lesser access routes to the Klondike (behind Skagway and Dyea) at the head of what became known as the Jack Dalton Trail into Canada. At about the same time, gold was discovered much closer to home—in Porcupine, just 36 miles away—and that strike drew even more prospectors to Haines. The gold quickly petered out, though, and Porcupine is no more.

Its gold history, its military background, and its Native heritage are the significant tourist draws in Haines. So are **eagles.** The place is a magnet for these magnificent creatures, a couple hundred of which are year-round residents of the area. Unfortunately, cruise passengers are unable to experience one of Haines's most spectacular avian events, the annual **Gathering of the Eagles,** which occurs in winter (say, Oct until mid-Feb), after the cruise season, and which brings as many as 4,000 birds from all over the Pacific Northwest to the area in

Haines

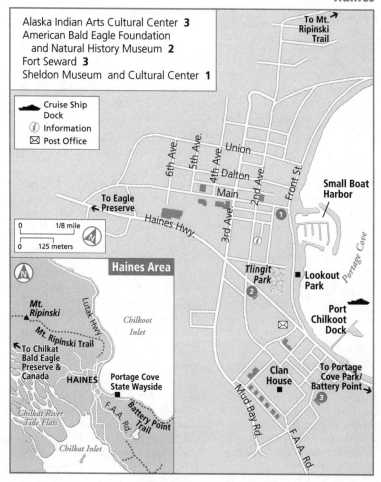

Alaska Indian Arts Cultural Center **3**
American Bald Eagle Foundation
  and Natural History Museum **2**
Fort Seward **3**
Sheldon Museum and Cultural Center **1**

Cruise Ship Dock
ⓘ Information
✉ Post Office

To Mt. Ripinski Trail

6th Ave.
5th Ave.
4th Ave.
Union
Dalton
Main
2nd Ave.
Front St.
3rd Ave.

Small Boat Harbor

To Eagle Preserve

Haines Hwy.

0   1/8 mile
0   125 meters

Portage Cove

Haines Area

Tlingit Park

Lookout Park

Mt. Ripinski

Lutak Hwy.

Chilkoot Inlet

Mt. Ripinski Trail

To Chilkat Bald Eagle Preserve & Canada

HAINES

Portage Cove State Wayside

F.A.A. Rd.

Battery Point Trail

Chilkat River Tide Flats

Chilkat Inlet

Port Chilkoot Dock

Clan House

Mud Bay Rd.

To Portage Cove Park/ Battery Point

F.A.A. Rd.

search of salmon, which can't be found anywhere else during those months. During this time, trees along a 5-mile stretch of the river (in an area known as the **Alaska Chilkat Bald Eagle Preserve**) are thick with rows of these snow-headed raptors—often a dozen or more sharing a limb, from which they swoop down to carry off their favorite takeout food. But even during the cruise season, you're likely to spot at least an eagle or two. We spotted eight in various swooping and tree-sitting poses on a bike ride out to Chilkoot Lake (about 10 miles from the cruise ship pier) last May.

For ages, one of the most popular attractions in Haines was a performance by the **Chilkat Dancers** dance troupe, which performed in space on the Fort William Seward parade ground. The troupe lost its lease last year, though, and ended up canceling both its 2000 and 2001 seasons. No word at press time whether they'll be back in 2002. For updated information, call ⓒ/fax **907/ 766-2160**.

COMING ASHORE   Ships either dock at the Port Chilkoot Dock, directly opposite Fort Seward, or tender passengers in, dropping them either at Port

Chilkoot or at the small-boat harbor in the downtown area, less than a mile away.

INFORMATION   Pick up some walking-tour information on Haines at the visitor center on Second Avenue (© **800/458-3579** or 907/766-2234). It's easy to explore the town on foot, or you can rent a bike at **Sokeye Cycle,** on Portage Street right up the street from the cruise-ship dock (© **907/766-2869**) for $6 an hour or $20 for a half day. (The company also offers guided bike tours.)

SHORE EXCURSIONS

Chilkat Nature Hike (4 hr.; $61–$65): This hike takes you through a rain forest and includes a narrative on forest flora and fauna by a naturalist. You might spot a bald eagle or two. Moderately difficult hiking.

Chilkat Bald Eagle Preserve Jet-Boat Tour (3½ hr.; $84–$98): A bus takes you to the world famous Bald Eagle Preserve, where you board small boats specially designed to traverse the narrows of the Chilkat River into the Alaskan wilderness. Eagle-spotting is the thing on this excursion, and you may also see bears, moose, and beavers.

Best of Haines by Classic Car (1 hr.; $38): Explore Haines in style in a 1930s or '40s vintage automobile. The entertaining guides share the history of the area, and you'll get an insight into how Hainesians live and make their livings.

Chilkat Bicycle Adventure (1½ hr.; $42): Tour the Fort Seward area and then along the Chilkat River estuary by bicycle. You'll hit some minor hills but nothing too challenging. And you may even spot a few eagles. Bike, helmet, and rain gear provided.

TOURING THROUGH LOCAL OPERATORS

Chilkat Guides (© **907/766-2491**), on Portage Street, offers a rafting trip twice a day during the summer down the Chilkat to watch eagles. The rapids are pretty easy—there's a chance you may be asked to get out and push—and you'll see lots of eagles. The 4-hour trip, with a snack, costs $75 plus tax for adults and $37.50 plus tax for children. **Alaska Nature Tours** (© **907/766-2876**) offers a variety of escorted tours including a 3-hour bus and walking tour to the Chilkat Bald Eagle Preserve for $50 per person ($60 with lunch).

ON YOUR OWN: WITHIN WALKING DISTANCE

Alaska Indian Arts Cultural Center   On the south side of the parade grounds. Open 1–5pm Mon–Fri and when cruise ships are in town.

Located in the old fort hospital on the south side of the parade grounds, the Center has a small gallery and a carvers' workshop where you may be able to see totem-carving in progress.

The American Bald Eagle Foundation and Natural History Museum   At Second Ave. and Haines Hwy. © 907/766-3094. Admission $3 adults, $1 kids 8–12, under 8 free.

The foundation celebrates Haines's location in the "Valley of the Eagles" with a huge diorama depicting more than a hundred eagles.

Fort William Seward   Just above the cruise-ship dock.

The central feature of the town, rising right above the docks, Fort Seward was retired after World War II and redone by a group of returning veterans. It's not the kind of place one thinks of when envisioning a fort. It has no parapets, no walls, no nothing—just an open parade ground surrounded by large, wood-frame former barracks and officers' quarters (which have today been converted into private homes, a hotel, a gallery and studio, and the Alaska Indian Arts Cultural Center; see above). In the center of the sloping parade ground, you'll find a replica of a Tlingit tribal house.

The Sheldon Museum and Cultural Center Corner of Main and Front sts. © 907/766-2366. Admission $3 (under 12 free).

Not to be confused with the Sheldon Jackson Museum in Sitka, this place was established by a local man, Steve Sheldon. Small by some museum standards, it nevertheless has a wonderful collection of Hainesiana: Tlingit artifacts, gold-rush-era weaponry, military memorabilia, and so on.

13 Skagway

No port in Alaska is more historically significant than this small town at the northern end of the picturesque Lynn Canal, where a steady stream of prospectors began the long trek into Canada's Yukon Territory at the turn of the century, seeking the vast quantities of Klondike gold that had been reported in Rabbit Creek (later renamed Bonanza Creek). Not many of them realized the unspeakable hardships they'd have to endure before they could get close to the stuff. They first had to negotiate either the **White Pass** or the **Chilkoot Pass** through the coastal mountain range to the Canadian border. To do so, they had to hike 20 miles, climbing nearly 3,000 feet in the process. And, by order of Canada's North West Mounted Police, they had to have at least a year's supply of provisions with them before they could enter the country. Numbed by temperatures that fell at times into the minus-50s, and often blinded by driving snow or stinging hail (they were, after all, hiking through the mountain passes that gave Skagway its name—in Tlingit, Skagua means "Home of the North Wind"), they plodded upward, ferrying part of their supplies up part of the way, stashing them, and returning to Skagway to repeat the process with another load, always inching their way closer to the summit. The process took as many as 20 stages for some, and often enough their stashes were stolen by unscrupulous rivals or opportunistic locals. Some who thought themselves lucky enough to be able to afford horses or mules found their pack animals to be less than sound of limb. Not for nothing is one stretch of the trail through the White Pass (the more popular of the two routes through the mountains) called **Dead Horse Gulch.**

That first leg, arduous as it was, was just the beginning. From the Canadian border, their golden goal lay a long and dangerous water journey away, part of the way by lake (and thus relatively easy), but most of it down the mighty Yukon River and decidedly dangerous.

The gold rush brought to Skagway a way of life as violent and as lawless as any to be found in the frontier west. The Mounties (the law in Canada) had no jurisdiction in Skagway. In fact, there was no law whatsoever in Skagway. Peace depended entirely on the consciences of the inhabitants, and the smell of gold and the realization that there were opportunities for profit without ever setting foot in the Klondike drew to the town many for whom conscience would never be a factor—saloon keepers, gamblers, scarlet women, and desperadoes of every stripe.

The most notorious of the Skagway bad men was Jefferson Randolph "Soapy" Smith, a thug and an accomplished con man. He'd gotten his nickname in Denver, Colorado, by persuading large numbers of people to buy bars of cheap soap for $1 in the belief that some of the bars were wrapped in larger denomination bills. They weren't, of course, but the scam made Smith a lot of money.

In Skagway, he and his gang engaged in all kinds of nastiness, charging local businesses large fees for "protection"; exacting exorbitant sums to "store" prospectors' gear (and then selling the equipment to others); setting up a telegraph station and charging prospectors to send messages home (though the telegraph wire went no farther than the next room); involving themselves in gambling, prostitution, and thuggery; and generally practicing any other kind of nefarious activity to separate the starry-eyed gold-seekers from their cash.

The gold-rush days of Skagway had its heroes as well, of course, one of them the man who finally put an end to Soapy's reign of terror. He was city surveyor Frank Reid, who shot Smith dead and was himself mortally wounded in the gunfight. In his honor, the local citizenry erected an impressive granite monument (which reads, in part, "He gave his life for the honor of Skagway") over his grave in the Gold Rush Cemetery; Smith's marker, on the other hand, is very simple, and his remains aren't even underneath it (they're 3 ft. to stage left, outside consecrated ground). Perversely, though, perhaps because he was the more colorful character, it is the villain Smith whose life is commemorated each July 8, with songs and entertainment.

Another memorable figure of the day was Mollie Walsh, "The Angel of the White Pass." Moved by the suffering of the prospectors trekking into Canada, the pious Walsh opened an eatery in a tent at the summit of the White Pass, from which she dispensed hot soup and coffee to the often frozen gold-seekers. Her life is commemorated in a bronze bust in Mollie Walsh Park at Sixth Avenue and Spring Street, downtown. It says much about the nature of Skagway and the kind of people it attracted at the turn of the century that the man Walsh met and married there murdered her in 1902 and then committed suicide.

Unlike many other Alaska frontier towns, Skagway has been spared the ravages of major fires and earthquakes, and some of the original buildings still stand, protected by the National Park Service. The Klondike Gold Rush National Historic District, which comprises much of the downtown area, contains some striking examples of these. Other little touches of history are preserved around town, such as the huge watch painted on the mountainside above town—it was an early billboard for the long-gone Herman Kirmse's watch-repair shop. Also remaining from back in the day is the White Pass and Yukon Route narrow-gauge railroad, opened in 1900 to carry late stampeders in and gold out, and now a must for visitors. The round-trip to the summit of the pass, following a route carved out of the side of the mountain by an American/Canadian engineering team backed by British money, takes 3 hours from a departure site conveniently located a short walk (or an even shorter shuttle bus ride) from the cruise-ship piers.

Having a sweet little historic town is nice for Skagway's 860 or so year-round residents, of course, but by itself, historicism doesn't pay the bills. So, though Skagway is trying to hang on to its gold-rush heritage, it's also trying to make money off it—so much so, and so successfully, that on any given day in the summer, thousands of seasonal workers will be around to reap the profits from the summer influx of visitors, principally from cruise ships. New businesses, including restaurants and jewelry stores, are sprouting up as well, many of which have gold-rush connotations only in the sense that they've opened to cash in on tourist gold.

A few years back, we were struck that one of the first things that greeted us as we walked from the ship, on the wall of the Mercantile Building on Second

Alaska Wildlife Adventure
  Museum **7**
The Arctic Brotherhood Hall **8**
Case-Mulvihill House
  & Nye House **2**
Eagles Hall **5**
Gault House **3**
Gold Rush Cemetery **1**
Golden North Hotel **9**
Klondike Gold Rush
  National Historic Park
  Visitor Center **9**
Mollie Walsh Park **4**
Moore Cabin **6**
Red Onion Saloon **8**
White Pass and Yukon Route
  Railway **10**

Cruise Ship Dock
Information
Post Office

Avenue, was the most 21st century of all logos: Starbucks Coffee! Then last year, we were actually given a verbal come-on by a clerk at one of those fancy jewelry stores that have followed cruise passengers here from the Caribbean. We know he was only doing his job, but really, you used to be able to window shop in Skagway in peace without having to worry about being lured in.

For a respite from shopping, check out the $3 beer specials at the 1898 Red Onion Saloon (at Broadway and Second Ave.), or down Broadway, test the product at the **Skagway Brewing Company,** where you can have a beer and also check your e-mail.

COMING ASHORE Ships dock at the cruise pier, at the foot of Broadway or off Congress Way. From the farthest point, it's about a 5-minute walk from the pier across the train tracks to downtown, but shuttle buses are also offered. The only street you really need to know about is Broadway, which runs through the center of town and off which everything branches.

INFORMATION Walking maps are available at the **Skagway Convention and Visitors Bureau** (© 907/983-2854) at the Arctic Brotherhood Hall (on Broadway between Second and Third aves.). Free guided tours leave several times a day from the Klondike Gold Rush National Historic Park visitor center at Broadway and Second Avenue and visit the White Pass & Yukon Railway Depot, Soapy's Parlor, Moore House, and the Mascot Saloon. (You can also watch a free 30-min. film, *Days of Adventure Dreams of Gold*, at the visitor center, while you're waiting for the tour to begin.)

SHORE EXCURSIONS

Chilkoot Pass Helicopter Tour (1½ hr.; $179–$186): If the prospectors had known you could take a helicopter over the Chilkoot Trail, maybe they would have just waited. But would there then be a trail to see? Ah, a philosophical quandary. In any case, the trip overflies the trail, then takes you to the Chilkat glacier system, where you'll get to view glaciers in their high mountain peaks, and then lands on one for an ice-age thrill. There are also more elaborate helicopter tours, including one that visits a dogsled camp (2 hr.; $325–$365).

Glacier Flight & Bald Eagle Float (4½–5½ hr.; $164–$215): Board your plane in Skagway for a scenic flight over peaks and glaciers, then hop a raft in Haines for a gentle float trip through the Chilkat Bald Eagle Preserve to see eagles, wolves, moose, and bears. You rejoin your ship in Haines. There are also less-expensive options that involve a cruise to Haines, but you miss the aerial view of the peaks.

Skagway by Streetcar (2 hr.; $36–$40): As much performance art as historical tour, guides in period costume relate tales of the boomtown days as you tour the sights both in and outside of town aboard vintage 1930s Kenworth, Dodge, and White sightseeing limousines. Though theatrical, it's all done in a homey style, as if you're getting a tour from your cousin Martha. The guide is as likely to point out funky small-town oddities as major historical sights (example: "And that's Buckwheat's old truck; his niece Kelly's husband uses it," said while pointing to an old blue pickup belonging to local performer/tourism booster Buckwheat Donahue). After seeing the Historic District, the Lookout, the Gold Rush Cemetery, and other sights, guests see a little song-and-dance and film presentation about Skagway history and become honorary members of the Arctic Brotherhood. This part is very hokey.

White Pass & Yukon Route Railway (3 hr.; $79–$89): The sturdy engines and vintage parlor cars of this famous narrow-gauge railway take you from the dock past waterfalls and parts of the famous "Trail of '98" to the White Pass Summit, the boundary between Canada and the United States. Don't take this trip on an overcast day—you won't see anything. If you're lucky and have a clear day, though, you'll be able to see all the way down to the harbor, and you might see the occasional hoary marmot or other critter fleeing from the train's racket.

Horseback Riding (3½–5½ hours; $120–$139): Giddy-up on horseback to see the remnants of Dyea, once a booming gold-rush town, and explore the scenic Dyea Valley; or on longer tours, take in the breathtaking scenery across the border in Canada, including forests, streams, and a waterfall. Participants must be able to mount a horse and maintain balance in a saddle.

TOURING THROUGH LOCAL OPERATORS

There are independent tours sold at a tour center at Seventh and Broadway. Tours are offered here by a number of operators and are priced in the $35 range for a 2½-hour city and White Pass Summit tour by van. **Haines-Skagway Water Taxi** (© 888/766-3395) operates Lynn Canal sightseeing cruises that take you to Haines, about an hour away, for $35. The cruises leave Skagway at 10:45am and return at 3:45pm; it's about an hour's trip each way. There is also **Chilkat Cruises** (© 888/766-2103), which offers a fast ferry that takes about 35 minutes and runs several trips a day.

ON YOUR OWN: WITHIN WALKING DISTANCE

Alaska Wildlife Adventure Museum Fourth Ave. and Spring St. ☎ 907/983-3601. Admission $19 adults, $7.50 kids, children 5 and under free.

This funky place, shown by the owners by way of guided tours, holds an impressive and incredibly diverse collection of Alaskana and just plain collectables (everything from Elvis memorabilia to guns) with a special section devoted to mounted animals.

The Arctic Brotherhood Hall On Broadway, between Second and Third aves. ☎ 907/983-2420.

Originally the headquarters of a secret fraternal society, and now home to the Skagway Vistor Center, the hall is one of the most popular sights in town. You can't miss it: It's the building everybody's taking pictures of. (The building's facade is constructed from an estimated 20,000 pieces of driftwood.)

The Case-Mulvihill House, the Gault House & the Nye House On the western edge of town, near Alaska St.

All within a block of one another, the three are striking examples of gold-rush-era Skagway architecture.

Eagles Hall & Days of '98 Show Southeast corner of Sixth Ave. and Broadway. ☎ 907/983-2234. Daytime performances $14, kids $6.

This is the venue for Skagway's long-running (since 1927) "Days of '98" show, a live melodrama of the Gay '90s featuring dancing girls, ragtime music, Smith and Reid in their historic shoot-out (naturally), and more. Daytime performances are offered at 10:30am and 2:30pm, timed so cruise passengers can attend. (Mon there is only a 2:30pm show, and Sat there is only a nighttime show.)

The Golden North Hotel Third Ave. and Broadway. ☎ 888/222-1898 or 907/983-2294.

The Golden North is one of the tallest buildings in Skagway (it's all of three stories) and is said to be the oldest operating hotel in Alaska. Its Gold Bar Pub and Restaurant has a really lovely 19th-century look and is a good spot for lunch or dinner. You can enjoy the grub or just hop onto a stool at the fabulously long polished wood bar for a pint of the on-site Skagway Brewing Company's Oosik Stout or Chilkoot Trail Ale. (Good stuff!)

Historic Moore Homestead Fifth Ave. and Spring St. Tours $2 adults, $1 kids.

The Moore Cabin was built in 1887 as the home of Capt. William Moore, the founder of Skagway. The cabin was restored recently by the National Park Service.

Jefferson Smith's Parlor Second Ave., just off Broadway.

Also known as Soapy's Parlor, Jefferson Smith's Parlor was the saloon and gambling joint operated by the notorious bandit in the late 1890s. The building, which tourists can inspect only from the outside, has been relocated twice over the decades but looks pretty much as it did at the time of Smith's death.

The Red Onion Saloon 205 Broadway, at the corner of Second Ave. ☎ 907/983-2222.

Located near the Arctic Brotherhood Hall in what was originally a dance hall and honky-tonk bar (ca. 1898) with the obligatory bordello upstairs, the Red Onion's barkeepers still serve drinks over the same mahogany bar as did their turn-of-the-century predecessors. The waitresses wear dance hall outfits, and there's often live entertainment.

Skagway City Hall Spring St. and Seventh Ave.

This is not, strictly speaking, a tourist site, but as the town's only stone building, it's worth eyeballing.

Skagway Museum & Archives Seventh and Spring sts. ℂ **907/983-2420.** Admission is $2 adults, $1 students, 12 and under free.

Now back in its original and newly renovated location at the historic McCabe College building (built 1899–1900), the museum offers a look at Skagway's history through artifacts, photographs, and historical records. Items on display include a Tlingit canoe and Bering Sea kayaks, as well as a collection of gold-rush supplies and tools and Native American items including baskets and bead-work. There's also a big, stuffed, and standing brown bear.

ON YOUR OWN: BEYOND WALKING DISTANCE

The Gold Rush Cemetery About 1½ miles away from the center of downtown, up State St. (Walkable if you have the time and inclination.)

This is the permanent resting place of Messrs. Smith and Reid. The cemetery is small and lies a short walk from the scenic Reid Falls, named after the heroic one-time surveyor. Aside from Reid's impressive monument, most of the headstones at the cemetery are whitewashed wood and are replaced by the park service when they get too worn.

10

Ports & Wilderness Areas Along the Gulf Route

Remember what we said back in chapter 3: Going on a Gulf cruise does not mean that you miss out on the ports and natural areas of the Inside Passage. It just means that, whereas Inside Passage cruise itineraries typically begin and end in Vancouver, the Gulf routing is one-way—from Vancouver to Anchorage/Seward or the reverse—and may sail an itinerary that includes Inside Passage ports and attractions like Ketchikan, Juneau, Skagway, and Glacier Bay, plus Gulf ports and attractions like Hubbard Glacier, College Fjord, and Seward.

See chapter 7 for information on shore excursions and a few tips on debarkation, what to bring along with you while ashore, and little matters such as not missing the boat.

1 Hubbard Glacier

Said to be Alaska's longest ice face—it's about 6 miles across—Hubbard lies at the northern end of **Yakutat Bay.** The glacier has a rather odd claim to fame: It is one of the fastest moving in Alaska. So fast did it move about a dozen years ago that it created a wall across the mouth of **Russell Fjord,** one of the inlets lining Yakutat Bay. That effectively turned the fjord into a lake and trapped hundreds of migratory marine creatures inside. Scientists still can't tell us why Hubbard chose to act the way it did, or why it receded to its original position several months later, reopening Russell Fjord.

Cruise ships in Yakutat Bay offer spectacular views of the glacier, which, because of the riptides and currents, is always in motion, calving into the ocean and producing lots of white thunder. It should be noted, however, that only one ship can get close to the glacier at a time, and if another ship is hogging the space, your ship may have to wait or may not get close at all.

There is one footnote to the Yakutat Bay cruise experience, a reflection of the desire of some in the state to make visitors pay for the privilege. Some residents of the **village of Yakutat,** at the mouth of the bay, recently proposed imposing a $1.50 head tax on all ship passengers visiting Hubbard Glacier—even though ships NEVER call at Yakutat! At press time, it was unclear whether the initiative would be approved or be enforceable.

2 Prince William Sound

Located at the northern end of the underside of the Kenai Peninsula, this is truly one of Alaska's most appealing wilderness areas, though it suffered mightily following the *Exxon Valdez* oil spill in 1989. The area has recovered nicely (although not completely) from the ravages of that infamous spill, and today, visitors are absolutely guaranteed wildlife—whales, harbor seals, eagles, sea lions, sea otters, puffins, and much more.

The Kenai Peninsula & Prince William Sound

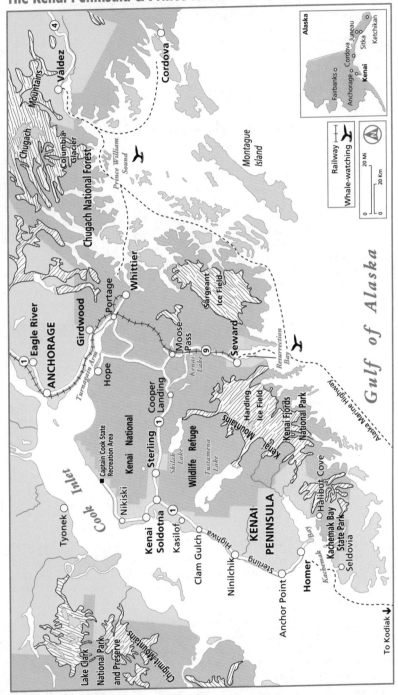

If your cruise doesn't spend enough time on the Sound for your taste, day cruises are available out of Whittier and Seward. One company, **Phillips Tours and Cruises,** 519 W. Fourth Ave., Suite 100, Anchorage, AK 99501 (© **800/ 544-0529** or 907/276-8023; www.26glaciers.com), markets what it calls a "26 Glaciers Cruise." All in 1 day! That tells you just about as much as you need to know about the scenic beauty of the Sound. The cruise—$122.50 per person— is well worth taking.

Perhaps the most spectacular of the Sound's ice faces is **Columbia Glacier,** whose surface spreads over more than 400 square miles and whose tidewater frontage is nearly 6 miles across. Columbia is receding faster than most of its Alaska counterparts. Scientists reckon it will retreat more than 20 miles in the next 20 to 50 years, leaving behind nothing but another deep fjord—just what Prince William Sound needs.

3 Valdez

Until one miserable, overcast day in 1989, probably not many people could have located Valdez (pronounced val-*deez*) on a map. The town seldom appeared on tourist agendas, even though its interesting history includes both the gold rush and a devastating earthquake in 1964 (registering 9.2 on the Richter scale). Then, with a grinding and a gurgling, the supertanker *Exxon Valdez,* having just left the harbor there, grounded on Bligh Rock and disgorged 11 million gallons of crude oil into the hitherto pristine waters of Prince William Sound. Suddenly, the eyes of the world were on Valdez. Newspapers carried stories, invariably illustrated with a map insert showing the affected region, and all at once, everybody knew where Valdez was.

Nowadays, you can take a boat into the Sound without seeing much evidence of the oil spill, unless you're in a canoe or similar small craft and get close to the walls of the surrounding fjords. In some of them, you can still see the scum marks on the rocks and shoreline—like a bathtub that's been used and not cleaned afterward.

A town's tourism image could be seriously damaged by a catastrophic event like the *Exxon Valdez* grounding. Valdez, though, didn't have much of a tourism image to start with. It still doesn't, to be perfectly frank. The town's position as the southern terminal of the 800-mile-long **Trans-Alaska Pipeline** conjures up in people's minds all kinds of negative visions—storage tanks, pipes, heavy equipment, tankers lined up waiting to get into the always ice-free, deep-water harbor. The reality is not as bad as that, but there's no doubt that Valdez is an industrial center. And even though it has about 4,000 inhabitants, a great many of these are there to work for the oil companies and have no intention of remaining beyond the period of their contracts. Consequently, the sense of community that you get in places like Juneau, Sitka, and the rest just doesn't seem to exist here.

Downtown, there are a few shops selling T-shirts, jewelry, and other souvenirs, and you'll also find a couple of places where you can get a latte (including a booth at the grocery store).

ESSENTIALS

ARRIVING   Ships dock at a huge commercial facility a couple of miles from the town center. Shuttle buses ferry visitors to the information center in town.

VISITOR INFORMATION   Valdez is tiny, and there's really not much to see in the town itself. At the **Valdez Convention and Visitors Bureau** information

Valdez

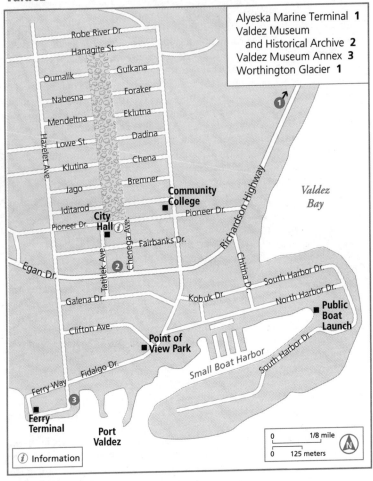

Alyeska Marine Terminal **1**
Valdez Museum
  and Historical Archive **2**
Valdez Museum Annex **3**
Worthington Glacier **1**

center on Fairbanks Drive (© **800/770-5954** or 907/835-4363), you can pick up a free town map.

ATTRACTIONS WITHIN WALKING DISTANCE

The Valdez Museum and Historical Archive 217 Egan Ave. © 907/835-2764. Admission $3 adults, $2 for ages 14–18, free for children under 14.

The museum contains an exceptional display that follows the history of the area, from early white exploration through the oil spill, and includes such unusual items as parkas made of bear and seal gut.

The Valdez Museum Annex Hazelet Ave. (at the ferry dock). © 907/835-5407. Admission $1.50.

The museum annex, located about 4 blocks from the main museum (near the ferry terminal), has a 1:20 scale replica of Valdez as it appeared before the 1964 earthquake destroyed much of the town.

THE BEST SHORE EXCURSIONS

Canyon Rafting (2¼ hr.; $62–$77): You can't beat the rafting in Keystone Canyon. There are a few thrilling hiccups along the 4½-mile, Class III run, but it's mild for the most part, and the sheer canyon walls and waterfalls pounding into the Lowe River are stunning. Knowledgeable guides and all equipment are provided.

Helicopter Flightseeing (1½–3¾ hr.; $195–$229): This quick helicopter adventure zips you over old Valdez (destroyed in the 1964 earthquake), the Trans-Alaska Pipeline, the crevasses of the Columbia Glacier, Prince William Sound, and Anderson Pass, then lands on the beach at the face of Shoup Glacier for a little ground-level gawking. Some tours, billed as heli-hiking, include a wilderness hike.

Thompson Pass & Worthington Glacier Bus Tour (2¼–3 hr.; $39): This tour takes you past the old town site, through narrow Keystone Canyon, and up to Thompson Pass to get a look at the Trans-Alaska Pipeline before reaching the Worthington Glacier Recreation Site, a prime spot to snap some photos.

Trans-Alaska Pipeline Tour (2½ hr.; $26–$29): If the pipeline project and Alaska's "black gold" are of interest to you, sign up for the tour of the Alyeska Marine Terminal. You'll see the storage tanks and tanker berths, and maybe see the giant ships getting tanked up.

Valdez Sport-Fishing (4 hr; $129): It might sound odd, given the oil spill and all, but Valdez is a wonderful fishing destination, especially for Coho salmon. The excursion, operated mid-July to early September only, is designed for beginners and experienced fishermen alike. Equipment, tackle, and bait are provided. You need to buy a $10 fishing license on the boat.

ALTERNATIVE TRANSPORTATION & TOURS

Valdez Tours (© **907/835-2686**) operates coach tours of the pipeline marine terminal—the only way visitors can get into the facility (unless you book a shore excursion).

4 College Fjord

College Fjord is in the northern sector of Prince William Sound, roughly midway between Whittier and Valdez. It's not one of the more spectacular Alaska glacier areas, being very much overshadowed by Glacier Bay, Yakutat Bay (for Hubbard Glacier), and others, but it's scenic enough to merit a place on a lot of cruise itineraries, mostly for **Harvard Glacier,** which sits at its head.

The fjord was named in 1898 by an expedition team that opted to give the glaciers lining College Fjord and its neighbor, Harriman Glacier, the names of Ivy League and other prominent eastern universities. Hence, Harvard, Vassar, Williams, Yale, and so on.

5 Seward

Seward is the main northern embarkation/debarkation port for north- and southbound Alaska cruises. For information on attractions, shore excursions, tours, accommodations, and dining, see chapter 8, "The Ports of Embarkation."

11

Cruisetour Destinations

No matter how powerful your binoculars, you can't see all of Alaska from a cruise ship, and that's why the cruise lines invented the cruisetour. In this chapter, we'll give you some info on the most popular cruisetour destinations. (See chapter 3 for a discussion of the various cruisetour packages offered; for much more in-depth information on these destinations, pick up a copy of *Frommer's Alaska*.)

1 Denali National Park & Preserve

This is Alaska's most visited—environmentalists say overly visited—wilderness area, with almost 1 million people a year entering by bus and train to soak up its scenic splendor.

Wildlife is the thing in Denali—somewhere in the realm of 161 species of bird, 37 species of mammal, and no fewer than 450 species of plant are to be found there.

The **Alaska Railroad** operates daily service from Anchorage and Fairbanks into the park, towing the private railcars of Holland America Line, Princess Cruises, and Royal Caribbean, as well as their own, more basic (but less expensive and perfectly adequate) carriages.

Besides the wildlife, the focal point of the park is North America's highest peak, **Mount McKinley** (commonly known to Alaskans by its original Native name, "Denali," which means "The Great One"). In fact, you could argue that McKinley is the two highest peaks in North America: Its north face towers over the Alaska Range at 20,320 feet, while its south face rises to 19,470 feet. On all sides are impressive, permanently snow-covered mountains.

Now a word of warning: There's no guarantee that you'll be able to see McKinley when you visit. As with all enormous mountains, the Great One creates its own weather system, and "foggy" seems to be its favorite flavor.

2 Fairbanks

Alaska's second largest city (after Anchorage) is friendly, unpretentious, and easygoing in the Alaska tradition, although its downtown area is drab and, frankly, sort of depressing. The major attraction in Fairbanks is the *Riverboat Discovery III*, a three-deck stern-wheeler that operates 3½-hour cruises twice a day throughout the summer on the Chena and Tanana rivers. The trip features visits to a re-created Indian village, a sled-dog training school, a viewing (with narration) of an Athabascan Indian fish camp, and a flyby performed by a genuine Alaskan bush pilot. The Binkleys, the family that owns the stern-wheeler, also owns **El Dorado Gold Mine,** where visitors pan for gold and, while riding on the open-sided Tanana Valley Railroad, study the workings of the mine just as it was a century ago. It's all good fun.

Alaskaland, right next to the gold mine, is a low-key Native culture–themed park with a couple of small museums, a playground, and a little tour train. The entire mine/Alaskaland complex is located an easy half-mile ride from downtown.

Your cruisetour may include a tour of the gold mine or a visit to **Gold Dredge No. 8,** a huge monster of a machine that dug gold out of the hills until 1959 and is now open for visitors. Shore excursions and cruisetours generally include the *Riverboat Discovery III.*

3 Prudhoe Bay

Prudhoe Bay is located at the very end of the Dalton Highway, also known locally as the Haul Road, a 414-mile stretch built to service the Trans-Alaska Pipeline. The road connects the Arctic coast with Interior Alaska, and passes through wilderness areas that include all sorts of scenic terrain—forested rounded hills, the rugged peaks of the Brooks Range, and the treeless plains of the North Slope included. Along the way will be lots of wildlife-spotting opportunities, likely to include caribou, Dall sheep, moose, and bear.

But the real reason to come way up here is the **Prudhoe Bay Oilfield.** Although touring an oil field may not be high on your vacation must-do list, the bay complex is no ordinary oil field. It's a historic and strategic site of great importance and a great technological achievement. The industry coexists here with migrating caribou and waterfowl on wet, fragile tundra that permanently shows any mark made by vehicles.

To get here, you usually drive the Dalton Highway in buses one way and fly the other, with either **Fairbanks** or **Anchorage** being the other connecting point. The trip includes an overnight in **Coldfoot.**

4 Nome & Kotzebue

There's no place like Nome. Well, we had to say it. But this arctic frontier town is a special place, combining a sense of history, a hospitable if somewhat silly attitude (we're talking about a place that holds an annual Labor Day bathtub race), and an exceptional location on the water in front of a tundra wilderness.

The name Nome was actually a mistake. A British naval officer in 1850 wrote "? Name" on a diagram, and the scrawl was misinterpreted by a mapmaker as "Nome." The population boom here in 1899 also happened by chance, when a prospector from the 1898 gold rush was left behind on the beach due to an injury. He panned the sand outside his tent and found that it was full of gold dust.

Undoubtedly on your visit, you'll find time to try your own hand at gold panning. The city also offers a still sloppy, gold rush–style saloon scene, and bargains on **Inupiat Eskimo** arts and crafts.

Your tour will include a visit to **Kotzebue** (pronounced *kotz*-eh-biew) to the north, one of Alaska's largest and oldest Inupiat Eskimo villages. Here, you'll tour the **NANA Museum of the Arctic,** run by a regional Native corporation representing the roughly 7,000 Inupiat people who live in the Northwest Arctic region.

To get here, you fly from Anchorage, fly between Nome and Kotzebue, and fly back to Anchorage, as part of itineraries that typically include an overnight in Anchorage and a visit to Denali and Fairbanks.

5 The Kenai Peninsula

The Kenai (*Kee*-nye) Peninsula, which divides Prince William Sound and Cook Inlet, offers glaciers, whales, legendary sport-fishing, spectacular hiking trails, bear, moose, and high mountains. And it's easy to get to, to boot.

People from Anchorage come here for the weekend to hike, dig clams, paddle kayaks, and, particularly, to fish. There's a special phrase for what happens when the red salmon are running in July on the Kenai and Russian rivers: **combat fishing.** Fishers stand elbow to elbow on a bank, each casting into his or her yard-wide slice of river, and still catch plenty of fish.

Cruisetours to the Kenai Peninsula include options for fishing, **river rafting,** and other soft-adventure activities.

You will typically drive here in buses from **Seward.** Princess includes an overnight at its Kenai Princess Lodge, a wilderness resort. Some tours include an overnight in **Anchorage,** and then go on to **Denali/Fairbanks.**

6 The Yukon Territory

You'll pass plenty of beautiful scenery along the way, but today the real reason to cross the Canadian border into this region is the same as it was 100 years ago: **gold** (or, rather, gold-rush history).

Gold was discovered on Bonanza Creek in Canada's Klondike in 1896, and in a matter of months, tens of thousands of people descended into the Yukon for the greatest gold rush in history, giving birth to Dawson City, Whitehorse, and a dozen other tent communities.

Once part of the Northwest Territories, the Yukon is now a separate Canadian territory bordered by British Columbia and Alaska. The entire territory has a population of just over 33,000, two-thirds of them living in **Whitehorse,** the capital of the region since 1953. Located on the banks of the Yukon River, Whitehorse was established in 1900, 2 full years after the stampeders swarmed into Dawson City. Today, the city serves as a frontier outpost, its tourism influx also giving it a cosmopolitan tinge complete with nightlife, good shopping opportunities (with some smart boutiques and great outdoors shops), fine restaurants, and comfortable hotels.

Dawson City was once the biggest Canadian city west of Winnipeg, with a population of 30,000, but it withered to practically a ghost town after the gold-rush stampeders stopped stampeding. Dawson today is the nearest thing to an authentic gold-rush town the world has to offer, with old buildings, vintage watering holes, dirt streets flanked with raised boardwalks, shops (naturally), and some particularly good restaurants (such as Marina's, a fine Italian place on Fifth Ave., and Klondike Kate's).

If you're on a Holland America cruisetour—which is likely, as they operate more Yukon cruisetours than Princess—you'll travel between Dawson City and the tiny Alaskan town of Eagle via the MV *Yukon Queen II,* a high-speed, 115-passenger catamaran that makes the trip along the Yukon River in 5 hours, passing through beautiful, remote scenery, where the only signs of civilization are the occasional fisherman.

7 The Canadian Rockies

Canadian Rockies cruisetours typically include travel by bus and/or train between Vancouver and either Seattle or Calgary.

Highlights of the tour include a visit to the parks at **Jasper** and **Banff,** which together comprise 6,764 square miles. The parks are teeming with wildlife, with some animals—like bighorn sheep, mountain goats, deer, and moose—meandering along and across highways and hiking trails. There are also coyotes, lynx, and occasional wolves (though they tend to give humans a wide berth), as well as grizzlies and black bears, both of which are unpredictable and best photographed with a telephoto lens.

The two "capitals," Banff and Jasper, are 178 miles apart, and connected by scenic Highway 93. **Banff** is in a stunningly beautiful setting, with the mighty Bow River, murky with glacial till, coursing through town.

The **Banff Springs Hotel** was built in 1888 as a destination resort by the Canadian Pacific Railroad, and tourists have been visiting this area ever since for its scenery and hot springs and nearby fishing, hiking, and other outdoor activities. Today, the streets of Banff are also an attraction, lined with trendy cafes and exclusive boutiques offering the latest names in international fashion.

Lake Louise is located 35 miles north of Banff and is a famed beauty spot, deep green from the minerals it contains (ground by the glaciers above the lake) and surrounded by forest-clad snowcapped mountains. The village near the lake is a resort destination in its own right. Nearly as spectacular as the lake is **Chateau Lake Louise** (111 Lake Louise Dr., Lake Louise, Alberta Canada T0L 1E0; ✆ **800-441-1414,** or 403/522-3511; fax 403/522-3834; www.fairmont. com), built by the Canadian Pacific Railroad and one of the most celebrated hotels in Canada.

Between Lake Louise and Jasper is the **Icefields Parkway,** a spectacular mountain road that climbs through three deep river valleys, beneath soaring, glacier-notched mountains and past dozens of horn-like peaks. Capping the route is the **Columbia Icefields,** a massive dome of glacial ice and snow that is the largest nonpolar ice cap in the world.

Jasper isn't Banff. It was born as a railroad division point, and the town does not offer the glitz of its southern neighbor. **Jasper National Park** is Canada's largest mountain park and offers an outdoor-oriented experience with opportunities to hike, ride horses, fish, or even climb mountains.

Appendix: Alaska in Depth

An old photo album opens, emitting a scent of dust and dried glue. Inside, pale images speak wanly of shrunken mountains and glaciers, a huge blue sky, water and trees, a moose standing way off in the background. No family photographer can resist the urge to capture Alaska's vastness in the little box of a camera, and none, it seems, has ever managed it. Then, turning the page, there it is—not in another picture of the landscape, but reflected in a small face at the bottom of the frame: my own face, as a child. For anyone who hasn't experienced that moment, the expression is merely enigmatic—slightly dazed, happy but abstracted. But if you've been to Alaska, that photograph captures something familiar: It's an image of discovery. I've seen it on the fresh, pale faces in photographs stamped with the dates of my family's first explorations of Alaska 35 years ago. And then, researching this book, I got to see it once again, on my own young son's face. And I knew that, like me, he had discovered something important.

So what, exactly, am I talking about? Like anything worth experiencing, it's not simple to explain.

Tour guides try to get it across with statistics. Not much hope of that, although some of the numbers do give you a general idea of scale. Once you've driven across the continental United States and know how big that is, seeing a map of Alaska placed on top of the area you crossed, just about spanning it, provides some notion of size. Alaskans always like to threaten that we'll split in half and make Texas the third-largest state. Alaska has 627,000 residents. If you placed them an equal distance apart, each would be almost a mile from any other. Of course, that couldn't happen. No one has ever been to some parts of Alaska.

But none of that expresses what really matters. It's not just a matter of how big Alaska is or how few people it contains. It's not an intellectual concept at all. None of that crosses your mind when you see a chunk of ice the size of a building fall from a glacier and send a huge splash and wave surging outward, or when you feel a wave lift your sea kayak from the fall of a breaching humpback whale. Or when you hike for a couple of days to stand on top of a mountain, and from there see more mountaintops, layered off as far as the horizon in unnamed, seemingly infinite multiplicity. A realization of what Alaska means also can come in a simple little moment. It can come at the end of a long day driving an Interior Alaska highway, as your car climbs into yet another mountain range, the sun still hanging high in what should be night, storm systems arranged before you across the landscape, when you realize that you haven't seen another car in an hour. Or standing on an Arctic Ocean beach, it could happen when you look around at the sea of empty tundra behind you, the sea of green water before you, and your own place on what seems to be the edge of the world. Or you might simply be sitting on the sun-warmed rocks of a beach in Southeast or Southcentral Alaska when you discover that you're occupying only one of many worlds—a world of intermediate size, lying in magnitude between the tiny tide-pool universes of life all around you and the larger world as seen by an eagle gliding through the air high above.

What's the soul alchemy of such a moment? I suppose it's different for each person, but for me it has something to do with realizing my actual size in the world, how I fit in, what it means to be just another medium-sized mammal, no longer armed with the illusions supplied by civilization. On returning to the city from the wilderness, there's a re-entry process, like walking from a vivid movie onto the mundane, gray street outside—it's the movie that seems more real. For a while, it's hard to take human institutions seriously after you've been deep into Alaska.

Some people never do step back across that boundary. They live their lives out in the wilderness, away from people. Others compromise, living in Alaskan cities and walking out into the mountains when they can, the rest of the time just maintaining a prickly notion of their own independence. But with the courage to come to Alaska and the time to let the place sink in, anyone can make the same discovery. You don't have to be an outdoors enthusiast or a young person. You only have to be open to wonder and able to slow down long enough to see it. Then, in a quiet moment when you least expect it, things may suddenly seem very clear and all that you left behind oddly irrelevant.

How you find your way back to where you started is your affair.

1 Natural History: Rough Drafts & Erasures
THE SURGING ICE

In 1986, Hubbard Glacier, north of Yakutat, suddenly decided to surge forward, cutting off Russell Fjord from the rest of the Pacific Ocean. A group of warm-hearted but ill-advised wildlife lovers set out to save the marine mammals that had been trapped behind the glacier. Catching a dolphin from an inflatable boat isn't that easy—they didn't accomplish much, but they provided a lot of entertainment for the locals. Then the water burst through the dam of ice, and the lake became a fjord again, releasing the animals anyway.

Bering Glacier can't decide which way to go. Surging and retreating on a 20-year cycle, it recently reversed course after bulldozing a wetland migratory bird stopover, and speedily contracted back up toward the mountains. Yanert Glacier surged 100 yards a day in 2000 after moving 100 yards a year since 1942. In 1937, surging Black Rapids glacier almost ate the Richardson Highway. Mount McKinley's glaciers take off regularly. In Prince William Sound, Meares Glacier has plowed through old-growth forest. On the other hand, some glaciers are so stable that they gather a layer of dirt where trees and brush grow to maturity. When Malspina Glacier retreated, the trees on its back toppled. And on a larger scale, all the land of Glacier Bay—mountains, forests, sea floor—is rising 1½ inches a year as it rebounds from the weight of melted glaciers that 100 years ago were a mile thick and 65 miles longer.

Yet these new and erased lands are just small corrections around the margins compared to all the earth has done in setting down, wiping out, and rewriting the natural history of Alaska. In the last Ice Age, 15,000 years ago, much of what is Alaska today was one huge glacier. Looking up at the tops of granite mountains in Southeast Alaska, especially in the Lynn Canal, you can see a sort of high-water mark—the highest point the glaciers came in the Ice Age. Even looking from the deck of a boat, thousands of feet below, you can see where mountain shoulders, rounded by the passage of ice, are much smoother than the sharp, craggy peaks just above, which stuck out of that incredible sheet of ice.

Some 7-year-old children worry about the bogeyman or being caught in a house fire. When I was that age, living with my family in Juneau, I learned how Gastineau Channel was formed and then went to see Mendenhall Glacier. I was told how it was really a river of ice, advancing and retreating, and with this knowledge I developed a deeper fear: ice. I was afraid that while I slept, another Ice Age would come and grind away the city of Juneau.

It's possible that a glacier *could* get Juneau—the city fronts on the huge Juneau Ice Field—but there would be at least a few centuries' warning before it hit. Glaciers are essentially just snow that doesn't get a chance to melt. It accumulates at higher altitudes until it gets deep enough to compress into ice and starts oozing down the sides of the mountain. When the ice reaches the ocean, or before, the melt and calving of icebergs at the leading edge reaches a point of equilibrium with the snow that's still being added at the top. The glacier stops advancing, becoming a true river of ice, moving a snowflake from the top of the mountain to the bottom in a few hundred years. When conditions change— more snow or colder long-term weather, for example—the glacier gets bigger; that's called advancing, and the opposite is retreating. Sometimes, something strange will happen under the glacier and it will surge. Bering Glacier started to float on a cushion of water, and Yanert Glacier slid on a cushion of mud. But most of the time, the advance or retreat is measured in inches or feet a year.

It took some time to figure out how glaciers work, and the living glaciers of Alaska, like living fossils from the last Ice Age, helped show the way. In the 1830s, scientists in Switzerland found huge rocks (now called glacial erratics) that appeared to have moved miles from where they once had been a part of similar bedrock. They developed the theory that ancient glaciers shaping the Alps must have moved the rocks. **John Muir,** the famous writer and naturalist, maintained in the 1870s that the granite mountains of Yosemite National Park had been rounded and polished by the passing of glaciers that melted long ago (he was only partly right). He traveled to Alaska to prove it. Here, glaciers were still carving the land—they had never finished melting at the end of the last glacial period—and Muir could see shapes like those at Yosemite in the act of being created. Glacier Bay, which Muir "discovered" when guided there by his Alaska Native friends, was a glacial work in progress, as it still is today.

When you visit, you can see for yourself how the heavy blue ice and white snow are streaked with black rock and dust that were obviously gouged from mountains and left in hills at the face and along the flanks of the glaciers in debris piles called moraines. At Exit Glacier in Kenai Fjords National Park, you can stand on a moraine that wraps the leading edge of the glacier like a scarf and feel the cold streaming off spires of clicking ice—like standing in front of a freezer with the door open. Find another hill like that, no matter where it is, and you can be pretty sure a glacier once came that way. Likewise, you can see today's glaciers scooping out valleys in the mountains. Fjords and valleys all over Alaska surely were made by the glaciers of the 50 ice ages that have covered North America in the last 2.5 million years.

We still don't know exactly why these glacial periods come and go. The best theory to date holds that the wobbles and imperfections in the earth's spin and orbit around the sun alter energy flow into the climate enough to bring on the ice. Indeed, ancient ice samples suggest that the last 10,000 years, in which mankind developed agriculture and civilization, have been an extremely rare period of benign and stable climatic conditions. That stability could be ending. The earth is warming, probably aided by human release of carbon dioxide into the atmosphere, and the effects are being felt more strongly in the Arctic than anywhere else on earth. Forests are moving north, wetlands are drying, sea ice is withdrawing, and permanently frozen ground is warming. But no one knows how glaciers will change. If global warming brings more precipitation, they may grow.

Today, Alaska's 100,000 glaciers cover about 5% of its landmass, mostly on the southern coast. There are no glaciers in the Arctic—the climate is too dry to produce enough snow. The northernmost large glaciers are in the Alaska Range, such as those carving great chasms in the side of Mount McKinley. The mountain's height creates its own weather, wringing moisture out of the atmosphere and feeding its glaciers. The Kahiltna Glacier flows 45 miles from the mountain, losing 15,000 feet downhill over its course. The Ruth Glacier has dug a canyon twice as deep as the Grand Canyon, half-filled with mile-deep ice.

THE TREMBLING EARTH

Despite my early glacier phobia, I never had a similar fear of earthquakes. Living in Anchorage, I'd been through enough of them that, as early as I can remember, I generally didn't bother to get out of bed when they hit. Alaska has an average of 13 earthquakes a day, or 11 percent of all the earthquakes in the world, including three of the six largest ever recorded. Of course, Alaska is large; in Anchorage, we feel only a few earthquakes a year.

It's all part of living in a place that isn't quite done yet. Any part of Alaska could have an earthquake, but the Pacific Rim from Southcentral Alaska to the Aleutians is the shakiest. This is where Alaska is still under construction. The very rocks that make up the state are something of an ad hoc conglomeration, still in the process of being assembled. The floor of the Pacific Ocean is moving north, and as it moves, it carries islands and mountains with it. When they hit the Alaska plate, these pieces of land, called **terranes,** dock like ships arriving, but slowly—an island moving an inch a year takes a long time to travel thousands of miles. Geologists studying rocks near Mount McKinley have found a terrane that used to be tropical islands. In Kenai Fjords National Park, fossils have turned up that are otherwise found only in Afghanistan and China. The slowly moving crust of the earth brought them here on a terrane that makes up a large part of the south coast of Alaska.

The earth's crust is paper thin compared to the globe's forces, and, like paper, it is folding where the two edges meet. Alaska's coast is bending down; and farther inshore, where McKinley stands, it is bowing up. The steep little rock islands you see flocking with birds at Kenai Fjords National Park are old mountaintops; the monolith of McKinley is a brand-new one.

Here's how it works: Near the center of the Pacific, underwater volcanoes and cracks that constantly ooze molten new rock are adding to the tectonic plate that forms the ocean floor. As it grows from the middle, the existing sea floor spreads at a rate of perhaps an inch a year. At the other side of the Pacific plate, where it bumps up against Alaska, there's not enough room for more crust, so it's forced, bending and cracking, downward into the planet's great, molten recycling mill of magma. Landmasses that are along for the ride smash into the continent that's already there. When one hits—the so-called Yakutat block is still in the process of docking—a mountain range gets shoved up. Earthquakes and volcanoes are a byproduct.

Living in such an unsettled land is a matter of more than abstract interest. The Mount Spurr volcano, which erupted most recently in 1992, turned day to night in Anchorage, dropping a blanket of ash all over the region. A Boeing 747 full of passengers flew into the plume and lost power in all its engines, falling in darkness for several minutes before pilots were able to restart the clogged jets. After that incident, the airport was closed until aviation authorities could find a way to keep volcanic plumes and planes apart. More than 80 volcanoes have been active in Alaska in the last 200 years. Earthquakes between 7 and 8 on the Richter scale—larger than the 1994 Los Angeles quake—occur once a year on average, and huge quakes over 8 averaged every 13 years over the last century.

The worst of the quakes, on March 27, 1964, was the strongest ever to hit North America. It ranked 9.2 on the Richter scale, lowering an entire region of the state some 10 feet and moving it even farther laterally. No other earthquake has ever moved so much land.

The earthquake destroyed much of Anchorage and several smaller towns, and killed about 131 people, mostly in sea waves created by underwater landslides. In Valdez, the waterfront was swept clean of people. In the Prince William Sound village of Chenega, built on a hill along the water, people started running for higher ground when the wave came. About half made it. But the earthquake could have been much worse. It occurred in the early evening, on Good Friday, when most public buildings were empty. An elementary school in Anchorage that broke in half and fell into a hole had no one inside at the time.

But even that huge earthquake wasn't an unusual occurrence, at least in the earth's terms. Geologists believe the same Alaska coast sank 6 feet in an earthquake in the year 1090.

THE FROZEN TUNDRA

The Interior and Arctic parts of the state are less susceptible to earthquakes and, since they receive little precipitation, they don't have glaciers, either. But there's still a sense of living on a land that's not quite sure of itself, since most of northern Alaska is solid only by virtue of being frozen. When it thaws, it turns to mush. The phenomenon is caused by **permafrost,** a layer of earth a little below the surface that never thaws—or at least, you'd better hope it doesn't. Buildings erected on permafrost without some mechanism for dispersing their own heat—pilings, a gravel pad, or even refrigerator coils—thaw the ground below and sink into a self-made quicksand. You occasionally run across such structures. There's one in Dawson City, Yukon Territory, still left from the gold rush, that leans at an alarming angle with thresholds and lower tiers of siding disappearing into the ground.

Building sewer and water systems in such conditions is a challenge still unmet in much of Alaska's Bush, where village toilets are often "honey buckets" and the septic systems are sewage lagoons on the edge of town where the buckets are dumped. Disease caused by the unsanitary conditions sweeps the villages as if rural Alaska were a Third World country. Large state and federal appropriations are resolving the problem one village at a time, but many years of work are still left.

Permafrost makes the land do other strange things. On a steep slope, the thawed earth on top of the ice can begin to slowly slide downhill like a blanket over a pile of pillows, setting the trees at crazy angles. These groves of black spruce—the only conifer that grows on this kind of ground—are called drunken forests, and you can see them in Denali National Park and elsewhere in the Interior. Permafrost also can create weird ground with shaky tussocks the size of basketballs that sit a foot or two apart on a wet, muddy flat. From a distance, it looks smooth, but walking on real basketballs would be easier.

The Arctic and much of the Interior is a swampy desert. Annual precipitation in Barrow is the same as in Las Vegas. Most of the time, the tundra is frozen in white; snow blows around, but not much falls. It melts in the summer, but it can't sink into the ground, which remains frozen. Liquid water on top of the permafrost layer creates huge, shallow ponds. Alaska is a land of 10 million lakes, with three million larger than 20 acres. Birds arrive to feed and paddle around those circles and polygons of deep green and sky blue. Flying over the Arctic in a small plane is disorienting, for no pattern maintains in the flat green tundra, and irregularly shaped patches of water stretch as far as the eye can see. Pilots find their way by following landmarks like tractor tracks etched into the tundra. Although few and far between, the tracks remain clearly delineated for decades after they're made, appearing as narrow, parallel ponds reaching from one horizon to the other.

The permafrost also preserves much older things. The meat of prehistoric mastodons, still intact, has been unearthed from the frozen ground. On the Arctic Coast, the sea eroded ground near Barrow that contained ancient ancestors of the Eskimos that still inhabit the same neighborhood. In 1982, they found a family that apparently was crushed by sea ice up to 500 years ago. Two of the bodies were well preserved, sitting in the home they had occupied and wearing the clothes they had worn the day of the disaster, perhaps around the time Columbus was sailing to America.

Sea ice is the frozen ocean that extends from northern Alaska to the other side of the world. For a few months of summer, it pulls away from the shore. Then, in September, when the ocean water falls below 29°F, ice forms along the beach and expands from the North Pole's permanent ice pack until the two sides meet. The clash of huge ice floes creates towering pressure ridges, small mountains of steep ice that are difficult to cross.

At its extreme, in March, the ice extends solidly all the way south to the Pribilof Islands, when it becomes possible to drive a dog team across the Bering Sea to Siberia. The National Weather Service keeps track of the ice pack and issues maps and predictions you can find on the Internet (www.alaska.net/~nwsar). Crab boats like to tempt its south-moving edge in the fall and shippers look for the right moment in the summer to venture north with barges of fuel and other supplies for the coast of the Arctic Ocean—they barely have time to get there and back before the ice closes in again in the fall.

The Arctic and Interior are biologically relatively barren compared with the southern coastal areas of the state. Polar bears wander the Arctic ice pack, but they, like the Eskimos, feed more on marine mammals than on anything found on the shore. A 1,200-pound adult polar bear can make a meal of a walrus, and they're expert at hunting seal. In the summer, herds of caribou counted in the tens of thousands come north to their Arctic calving grounds, but they migrate south when the cold, dark winter falls unremittingly on the region.

> **Higher, Higher**
> The Eskimo blanket toss—the game of placing a person in the center of a walrus-skin blanket and bouncing him or her high in the air—traditionally was used to get hunters high enough to see over the pressure ridges so they could spot game.

In Barrow, the sun doesn't rise for more than 65 days in the winter. In February, the average daily high temperature is −12°F, and the average low is −24°F. The Inupiat people learned to survive in this climate for millennia, but life was short and terribly hard. Today, they've made some sensible allowances while holding onto many cultural traditions. For example, the school in Barrow has wide, light hallways and a large indoor playground.

THE RAIN FOREST

By comparison, southern coastal Alaska is warm and biologically rich. Temperate rain forest ranges up the coast from Southeast Alaska into Prince William Sound, with bears, deer, moose, wolves, and even big cats living among the massive western hemlock, Sitka spruce, and cedar. This old-growth forest, too wet to burn in forest fires, is the last vestige of the virgin, primeval woods that seemed so limitless to the first white settlers who arrived on the east coast of the continent in the 17th century. The trees grow on and on, sometimes rising more than 200 feet high, with diameters of 10 feet, and falling only after hundreds of years. When they fall, the trees rot on the damp moss of the forest floor and return to soil to feed more trees, which grow in rows upon their nursery trunks.

Here at least, Alaska *does* seem permanent. That sense helps explain why cutting the rain forest is so controversial. Just one of these trees contains thousands of dollars' worth of wood, a prize that drives logging as voraciously as the federal government, which owns most of the coastal forest, may choose to allow. Already the vast Southeast lands owned by Alaska Native corporations have been stripped of their old trees.

The rivers of the great coastal forests bring home runs of big **salmon,** clogging in spawning season like a busy sidewalk at rush hour. The fish spawn only once, returning by a precisely tuned sense of smell to the streams where they were hatched as many as 7 years before. When the fertilized eggs have been left in the stream gravel, the fish conveniently die on the beach, making a smorgasbord for bears and other forest animals. The huge **Kodiak brown bear,** topping 1,000 pounds, owes everything to the millions of salmon that return to the island each summer. By comparison, the grizzly bears of the Interior—the same species as browns, but living on grass, berries, and an occasional ground squirrel—are mere midgets, their weight counted in the hundreds of pounds. Forest-dwelling black bears grow to only a few hundred pounds.

TAIGA & FIRE

Rain forest covers only a small fraction of Alaska. In fact, only a third of Alaska is forested at all, and most of this is the boreal forest that covers the central part of the state, behind the rain-shadow of coastal mountains that intercept moist clouds off the oceans. Ranging from the Kenai Peninsula, south of Anchorage, to the Brooks Range, where the Arctic begins, this is a **taiga**—a moist, subarctic forest of smaller, slower-growing, hardier trees that leave plenty of open sky between their branches. In well-drained areas, on hillsides and southern land less susceptible to permafrost, the boreal forest is a lovely, broadly spaced combination of straight, proud white spruce and pale, spectral paper birch. Along the rivers, cottonwoods grow, with deep-grained bark and branches that spread in an oaklike matrix—if they could speak, it would be as wise old men. Where it's wet and swampy, over more and more land as you go north, all that will grow are low, brushy willow and the glum black spruce, which struggles to become a gnarled stick a mere 3 inches thick in 100 years, if it doesn't burn first. As the elevation grows, the spruce shrink, turning into weirdly bent, ancient shrubs just before the tree line and the open alpine tundra.

Forest fires tear through as much as a million acres of Alaska's boreal forest each summer. In most cases, forest managers do no more than note the occurrence on a map. There's little commercially valuable timber in these thin stands, and, anyway, it isn't possible to halt the process of nature's self-immolation over the broad expanse of Alaska. The boreal forest regenerates through fire—it was made to burn. The wildlife that lives in and eats it needs new growth from the burns as well as the shelter of older trees. When the forest is healthiest and most productive, the dark green of the spruce is broken by streaks and patches of light-green brush in an ever-changing succession.

This is the land of the **moose.** They're as big as large horses, with long, bulbous noses and huge eyes that seem to know, somehow, just how ugly they are. Their flanks look like a worn-out shag carpet draped over a sawhorse. But moose are survivors. They thrive in land that no one else wants. In the summer, they wade out into the swampy tundra ponds to eat green muck. In the winter, they like nothing better than an old burn, where summer lightning has peeled back the forest and allowed a tangle of willows to grow—a moose's all-time favorite food. Eaten by wolves, hunted and run over by man, stranded in the snows of a hard winter, the moose always come back. In the summer, the moose disperse and are not easily seen in thick vegetation. In the winter, they gather where walking is easy, along roads and in lowlands where people also like to live. Encounters happen often in the city, until, as a resident, you begin to take the moose for granted. Then, skiing on a Nordic trail one day, you round a corner and come face to face with an animal that stands 2 feet over you. You can smell the beast's foul scent and see his stress, the ears pulled back on the head and the whites of the eyes showing, and you know that this wild creature, fighting to live until summer, can easily kill you.

THE LIGHT & THE DARKNESS

There's no escaping the stress of winter in Alaska—not for moose or people— nor any shield from the exhilaration of the summer. In summer, it never really gets dark at night. In Fairbanks in June, the sun sets in the north around midnight, but it doesn't go down far enough for real darkness to settle, instead rising again 2 hours later. It's always light enough to keep hiking or fishing, and, in clear weather, always light enough to read by. You may not see the stars from early May until sometime in August (the climate chart in chapter 2, "Alaska 101: A Cruise-Goer's Companion," gives seasonal daylight for various towns). Visitors have trouble getting used to it: Falling asleep in broad daylight is hard. Alaskans deal with it by staying up late and being active outdoors. In the winter, on the other hand, you forget what the sun looks like. Kids go to school in the dark and come home in the dark. The sun rises in the middle of the morning and sets after lunch. At high noon in December, the sun hangs just above the southern horizon with a weak, orange light, a constant sunset. Animals and people go into hibernation.

As you go north, the change in the length of the days gets larger. In Ketchikan, the longest day of the year, the summer solstice is 17 hours, 28 minutes; in Fairbanks, 21 hours, 48 minutes; and in Barrow, the longest day is more than 2 months. In contrast, in Seattle the longest day is 16 hours, and in Los Angeles 14 hours, 26 minutes. On the equator, days are always the same length, 12 hours. At the North and South poles, the sun is up half the year and down the other half.

2 Politics & History: Living a Frontier Myth

The occupations of prospector, trapper, and homesteader—rugged individualists relying only on themselves in a limitless land—would dominate Alaska's economy if the state's image of itself were accurate. Alaskans talk a lot about the Alaskan spirit of independence, yearn for freedom from

Dateline

- Approximately 15,000 years ago First human explorers arrive in Alaska from Asia.
- 1741 Vitus Bering, on a mission originally chartered by Peter the Great, finds Alaska; ship's surgeon and

continues

government, and declare that people from "Outside" just don't understand us when they insist on locking up Alaska's lands in parks and wilderness status. The bumper sticker says, simply, "We don't give a damn how they do it Outside." A state full of self-reliant frontiersmen can't be tied down and deterred from their manifest destiny by a bunch of Washington bureaucrats. At the extreme, there has even been a movement to declare independence as a separate nation so that Alaskans can extend the frontier, extracting its natural resources unfettered by bunny-hugging easterners.

But just because you wear a cowboy hat doesn't mean you know how to ride a horse. In Las Vegas, you find a lot more hats than horsemen, and Alaska is full of self-reliant pioneers who spend rush hour in traffic jams and worry more about urban drug dealing and air pollution than where to catch their next meal or dig the mother lode. As for self-reliance and independence from government, Alaska has the highest per capita state spending of any state in the nation, with no state income or sales taxes and an annual payment of about $2,000 a year to every man, woman, and child just for living here. The state government provides such socialistic benefits as retirement homes and automatic income for the aged; it owns various businesses, including a dairy, a railroad, and a subsidized mortgage lender; it has built schools in the smallest communities, operates a state ferry system and a radio and television network, and owns nearly a third of the landmass of Alaska. And although the oil money that funds state government has been in decline in recent years, forcing the legislature to dig into savings to balance its books, the independent, self-reliant citizens have successfully resisted having to pay any taxes.

That conflict between perception and reality grows out of the story of a naturalist Georg Steller goes ashore for a few hours on Kayak Island, the first white to set foot in Alaska.

- 1743 Russian fur traders enter the Aleutian Islands; Aleuts are enslaved to hunt sea otter and massacred; when they try to revolt, Aleut cultural traditions are eliminated, and over the coming decades, they are relocated as far south as California for their hunting skills.

- 1772 Unalaska, in the Aleutian Islands, becomes a permanent Russian settlement.

- 1776–79 British Capt. James Cook makes voyages of exploration to Alaska, seeking the Northwest Passage from the Pacific to the Atlantic, and draws charts of the coast.

- 1784 Russians build a settlement at Kodiak.

- 1799 Russians establish a fort near present-day Sitka, which will later become their capital; Tlingits attack and destroy the fort, but are later driven off in a counterattack; the Russian-America Company receives a 20-year exclusive franchise to govern and exploit Alaska.

- 1821 Russian naval officers are placed in control of the Russian-America Company, which begins to decline in profitability.

- 1824 Boundaries roughly matching Alaska's current borders are set by treaty between Russia, Britain, and the United States.

- 1839 The British Hudson's Bay Company, surpassing Russia in trade, begins leasing parts of Southeast Alaska and subsequently extends trading outposts into the Interior.

- 1843 First overtures are made by American officials interested in buying Alaska from the Russians so that U.S. instead of British power could expand there.

- 1867 In need of money and fearful that Russia couldn't hold onto Alaska anyway, Czar Alexander II sells Alaska to the United States; Secretary of State William Seward negotiates the deal for a price of $7.2 million, roughly 2¢ an acre; the American flag is raised in Sitka, and the U.S. military assumes government of Alaska.

century of development of Alaska. The state is a great storehouse of minerals, oil, timber, and fish. A lot of wealth has been extracted, and many people have gotten rich. But it has always been because the federal government let them do it. Every acre of Alaska belonged to the U.S. government from the day Secretary of State William Seward bought Alaska from Russia in 1867. Since then, the frontier has never been broader than Uncle Sam made it.

Yet the whole concept of ownership didn't fit Alaska well from the first. Did the Russians really own what they sold? Alaska Natives didn't think so. They'd been living on this land for more than 100 centuries, and at the time of the purchase, most had never seen a white face. How could Russia hold title to land that no Russian had so much as explored? As Americans flooded into Alaska to search for gold at the turn of the century, this conflict became obvious. Alaska Natives, never conquered by war or treaty, began their legal and political fight to recover their land early in the century—a fight they would eventually win.

The concept of ownership has changed in other ways, too. When the United States bought Alaska and, for the next 100 years afterward, the vast majority of the state was public domain—like the Old West of frontier lore—federal land and its surface and hard-rock resources were there for the taking. They belonged to everyone, but only until someone showed up to lay private claim. Today, amid deep conflicts about whether areas should remain natural or be exploited for natural resources, federal control stands out far more clearly than it did during the gold rush, when the land's wealth was free to anyone with strength enough to take it. Alaskans who want to keep receiving the good things that government brings today equate the frontier spirit of the past

■ **1870** The Alaska Commercial Company receives a monopoly on harvesting seals in the Pribilof Islands and soon expands across the territory. (The company remains a presence in the Alaska Bush today.)

■ **1879** Naturalist and writer John Muir explores Southeast Alaska by canoe, discovering Glacier Bay with Native guides.

■ **1880** Joe Juneau and Richard Harris, guided by local Natives, find gold on Gastineau Channel and found city of Juneau; gold strikes begin to come every few years across the state.

■ **1884** Military rule ends in Alaska, but residents still have no right to elect a legislature, governor, or congressional representative, or to make laws.

■ **1885** Protestant missionaries meet to divide up the territory, parceling out each region to a different religion; they begin to fan out across Alaska to convert Native peoples, largely suppressing their traditional ways.

■ **1898** After prospectors arrive in Seattle with a ton of gold, the Klondike gold rush begins; gold rushes in Nome and Fairbanks follow within a few years; Americans begin to populate Alaska.

■ **1906** Alaska's first (nonvoting) delegate in Congress takes office; the capital moves from Sitka to Juneau.

■ **1908** The Iditarod Trail, a sled dog mail route, is completed, linking trails continuously from Seward to Nome.

■ **1913** The first territorial legislature convenes, although it has few powers; the first automobile drives the Richardson Highway route, from Valdez to Fairbanks.

■ **1914** Federal construction of the Alaska Railroad begins; the first tents go up in the river bottom that will be Anchorage, along the rail line.

■ **1917** Mount McKinley National Park is established.

■ **1920** The first flights connect Alaska to the rest of the United States; aviation quickly becomes the most important means of transportation in the territory.

■ **1923** Pres. Warren Harding drives the final spike on the Alaskan Railroad at

continues

with their own financial well-being, whether that means working at a mining claim or at a desk in a glass office tower. But other Americans feel they own Alaska, too, and they don't necessarily believe in giving it away anymore. They may want the frontier to stay alive in another sense—unconquered and still wild.

White colonization of the territory came in boom-and-bust waves of migrants arriving with the goal of making a quick buck and then clearing out—without worrying about the people who already lived there. Although the gold rush pioneers are celebrated today, the **Klondike rush of 1898** that opened up and populated the territory was motivated by greed and was a mass importer of crime, inhumanity, and, for the Native people, terrible epidemics of new diseases that killed off whole villages. Like the Russians 150 years before, who had made slaves of the Natives, the new white population behaved as if the indigenous people were less than human. Until Franklin Roosevelt became president, federal policy was to suppress Alaska Native cultures; missionaries forbade Native peoples from telling the old stories or even speaking in their own languages. Segregation ended only after World War II. Meanwhile, the salmon that fed the people of the territory were overfished by a powerful, outside-owned canning industry with friends in Washington, D.C. Their abuses destroyed salmon runs. Formerly rich Native villages faced famine when their primary food source was taken away.

It was only with **World War II,** and the Japanese invasion of the Aleutian Islands, that Alaska developed an industry not based on exploitation of natural resources: the military industry. The war brought the construction of the territory's first road to the outside world, the Alaska Highway. After the war, military activity dropped off,

Nenana, then dies on the way home, purportedly from eating bad Alaska seafood.

- 1925 Leonhard Seppala and other dog mushers relay diphtheria serum on the Iditarod Trail to fight an epidemic in Nome; Seppala and his lead dog, Balto, become national heroes.

- 1934 Federal policy of forced assimilation of Native cultures is officially discarded and New Deal efforts to preserve Native cultures begin.

- 1935 New Deal "colonists," broke farmers from all over the United States, settle in the Matanuska Valley north of Anchorage.

- 1940 A military buildup begins in Alaska; bases built in Anchorage accelerate city's growth into a major population center.

- 1942 Japanese invade Aleutians, taking Attu and Kiska islands and bombing Dutch Harbor/Unalaska (a U.S. counterattack the next year drives out the Japanese); Alaska Highway links Alaska to the rest of the country overland for the first time, but is open to civilians only after the war.

- 1949 Massive cold war military buildup feeds fast economic growth.

- 1957 Oil is found on Kenai Peninsula's Swanson River.

- 1959 Alaska becomes a state.

- 1964 The largest earthquake ever to strike North America shakes Southcentral Alaska, killing 131 people, primarily in tsunami waves.

- 1968 Oil is found at Prudhoe Bay, on Alaska's North Slope.

- 1970 Environmental lawsuits tie up work to build the Alaska pipeline, which is needed to link the North Slope oil field to markets.

- 1971 Congress acknowledges and pays the federal government's debt to Alaska's indigenous people with the Alaska Native Claims Settlement Act, which transfers 44 million acres of land and almost $1 billion to new Native-owned corporations.

- 1973 The first Iditarod Trail Sled Dog Race runs more than 1,000 miles from Anchorage to Nome.

- 1974 Congress clears away legal barriers to construction of the trans-Alaska pipeline; Vice Pres. Spiro Agnew casts the deciding vote in the U.S. Senate.

but only briefly. By the late 1940s, Alaska was on the front line on the Cold War. Huge Air Force and Army bases were built and remote radar stations installed to detect and repel Soviet bombers and missiles. To this day, the federal government remains a key industry whose removal would deal the economy a grievous blow.

The fight for **Alaska statehood** also began after the war. Alaskans argued that they needed local, independent control of natural resources, pointing to the example of overfishing in the federally managed salmon industry. Opponents said that Alaska would never be able to support itself, would always require large subsidies from the federal government, and therefore should not be a state. But the advocates pointed out that Alaska's lack of self-sufficiency came about because its citizens did not control the resources—Alaska was a colony, with decisions and profits taken away by the mother country. If Alaskans could control their own land, they could use the resources to fund government. The discovery of oil on the Swanson River on the Kenai Peninsula in 1957 helped win that argument. Here was real money that could fund a state

■ **1977** The trans-Alaska pipeline is completed and begins providing up to 25% of the U.S. domestic supply of oil.

■ **1980** Congress sets aside almost a third of Alaska in new parks and other land-conservation units; awash in new oil wealth, the state legislature abolishes all taxes paid by individuals to state government.

■ **1982** Alaskans receive their first Alaska Permanent Fund dividends, interest paid on an oil-wealth savings account.

■ **1985** Declining oil prices send the Alaska economy into a tailspin; tens of thousands leave the state and most of the banks collapse.

■ **1989** The tanker *Exxon Valdez* hits Bligh Reef in Prince William Sound, spilling 11 million gallons of North Slope crude in the worst oil spill ever in North America.

■ **1994** A federal jury in Anchorage awards $5 billion to 10,000 fishermen, Natives, and others hurt by the Exxon oil spill; Exxon appeals continue today.

■ **1996** Wildfire rips through the Big Lake area, north of Anchorage, destroying 400 buildings.

■ **1999** Alaskans vote 87% against a plan to use Permanent Fund earnings to cover a state budget shortfall.

government. In 1959, Alaska finally became the 49th state. Along with the rights of entering the union, Alaska received a dowry, an endowment of land to develop and pay for all future government. The Statehood Act gave the new state the right to select 103 million acres from a total landmass of 365 million acres. Indeed, that land does pay for state government in Alaska, in the form of oil royalties and taxes—but to this day, the federal government still spends a lot more in Alaska than it receives.

Oil revenues supported the new state as it began to extend services to the vast, undeveloped expanse of Alaska. Anchorage boomed in the 1960s in a period of buoyant optimism. Leaders believed that the age-old problems of the wide-open frontier—poverty, lack of basic services, impenetrable remoteness—would succumb to the new government and new money, while the land still remained wide open. Then the pace of change redoubled in 1968 with the discovery of the largest oil field in North America at **Prudhoe Bay** on land that had been a wise state selection in the federal land-grant entitlement. The state government received as much money in a single oil lease sale auction as it had spent in total for the previous 6 years. This was going to be the boom of all booms.

The oil bonanza on the North Slope would change Alaska more than any other event since the gold rush. Once, opening the frontier meant letting a few

An Alaska Glossary

If Alaska feels like a different country from the rest of the United States, one reason may be the odd local usage that makes English slightly different here—different enough, in fact, that the Associated Press publishes a separate style-book dictionary just for Alaska. Here are some Alaskan words you may run into:

breakup   When God set up the seasons in Alaska, He forgot one: spring. While the rest of the United States enjoys new flowers and baseball, Alaskans are looking at melting snowbanks and mud. Then, in May, summer miraculously arrives. Breakup officially occurs when the ice goes out in the Interior's rivers, but it stands for the time period of winter's demise and summer's initiation.

bunny boots   If you see people wearing huge, bulbous, white rubber boots in Alaska's winter, it's not necessarily because they have enormous feet. Those are bunny boots, superinsulated footwear originally designed for Arctic air force operations—and they're the warmest things in the world.

cheechako   A newcomer or greenhorn. Not used much anymore because almost everyone is one.

dry or **damp**   Many towns and villages have invoked a state law that allows them to outlaw alcohol completely (to go dry) or to outlaw sale but not possession (to go damp).

Lower 48   The contiguous United States.

Native   When capitalized, the word refers to Alaska's indigenous people. "American Indian" isn't used much in Alaska, "Alaska Native" being the preferred term.

Native corporation   In 1971, Congress settled land claims with Alaska's Natives by turning over land and money; corporations were set up, with the Natives then alive as shareholders, to receive the property. Most of the corporations still thrive.

prospectors scratch the dirt in search of a poke of gold. But getting this immense pool of oil to market from one of the most remote spots on the globe would require allowing the world's largest companies to build across Alaska a pipeline that, when completed, could credibly claim to be the largest privately financed construction project in world history. With the stakes suddenly so much higher, it came time to figure out exactly who owned which parts of Alaska. The land couldn't just be public domain any longer.

That division wouldn't be easy. Much of the state had never even been mapped, much less surveyed, and there were some large outstanding claims that had to be settled. Alaska Natives, who had lost land, culture, and health in 2 centuries of white invasion, finally saw their luck start to turn. It wouldn't be possible to resolve the land issues surrounding the pipeline until their claims to land and compensation were answered. Native leaders cannily used that leverage to assure that they got what they wanted.

oosik   The huge penile bone of a walrus. Knowing this word could save you from being the butt of any number of practical jokes people like to play on cheechakos.

Outside   Anywhere that isn't Alaska. This is a widely used term in print and is capitalized, like any other proper noun.

PFD   No, not personal floatation device; it stands for Permanent Fund Dividend. When Alaska's oil riches started flowing in the late 1970s, the voters set up a savings account called the Permanent Fund. Half the interest is paid annually to every man, woman, and child in the state. With more than $26 billion in investments, the fund now yields more than $1,700 in dividends to each Alaskan annually.

pioneer   A white settler of Alaska who has been here longer than most other people can remember—25 or 30 years usually does it.

salmon   There are five species of Pacific salmon, each with two names. The king, or Chinook, is the largest, growing up to 90 pounds in some areas; the silver, or coho, is next in size, a feisty sport fish; the red or sockeye has rich red flesh; the pink, or humpy, and the chum, or dog, are smallish and not as tasty, mostly ending up in cans and dog lots.

Southeast   Most people don't bother to say "Southeast Alaska." The region may be to the northwest of everyone else in the country, but it's southeast of most Alaskans, and that's all we care about.

tsunami   Earthquake-caused sea waves are often called tidal waves, but that's a misnomer. The destructive waves of the 1964 Alaska earthquake were tsunamis caused by underwater upheavals like landslides.

village   A small, Alaska Native settlement in the Bush, usually tightly bound by family and cultural tradition.

In the early 1970s, America had a new awareness of the way its first people had been treated in the settlement of the West. When white frontiers expanded, Native traditional homelands were stolen. In Alaska, with the powerful lure of all that oil providing the impetus, Native people were able to insist on a fairer resolution. In 1971, with the support of white Alaskans, the oil companies, and President Richard Nixon, who threatened to veto any settlement that Natives did not support, Congress passed the **Alaska Native Claims Settlement Act,** called ANCSA. The act transferred 44 million acres of land and $962.5 million to corporations whose shareholders were all the Native people of Alaska. The new Native corporations would be able to exploit their own land for their shareholders' profit. In later legislation, Natives also won guaranteed subsistence hunting and fishing rights on federal land. Some Natives complained that they'd received only an eighth of the land they had owned before white contact, but it was still by far the richest settlement any of the world's indigenous people had received at that time. Today, the Native corporations are Alaska's largest and most powerful homegrown businesses.

It was a political deal on a grand scale. It's unlikely that Natives would have gotten their land at all but for the desire of whites to get at the oil and their need for Native support, nor could the pipeline have overcome environmental challenges without the Natives' dropping their objections. Even with Native support in place, legislation authorizing the pipeline passed the U.S. Senate by only one vote, cast by Vice President Spiro Agnew.

But there were other side effects of the deal that white Alaskans didn't like so well. The state still hadn't received a large portion of its land entitlement, and now the Native corporations also had a right to select the land they wanted. There still remained the question of who would get what, and of the wild lands that Congress, influenced by a strong new environmental movement, wanted to maintain as national parks and wilderness and not give away. That issue wasn't settled until 1980, when the **Alaska National Interest Lands Conservation Act** passed, setting aside an additional 106 million acres for conservation, an area larger than California. Alaska's frontier-minded population screamed bloody murder over "the lock-up of Alaska," but the act was only the last, tangible step in a process started by the coming of big oil and the need its arrival created to draw lines on the map, tying up the frontier.

When construction of the $9 billion pipeline finally got underway in 1974, a huge influx of new people chasing the high-paying jobs put any previous gold rush to shame. The newcomers were from a different part of the country than previously, too. Alaska had been a predominately Democratic state, but oil workers from Texas, Oklahoma, and other Bible Belt states helped shift the balance of Alaska's politics, and now it's solidly Republican. In its frontier days, Alaska had a strong Libertarian streak, but now it became more influenced by fundamentalist Christian conservatism. A hippie-infested legislature of the early 1970s legalized marijuana for home use. Conservatives at the time, who thought the government shouldn't butt into its citizens' private lives, went along with them. After the pipeline, times changed, and Alaska developed tough antidrug laws.

Growth also brought urban problems. As the pipeline construction boom waned in 1977, a boomtown atmosphere of gambling and street prostitution went with it, but other big-city problems remained. No longer could residents of Anchorage and Fairbanks go to bed without locking their doors. Both cities were declared "nonattainment" areas by the Environmental Protection Agency because of air pollution near the ground in cold winter weather, when people left their cars running during the day to keep them from freezing.

But the pipeline seemed to provide limitless wealth to solve these problems. For fear that too much money would be wasted, the voters altered the state constitution to bank a large portion of the new riches. The new Permanent Fund would be off limits to the politicians in Juneau, with half the annual earnings paid out to citizens as dividends. The fund now contains more than $26 billion in savings and has become one of the largest sectors of the economy simply by virtue of paying out more than $1 billion a year in dividends to everyone who lives at least a year in the state. All major state taxes on individuals were canceled, and people got used to receiving everything free from the government.

Then, in 1985, oil prices dropped, deflating the overextended economy. Housing prices crashed, and thousands of people simply walked away from their mortgages. All but a few of the banks in the state went broke. Condominiums that had sold for $100,000 went for $20,000 or less a year later. It was the bust that always goes with the boom, but it still came as a shock to many. The spending associated with the ***Exxon Valdez* oil spill** in 1989 restarted the economy, and it continued on an even keel for a decade after, but the wealth of the earlier oil years never returned.

Meanwhile, the oil from Prudhoe Bay started running out. Oil revenues, an irreplaceable 85% of the state budget, started an irrevocable downward trend in the early 1990s. The oil companies downsized. Without another boom on the horizon, the question became how to avoid, or at least soften, the next bust. At this writing, that question remains unanswered. In 1999, the governor and legislature asked the voters to approve reducing their Permanent Fund dividends to cover a $1 billion budget gap. Conservatives said the state should just cut the budget; liberals said reducing the dividend would amount to a head tax, hitting hardest the poor people who rely on the money for necessities. The plan failed, with 87% voting no. The legislature, with a temporary budgetary reprieve provided by higher oil prices, backed away from doing anything. With the political system in deadlock, the disadvantages of individualism seemed apparent. Some asked if Alaskans had lost their capacity for collective sacrifice. More asked when the next big project would get the good times rolling again, such as a natural gas pipeline from the North Slope to middle America or oil development in the Arctic National Wildlife Refuge (ANWR).

Culture moves slower than politics, and Alaskans still see themselves as gold rush prospectors or wildcat oil drillers, adventuring in an open land and striking it rich by their own devices. Even as the economy blends ever more smoothly into the American corporate landscape, Alaskans' myth of themselves remains strong. Today, the state's future is as little in its own hands as it has ever been. Whether anyone gets to explore for oil in ANWR will be decided in Congress and distant corporate boardrooms, not here. Ultimately, an economy based on exploiting natural resources is anything but independent.

Index

See also Accommodations and Restaurant indexes, below.

FROMMER'S® MEMORABLE WALKS

| Chicago | New York | San Francisco |
| London | Paris | |

FROMMER'S® GREAT OUTDOOR GUIDES

| Arizona & New Mexico | Northern California | Vermont & New Hampshire |
| New England | Southern New England | |

SUZY GERSHMAN'S BORN TO SHOP GUIDES

Born to Shop: France	Born to Shop: Italy	Born to Shop: New York
Born to Shop: Hong Kong,	Born to Shop: London	Born to Shop: Paris
Shanghai & Beijing		

FROMMER'S® IRREVERENT GUIDES

Amsterdam	Los Angeles	San Francisco
Boston	Manhattan	Seattle & Portland
Chicago	New Orleans	Vancouver
Las Vegas	Paris	Walt Disney World
London	Rome	Washington, D.C.

FROMMER'S® BEST-LOVED DRIVING TOURS

Britain	Germany	New England
California	Ireland	Scotland
Florida	Italy	Spain
France		

HANGING OUT™ GUIDES

| Hanging Out in England | Hanging Out in France | Hanging Out in Italy |
| Hanging Out in Europe | Hanging Out in Ireland | Hanging Out in Spain |

THE UNOFFICIAL GUIDES®

Bed & Breakfasts and Country	Florida with Kids	New Orleans
Inns in:	Golf Vacations in the	New York City
California	Eastern U.S.	Paris
New England	The Great Smokey &	San Francisco
Northwest	Blue Ridge Mountains	Skiing in the West
Rockies	Inside Disney	Southeast with Kids
Southeast	Hawaii	Walt Disney World
Beyond Disney	Las Vegas	Walt Disney World for
Branson, Missouri	London	Grown-ups
California with Kids	Mid-Atlantic with Kids	Walt Disney World for Kids
Chicago	Mini Las Vegas	Washington, D.C.
Cruises	Mini-Mickey	World's Best Diving Vacations
Disneyland	New England & New York	
	with Kids	

SPECIAL-INTEREST TITLES

Frommer's Adventure Guide to Australia & New Zealand
Frommer's Adventure Guide to Central America
Frommer's Adventure Guide to India & Pakistan
Frommer's Adventure Guide to South America
Frommer's Adventure Guide to Southeast Asia
Frommer's Adventure Guide to Southern Africa
Frommer's Britain's Best Bed & Breakfasts and Country Inns
Frommer's France's Best Bed & Breakfasts and Country Inns
Frommer's Italy's Best Bed & Breakfasts and Country Inns
Frommer's Caribbean Hideaways

Frommer's Exploring America by RV
Frommer's Gay & Lesbian Europe
Frommer's The Moon
Frommer's New York City with Kids
Frommer's Road Atlas Britain
Frommer's Road Atlas Europe
Frommer's Washington, D.C., with Kids
Frommer's What the Airlines Never Tell You
Israel Past & Present
The New York Times' Guide to Unforgettable Weekends
Places Rated Almanac
Retirement Places Rated

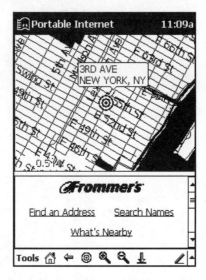